Translation Quality Assessment: A Model Revisited

翻译质量评估模式再研究

司显柱 著
芈 岚 司显柱 译

东华大学出版社·上海

图书在版编目（CIP）数据

翻译质量评估模式再研究 = Translation Quality Assessment: A Model Revisited：英文、中文 / 司显柱 著；芈岚, 司显柱 译. -- 上海：东华大学出版社, 2025.1. -- ISBN 978-7-5669-2413-1

Ⅰ．H059

中国国家版本馆 CIP 数据核字第 2024JF2367 号

Translation Quality Assessment: A Model Revisited 翻译质量评估模式再研究	司显柱 著 芈岚 司显柱 译	责任编辑 曹晓虹 封面设计 书研社

出版发行　东华大学出版社　（上海市延安西路 1882 号　邮政编码：200051）
编　辑　部　021-62379902
营销中心　021-62193056　62373056
天猫旗舰店　http://dhdx.tmall.com
出版社网址　http://dhupress.dhu.edu.cn
印　　　刷　上海龙腾印务有限公司
开　　　本　710mm×1000mm　1/16
印　　　张　26.5
字　　　数　997 千字
版　　　次　2025 年 1 月第 1 版
印　　　次　2025 年 1 月第 1 次 印刷

书　号　**ISBN** 978-7-5669-2413-1　　定　价：98.00 元

Preface

According to Holmes'discussion on the classification of translation studies, translation criticism belongs to the category of applied translation theory. However, when talking about translation criticism, people often make no distinction between several terms related to this concept, namely, translation criticism, translation assessment and translation evaluation. It is commendable that McAlester (2000:231) differentiated between these three terms and thus defined as such: (1) "translation evaluation" is to rate the translation, in other words, to give a score, even if it is only qualified/unqualified. The evaluation includes quantitative factors; (2) "Translation criticism" is to discuss whether the translation is appropriate, which also contains the meaning of value judgment, but it does not have to be quantified. Obviously, it contains the value judgment of the translation. (3) "Translation evaluation" includes translation *assessment* and translation criticism.

According to Newmark's (1988/2001: 184-192) explanation of the connotation of translation criticism, the steps and components of translation criticism are as follows: (1) a brief analysis of the SL text stressing its intention and its functional aspects; (2) the translator's interpretation of the SL text's purpose, his translation method and the translation's like readership; (3) a selective but representative detailed comparison of the translation with the original; (4) an evaluation of the translation—(a) in the translator's terms, (b) in the critic's terms; (5) where appropriate, an assessment of the likely place of the translation in the target language culture or discipline.

In *Chinese Translators Journal Dictionary*, translation criticism is defined as "a comprehensive evaluation of translation process as well as translation quality relying on certain criteria" (Lin 1997: 184). Specifically, it includes the following five aspects: (1) to analyze the original text with great emphasis on the author's intention and the function of the source text; (2) to analyze the target text identifying the translator's motivation, translation strategies and potential readers; (3) to conduct a detailed contrastive study of typical parts of the source text and the target text; (4) to assess the translated text from both the macro and micro perspectives, including its translation techniques as well as its translation quality; and (5) to evaluate the role or position of the translated text in the target culture.

If the discussion of translation criticism by Holmes, Newmark and domestic scholars is projected into the investigation of the concepts of "translation criticism", "translation assessment" and "translation evaluation", it is not difficult to find that, from the perspective of "genus" and "species", "translation assessment" does not include translation evaluation and translation criticism, but "translation criticism" dominates translation evaluation and translation assessment, That is, translation criticism is "species", and translation evaluation and translation assessment are "genus". Linguistically speaking, translation criticism is superordinate to both Text criticism and the theory of translation criticism as well as the criticism of translation thoughts and activities. Text criticism is also more from the social and cultural metaphysical level, such as Qian's *Lin Shu's Translation*. While translation evaluation and assessment are co-hyponyms which are both subordinate to translation criticism. They primarily evaluate the quality of translation from the perspective of the text itself. Therefore, we believe that there is no need to make a distinction between translation evaluation and translation assessment, and we can use translation assessment to refer to the value judgment of translation quality, which can be with or without quantitative indicators. In short, translation assessment is an integral part of translation criticism, not the opposite.

This book is a study of translation assessment. Specifically, it is a deepening of the author's doctoral thesis *Construction of Translation Quality Assessment Model-A Functional Linguistic Perspective*, which passed the oral defense in June 2006 at Sun Yat-sen University and later was published by Peking University Press in September 2007. This book stems from the author's original research which constructs a translation quality assessment model characterized by systematicness, completeness, operability and less subjectivity, and it boosts high academic value and status: "Professor Si is the first scholar in China to systematically conduct translation quality assessment research and publish his achievements in books. Guided by the theories of functional linguistics and text typology, he constructs a text-based translation quality assessment model. His research is groundbreaking in China." (Kang, 2010) "It is characterized by completeness, systematicness, operability, and less subjectivity. This independently created model is the first in China. Compared to the translation and review of foreign translation quality assessment models, it is undoubtedly a significant progress in academic research." (Lin et. al, 2010) However, the original model has the following two main problems:

Firstly, in the face of translation practices in various types and genres of texts, there is no universal assessment model that can be applied to all types of texts and can provide a scientific and comprehensive quality assessment of a wide variety of translated texts. This requires the exploration and establishment of more targeted and operational assessment models for different genres of texts. In particular, due to their obvious communicative purposes, applied genres have their own regularity in text structure and language use.

Therefore, from the perspective of translators, it is necessary to start with generic analysis, which includes the analysis of the textual characteristics of specific applied genres, the grasp of the overall intention and function of the source texts, the identification of the means by which authors convey the intention of the texts, and the selection as well as application of correct translation strategies and methods. From the perspective of translation assessment, it is also natural to use generic analysis as a tool to describe, analyze, and compare the original text with the translation in order to make a comprehensive and accurate judgment on the quality of the translation. Unfortunately, the original assessment model lacks generic analysis in terms of parameter settings.

Secondly, in addition to the obvious lack of detailed research on different genres of translated texts, the biggest problem of the original model is that it does not pay enough attention to the aesthetics or artistry of the translated texts. From the perspective of "faithfulness" and "smoothness", which measure translation quality standards, the original model pays more attention to whether the translated texts are "equivalent" and "faithful" to the source texts in terms of ideational and interpersonal meanings, but evades or is vague about whether the translated texts are "smooth" and "beautiful", making it difficult to evaluate the "smoothness" and "elegance" that fall within the aesthetic and artistic categories of the translated texts.

In view of this, based on analyzing the shortcomings of the original model and elaborating the two-dimensional criteria for translation quality, this study discusses the two-stage theory of translation quality assessment under the guidance of Systemic Functional Linguistics: In the first stage, evaluating the function and significance of the translated texts with respect to the source texts, focusing on "faithfulness" and "equivalence"; In the second stage, a new translation quality assessment model is constructed by evaluating whether the language of the translated texts is smooth and beautiful, focusing on "expressiveness and elegance". It can be seen that this study is the development and improvement of *The Construction of Translation Quality Assessment Models - A Functional Linguistic Perspective*, aiming to enrich the system of translation quality assessment models. This study not only intends to further research on translation quality assessment models, but also to continue translation research from the perspective of Systemic Functional Linguistics.

Of course, there are still shortcomings in this study, mainly including the following two points:

Firstly, this study aims to build a complete model that can evaluate whether the translation is "faithful" in meaning to the source texts, as welle as whether it is "smooth"; as for the path, a targeted evaluation model for the quality of applied generic text translation is established from the perspective of generic analysis. This naturally requires the analysis of different applied generic texts to grasp their generic characteristics and provide practical tools for constructing translation quality assessment models for this genre. However, how does one grasp the norms and characteristics of applied generic texts of the two languages involved in translation? From the perspective of research methods, a relatively feasible approach is to establish a small corpus of English, Chinese, and translated English of three types of applied generic texts (corporate profiles, sports news reports, and museum introductions) that this study focuses on, and to analyze and describe the macro structure (GSP model) and linguistic characteristics (manifestation style) of the three types of generic texts included in the three corpora, thus to summarize their respective characteristics and comparative analysis to identify similarities and differences. However, due to limited time and effort, the established corpora do not have a large sample size. Therefore, the structural and verbal features of a specific genre summarized based on limited samples may not accurately reflect the overall picture of that genre, and thus, judgments based on this may not necessarily be accurate and comprehensive in terms of translation quality. Secondly, no matter how to identify and judge the structure of texts in the self-built corpora, or how to identify and describe the process types, mood choices, and thematic types that embody the style, due to the lack of effective analysis software that can be used, the reliance on manual work and the huge differences between English and Chinese and the inevitable subjectivity, errors are still inevitable though with repeated speculation and verification.

Three special points need to be stated.

First, given the extremely complex nature of translation, researchers will explore it from different disciplinary perspectives, which is undoubtedly very necessary and beneficial. However, the essential attribute of translation is, after all, the use of a special language that reproduces the meaning carried by one language and characters in another language. Therefore, describing and interpreting it from a linguistic perspective aligns directly with the perspective of translation studies. Systemic Functional Linguistics is about the study of language use. In this way, the language theory developed based on it naturally has guiding and referential significance in terms of theory and logic for the exploration of translation phenomena that belong to the same category of language use.

Second, different translation perspectives lead to different translation standards, different translation strategies and methods, which also lead to different concepts of translation quality and different translation assessment methods. This study examines the nature of translation from the perspective of Systemic Functional Linguistics and proposes with demonstration a text-based translation quality assessment model. Therefore, it is only our opinion, and other analytical perspectives can not be excluded, such as Paepcke (1986), Stolze (1992) and Kupsch-Losereit (1994) from the perspective of neo-hermeneutic approaches，Graham (1985), de Man (1986), Benjamin (1989), Derrida (1985), Venuti (1992,1995) and Gentzler (1993) from the perspective of post-modernist and deconstructionist approaches, as well as Toury (1995) et al. from the perspective of descriptive translation studies. Due to the extremely complex nature of the problem, we insist that different views are complementary to each other rather than mutually exclusive.

Third, for some critics who believe that using this model to assess the actual workload is too large, especially for the lack of feasibility of tome translations, we believe that unless computer programming and manual analysis of translations and texts can be used, such problems always exist. For example, critical discourse analysis (CDA) of a masterpiece also faces the same dilemma, which is not exclusive to the use of this model to assess translated texts. However, on the other hand, during actual assessment, it is possible to conduct sampling of chapters in the translation based on the actual situation to reduce the workload when necessary.

Looking forward to criticism and correction from experts and scholars!

Xianzhu Si
Summer, 2024

Contents

Preface
Part I Theoretical Research // 1

Chapter 1 Introduction // 1
    1.1 Deficiencies in Existing Models // 3
    1.2 Systemic Functional Linguistics, Theory of Genre Analysis and Translation Quality Assessment of Applied Generic Texts // 9
    1.3 Research Approach and Structure of This Book // 11

Chapter 2 A Survey of Translation Quality Assessment Research // 15
    2.1 Review of Domestic Translation Quality Research // 15
    2.2 Review of International Translation Quality Research // 17
    2.3 Review of Representative Translation Quality Assessment Models at Home and Abroad // 20
        2.3.1 Reiss's Model // 20
        2.3.2 Introduction to House's Model // 22
        2.3.3. Introduction to Al Qinai's Model // 25
        2.3.4. Introduction to Williams' Model // 27
        2.3.5. Introduction to Jeremy Munday's Model // 30
    2.4 Conclusion // 31

Chapter 3 Systemic Functional Linguistics and Translation Research // 37
    3.1 Review of Translation Research of Systemic Functional Linguistics in Foreign Countries // 38
    3.2 Review of Translation Research of Systemic Functional Linguistics Approach in China // 42
        3.2.1 Pure Functional Theory and Translation Studies // 44
        3.2.2 Context Theory and Translation Studies // 45
        3.2.3 Evaluation Theory and Translation Studies // 46
        3.2.4 Grammatical Metaphor and Translation Studies // 49

    3.2.5 Systemic Functional Linguistics and the Construction of Translation Quality Assessment Model // 50
  3.3 Review of Translation Research in Systemic Functional Linguistics: Achievements and Shortcomings // 53

Chapter 4 Research on Genre and Translation from Genre Perspective Translation // 59
  4.1 Introduction to the Concept of Genre // 59
  4.2 Schools of Genre Research // 62
    4.2.1 Genre Research of Systemic Functional Linguistics School // 63
    4.2.2 ESP/EAP School Genre Analysis // 65
      4.2.2.1 Swales' Model of Moves and Steps // 66
      4.2.2.2 Bhatia's Seven-Move Model // 68
    4.2.3 New Rhetoric School // 69
  4.3 Genre Research of Systemic Functional Linguistics School // 71
    4.3.1 Introduction to Systemic Functional Linguistics Theory // 71
    4.3.2 Genre Theory of Halliday and Hasan // 73
    4.3.3 Martin's Genre Theory // 76
  4.4 Research on Three Applied Genre Texts and Their Translation // 81
    4.4.1 Corporate Profiles and Translation // 82
    4.4.2 News Discourse, Sports News and The Translation // 84
    4.4.3 Tourism Text, Museum Introduction and Translation // 88
  4.5 Genre Analysis Models of This Book // 90

Chapter 5 Construction of a Quality Assessment Model for Translation of Applied Genre Discourses // 97
  5.1 Construction and Development of Original Translation Quality Assessment Model // 97
  5.2 Construction of A Quality Assessment Model for Applied Discourse Translation // 106

Part II Empirical Study

Chapter 6 Research on the Translation Quality of The Genre of Enterprise Profiles // 118
  6.1 Construction of a Corporate Profile Genre Corpus // 119
    6.1.1 About GSP Model // 119

6.1.2 Constructing Corpus: Content, Steps and Methods // 121
6.2 Corpus-Based Discourse Schematic Structure of Corporate Profiles // 123
 6.2.1 Composition of the Genre Structure of Corporate Profiles // 123
 6.2.2 The GSP Model of English Corporate Profile Texts // 125
 6.2.3 GSP Model for English Translation of Chinese Corporate Profiles // 130
6.3 Corpus-based Discourse Features of Corporate Profiles // 136
 6.3.1 Verbal Features of English Corporate Profiles // 139
 6.3.2 Verbal Features of Chinese Corporate Profiles // 155
 6.3.3 Linguistic Features of English Translation of Chinese Corporate Profiles // 169
6.4 Corpus-based Contrastive Analysis of Corporate Profiles // 184
 6.4.1 Comparison of Schematic Structure of Three Types of Texts (GSP Model) // 184
 6.4.2 Comparison of the Presentation Styles of Three Types of Texts(Vocabulary and Grammar Level) // 186
6.5 Evaluation and Improvement of Translation Quality for Corporate Profiles // 195
 6.5.1 Judgment and Modification Suggestions on the Quality of the Translation from the Perspective of Structure // 195
 6.5.2 Judgment and Modification Suggestions on the Quality of the Original Translation from the Perspective of Representation Style // 200

Chapter 7 Research on the Translation Quality of Sports News Discourses //209

7.1 Construction of the Corpus of Sports News Discourses // 209
7.2 Corpus-based Generic Structure of Sports News Discourses // 213
 7.2.1 Components of Generic Structure of Sports News // 213
 7.2.2 The GSP Model of BBC English Sports News // 215
 7.2.3 The GSP Model of Xinhua Sports News // 219
 7.2.4 Structure of Translated English Sports News on Xinhua Net // 224
7.3 Corpus-based Linguistic Analysis of Sports News Discourses // 229
 7.3.1 Linguistic Characteristics of BBC English Sports News Discourses // 230
 7.3.2 Linguistic Features of Chinese Sports News Texts on Xinhua Net // 242
 7.3.3 Linguistic Features of Translated English Sports News Texts // 257
7.4 Corpus-based Comparative Analysis of Sports News Discourses // 274
 7.4.1 Structural Comparison of Three Types of Texts (GSP Model) // 274
 7.4.2 Comparison of Vocabulary and Grammar among Three Types of Texts // 278
7.5 Assessment and Improvement of Translation Quality of Sports News // 283

7.5.1 Quality Judgment and Modification Suggestions for the Original Translation from the Perspective of Generic Structure // 284
7.5.2 Judgment and Improvement Suggestions on the Quality of the Original Translation from the Perspective of Representation Style // 289

Chapter 8 Translation Quality Studies of Museum Introduction Discourses // 296

8.1 Construction of Corpus of Museum Introduction Discourses // 296
8.2 Corpus-based Generic Structure of Museum Introductions // 299
    8.2.1 Structural Elements of Museum Introductions // 299
    8.2.2 The GSP Model of English Introductions to Foreign Museums // 300
    8.2.3 The GSP Model of Chinese Introductions of Domestic Museums // 306
    8.2.4 The GSP Model of English Translation of Domestic Museum Introductions // 311
8.3 Corpus-based Analysis of Characteristics of Museum Introductions // 316
    8.3.1 Linguistic Features of English Introductions of Foreign Museums // 316
    8.3.2 Linguistic Features of Chinese Introductions of Domestic Museums // 334
    8.3.3 Linguistic Features of the English Translation of Domestic Museum Introductions // 351
8.4 Corpus-based Comparative Analysis of Museum Introductions // 368
    8.4.1 Comparison of Schematic Structure of Three Types of Texts (GSP Model) // 369
    8.4.2 Comparison of the Presentation Style of Three Types of Texts (at the lexical and grammatical level) // 372
8.5 Assessment and Improvement of Translation Quality of Museum Introduction Discourses // 381
    8.5.1 Judgment and Improvement Suggestions on the Quality of the Original Translation from the Perspective of Schematic Structure // 381
    8.5.2 Judgment and Improvement Suggestions on the Quality of the Original Translation from the Perspective of Representation Style // 387
    8.5.3 Some Thoughts // 403

Chapter 9 Conclusion // 405

Part I Theoretical Research

Chapter 1 Introduction

This chapter reviews the construction thinking and social repercussions of the original translation quality assessment model, analyzes the main problem within the model, and discusses why this defect is particularly significant for the evaluation of translation quality in applied genre. It also expounds the objectives, theoretical basis, research ideas, and framework of this study.

In *Functional Linguistics and Translation Studies - Construction of Translation Quality Assessment Models*[1], we explained that language use or verbal communication, including translation, occurs within the framework of verbal communication. This framework for verbal communication includes three systems: context, function, and form. The elements and interrelationships of these three systems can be summarized as follows: context generally includes context of situation and context of culture. The register that reflects context of situation has three variables: field, tenor, and mode. The functional (meaning) system includes ideational function (meaning), interpersonal function (meaning) and textual (functional) meaning. The form system refers to the transitivity system, mood system, and thematic system in the lexical-grammatical system of a language. The relationship among the three is that context determines meaning (function), meaning (function) is embodied by form, and in turn, form also constructs context. Specifically, the three variables of register, field, tenor, and mode correspond respectively to and determine the ideational, interpersonal, and textual meanings in the functional (meaning) system, while ideational meaning, interpersonal meaning, and textual meaning correspond to and are embodied in the transitivity system, mood system, and thematic system of the form (linguistic) system.

From this point of view, translation, as a form of verbal communication, is essentially "seeking to have the same meaning and function in the same overall context of texts in two languages", and " a good translation needs to be equivalent to the source text in all

---

[1] Si Xianzhu. *Functional Linguistics and Translation Studies - Construction of a Translation Quality Assessment Model* [M]. Beijing: Peking University Press, 2007.

three senses"[1]. However, in the setting of assessment parameters, when describing whether the translation is functionally equivalent or deviated from the source text, it is only necessary to set two parameters: ideational and interpersonal function. Textual meaning shall not be taken into consideration. This is because textual meaning only assists in the realization of ideational and interpersonal meaning, and does not represent "content" in itself, which is not on the same level as ideational and interpersonal meaning. On the other hand, in order to achieve the equivalence in both ideational and interpersonal meaning to the source texts, the translated texts must be organized at the textual level, namely the equivalence in textual meaning.

In terms of assessment tools, since the ideational meaning, interpersonal meaning and textual meaning of a language correspond to respectively and are reflected in the transitivity, mood, and thematic systems of the lexico-grammatical system of the language, then the vocabulary-grammar system of a language is naturally a good tool for exploring the functions and meanings between the source texts and the translation. In other words, through transitivity, mood, modality, appraisal, and thematic analysis of the clauses of the source texts and translations, by revealing and describing their ideational and interpersonal meanings, it is possible to judge comprehensively and systematically whether or where the translation deviates from the source texts[2].

After the introduction of this model, it has received considerable attention from the academic community. Yang (2008)[3], Kang and Zhang (2010)[4], Kou (2010)[5], and Liu (2010)[6] introduced and commented on the model; Lv (2010)[7] conducted an empirical analysis of the model in two translations of *Autumn in the Old Capital*, verifying its applicability and feasibility; Sun and Wang (2011)[8] applied the model to evaluate the

---

[1] Hu Zhuanglin et al. *Introduction to Systemic Functional Grammar* [M]. Hunan Education Press, 1989:9.
[2] See Si Xianzhu 2007:44, 81, 120, 135, 198 for details.
[3] Yang Rufu. "A stone from another mountain can be used to attack a jade—A review of *Functional Linguistics and Translation Studies—Construction of a Translation Quality Assessment Model*"[J]. *Foreign Language and Foreign Language Teaching*, 2008 (11): 63-64.
[4] Kang Leiming, Zhang Wenhui. "Book Review of Si Xianzhu's Translation Quality Assessment Model" [J]. *Journal of Heilongjiang Institute of Education*, 2010 (12): 148-150.
[5] Kou Liping. "A review of translation quality assessment models from the perspective of systemic functional linguistics" [J]. *Journal of Chinese Studies*, 2010 (6): 100-101.
[6] Liu Yi. "A Study of Chinese and Western Translation Quality Assessment Models" [D]. Master's Thesis of Ocean University of China, 2010.
[7] Lv Gui. "Evidence and reflection on the translation quality assessment model in systemic functional linguistics" [J]. *Foreign Language Research*, 2010 (2): 64-69.
[8] Sun Mengyi and Wang Xiaoyan. "The Application of Si Xianzhu's Translation Quality Assessment Model: A Review of the English Translation Quality of a University Online Current Affairs News" [J]. *China Electric Power Education*, 2011 (17): 186-187.

translation quality of a college online current affairs news, proving that the parameters, approaches, and methods of the model are basically feasible.

1.1 Deficiencies in Existing Models

In the practice of translation assessment based on this model, especially in the assessment of the quality of applied genre text translation, the most prominent drawback has been found to be the lack of generic analysis.

Because the texts that translation face are always examples of a certain genre, which is influenced by the genre norms of the text under specific cultural acculturation. Although reviewers can systematically detect and describe whether the translated texts deviate from the source texts in terms of ideational and interpersonal meaning with respect to transitivity, mood, and modality based on the existing model and existing parameters, it is difficult to describe and judge its appropriateness at the genre level. This is reflected in the following aspects:

1 The structure of texts of the same genre is often different in the source and target languages

Texts always exist in a certain context of culture. As a reflection of the influence of cultural factors on texts at the structural level, any text belongs to a certain genre and therefore exhibits a certain structure. However, due to differences between the two languages and cultures involved in translation, there are often differences in the text structure. When comparing cross-cultural texts, Jia[1] points out that the structure of Chinese discourse tends to gradually reach a climax, from secondary to primary, from background to task; while in Western languages, such as English, the structure of discourses is often of the retroactive type, with the "result" in front, the "cause" behind, the summary before, and the details behind. Consider the structure of a Chinese applied genre, such as an advertising discourse.

杭州市属7个县境内，北有超山，西有天目山，溯钱塘江而上，有富阳鹳山，桐庐瑶琳仙境、桐君山和严子陵钓台，建德灵栖三洞，新安江"千岛湖"等名胜，形成一个以西湖为中心的广阔旅游区。

This is a typical Chinese advertisement for tourist attractions. Its textual model is to divide it first and then summarize it. The final sentence "形成一个以西湖为中心的广阔

---

[1] Jia Yuxin. *Intercultural Communication* [M]. Shanghai: Shanghai Foreign Language Education Press, 1997.

旅游区" summarizes the entire text.

When Guo translated it into English, he fully considered the structural features of the English text, first summarizing it and then dividing it into parts. He started with "形成一个以西湖为中心的广阔旅游区" as the beginning (the first sentence) and then divided it into scenic spots in all directions including east, west, south and north. The text is clearly structured and layered.

The beauty spots in the seven nearby counties form a vast area for tourists with West Lake at its center. To the north of Hangzhou stands the Chao Hill, and to the west Mt. Tianmu. Coming up to the Qiantang River one finds oneself at Stork Hill in Fuyang county. Nearby in Tonglu County are the Yaolin Wonderland, the Tongjun Hill and the Terrace where Yan Ziling, a hermit of the Eastern Han Dynasty (25-220), loved to go angling by the Fuchun River. Jinde County boasts of the three Linqi Caves and the Thousand-Islet Lake at the source of the Xin'anjiang River[1].

According to Zhou and Zhou's[2] research on the internal structure of advertising, the commonly used text structures or discourse patterns in English advertising include "general specific", "background problem", "solution evaluation", "cause result", and "hypothesis fact". Therefore, it is necessary to adjust the structure of Chinese-English advertisements being translated in accordance with the reading habits of English readers. For instance:

无线电工厂

无线电工厂是全国著名企业之一，专业生产收音机、收录机、通信机、无线扩音机和音响设备。冠以"红灯"著名商标，享誉国内外。该产品款式新颖、音质优美、质量可靠、功能齐备，它将赢得您的喜爱，并给您的家庭带来欢乐。

One version of translation is:

The Elegance of Audio Systems "Red Lantern"

Present You with the Most Wonderful Experience

When picking up an audio system you certainly want it to deliver stunning sound

---

[1] Guo Jianzhong. "The translation unit of Chinese-English translation" [J]. *Foreign Language*, 2001 (6): 49-56.
[2] Zhou Xiao, Zhou Yi. *Modern English Advertising* [M]. Shanghai: Shanghai Foreign Language Education Press, 1998:93-128.

reproduction, to be equipped with a complete range of functions and attractive novel design.

The perfect answer lies in "Red Lantern"produced by...... Radio Factory.

We specialize in the production of radios, radio-recorders, communication equipments, radio amplifiers and other audio systems.

Our Brand"Red Lantern"is renowned both in China and throughout the world.

"Red Lantern": brings happiness to your family.

By using the "problem solving" discourse model, the translation first proposes the "novel style, beautiful sound quality, reliable quality, and complete functionality"in the original text as a problem, then presents the "solution", and finally provides evaluation (renowned both in China and through the world). At the same time, according to English advertising habits, emphasis is placed on the trademark of the product rather than the manufacturer, so the manufacturer name only appears once in the translation, while the trademark name appears four times. This conforms to the structure of English advertising discourse, caters to the reading and aesthetic expectations of British and American readers, and undoubtedly will produce better reader response effects.

Another example is the famous Chinese literary master and translator Lin Yutang. In order to achieve a comprehensive understanding of Confucius'philosophical thoughts for ordinary Western readers, he adopted the translation strategy of domestication and adapted the text of this book according to the reading habits of Western readers: Putting aside the textual structure of the quotation form of the source text and classifying it into categories, making it a book with thorough logic, beginning and end, and strong readability, which has had a wide impact on Western readers and promoted cultural exchanges between China and the West.

In other words, due to the structural differences between English and Chinese texts, it is required to make necessary adjustments to the macro structure during translation. Undoubtedly, when evaluating the quality of a translation, only by taking this factor into account can a fair and appropriate assessment be made.

2 Although the structure of a text of the same genre is the same in both languages and cultures, its manifestation styles differ from each other

On the other hand, in most cases, the "structure" of English and Chinese texts is basically the same. However, due to differences in cultural environments, it is often like this: When translating a text of the same genre into the target language, although there is no need to make any changes to its structure, its style of expression needs to be changed in response to the new context. For instance:

一流大学，首先是教学、科研水平达到世界一流，但能否想象，到那时（2011年）我校两万多名师生员工还敲着饭碗，拿着饭票，排着长队买饭呢？我看是不行的。这就给我们提出了一个问题：清华大学要建成世界一流大学，我们后勤怎么办？我们饮食中心怎么办？

This is a typical Chinese text with the theme or central message of "一流大学不仅教学、科研要达到世界一流，其后勤服务也必须是一流的"(first-class universities not only need to achieve world-class teaching and scientific research, but also must provide first-class logistics services). However, this theme is not directly expressed in the text, but it is not difficult for readers to "realize the whole"through "visualizing"——"敲着饭碗，拿着饭票，排着长队买饭" (knocking on bowls, holding meal tickets, and queuing in long lines): Tsinghua University's logistics are currently not first-class, so what should we do? However, when translating this text into English, in order to ensure the transmission of this topic information and achieve smooth communication in the translated text, the translation should be explicitly adjusted in accordance with the embodiment style of the English text——placing the topic sentence in the prominent position of the text. Here is the translation:

If Tsinghua is turned into a first-class university, not only should its academic level live up to the standard, but also its catering services. You can not imagine about 20000 staff and students are still lining up in the queue for meals in canteens by the year 2011.Therefore, the issue of how to improve our catering services should be put on the top of the agenda. [1]

In contrast, it is not difficult to see that the theme of Chinese discourse is often implicit, while the theme of English discourse is often overt. The differences in presentation styles between English and Chinese texts are often manifested in the opposition between "explicit" and "implicit" in the processing of textual central information.

Therefore, text translation must focus on rendering the macro theme of the entire text. Therefore, in translation, translators often need to adjust the construction mode and

---

[1] Ren Xiaoping. Flexibility in Diplomatic Interpretation [J]. *China Translation*, 2000 (5): 40-44

manifestation style of the source text to a certain extent according to the construction characteristics of the target text. Otherwise, "if in translation, the existence of corresponding structures in the target language is disregarded, and the grammatical structure in the target language is not used to replace the grammatical structure in the source language, then the grammatical structure in the translation is actually the formal structure in the (untranslated) source language, rather than the equivalent or corresponding form in the target language, meaning will thus inevitably be lost or distorted to varying degrees."[1]

In fact, the manifestation of a genre, or the linguistic features of a genre, actually represents a stylistic representation from a stylistic perspective. Different styles naturally emphasize different stylistic representations. From the perspective of the correlation between language form and stylistic theme, the weight given to language forms with stylistic significance in a text is directly proportional to their correlation with the thematic meaning of the text: the more thematic language forms are, the greater the weight they are given; the core linguistic forms involved in the construction of textual thematic meaning must be reflected or compensated in the corresponding forms in the translation. The following are an English sports news text and its two Chinese Translators Journals:

After three championships with the Chicago Bulls, a second gold medal with the U.S. team at the 1992 Olympic, and all the accolades the game can bestow, Jordan felt his motivation slipping away. "I'm at the pinnacle," he told a thronged press conference. "I just feel I don't have anything else to prove."

The first version of translation:
在芝加哥公牛队打球连得三次冠军，在美国队打球于1992年奥林匹克运动会上获第二枚金牌，并获得篮球所能给予的一切荣誉之后，乔丹说他打球的动力在消退。"我已经到了顶点，"他在一次熙熙攘攘的记者招待会上说。"我觉得我再没有什么东西要去证明了。"

The second version of translation:
在<u>效力</u>芝加哥公牛队连获三冠，<u>加盟</u>美国队于1992年再获奥运金牌，并<u>囊括</u>篮球运动各项殊荣之后，乔丹觉得自己打球的动力日见消退……[2]

Obviously, due to the adoption of commonly used words (underlined parts) in

---

[1] Shen Dan. On Formal Equivalence in Translation [J]. *Foreign Language Teaching and Research*, 1997 (2): 34-39.
[2] Liu Junbiao: The Application of Register Theory in Translation [J]. *Journal of Zhengzhou Institute of Aviation Industry Management,* 2009 (4): 103-106.

Chinese sports news reports, the second version reproduces the formal features of the source text in terms of language form; in terms of meaning, it realizes the care for the thematic meaning of this genre or style, achieving a "combination of form and spirit" in translation, as if it were "the re creation of the source language author by using the translated language".

As for applied genre texts, due to their obvious communicative purposes, they generally have relatively obvious genre markers or genre markers. For example, the beginning of a story or narrative is usually "Once upon a time..."or "It is said that...", therefore, from the perspective of translation, we must pay attention to the markedness of a genre and respond formally when translating. For example, the opening sentence of "The Romance of the Three Kingdoms" is: "话说天下大势，分久必合，合久必分". "话说" in this sentence is a genre marker that cannot be ignored!

One version of translation is:

Domains under heaven, after a long period of division, tends to unite; after a long period of union, tends to divide.[1]

Another version of translation is:

Here begins our tale. The empire, long divided, must unite; long united, must divide.[2]

The first version omits the word "话说", which is a deviation from the genre marker in language level. By retaining the word "words", the second version pays attention to the marks on specific parts of this genre of text, and translates it into a single sentence independently, highlighting the importance of equivalence in forms during translation.

The genre of applied text is very complex and diverse. According to content, the translation of applied genre text can be divided into legal translation, tourism translation, academic translation, advertising translation, etc. What's more, various genres can also be further categorized, such as scientific and technological translation, which can be divided into legal text (such as patent specifications, technical contracts, etc.) translation, academic translation, and popular science translation based on different styles and content. The classification principles and methods of applied genres vary from one to another, and the text structure and language use of each genre have their own regularity. Therefore,

---

[1] Shi Changyu. "Forward to *The Romance of the Three Kingdoms in Chinese and English*" [A]. Luo Guanzhong, translated by Moss Roberts. *The Romance of the Three Kingdoms in Chinese and English*. Beijing: Foreign Language Press, 2000:17-30.
[2] Luo Guanzhong, translated by Moss Roberts. *The Romance of the Three Kingdoms in Chinese and English*. Beijing: Foreign Language Press, 2000.

applied text genre analysis directly affects the selection and application of translation methods. As Zhou[1] said, "It is necessary for translators to analyze the characteristics of specific textual genres, to grasp the overall intention and function of the source text, to identify the means by which the author conveys the intention of the text, and thus to correctly choose translation strategies."

From this perspective, it is not difficult to see the shortcomings of the original assessment model in the setting of genre analysis parameters, especially in the assessment of applied genre text translation quality.

The above analysis of the defects of the original model fundamentally fails to pay enough attention to the context system within the framework of verbal communication on which the aforementioned verbal communication, including translation, relies: the original model only pays attention to the influence of situational context, that is, register, on meaning construction and language form selection, but relatively ignores the influence of context of culture, that is, genre factors, on translation production.

From the perspective of genre analysis, based on systemic functional linguistics and on the basis of existing models, this research attempts to establish a more targeted and operable assessment model for the translation quality of applied genre texts to enrich the theoretical system of translation evaluation.

1.2 Systemic Functional Linguistics, Theory of Genre Analysis and Translation Quality Assessment of Applied Generic Texts

As an interdisciplinary subject, translation needs to consciously apply the achievements of other disciplines, such as linguistics, philosophy, literature, human culture, cognitive science, semiotics, psychology, communication, sociology, etc. In adopting theories from other disciplines to conduct translation studies, linguistics provides the most direct guidance to translation research. This stems from the fact that translation is first and foremost a linguistic activity. Moreover, other activities of translation will ultimately manifest themselves in the choice and manipulation of language. For example, the cultural school of translation studies focuses on cultural and political activities such as post-colonialism and imperialism behind translation.

As one of the most influential linguistic theories today, systemic functional linguistics originates from the anthropological tradition of language research such as Protagoras and Plato. Focusing on the human nature and social aspects of language,

---

[1] Zhou Xuanfeng. Genre Analysis and Translation Strategies [J] *Journal of Xiangtan Normal University* (Social Science Edition), 2004 (5): 102-103.

following the policy of meaning rather than form advocated by Firth, functional linguistics has always taken the meaning expressed in actual situational contexts, that is, the function of language, as the focus of language research. Translation studies have always been "meaning oriented": Hatim and Mason regard "meaning interpretation as the center of translators'work" in translation studies[1], Matthiessen understands the act of translation as "the process of reconstructing the meaning of the target language"[2]. It is evident that there is a close relationship between systemic functional linguistics and translation studies, which can become the ideological basis and theoretical basis for our study of translation issues. In fact, in recent years, the founder of systemic functional linguistics has repeatedly referred to his functional linguistics as "applicable linguistics", which can be applied to many aspects, including translation studies[3].

The study of language use in a text requires not only that the language be grammatically consistent at the formal level, but also that the language of the text reflect the culture to which it belongs at the pragmatic level. To assess the appropriateness of the language form selection of a text, including a translated text, it is necessary to go beyond the limitations of the text and consider factors such as cultural context and situational context[4]. The most direct impact of cultural context on language use, as mentioned above, is the schematic structure and expressive style of a genre. Therefore, the fundamental purpose of genre research or genre analysis, is to study the communicative purposes and language use strategies of discourse with the aim of answering the question of why people tend to choose words, sentences, and layout in this way rather than in that way when constructing certain types of discourse[5].

Of course, there are many methods for genre analysis, and we will elaborate on them later (Chapter 4). However, in view of the above value of systemic functional linguistics for translation research, this topic will mainly explore the construction of a quality assessment model for applied genre text translation based on genre analysis theory of systemic functional linguistics.

---

[1] Hatim, B.& &I. Masion. *Discourse and the Translator* [M]. London: Longman./ Shanghai: Shanghai Foreign Language Education Press,1990/2001: 25.
[2] Matthessian, C. The environment of translation [A]. In E. Steiner &C. Yallop (eds.). Exploring Translation and Multilingual Text Production: Beyond Context [C]. Berlin: Mouton de Cruyter, 2001, 51-64.
[3] Huang Guowen. "Systemic Functional Linguistics as Applied Linguistics"[J]. *English Studies*, 2006a (4): 1-6
[4] Huang Guowen. *A Linguistic Exploration of Translation Studies: A Linguistic Analysis of English Translations of Ancient Poems* [M]. Shanghai Foreign Language Education Press, 2006b: 176.
[5] Qin Xiubai. "Introduction to 'Genre Analysis'" [J]. *Foreign Language,* 1997 (6): 8-15

1.3 Research Approach and Structure of This Book

This study is based on the original model, especially the aforementioned defects found in the quality assessment of applied genre text translations of the original model, and constructs a quality assessment model for applied genre text translation from the perspective of systemic functional linguistics genre analysis. Therefore, this study is an inheritance, revision, and improvement of the original model, aiming to enrich the system of translation quality assessment models. It not only intends to further research on translation quality assessment models, but also to continue translation research from the perspective of systemic functional linguistics. As an introduction, the first chapter of the book reviews the construction thinking and social repercussions of the original translation quality evaluation model, analyzes the seriousness of the lack of genre analysis for the evaluation of applied genre text translation quality, and expounds the objectives, theoretical basis, research ideas, and framework structure of this research project. Chapter 2 provides an overview of translation quality and its evaluation models from the perspective of research trends and literature review. Chapter 3 reviews the achievements and problems of translation research from the perspective of systemic functional linguistics. Due to the inadequacy of the original model, this study designed and constructed a genre-oriented text translation quality evaluation model from the perspective of genre analysis. Chapter 4 discusses the concept of genre and its main analysis modes, expounds the genre analysis modes adopted in this topic, and introduces the text features of applied genre, especially the three types of applied genre text focused on in this topic, such as corporate profiles, sports news reports, and museum introductions. Because the text structure and language use of each genre have their own regularity, it is necessary to establish a targeted evaluation model for the translation quality of applied genre texts. Naturally, it is necessary to analyze different applied genres in order to grasp their genre characteristics and provide practical tools for constructing such a genre translation quality evaluation model. However, how can we grasp the norms and characteristics of applied genre texts in the two languages involved in translation? From the perspective of research methods, a relatively feasible approach is to establish a small corpus of English, Chinese, and Chinese Translators Journals of the three types of applied genre texts (corporate profiles, sports news reports, and museum introductions) that this topic focuses on, so that we are able to analyze the macro structure (schematic e and describe language features (patterns of expression) to summarize their respective characteristics and compare them to identify similarities and differences. Therefore, chapter 5 briefly explains the concepts of corpus and translation corpus, and introduces the situation of the small corpus to be established in this topic. On the basis of the above discussion, Chapter 6 discusses the construction ideas, procedures, parameters, development and achievements of the original model, analyzes the existing shortcomings, and expounds the translation quality evaluation standards and the purpose and characteristics of applied genre text translation. On this basis, it discusses how to inherit the effective parts of the original model and integrate genre analysis into the translation assessment parameter system, constructing a new translation quality assessment model.

As mentioned above, the first part of this study consists of six chapters, Chapter 1 is introduction, Chapter 2 investigates translation quality assessment research, Chapter 3 covers systemic functional linguistics and translation research, Chapter 4 explores genre and perspective translation research, Chapter 5 focuses on corpus-driven speech and translation research, and Chapter 6 discusses the construction of applied genre text translation quality assessment model. However, the above constructed model for evaluating the quality of applied genre text translation is only a theoretical product and has not yet been verified, so it can only be a model hypothesis at best. To achieve the transformation from model hypothesis to model, it is necessary to undergo practical testing. Therefore, the second part of this monograph is an empirical study consisting of Chapter 7, 8 and 9, which conduct genre analysis of the English, Chinese, and Chinese-English translations of three applied genres: corporate profiles, sports news reports and museum introductions. On this basis, the aforementioned new model is used to evaluate the quality of the translated text, and countermeasures are proposed to improve it in order to complete the verification of the model. Finally, Chapter 10 summarizes the value and innovation of this study, pointing out the shortcomings.

References:

[1]Hatim, B.& &I. Masion. *Discourse and the Translator* [M]. London: Longman./ Shanghai: Shanghai Foreign Language Education Press,1990/2001.

[2]Matthessian, C. "The environment of translation" [A]. In E. Steiner &C. Yallop (eds.). *Exploring Translation and Multilingual Text Production: Beyond Context* [C]. Berlin: Mouton de Cruyter, 2001.

[3]Guo Jianzhong. "The translation unit of Chinese-English translation" [J]. *Foreign Language*, 2001 (6): 49-56.

[4]Hu Zhuanglin et al. *Introduction to Systemic Functional Grammar* [M]. Hunan Education Press, 1989.

[5]Huang Guowen. "Systemic Functional Linguistics as Applied Linguistics" [J]. *English Studies*, 2006a (4): 1-6.

[6]Huang Guowen. *A Linguistic Exploration of Translation Studies: A Linguistic Analysis of English Translations of Ancient Poems* [M]. Shanghai Foreign Language Education Press, 2006b

[7]Jia Yuxin. *Intercultural Communication* [M]. Shanghai: Shanghai Foreign Language Education Press, 1997.

[8]Kang Leiming, Zhang Wenhui. "Book Review of Si Xianzhu's Translation Quality Evaluation Model"[J]. *Journal of Heilongjiang Institute of Education*, 2010 (12): 148-150.

[9]Liu Junbiao. "The Application of Register Theory in Translation"[J]. *Journal of Zhengzhou Institute of Aviation Industry Management*, 2009 (4): 103-106.

[10]Liu Yi. *A Study of Chinese and Western Translation Quality Assessment Models* [D]. Master's Thesis of Ocean University of China, 2010.

[11]Luo Guanzhong, translated by Moss Roberts*"The Romance of the Three Kingdoms" in Chinese and English*[M]. Beijing: Foreign Language Press, 2000.

[12]Lv Gui. "Evidence and reflection on the translation quality assessment model in systemic functional linguistics"[J]. *Foreign Language Research*, 2010 (2): 64-69.

[13]Koulipin. "A review of translation quality assessment models from the perspective of systemic functional linguistics"[J]. *Journal of Chinese Studies*, 2010 (6): 100-101.

[14]Qin Xiubai. "Introduction to 'Genre Analysis'" [J]. *Foreign Language*, 1997 (6): 8-15.

[15]Ren Xiaoping. "Flexibility in Diplomatic Interpretation"[J]. *Chinese Translators Journal*, 2000 (5): 40-44.

[16]Shen Dan. "On Formal Equivalence in Translation"[J]. *Foreign Language Teaching and Research*, 1997 (2): 34-39.

[17]Si Xianzhu. *Functional Linguistics and Translation Studies - Construction of a Translation Quality Assessment Model* [M]. Beijing: Peking University Press, 2007.

[18]Shi Changyu. "Introduction to *The Romance of the Three Kingdoms* in Chinese and English"[A] Luo Guanzhong, translated by Moss Roberts *The Romance of the Three Kingdoms in Chinese and English*[M]. Beijing: Foreign Language Press, 2000:17-30.

[19]Sun Mengyi, Wang Xiaoyan. "The Application of Si Xianzhu's Translation Quality Assessment Model: A Review of the English Translation Quality of a University Online Current Affairs News"[J]. *China Electric Power Education*, 2011 (17): 186-187.

[20]Yang Rufu. "A stone from another mountain can be used to attack a jade. A review of *Functional Linguistics and Translation Studies—Construction of a Translation Quality Assessment Model*"[J]. *Foreign Language and Foreign Language Teaching*, 2008 (11): 63-64.

[21]Hou Xuanfeng. Genre Analysis and Translation Strategies [J] Journal of Xiangtan Normal University (Social Science Edition), 2004 (5): 102-103.

[22]Zhou Xiao, Zhou Yi. *Modern English Advertising*[M]. Shanghai: Shanghai Foreign Language Education Press, 1998.

Chapter 2 A Survey of Translation Quality Assessment Research

This chapter reviews the history of translation quality assessment research, introduces and comments on representative foreign translation quality assessment models, summarizes the achievements made and analyzes the existing problems. On this basis, it expounds how to further promote the study of translation quality assessment models.

From the beginning of translation activities, there has been concern about translation quality issues. The recorded history of human translation shows that translation quality has always been accompanied by translation principles and criteria. Although translation principles and standards are behavioral norms that guide and regulate translation practice, the demand for translation quality lies behind. Translation quality assessment should also have its own standards, without which it is difficult to clarify the quality of translation. However, in the early stages of linguistics, there was a lack of clear and systematic standards for translation quality assessment, which are integrated with the guiding principles and standards of translation. At that time, there was only a macro and general grasp of translation quality, and it was difficult to have specific and micro evaluation parameters which further led to the lack of operability. Since the introduction of linguistic methods into translation research, its research procedures and methods have been characterized by systematization and scientificity. The same is true of translation quality assessment, which has become increasingly operational since the linguistic era. However, due to its disciplinary nature, the influencing factors of translation quality assessment activities are difficult to be exhaustive and accurately grasped, and a combination of macro and micro, subjective and objective approaches must be taken. Tracing the history of translation quality assessment activities and examining the historical trajectory of translation quality search can help to propose more feasible assessment models.

2.1 Literature Review of Domestic Translation Quality Research

Domestic translators and scholars have long been concerned about the quality of translation. Zhi put forward that "Importance should be attached to the meaning of the translated texts instead of word choices". According to Dao, the discourse is the most important. Kumarashi said that "Faithfulness to the source language comes first, then follows the elegance of the target language". Hui proposed the combination of literal translation and free translation. Seng made a further step by putting forward that the elegance of the target language (especially Chinese) should be maintained as much as possible. In Yan's point of view, faithfulness to the source language should be preferred to the graceful expression of the target language, and translators should possess "eight qualifications". Xuan Zang proposed "five non-translations" and "perfect harmony". Zan listed "six examples of translating scriptures". Liang suggested "it is necessary to seek both faithfulness and expressiveness". Ma advocated for "suitable translation". He Lin studied the relationship between meaning and expression. Yan raised the famous "faithfulness, expressiveness and elegance". Lu preferred "literal translation". Guo advised "graceful translation" and "translating poems with poems". Fu suggested "be alike in spirit". Qian preferred "perfection in translation"[1]. Liu put forward "faithfulness, expressiveness and closeness"[2]. Xu raised "beauty in sense, sound and form"[3]. Gu established "the Multiple Complementarity of Translation Criteria"[4]. Wang put forward "spirit transmission and meaning conveyance". Cai believed in "the ontology of meaning". Accompanied by these translation standards and principles as well as translators' continuous pursuit of higher qualification, is the tireless search by translators and translation theorists for what constitutes good translation and high-quality translation. Although these summaries and statements are the summary of the experience of masters who have devoted themselves to translation practice, due to the aesthetic limitations of traditional Chinese philology and literary studies, it is inevitable that there is a lack of dissipation and casual feeling, and the role of standards and principles in translation quality assessment practice is limited. Thus there is an inevitable sense of ambiguity and

---

[1] Luo Xinzhang ed. *Translation Essays* [M]. Beijing: Commercial Press, 2009:1-20.
[2] Liu Chongde. "Three discussions on the principle of " faithfulness, expressiveness, and integrity " - and discussing the issue of academic style with Peng Jun" [J]. *Fujian Foreign Language Journal*, 2000 (4): 44-50.
[3] Xu Yuanchong. *The Art of Translation* [M]. Beijing: Wuzhou Communication Press, 2006:73.
[4] Gu Zhengkun. "The Theory of Multiple Complementarity of Translation Criteria" [J]. *Chinese Translators Journal*, 1989 (1): 16-20.

obscurity in these standards and principles.

In recent years, the domestic translation community has published a number of theoretical works on Translation criticism that have direct guiding significance for the evaluation of translation quality, including Xu (1992)[1], Wang (2000)[2], Yang (2005)[3], Wang (2006)[4], Chen (2008)[5], Lu and Hou (2009)[6], Zhao and Zhao (2010)[7], etc. The common feature of these works is that they have deviated from the traditional macro approach of discussing translation quality based on standards and principles and gradually moved towards a micro level, thus strengthening their guiding significance for translation quality assessment practice.

2.2 Review of International Translation Quality Research

In foreign countries, there are "translations as an orator" by Cicero[8]; Horace's "original imitation"[9]; Jerome's "sense for sense"[10]; Alfred's' "plain and clear"[11]; Luther's "reader oriented translation"[12]; Dolet's "the five principles of translation"[13]; Dryden's "translation trichotomy"[14]; Johnson's "change nothing but the language"[15]; Tytler's "the complete transfer of advantages of the source text into the target language is a good translation" and

---

[1] Xu Jun. "Reflections on Literary Translation criticism" [J]. *Chinese Translators Journal*, 1992 (4): 30-33.
[2] Wang Shouyuan. "On Language Learning Strategy Training" [J]. *Journal of the School of Foreign Languages, Shandong Normal University*, 2000 (1): 7-10.
[3] Yang Xiaorong. "Analysis of Constraints on Translation Standards" [J]. *Journal of Shanghai International Studies University*, 2005 (6): 51-58.
[4] Wang Hongyin. *Literary Translation Criticism* [M]. Shanghai: Shanghai Foreign Language Education Press, 2006.
[5] Chen Hongwei. "It may seem easy, but in reality it's not easy" [J]. *Chinese Translators Journal*, 2008, 29 (1): 88-90.
[6] Lv Jun, Hou Xiangqun. *An introduction to the science of translation criticism*[M]. Shanghai: Shanghai Foreign Language Education Press, 2009.
[7] Zhao Xiuming, Zhao Zhangjin. *Literature Translation criticism: Theory, Method and Practice*[M]. Changchun: Jilin University Press, 201.
[8] Robinson, D. *Western Translation Theory: from Herodotus to Nietzsche* [M]. Beijing: Foreign Language Teaching and Research Press, 2006:9.
[9] Ibid.
[10] Ibid.
[11] Ibid.
[12] Ibid.
[13] Ibid.
[14] Ibid.
[15] Ibid.

"three standards"[1]; Goethe's "two principles of translation"[2] and so on. In the pre-linguistic period of translation studies, the quality pursuit reflected in these translation practice principles was either "influenced by classical epistemology philosophy, overemphasizing' intuition'and' inspiration', which shrouded everything in a mysterious color"; or "it is to use the proportion of right and wrong to judge the quality of the translation, and to a large extent, consider and evaluate the quality and style of the translation based on the language content and style tone of the original work"[3]. Later on, there are Nida's theory of equivalence[4]; Catford's "translation transformation"[5]; Reiss's "text types and translation"[6]; Vermeer's "teleology"[7]; Nord's"function plus loyalty"[8]; Lefevere et al.'s"priority of ideological and poe'tic factors over linguistic factors in translation"[9]; Simon et al.'s "strategies of pursuing translation and language as advocates for women"[10]; Niranjan's redefinition of translation by introducing post-colonialism rights theory[11]; Venuti calls for"impedance based"translation to allow translators and their translations to"take shape" in the target language[12]; Lewis'"indulgent loyalty"[13]; Benjamin's "pure language" of translation[14]; Pound's creative translation of "imagism"[15] and so on, just to name a few. These translation theories are also the principles, standards, or strategies that speakers adhere to in their translation practice, and they also embody

---

[1] Ibid.
[2] Ibid.
[3] Xiao Weiqing. *Research on the Mode of Translation criticism* [M]. Shanghai: Shanghai Foreign Language Education Press, 2010: 270.
[4] Venuti, L. *The Translation Studies Reader* [M]. London & New York: Routledge, 2000: 126.
[5] Venuti, L. *The Translation Studies Reader* [M]. London & New York: Routledge, 2000: 141.
[6] Reiss, K. *Translation Criticism—the Potentials and Limitations: Categories and Criteria for Translation Quality Assessment* [M]. Manchester: St. Jerome Publishing, 2000.
[7] Venuti, L. *The Translation Studies Reader* [M]. London & New York: Routledge, 2000:221.
[8] Nord, C. *Translating as a Purposeful Activity: Functionalist Approaches Explained*[M].Manchester: St Jerome,1997:125.
[9] Lefevere, A. *Translation, Rewriting and the Manipulation of Literary Fame* [M]. London and New York: Routledge,1992: 9.
[10] Simon, S. *Gender in Translation: Cultural Identity and the Politics of Transmission*[M]. London & New York: Routledge, 1996: 15.
[11] Niranjana, T. *Siting Translation: history, post-structuralism, and the colonial context*[M]. Berkeley. Los Angeles. Oxford: University of California Press, 1992.
[12] Venuti. L. *The Translator's Invisibility*[M]. Shanghai: Shanghai Foreign Language Education Press, 1995:16-17.
[13] Venuti. L. ed. *The Translation Studies Reader*[M]. London and New York: Routledge, 2000:268-273.
[14] Ibid: 15-25.
[15] Ibid: 26-33.

their pursuit of translation quality to some extent, expressing their vision of what a good translation is. However, due to the fact that these translation theories do not directly address translation quality issues and lack systematicity, they can only serve as behavioral guidelines for individual translation practices and cannot be well applied to systematic translation quality assessment practices.

Undoubtedly, translation quality assessment is an important component of translation research. In the latter half of the 20th century, inspired by linguistics, research on translation quality assessment began to systematize. In the West, the systematic translation quality assessment model originated from House[1]. Based on the register framework of functional linguistics, House proposed eight contextual parameters according to the dimensions of language users and language use. Reiss[2] introduced text type as the most important variable in translation quality assessment. House later revised the original model by further adopting speech act theory, discourse theory and other pragmatic knowledge. Al Qinai[3] proposed seven parameters for quality assessment: text type, formal correspondence, thematic coherence, cohesion, discourse pragmatic equivalence, lexical properties, and the equivalence of grammar-syntactic. Williams[4] proposed a new argumentation evaluation model, which sets core parameters such as argumentation schema, propositional function/conjunction/inference indicators, argumentation type and narrative strategy; specific parameters such as terms, figures of speech, format and target language quality, and assigns values to each parameter. Based on the translation definition of "usually paid by customers, with fixed terms and usage purposes,and with certain requirements"[5], Drugan analyzed in detail the huge differences between the academic and commercial translation quality models in the era of industrialization translation from the practical perspective of translation industrialization and professionalization. Through groundbreaking empirical research, he considered both the translation process and the

---

[1] House, J. *Translation Quality Assessment: A Model Revisited* [M]. Tübingen: Gunter Narr Verlag,1997.
[2] Reiss, K. *Translation Criticism—the Potentials and Limitations: Categories and Criteria for Translation Quality Assessment* [M]. Manchester: St. Jerome Publishing, 1971/2000.
[3] Al-Qinai J. *Translation quality assessment. Strategies, parameters and procedures*[J]. Meta: Journal des traducteurs Meta:/Translators'Journal, 2000, 45(3): 497-519.
[4] Williams, M. *Translation Quality Assessment: An Argumentation--Centered Approach [M]*. Ottawa: University of Ottawa Press, 2004.
[5] Drugan, J. *Quality in Professional Translation: Assessment and Improvement* [M]. London: Bloomsbury, 2013.

translation results by paying comprehensive attention to all aspects of translation quality from top down and bottom up perspectives. The book proposes a series of translation practice plans, dedicating others'rich translation practice experience and lessons to readers. The author also draws on over a decade of experience in using modern translation technology tools, such as translation memory software, to depict the prospects for improving translation quality.

These works completely break away from the traditional macro approach of discussing translation quality based on standards and principles and enter the micro level. Through micro operations, they achieve a grasp of macro quality, thus providing greater guidance for translation quality assessment practice.

2.3 Review of Representative Translation Quality Assessment Models at Home and Abroad

This section selects several major systematic and operational translation quality assessment models both domestically and internationally for a detailed introduction. It is necessary to make two clarifications here. Firstly, in the commentary process, we stand from the perspective of the current translation field. The intention of doing so is not to negate the achievements of predecessors, but to stand on the shoulders of giants to highlight their historical limitations. The second is that when it comes to the concepts of "translation industry" and "translation profession", we, like Drugan, do not make a distinction because the two are basically born together in the same era. Here we only take into account the commonalities of the era without considering the heterogeneity of their content[1].

2.3.1 Reiss's Model,

Reiss's contribution to translation quality assessment mainly lies in three aspects. Firstly, the three major categories of translation quality assessment practice are clearly proposed: literary, linguistic and pragmatic. The category of literary examines text-type; the linguistic category refers to the linguistic factors that constitute a certain type of

---

[1] Drugan, J. *Quality in Professional Translation: Assessment and Improvement* [M]. London: Bloomsbury, 2013, 7.

discourse; pragmatic category refers to contextual factors outside of language.

Reiss's second major contribution is to clarify the specific focus of inspection in the three major categories of quality assessment. In the first category, the relationship among text function, text-type, translation strategy and its quality assessment is discussed. Texts can be divided into four categories based on their function: content-focused, form-focused, appealing-focused and audiovisual. The first type of text focuses on information; the second type focuses on emotional and aesthetic functions; the third type focuses on the effect of the text on readers. According to Reiss, different text types require different criteria of assessment. For the translation assessment of the first type, the most important thing is to see whether the translation accurately conveys the information of the source text. The quality of the second type should be assessed by whether it adopts the same or similar text form as the source text and achieves the same or similar aesthetic effect. For the third type of text, it should be determined whether its effect on target readers is the same as that of the source text on its target audience. The quality of the final type of translation depends on whether it combines various nonverbal means to produce the same effect on the audience. In the second category, Reiss believes that quality assessment should examine factors at various levels of language, namely semantics, vocabulary, grammar and style. At the semantic level, the examination is to check whether the semantics and content are preserved, and to pay attention to the semantic mismatch between polysemous words and homophones. At the lexical level, to examine the translation quality of translators' technical terms and customary expressions. At the grammatical level, the examination should check whether the translation's morphology and syntax meet the requirements of semantics and style of the target language. Finally, it is to examine whether the translation reproduces the style of the source text. Semantic, lexical, grammatical and stylistic factors are all considered in the translation to preserve the meaning of the source text. In the field of pragmatics, the main consideration is the contextual factors that affect translation, such as theme, time, location, reader, speaker and emotional factors. Here, Reiss combines the linguistic and pragmatic functional criteria of the text, making her assessment criteria more objective.

Reiss's third major contribution lies in discussing the limitations of translation quality assessment from both subjective and objective perspectives. There are two subjective limitations: firstly, the translator's interpretation of the source text is Inevitably subjective; secondly, translators have different academic temperaments. Translators and reviewers should fully consider these two subjective factors. There are also two types of objective limitations. Firstly, the quality of translation is limited by the specific purpose of the translation; secondly, the quality of translation is limited by the special readership set for translation activities. Reiss points out that translators and reviewers must fully consider the four subjective and objective factors that determine quality.

Reiss's quality assessment model comprehensively considers the knowledge of text typology, linguistics, pragmatics and aesthetics, and it is the first model with strong systematicness and feasibility which combines subjective and objective perspectives. However as she herself points out, there is no translation quality assessment theory that covers all phenomena, and each theory has its own limitations[1]. She does not specify how language achieves a certain function, how to specifically determine the text type of the source text, nor does she realize the coexistence of multiple texts dominated by a certain text.

2.3.2 Introduction to House's Model

When summarizing the current situation of translation assessment research, Mcalester points out that there are only two books dedicated to translation assessment so far, one is House's *Translation Quality Assessment Model* and its revised version *Translation Quality Assessment: A Model Revisited*, the other is Reiss's *Translation Criticism: Foreground and Limitations*[2].

House classifies quality assessment into three main types: individual subjective, equivalent response and text-based[3].

House regards the first type of quality assessment method as a professional one. She classifies all translation quality assessment methods before translation research became a

---

[1] Reiss, K. *Translation Criticism—the Potentials and Limitations: Categories and Criteria for Translation Quality Assessment* [M]. Manchester: St. Jerome Publishing, 2000:6-7.
[2] Mcalester G. *The evaluation of translation into a foreign language*[J]. BENJAMINS TRANSLATION LIBRARY, 2000, 38: 229-242.
[3] House, J. *Translation Quality Assessment: A Model Revisited* [M]. Tübingen: Gunter Narr Verlag,1997.

discipline into this category. These methods have been advocated by translators, philosophers, linguists, writers, etc. She believes that these methods lack theoretical depth, systematicity, and universality. The second type of quality assessment of House is based on the equivalence between the translated text and the source text, which compares and evaluates the reactions of the target language readers or users with those of the source text readers and users. House adopts psycholinguistic and behavioral methods, and believes that the main drawback of these methods is that they all rely on the black box of the human brain. The third assessment type of House is based on texts, including Reiss's and Vermeer's quality assessment methods, which focuses on detailed analysis and comparison of the source text and translation. House believes that these three types have limitations because translation is constrained by many aspects of both the source text and the cultural system of the target language, and all translation assessment should start from this fact.

The model proposed by House avoids personal subjectivity and covers two types of assessment: equivalent response and text analysis. She proposes three important concepts: overt translation, covert translation, and culture filtering. Explicit translation is the use of another language to enable its readers to appreciate the function of the source text in the cultural environment of the source language; Implicit translation pursues equivalence in a new language, and through the pursuit of the same functions as the source text in the source language and culture, the translated text does not read like a translation.

The early quality assessment model of House is divided into three steps:

The first is to analyze the source text and state its functions. She analyzed and identified the characteristics of the source text from five aspects: text style, participation situation, relationship of social players, social attitudes and domains. Text style refers to the presentation form of a text, which can be spoken or written. Participation refers to whether the text is monologue, dialogue or both. The relationship of social players refers to the relationship between the speaker of the source text and the reader, user, or audience. These relationships can be symmetric or asymmetric. Social attitude is related to the degree of formality in language, and there are five styles: reservation, formality, negotiation, casualness, and familiarity. The scope of domain is relatively broad, referring to the professional activity scope of text producers, the language field and theme of text language activities, including the register. By analyzing these five parts, House examined the relevant dimensions of language use, such as syntax, morphology and the use of discourse devices. House also analyzed and examined the situation of language users (such as the background and social class of the source text author, the time of original creation, etc.).

The second step is to compare the source text with the translated text. House compared the source text and translation from the above five dimensions to determine translation errors. Errors are divided into overt errors and covert errors. The former refers to syntax errors in the translation and misuses of the meaning of the translation relative to the source text. The latter refers to the situation where the translation does not match the source text in the above five dimensions. House believed that overt errors had always been taken seriously in quality assessment. And covert errors had always been ignored.

The third step is the statement of the quality situation. After conducting a detailed comparison between the source text and translation as well as confirming the errors, she made comprehensive statement on the quality of a certain translation.

Twenty years later, House revised her model. The revised mode still consists of three steps:

The first step is to analyze the source text. The terms and statements used in analysis are simpler and more direct than the old model, and their theoretical basis is Halliday's linguistics, which focuses on several aspects such as field, tenor, mode, and genre. The field includes the theme and content of the source text. Description of participants: the author and readers, as well as the relationship between the two, including the author's time, location, and social domain. The revised model only considers three types of writing styles: formal, negotiation, and informal. The language style includes two parts: the text style in the original model and the participation situation, which refers to the communication channel between the author and readers, whether it is spoken or written. The former can also be divided into monologues and dialogues. The genre definition is relatively detailed and serves as an intermediate concept between register and stylistic function. After analyzing these four aspects, House made a comprehensive statement on the functionality of the source text.

The second step is to compare the source text with the translated text. The translation is analyzed from the four new dimensions of the first step above and is compared with the source text with the aim of identifying translation errors.

The third step is the statement of the translation quality. After a detailed comparison between the translation and the source text and the identification of mistranslations, House provided a comprehensive quality statement for a particular translation.

The criticism of House's revised model mainly focuses on four aspects. Firstly, the sample provided by House to verify her model is only one language pair. The direction of translation is only from English to German, and texts are relatively short, so the scope of her model was unknown. Secondly, the source texts selected by House rarely fall within the scope of professional translators' choices, and the text format is single, in which complex network and software texts are not included. Thirdly, it is difficult to apply her model to assess translation quality in a professional environment. She also entrusted future detailed empirical quality assessments to experienced translation teachers rather than translation practitioners, which goes against reality. Fourthly, the translation of commission letters, the writing context of the source text and the conditions for the production of the translation are seldom involved in House's model. Her inference was not based on a specific translation process, was not concerned with the deadline for translation activities, translation tools and reference materials, nor did it involve customer details which are important factors affecting the quality of professional translation. House also did not explicitly indicate that she had communicated with the source text author and the translator of the translated text, and all of her views were based on her reading of the source text and translation, which was too subjective. Finally, error correction is the main purpose of the House translation assessment model, while the focus of professional translation is to pursue appropriate and acceptable translation products. In view of this, in professional translation quality assessment, the practice of polishing the source text to improve quality in the translation is highly recommended, but in House's model, these situations would be considered as mistranslations[1].

2.3.3. Introduction to Al Qinai's model

Al Qinai proposed an empirical and compromised translation quality assessment

---

[1] Drugan, J. *Quality in Professional Translation: Assessment and Improvement* [M]. London: Bloomsbury, 2013.

model. His model was based on text analysis and specifically examined a series of factors, including text type, correspondence in forms, thematic coherence, referential cohesion, pragmatic equivalence and lexical and syntactic features[1]. The theoretical basis of the Qinai model was also a compromised one. He drew on House's initial model and pointed out that the goal of quality evaluation theory should be objective positivity rather than subjective impression. The difference between him and House is that his model did not examine whether translation was equivalent, but rather whether translation was appropriate. Al Qinai identified seven sets of parameters:

1. Text type and mode. Including the language and narrative structure and discourse functions of the source text and the translation. The discourse functions include preaching, information, instruction, persuasion or advice.

2. Correspondence in form. The comparison between the source text and the translated text in terms of length, arrangement, paragraph division and punctuation system.

3. Coherent thematic structure. Referring to the coherence and consistency between the source text and the translated text in terms of thematic progression.

4. Cohesion. In terms of cohesion, Al Qinai focuses on the translated text, examining to what extent it is deviated from the rhetorical and ideological context of the source text.

5. Discourse-pragmatic (dynamic) equivalence. Inspecting whether the translation achieves a predetermined effect similar to the source text (such as meeting readers' reading expectations).

6. Lexical features (including register and phrases such as jargon, idioms, and collocations). Comparing the source text and the translated text to determine translation strategies, including style changes due to language differences.

7. Grammatical/syntactic equivalence. Comparing the source and translated texts in terms of word order, consistency (number, gender, person), etc.

Al Qinai did not provide reasons for his selection of these seven parameters, nor did he explain why he excluded the consideration of other aspects. He only selected two

---

1 Al-Qinai, J. *Translation quality assessment: Strategies, parameters and procedures* [J]. Meta: Journal des traducteurs Meta:/Translators' Journal, 2000, 45(3): 497-519.

English-Arabic translated articles and used these seven parameters as sample analysis. Qinai emphasized that translation acceptance was the ultimate assessment of translation quality, and he proposed that any text translation with a common purpose should be put into the market to verify whether the expectations of the source language author and the translation readers had been met.

Qinai's model attaches more importance to the professionalism of translation than House's model. For example, he believed that 'a low-quality source text does not necessarily have to be translated into a low-quality translation'[1]. Qinai's model not only focuses on the mismatches and inconsistencies between the translation and the source text, but also on their coordination, which is more reasonable than the House model.

However, the Qinai model also has its shortcomings: the number of words in the selected samples is too small and there is only one language pair; insufficient consideration is given to factors such as power of attorney, deadline, working conditions, translation tools, and reference materials during the production and translation process of the source text; no consideration is given to the translator's selection and customers' requirements. Qinai also does not provide a comprehensive description of the appropriateness of translation. In addition, he does not specify the weights of the seven proposed parameters: if there is more compatibility than difference between the translation and the source text, can this alone determine the extent of acceptance of the translation? As Qinai believes that the highest criterion for translation quality assessment is the acceptability of the translation, more problems arise: since the market and users' acceptance of the translation is the highest criterion, this model loses its significance, and translation clients can directly focus on the market and the acceptance of the translation without worrying about assessing the quality of the translation[2].

2.3.4. Introduction to Williams' Model

Williams drew inspiration from the argumentative theory in discourse analysis and proposed his own micro discourse translation quality assessment framework. His model

---

[1] Drugan, J. *Quality in Professional Translation: Assessment and Improvement* [M]. London: Bloomsbury, 2013:58.
2 Ibid.: 59-60.

analyzed the source and translated texts, examined the translation of the topic and referred to the situational context generated by translation practice. When demonstrating his own model, Williams selected four pairs of texts, two of which were about the Canadian government's discussion of statistics and energy, and the other two were about criminology and law. This is more practical than the models of House and Qinai. These texts are all original, unrevised and of varying lengths, provided by freelance translators and general translation clients. Among them, two texts are about controversial topics, while the other two texts are about uncontroversial factual statistics. In this way, it can be detected that the effectiveness of his model is not affected by the argument of the topic. Williams'translation quality assessment is divided into four stages[1]:

1. Analyzing the source text. Analyzing the source text to determine its topic schema, specific structure of organization to clarify which parts contain basic textual information.

2. Analyzing the translation. Evaluating the overall coherence of the translation by examining it separately to determine whether the overall layout of the text has been preserved or appropriately adjusted. From the perspective of the target language, examining whether there are any issues concerned with the readability or acceptability of the text.

3. Comparative assessment. Comparing the source text and translation with the argument parameters set. The parameters include topic schema, topic layout, relationships of organizational structure, functions of the topic, related words, other inference markers, topic types, rhetoric, and narrative strategies. Williams defines each parameter and clarifies their relationship with translation quality assessment practices.

4. Overall quality statement. The final stage presents the overall translation quality under the argument-centered translation assessment model, and compares it with previous micro quantitative quality assessment methods.

Williams also abandoned general translation quality grading methods such as "precision"or"faithfulness"and proposed quality standard reference tools:

---

[1] Williams, M. *Translation Quality Assessment: An Argumentation—Centered Approach* [M]. Ottawa: University of Ottawa Press, 2004.

1. Publication standard. The translation accurately translates all aspects of the argumentative schema, meeting all parameter requirements of the translated language and other specific parameters of the selected translation domain. There are no critical errors.

2. Information standard. The translation accurately translates all aspects of the argumentative schema, meeting the parameters of the specific field of use of the selected translation. There are no critical errors.

3. Minimum standard. The translation accurately translates all aspects of the argumentative schema. There are no critical errors.

4. Secondary standard. The translation does not have a translation argumentation schema (at least one critical error) or does not meet the parameters of more than one specific field of use in the paper.

This standard setting is open and other grading standards can be attached. If it is a technical text, then the technical translation standards can be set as the translation quality grading parameters.

Williams'model of translation quality assessment focuses on the determination of quality based on functions of translation and the final use, emphasizing the professional feasibility of its model. His model also considers different quality grading and flexibility in different contexts. However, quality assessment practitioners have also raised some criticisms of his model. Like House and Qinai, Williams overlooked some macro factors that affect translation quality, such as the ability of translators in professional translation, translation process, translation tools, etc. There are also some other issues: Williams'empirical language pair is singular—only between French and English; Whether the topic structure is equally important in professional translated texts; If not, how should practitioners apply this pattern; How effective is the quality assessment method centered on debate in modern professional translation under team translation conditions, as team members sometimes have vastly different working environments and conditions; Team members sometimes lack access to standardized translations, and these translations are constantly being updated, especially in the localized industry; The source text has been constantly changing for decades, supplemented by multiple authors and translated by multiple translators with the same translation memory tool for a long time, then how to apply this model in this situation; The text that needs to be translated is only a part of the subsidiary texts of certain source texts, with various specific forms that have deviated from the original topic structure. In this case, whether the Weiss quality assessment model is still applicable; How to apply this model to online translation and computer game translation; Finally, using this mode is time-consuming and can be cumbersome in professional translation environments[1].

2.3.5. Introduction to Jeremy Munday's Model

Munday applied the evaluation theory developed by James R. Martin, David Rose and Peter R.R. White to translation assessment. This theory is based on the interpersonal function in Functional Linguistics and reveals the value orientation of language users through language analysis which consists of three dimensions: attitude, graduation and engagement. These three dimensions can be further systematized into their respective subsystems, forming a systematic assessment resource network[2].

Munday believes that evaluation is the core of communication and also the core of translation. Translation is a continuous evaluation process, which involves the translator comprehensively evaluating various possible expressions of the source text and ultimately making choices. Although evaluations may intentionally or unintentionally fill lines of the text, there are always parts of the text that are relatively susceptible to value manipulation, change, interpretation and evaluation in translation, which best reflect the translator's values. Munday called these parts "critical points". The focus of Munday is to explore what these critical points are, what their characteristics are and what laws should be followed in translation. Due to the significant differences in form and properties of key points, Munday introduced the "Appraisal Theory" model to increase the systematicness of the research. The operation of the model is based on the "Evaluation Theory". By analyzing evaluation, identifying these critical points and discovering their translation patterns, the operational process of translation at the micro linguistic level can be better

---

[1] Drugan, J. *Quality in Professional Translation: Assessment and Improvement* [M]. London: Bloomsbury, 2013:63-64.

[2] Munday, J. *Evaluation in Translation: Critical Points of Translator Decision-Making*[M]. London & New York: Rutledge, 2012.

understood.

By taking different types of texts such as political speech translation, technological translation, literary translation, and translation by quasi translators as examples, Munday conducted empirical research based on the evaluation theory model. His empirical selection covered a wide range of topics, including translation models, text styles, languages involved and translators' qualifications. His research methods were diverse, including expert interviews, online forums, translating manuscripts and translators' communication. On the one hand, this was to demonstrate the value of assessment theory in translation research; On the other hand, it was necessary to identify critical translation points in different text styles and languages, as well as the processing methods of different translators in translation.

The Munday model focuses on cultural factors in translation, but its focus on cultural factors still lays upon language and texts ultimately. This can be said to partially bridge the gap between different cultural schools and traditional translation studies. It is from this perspective that his model has pioneering academic value.

Munday's empirical research has many advantages, but its focus is clearly still on the lexical level. Although there have been mentions of attitude evaluation at the syntactic and discourse levels, it is not yet sufficient. In addition, there are certain rules that cannot be explained between the critical points of different types of texts he explores and their translations. The lack of systematization of critical points makes them trivial and therefore lacks applicability[1]. Of course, the Munday model also has limitations of the time, similar to some aspects of Drugan's criticism of the House, Qinai, and Williams models mentioned earlier.

2.4 Conclusion

The above review indicates that since the introduction of linguistics, research on translation quality assessment has begun to break free from the characteristics and limitations of casual and impressionistic comments that previously relied on translation

---

[1] Munday, J. *Evaluation in Translation: Critical Points of Translator Decision-Making*[M]. London & New York: Rutledge, 2012: 55.

principles and standards, and has gained systematic, actionable, and objective qualities. However, deficiencies still exist. For example, in the face of a vast amount of text translation practices of various types and genres, there is no universal assessment model that can be applied to scientifically and comprehensively assess the quality of translated texts.

At the same time, in the process of sorting out translation quality research, we also propose the following insights for the future development of translation quality research:

As the focus of translation studies turns again and again, the quality of translation has also been re-categorization. After the introduction of linguistics into translation research, although the evaluation of translation quality is relatively mechanical and static, it is quite systematic and scientific. Next is the cultural shift in translation research, which places translation quality under the context of cross-cultural communication. Although there is a sense of castles in the air and difficulty in operation, it reflects an improvement in the awareness of pursuing translation quality. Then comes the sociological turn, examining the fact that translation quality shifts with the will of the dominant actors in the field of translation. In the future, there may be an economic shift that emphasizes translation behavior as a link in the translation industry chain, and the inspection of its product quality should be placed in the overall efficiency of the entire industry operation[1]. The pursuit of translation quality is becoming increasingly practical, and micro factors have entered the view of scholars in the field of translation studies one after another. If we examine translation quality from a historical perspective, its pros and cons will change with historical changes, whether it is literary, historical, religious, or scientific translation. The inspection of translation quality gradually tends to deviate from the translation behavior and the translation product itself, after all, nothing can be separated from its environment. Once separated, it has no life and loses its own value, let alone quality. That is to say, it is necessary to connect translation quality with the effectiveness, functionality and value of translation products to inspect. The interdisciplinary nature of translation is becoming increasingly evident, and the connotation and extension of translation are constantly changing. The standards for translation quality have also become blurred in

---

[1] Si Xianzhu and Yao Yazhi. "Research on China's Translation Industry: From the Perspective of Industrial Economics" [J]. *Chinese Translators Journal*, 2014 (5): 67-71.

terms of correspondence and equivalence. Good translation may not necessarily be equivalent, and equivalent translation may not necessarily be good translation. Wu Guangjun pointed out that "a reasonable translation quality assessment model in the future should include two levels: fuzzy evaluation in general and accurate evaluation in parts. Fuzzy evaluation reflects the subjectivity of translation quality assessment. Accurate evaluation reflects the objectivity of translation quality assessment"[1]. Theory is used to guide practice, and translation quality assessment always has a relatively accurate foundation that can be grasped in tangible aspects such as text and genre. In the future, however, translation quality assessment will focus more on comprehensive linguistic research in various fields, combining research achievements in cultural studies, sociology, economics, translation professionalization, modern science and technology (localization), and develop towards a more systematic and detailed direction which is closer to the actual field context. We should not only keep in mind Zhuangzi's admonition to Shi Hui: "'There is no universal standard in the world to judge which one is right, but each is their own way is right,' and not everyone of us can be 'Yao'; it is also necessary to know 'the seven natural laws'[2] and 'follow the natural law'[3], and that is the principle translation assessment should stick to."

In short, with the increasingly prominent interdisciplinary nature of translation research, the connotation and extension of translation are also constantly changing. The future of translation quality assessment research will inevitably absorb the latest research results from disciplines such as linguistics, combined with cultural studies, stylistics, sociology, information science, economics, etc., in order to adapt to the development of translation professionalization and industrialization, and develop towards a more systematic, diverse and practical direction.

---

[1] Wu Guangjun. "Progress, Meta evaluation, and Development Direction of Contemporary Chinese and Western Translation Quality Evaluation Models" [J] *Foreign Language Research*, 2007 (4): 73-79.
[2] Seven major factors: knowing the first year of college, knowing the great yin, knowing the great eye, knowing the great equality, knowing the generosity, knowing the great faith, knowing the great determination, that's all! The great one is connected, the great Yin is resolved, the great vision is seen, the great unity is formed, the great body is formed, the great faith is formed, and the great determination is held.
[3] Meaning: Let nature take its course, there will be clarity in the heart, and everything will eventually have a solution. Concealing all things, standing in the center of the circle, not opposing any party. After all, it's still the natural way that works.

References:

[1] Al-Qinai J. *Translation quality assessment. Strategies, parameters and procedures* [J]. Meta Journal des traducteurs Meta:/Translators'Journal, 2000, 45(3): 497-519.

[2] Catford, C.J. *A Linguistic Theory of Translation* [M]. London: Oxford University Press,1965.

[3] Drugan, J. *Quality in Professional Translation: Assessment and Improvement* [M]. London: Bloomsbury, 2013.

[4] House, J. *Translation Quality Assessment: A Model Revisited* [M]. Tübingen: Gunter Narr Verlag, 1997.

[5] Lefevere, A. *Translation, Rewriting and the Manipulation of Literary Fame* [M]. London and New York: Routledge,1992.

[6] Mcalester G. The evaluation of translation into a foreign language [J]. BENJAMINS TRANSLATION LIBRARY, 2000, 38: 229-242.

[7] Munday, J. *Evaluation in Translation: Critical Points of Translator Decision-Making* [M]. London & New York: Rutledge, 2012.

[8] Niranjana, T. *Siting Translation: history, post-structuralism, and the colonial Context* [M]. Berkeley. Los Angeles. Oxford: University of California Press, 1992.

[9] Nord, C. *Translating as a Purposeful Activity: Functionalist Approaches Explained* [M]. Manchester: St Jerome,1997.

[10] Reiss, K. *Translation Criticism—the Potentials and Limitations: Categories and Criteria for Translation Quality Assessment* [M]. Manchester: St. Jerome Publishing, 2000.

[11] Robinson, D. *Western Translation Theory: from Herodotus to Nietzsche* [M]. Beijing: Foreign Language Teaching and Research Press,2006.

[12] Simon, S. *Gender in Translation: Cultural Identity and the Politics of Transmission* [M] London & New York: Routledge, 1996.

[13] Venuti. L. *The Translator's Invisibility* [M]. Shanghai: Shanghai Foreign Language

Education Press, 1995.

[14] Williams, M. *Translation Quality Assessment: An Argumentation--Centered Approach* [M]. Ottawa: University of Ottawa Press, 2004.

[15] Cai Xinle. *Artistic Philosophy of Literary Translation* [M]. Kaifeng: Henan University Press, 2001.

[16] Chen Hongwei. *It may seem easy, but in reality it's not easy* [J] Chinese Translators Journal, 2008, 29 (1): 88-90.

[17] Gu Zhengkun. *The Theory of Multiple Complementary Translation Criteria* [J]. Chinese Translators Journal, 1989 (1): 16-20.

[18] Liu Zhongde. "The Third Talk on the Principle of"Faithfulness, Darkness, and Cuteness "– Discussion on the Study Style with Peng Jun" [J]. *Fujian Foreign Language Journal*, 2000 (4): 44-50.

[19] Luo Xinzhang ed. *Translation Essays* [M]. Beijing: Commercial Press, 2009.

[20] Lv Jun, Hou Xiangqun. *Introduction to Translation criticism: An introduction to the science of translation criticism*[M]. Shanghai: Shanghai Foreign Language Education Press, 2009.

[21] Si Xianzhu & Yao Yazhi. "Research on China's Translation Industry: From the Perspective of Industrial Economics" [J]. *Chinese Translators Journal*, 2014 (5): 67-71.

[22] Wang Hongyin. *Literature Translation Criticism* [M]. Shanghai: Shanghai Foreign Language Education Press, 2006.

[23] Wang Rongpei."Translation Art of Book of Songs" [J]. *Foreign Language and Foreign Language Teaching*, 1994 (4): 11-15.

[24] Wang Shouyuan. "Discussion on Language Learning Strategy Training"[J]. *Journal of the School of Foreign Languages, Shandong Normal University*, 2000 (1): 7-10.

[25] Wu Guangjun."Progress, Meta evaluation, and Development Direction of Contemporary Chinese and Western Translation Quality Evaluation Models" [J] *Foreign Language Research*, 2007 (4): 73-79.

[26] Xiao Weiqing. *Research on the Mode of Translation criticism* [M]. Shanghai: Shanghai Foreign Language Education Press, 2010.

[27] Xu Jun."Reflections on Literature Translation criticism" [J]. *Chinese*

Translators Journal, 1992 (4): 30-33.

[28] Xu Yuanchong. *The Art of Translation* [M]. Beijing: Wuzhou Communication Press, 2006.

[29] Yang Xiaorong."Analysis of Constraints on Translation Standards" [J]. *Journal of Shanghai International Studies University*, 2005 (6): 51-58.

[30] Zhao Xiuming & Zhao Zhangjin. *Literature Translation criticism: Theory, Method and Practice*[M]. Changchun: Jilin University Press, 2010.

Chapter 3　Systemic Functional Linguistics and Translation Research

This chapter elaborates on the disciplinary nature and characteristics of translation research and Systemic Functional Linguistics, discusses the close correlation between the two as well as the reference and guiding significance of the latter for the former. Based upon this, the author provides a clear description about the approach of Systemic Functional Linguistics towards translation research by analyzing and summarizing the successes and failures of people in exploring this field, and points out the future research direction and focus.

Due to the complexity of translation phenomena, the description and explanation of them cannot be limited to a single theory and perspective. As an interdisciplinary subject, translation studies need to absorb nutrition and essence from other disciplines, such as linguistics, philosophy, literature, cognitive science, semiotics, psychology, communication, sociology, etc. The fact is exactly the same. As Huang Guowen said, "Translation studies should be like the sea to hold all rivers, and should attract more and more scholars from different disciplines to work hard in this field."[1]

Given the extremely complex nature of translation, it is undoubtedly necessary and beneficial for researchers to explore it from different disciplinary perspectives. However, the essential attribute of translation is, after all, the use of a special language that reproduces the meaning carried by one language with another language. Therefore, describing and interpreting it from a linguistic perspective can be described and explained from a disciplinary perspective of translation research, which can be directly towards the essence. Based on the study of actual language use, Systemic Functional Linguistics naturally provides guidance and reference for the exploration of translation phenomena that belong to the same category of language application in terms of theory and logic.

---

[1] Huang Guowen. "Introduction: About Discourse and Translation" [J]. *Foreign Language and Foreign Language Teaching*, 2002 (7): 1-2.

3.1 Review of Translation Research of Systemic Functional Linguistics in Foreign Countries

According to our (Si, 2007a) analysis of literature in this field, the theory of Systemic Functional Linguistics has been applied to translation research for over thirty years. As early as 1965, Catford consciously applied Halliday's theory of level and category grammar (an early form of systemic functional linguistics) to systematically explore the nature, types, methods, conditions, and limitations of translation. He used linguistic concepts, such as level, category and rank to discuss the basis for interlingual switching. He further pointed out that translation can be divided into word-by-word translation, literal translation and free translation based on the"level"of language, namely morphemes, words, phrases or meaning groups, clauses or sentences. Word-by -word translation is an equivalent relationship established on the"level"of words; the free translation is "unrestricted...changing between superiors and subordinates, always tending towards higher level changes... even surpassing sentences"; Literal translation is "between word-by-word translation and free translation". He also proposed that translation equivalence can only be discourse equivalence and functional equivalence, opening up a new path for translation theory research. As long as there is translation, there will be translation reviews, which can be said to accompany translation activities themselves. To conduct a systematic evaluation of the quality of translations, it is necessary to apply a certain assessment model, so constructing such a model is undoubtedly the responsibility of translation theorists. Juliane House, a renowned scholar in the German translation research community, has devoted almost all of her research energy to exploring such a model, which has not stopped for nearly 20 years. Firstly, she chose this topic as her doctoral research topic and wrote a paper titled "Translation Quality Assessment Model"in 1976 to obtain her doctoral degree; Afterwards, after a year of processing, it was officially published in the form of a monograph in 1977; In 1981, the second edition was revised again; Eleven years later, the third edition was published as *Translation Quality Assessment: A Revised Model*[1] in 1997; In 2001, she wrote an article on translation assessment in the international translation research journal *Meta* (see Chapter 2, Section 2.3.4).

Ms. Mona Baker, a renowned contemporary international translation theorist,

---

[1] House, J. *Translation Quality Assessment: A Model Revisited*[M]. Tubingen: Gunter Narr, 1997.

published *In other words: A Coursebook on Translation*[1] in 1992. This book systematically discusses some important concepts in modern linguistic theories (mainly systemic functional linguistics, pragmatics, etc.), and their enlightenment and guiding significance for dealing with many complex and difficult problems in translation. This book is truly a textbook for training translators. The entire book adopts a bottom-up, easy-to-difficult approach, starting from word equivalence in translation, through word and phrase matching, sentence equivalence, to the text equivalence. In the main section of the book titled"Text Equivalence"(which accounts for almost half of the book's length), Baker comprehensively discusses how to achieve translation equivalence at the textual level by utilizing the concepts of thematic structure and information structure in Halliday's Systemic Functional Linguistics, as well as the five cohesive means of word coherence, namely referential, substitution, ellipsis, connection, and lexical cohesion.

If Baker and others use the discourse analysis model of Systemic Functional Linguistics to discuss translation issues, they mainly elaborate on the functional level of the text, focusing on how to use thematic, cohesive, coherent and other resource means to achieve textual equivalence. Another scholar who discusses translation issues at the level of discourse cohesion and coherence is Blum-Kulka (2000)[2]. Through an analysis of a Hebrew translation selected from Pinter's work *Old Times*, she discussed how the functional changes in the translation were caused by changes in coherence. Hatim & Mason (1997)[3] used the discourse analysis model of Systemic Functional Linguistics to discuss translation. In addition to examining the matching between the translated text and the source text in terms of textual level, such as theme, coherence, etc., they also went deep into the concept of the translated text and the situation of interpersonal functions relative to the source text. Through transitivity analysis of a passage in Albert Camus'novel, they revealed how the change in transitivity types of small sentences in English translations resulted in a deviation from the source in conceptual function. By using the tool of register analysis, they also analyzed how the translator, under the

---

[1] Baker, M. *In Other Words: A Coursebook on Translation*. London: Routledge [M]. Beijing: Foreign Language Teaching and Research Press, 1992 / 2000.
[2] Blum-Kulka, S. "*Shifts of Cohesion and Coherence in Translation*", in L. Venuti(ed.) *The Translation Studies Reader*[J]. London: Routledge,2000: 221-232.
[3] Hatim, B. & Mason, I. *The Translator as Communicator*[M]. London: Routledge, 1997:7-10.

influence of their own ideology, changed the interpersonal function of the source text through purposeful manipulation of vocabulary grammar resources in the target language, thereby weaving the original intention that the source text did not have into the translated text and acting as a spokesperson for the interests of a certain social class.

Thus, as Munday (2001)[1] pointed out, Hatim & Mason's (1997)[2] discourse analysis model reflects and transcends the scope of House's register analysis and Beck's pragmatic analysis, and believes that language and discourse are the embodiment of socio-cultural information and power relations. Its biggest feature is that Halliday's views on social semiotics of language, culture and ideology are applied to translation studies.

Roger Bell is a famous linguist in the UK. By systematically applying linguistic theories to translation studies, he wrote his monograph *Translation and Translation Process: Theory and Practice* and thus became a representative figure of the linguistic school of translation studies. Halliday once said, "If a linguistic model could be used to describe the translation process, it would be very meaningful. We should describe it based on the language activity itself, rather than using preconceptions to describe it from outside the field of language research"[3]. Bell attempted to make translation studies from the perspectives of Systemic Functional Linguistics and discourse linguistics, striving to find an "objective" method to describe translation phenomena. He studies translation from the perspective of Systemic Functional Linguistics, Chapter 4 of his book is the best epitome. Bell not only introduces in great detail the three metafunctions of language - ideational function, interpersonal function and textual function - discussed by Systemic Functional linguistics, but also organically connects the three functions outlined by Systemic Functional Linguistics with the three systems of language logic, grammar and rhetoric, and discusses the cognitive meaning, communicative meaning and discourse meaning of language, as well as how they are reflected through transitivity, modality and thematic system of language. (In fact, the cognitive and communicative meanings here are the same as the ideational and interpersonal meanings elaborated in systemic functional linguistics.) Here, his exploration into the essence of translation studies - meaning - has shifted from

---

[1] Munday, J. *Introducing Translation Studies*[M]. London: Routledge, 2001:100.
[2] Hatim, B. & Mason, I. *The Translator as Communicator*[M]. London: Routledge, 1997:7-10.
[3] Bell, R.T. *Translation and Translating: Theory and Practice. London: Longman*[M]. Beijing: Foreign Language Teaching and Research Press, 1991: XVI.

static to dynamic, from semantics to communication, from words and sentences that are disconnected from context to discourse that relies on context - the actual unit of translation. Therefore, the idea of attaching importance to context, pragmatics and function, which runs through the language study of Systemic Functional Linguistics, has become his epistemology and methodology to study translation and to construct translation theories. Mund's doctoral thesis "The System of Translation: A Functional Path Analysis of Machine-Aided Systems for Translated Text of Cassia Marquez's Works"compares the English translations of the Spanish novel *Doce contens peregrinos* by Colombian Nobel Prize winner Garcia Marquez with the English translations of American translator Edith Grossman, to study shift and its trends in translation. In the process of exploring this issue and analyzing the text of the corpus, he consciously applied the language analysis model of Systemic Functional Linguistics as the theoretical basis. The reason for this is, as he himself put it:"The analytical model of Systemic Functional Linguistics focuses on the function of language as a communicative behavior in practical use, viewing language as a'system of meaning potential'[1] (Halliday 1978). That is to say, it compares the author's actual choices with possible choices and grasps the meaning of the chosen words. Therefore, it seems quite appropriate to use it to analyze the transfer and the "decision-making process" referred to by Lèvy in translation. Moreover, this model systematically links linguistic choices with individual, social, cultural and ideological aspects of society, thus providing a socio-cultural framework for exploring transfer in translation."[2] In his book *Introduction to Translation Studies*, he also analyzed the merits and demerits of House, Hatim, Mason, Baker and others who used the text analysis model of Halliday to study translation.

As mentioned earlier (Chapter 2.3.5), Munday applied the evaluation theory developed by James R. Martin, David Rose, and Peter R.R. White to translation evaluation. This theory is based on the interpersonal function in Systemic Functional Linguistics and reveals the value orientation of language users through language analysis. It consists of three dimensions: attitude, graduation, and engagement. These three dimensions can be

---

[1] Halliday M. "Language as Social Semiotic: The Social Interpretation of Language and Meaning" [J]. *Language in Society*, 1978:39.
[2] Munday, J. *System in Translation: A Computer-assisted Systemic Approach to the Analysis of the Translation of Garcia Marquez*. [D]. University of Bradford, 1997:3.

further systematized into their respective subsystems, forming a systematic evaluation resource network.

Starting from the meta-functional theory of language, Munday points out that generally speaking, "translation equivalence" is viewed from the perspective of ideational function. If a discourse and its source text are conceptually asymmetrical, it cannot be called translation, and the question of whether it is an excellent translation cannot be discussed.

3.2 Review of Translation Research of Systemic Functional Linguistics Approach in China

In China, Hu Zhuanglin was the first to use Halliday's linguistic theory to discuss translation studies. He (Hu et al., 1989) used systemic functional grammar to explore and analyze the connotation of the important concept of "equivalence" in translation studies, and thus discussed the essence and standards of translation: "Translation generally seeks the equivalence in meaning between the source text and the translated text…Translation should seek to have the same meaning and function in two languages' discourse within the same overall situational context." "The equivalence in translation cannot be based solely on one meaning (usually ideational meaning); While seeking ideational equivalence in discourse between two languages, it is also necessary to seek equivalence in interpersonal meanings such as the speaker's attitude, motivation, judgment and role, as well as in discourse meanings such as medium, channel and rhetorical device. In general, a good translation needs to be equivalent to the source text in all three senses."[1]

Though Hu et al. applies the theory of Systemic Functional Linguistics to study translation problems, it remains general and lacks empirical evidence. The fact that this is not satisfactory is understandable because as an introductory book on Systemic Functional Linguistics, their original intention was not to elaborate on the application of Systemic Functional Linguistics to translation research, but rather to demonstrate to readers that the application field of Systemic Functional Linguistics covers translation research.

The systematic and comprehensive application of Halliday's linguistic theory to explore translation issues is Huang Guowen. He published "Functional Linguistic

---

[1] Hu Zhuanglin, Zhu Yongsheng and Zhang Delu. *Introduction to Systemic Functional Grammar*[M]. Changsha: Hunan Education Publishing House, 1989:188.

Approaches to Translation Research"[1], outlining the attempts of functional linguistics in translation research and introducing the six steps in the research process. The paper illustrates the possibility and feasibility of this functional linguistic approach through examples. The author indicates through discussion that different approaches can be adopted for academic exploration of translation issues. The direction of literary research and literary criticism is different from that of functional linguistics, and they cannot be simply compared, nor can they be measured by the standards (rules). In the same year, Si Xianzhu wrote articles "On the Systemic Functional Linguistic Model of Translation Research"[2] and "On the Study of Translation Quality Assessment Model from the Perspective of Functional Linguistics"[3], which not only discussed specific translation issues such as how to view translation essence, standards and construct translation quality assessment models from the perspective of Systemic Functional Linguistics, but also preliminarily elaborated on the path, methodology and value of translation research from the perspective of Systemic Functional Linguistics. In the same year, Li Fagen (2004)[4] attempted to evaluate different translations of the same original text from the six process types of the transitivity system, summarizing the formal differences between English and Chinese transitivity processes and their strategies for achieving equivalence. Therefore, it can be said that 2004 witnessed the integration of Systemic Functional Linguistics and translation research in China, laying the foundation for translation research from the perspective of Systemic Functional Linguistics. According to our research (Si and Tao, 2014), the achievements of translation research from the perspective of Systemic Functional Linguistics in China from 2004 to the present decade are reflected in the following five aspects: Pure Functional Theory and Translation Studies, Context Theory and Translation Studies, Evaluation Theory and Translation Studies, Grammar Metaphor Theory and Translation Studies, and Systemic Functional Linguistics and the Construction

---

[1] Huang Guowen. "Functional Linguistic Approaches to Translation Research" [J]. *Chinese Translators Journal*, 2004 (5): 15-19.
[2] Si Xianzhu. "Research on Translation Quality Assessment Model from the Perspective of Functional Linguistics" [J]. *Foreign Language Teaching*, 2004a (4): 52-54.
[3] Si Xianzhu. "On the Systemic Functional Linguistic Model of Translation Research"[J]. *Foreign Language and Foreign Language Teaching*, 2004b (6): 45-50.
[4] Li Fagen. "Transitivity Process Theory and Equivalent translation of English Chinese Semantic Functions" [J]. *Journal of Xi'an Foreign Studies University*, 2004 (2): 26-30.

of Translation Quality Assessment Models.

3.2.1 Pure Functional Theory and Translation Studies

According to Systemic Functional Linguistics, language has three meta functions: ideational function, interpersonal function and textual function. Huang Guowen (2006) pioneered the pure functional theory in translation research. Starting from the three meta-functions of language, he used the translation of Chinese classics and ancient poetry as specific research corpus to explore the guiding significance of functional linguistics for translation research. Afterwards, many scholars continue to analyze and criticize translated works along his path based on three meta-functions: Xie Zhijun and Wang Xianfeng (2006) analyzed the correspondence and translation of Chinese and English clauses, Yu Jianping (2007) explored the translation of scientific papers, and Chen Yang (2009) evaluated the three English translation versions of the Analects. The basic idea of these studies is to first interpret the meta functions of the source text, then to describe the corresponding functions of the translation, then to analyze the similarities and differences between the translation and the source text, and to explain this based on the characteristics of the two different language systems and the cultural background of the discourse, pointing out the faithfulness and deviation of the translation from the source text.

We believe that translation studies based on meta-functions can break away from the arbitrary and impressionistic criticism methods of traditional translation theory, which can enable multi-dimensional, three-dimensional, qualitative and quantitative scientific analysis of translation problems and translation works. However, in recent years, there has been a lack of innovation in the path of research, and the methods are similar. Most of them dissect and evaluate the selected text from the perspectives of transitivity, mood, and thematic analysis. On the other hand, the analysis of texts mainly focuses on literary genres, with less involvement in applied texts such as news, technology, advertising and law. In order to strengthen the necessity and feasibility of Systemic Functional Linguistics and its meta-function theory in translation research, we believe that innovation and expansion must be made in research ideas and genre diversity of translation corpora. For example, the aforementioned analysis of the source text and translation of large English Chinese parallel corpora can be effectively compensated for by adopting corpus analysis, which should be the direction of future research.

3.2.2 Context Theory and Translation Studies

Translation is a special type of verbal communication activity that, like other verbal communication activities, occurs in a certain context. Therefore, the equivalence that translation seeks is contextual equivalence. According to the theory of Systemic Functional Linguistics, context can be divided into four levels: context, situational context (register), cultural context (genre) and ideology. In terms of the hierarchical relationship between context and the decoding and encoding tension involved in the translation process, Si (2007b)[1] concludes that from the perspective of speech decoding, context with lower levels of abstraction is easier to read, while cultural context with higher levels of abstraction is less easily recognizable. From the perspective of the encoding force, contextual context is the most direct, while cultural context is more subtle and indirect. In this way, the higher the level of abstraction, the greater the tension of the context on translation, the higher the requirements for the translator, and the greater the impact on the quality of the translation.

Dai (2007)[2] focuses on the impact of cultural context on translation. After a detailed comparison between the instructions on changing towels in Guangzhou hotels and their English translations with the relevant instructions in Australian hotels, she finds that the difference in environmental awareness is one of the cultural differences between China and Australia. In terms of language, the English translation of Guangzhou hotels adopts an inspiring and sincere attitude to remind guests of reusing personal towels as much as possible, giving them greater freedom because China is currently in the process of building environmental awareness. In Australia, where the awareness of environmental protection is deeply rooted, simple interpersonal communication is conducted only in the second person to persuade guests to reuse towels with less freedom. Taking pun rhetoric advertisements as an example, Li (2008)[3] pointed out that to achieve cultural context

---

[1] Si Xianzhu."On the Tension Relationship between the Hierarchy of Context and Translation"[J]. *Foreign Language and Foreign Language Teaching*, 2007b (2): 53-56.
[2] Dai Fan. "Discourse and Translation from the Perspective of Cultural Context" [J]. *Foreign Language Research*, 2007 (3): 77-81.
[3] Li Guoqing. "The Choice of Translation Strategies and the Equivalence of Cultural Context - Taking the

equivalence, the strategies of preserving pun ostentation, genre switching ostentation, and splitting and supplementing ostentation can be adopted. He believed that"the evaluation criteria of translation should be placed at the level of cultural context. As long as equivalence at the level of cultural context can be achieved, and the same intensity of contextual effects can be achieved, it is a good translation."

The above research explores how the translated work can make appropriate formal adjustments from the perspective of context, form, and meaning interaction, achieving functional meaning equivalence in the context of the translation relative to the source text. It is creative for breaking away from the narrow static and isolated perspective that used to be limited to form and meaning. However, there are two main problems: firstly, the exploration of the impact of cultural context on the reconstruction of translated discourse lacks a macro perspective of structure and remains at the traditional level of wording, and it is insufficient in description. Secondly, insufficient attention has been paid to the impact of ideology on translation, resulting in a lack of sufficient interpretation. No matter whether it is the schematic structure and manifestation style in the situational context, tenor, style, or cultural context, its impact on the construction of the translation is fundamentally due to ideological differences in the worldview, values, ethics and other aspects of the nation and community of a certain kind of language.

3.2.3 Evaluation Theory and Translation Studies

Evaluation theory is a new vocabulary grammar framework developed by James R. Martin based on the study of interpersonal meaning in Systemic Functional Linguistics. It consists of three subsystems: attitude, intervention, and gradation, and is a further extension of the mood system and modality system. Due to the fact that both evaluation theory and discourse translation view the language in use as specific symbols in different social contexts, Zhang (2007)[1] discussed the inspiration of evaluation theory for discourse translation: different resources for expressing attitudinal meanings can express the same attitudinal meanings. If there are no vocabulary in the target language that expresses

---

Translation of Pun Rhetorical Advertising with Interpersonal Function as an Example" [J]. *Journal of Foreign Languages*, 2008 (6): 117-120.

[1] Zhang Xiangang. "The Enlightenment of Evaluation Theory on Text Translation" [J]. *Foreign Language Teaching*, 2007 (6): 33-36.

attitudinal meanings in the source language, this attitudinal meaning can be transferred to other parts of the discourse, But it is necessary to ensure the effective communication of the corresponding ideational meaning. Zhang Wen's contribution lies in the inspiration for translation at the macro level, while lacking verification at the micro level. From a macro perspective, Liu (2012)[1] constructs a translation process model under the guidance of evaluation theory, elaborating on the construction principles of attitude model, intervention model and gradation model in the translation process in detail. He pointed out that the accurate communication of evaluation meaning should start from multiple levels such as vocabulary, syntax and discourse, and comprehensively consider the three subsystems, which is undoubtedly from a high perspective. However, the same deficiency is the lack of corpus support and validation.

Instead of the above qualitative research, Chai (2010)[2] used the quantitative research method to make a quantitative analysis of the "deviation" of evaluation resources in the process of English-Chinese translation, and discussed the means and ways to realize evaluation resources in the target language. He believes that differences in language expression and contextual factors constrain the reproduction of evaluative meaning in the target language. Translators can flexibly handle the evaluative meaning of the original work based on the characteristics of the source text and the language characteristics of the target language, and reasonably allocate the proportion of resources such as emotions, judgments, and appreciation in the translation, in order to improve the quality of the translation, enhance its readability and aesthetics.

Taking business discourse and its translation as an example, Fu (2010)[3] analyzes the expression patterns of attitude resources in business letters: when expressing pleasant information, explicit attitudes are often used; when expressing negative information

---

[1] Liu Shizhu."Translation Process Model under the Influence of Evaluation Theory"[J]. *Shandong Foreign Language Teaching*, 2012 (4): 24-28.
[2] Chai Tongwen. "The Reproduction of Evaluation Meaning in the Target Language: A Study of English Chinese Translators Journal Based on Evaluation Theory" [A]. Edited by Zhang Jingyuan. *Functional Linguistics and Translation Research*[C]. Beijing: Foreign Language Teaching and Research Press, 2010:192-205.
[3] Fu Lihua. "Expression and Translation of Attitudes in Business Discourse from the Perspective of Evaluation Theory" [J]. *China Science and Technology Translation*, 2010 (1): 28-30, 23.

implicit attitudes are often used. Xu (2011)[1] analyzes the attitude resources of business translation from the perspectives of vocabulary selection, appreciation analysis, explicit evaluation and implicit evaluation. Xu and Xia (2013)[2] use 20 English and Chinese company profiles as corpus to compare the similarities and differences in ways of realizing attitude resources, indicating the differences in thinking patterns and value orientations between China and the West.

Chen (2007)[3] briefly analyzes the significance of evaluation of attitude resource in news discourse. Qian (2007)[4] investigates the causes of "unfaithfulness" in the translation of perfume advertisements. Yu, Bai (2007)[5], Xia, Li (2009)[6], Liu (2010)[7], Yu (2010)[8], and others use literary translations as examples to examine the transmission of evaluation in the translation.

Although the history of applying evaluation theory into translation research has been relatively short, the achievements have been considerable in the objective and quantitative research methods, such as Chai's use of quantitative analysis methods to study the distribution characteristics and implementation methods of evaluation resources in different languages, as well as in the expansion of research on text genres, such as business, news, advertising, literature, etc. However, in terms of quantitative analysis of literature, the vast majority of articles focus on the analysis and explanation of attitude systems, with little exploration of intervention and gradation systems.

---

[1] Xu Jun. "Research on Business Translation from the Perspective of Evaluation Theory" [J]. *Journal of the PLA Foreign Languages College*, 2011 (1): 81-91.
[2] Xu Jun, Xia Rong. "A Comparative Study of English and Chinese Business Discourse from the Perspective of Evaluation Theory" [J]. *Foreign Language Teaching*, 2013 (3): 16-21.
[3] Chen Mingyao. "Analysis of Evaluation and Translation of Attitude Resources in News Discourse" [J]. *Shanghai Translation*, 2007 (1): 23-27.
[4] Qian Hong. "Explaining the phenomenon of 'unfaithfulness' by using evaluation theory - a case study of perfume advertisement translation" [J]. *Foreign Language*, 2007 (6): 57-63.
[5] Yu Jianping, Bai Litao. "Analysis of the English Translation of 'Hao Liao Ge' by Using Evaluation Theory" [J]. *Journal of Xi'an Foreign Studies University*, 2007 (2): 45-48.
[6] Xia Yun, Li Defeng. "The Transformation of Evaluation Meaning and the Translation Effect of Novel Character Images - Taking Two Translation Versions of *Gone with the Wind* as an Example"[J]. *Foreign Language and Foreign Language Teaching*, 2009 (7): 44-47.
[7] Liu Xiaolin. "Translation Studies from the Perspective of Evaluation: A Comparative Study of Two Translation Versions of *Dream of the Red Mansion*[J]. *Journal of Foreign Languages*, 2010 (3): 161-163.
[8] Yu Jiying. "The Significance of Evaluation and Translation Ideology - Taking the English Translation of *The True Story of Mr. Q* as an Example" [J]. *Foreign Language Teaching Theory and Practice*, 2010 (2): 83-90.

3.2.4 Grammatical Metaphor and Translation Studies

Grammatical metaphor is a supplement to "lexical metaphor" in traditional grammar from Systemic Functional Linguistics. It refers to a linguistic phenomenon that uses one grammatical means to replace another to express a given meaning. It is divided into ideational metaphor, interpersonal metaphor and textual metaphor. Huang (2009)[1] is one of the pioneers who apply the theory of grammatical metaphor to translation studies. He believes that in the process of code switching, translators face the choice of metaphorical and consistent forms, but there is no good or bad distinction between the two. This needs to be analyzed based on specific cultural contexts such as communication purpose, occasion, content, and the relationship between the two parties. However, on the other hand, distinguishing between the two helps to clarify their different communicative functions. Deng and Cao (2010)[2] conduct a specialized exploration of consistency and metaphorical expressions in English-Chinese translation, and conclude that the translator's subjectivity and cultural identity affect their choice of consistency and metaphorical expressions. Grammatical metaphor helps to explore the characters, social attributes, and personalities in a discourse, providing criteria for translators when choosing language"equivalents", and having a positive impact on improving the quality of translations. Liu (2008)[3] discusses the connection between consistent and metaphorical expressions in Chinese-English translation.

The functions of nominalization metaphor in simplifying grammatical structure, increasing the density of content words and enhancing information carrying capacity, all help to express the semantic meaning of scientific discourse. Because of this, some scholars have applied the theory of grammatical metaphor to the translation of scientific texts. Yu (2006)[4], Xu and Wu (2008)[5] analyze the working mechanism and function of

---

[1] Huang Guowen. "The Application of Grammar Metaphor in Translation Studies" [J]. *Chinese Translators Journal*, 2009 (1): 5-9.
[2] Deng Yurong, Cao Zhixi. "Consistency and Metaphor in English Chinese Translators Journal" [J]. *Journal of Foreign Languages*, 2010 (6): 114-116.
[3] Liu Zhuyan. "The Connection between Consistency and Metaphor in Chinese English Translation" [J]. *Journal of Tianjin University (Social Sciences Edition)*, 2008 (6): 553-555.
[4] Yu Jianping. "Ideational Metaphor: An Effective Way to Realize the Stylistic Features of Scientific English Discourse" [J]. *China Science and Technology Translation*, 2006 (2): 40-43.
[5] Xu Wu, Wu Lingjuan. "Translation of Scientific Texts from the Perspective of Ideational Metaphor" [J].

ideational metaphors in scientific and technological texts from the perspectives of process, functional components and vocabulary grammar transformation. They believe that ideational metaphors help achieve the formal, concise and objective stylistic features of scientific and technological texts, and are a shortcut for translating scientific and technological texts. Chen (2012)[1] also talks about the construction of metaphorical expressions in scientific language and its translation strategies, which can be translated at the same level or upgraded depending on how difficult it is. Yang (2013)[2] explores the cohesion function of nominalization in scientific English, pointing out that translators should choose appropriate parts of speech based on the characteristics and expression habits of English and Chinese languages, and try to find equivalent conversion methods as much as possible to achieve equivalent translation and coherence in the discourse.

The use of grammatical metaphor theory to study the choice of different expressions in translation is a new exploration. To achieve equivalence in meaning, form, and context between the translated text and the source text, translation practice cannot be separated from the guidance of grammatical metaphor theory. However, due to the late introduction of the concept of grammatical metaphor, the above research only broadens this research perspective from a macro perspective and has not yet delved into specific issues at the micro level. For example, it has not yet been defined whether the meaning reflected in the metaphorical form in the source language can also be translated into metaphorical form for functional equivalence. Therefore, in the future, on the one hand, it is necessary to further summarize the application rules of grammatical metaphor theory in translation, and on the other hand, it can be combined with the achievements of other theories of Systemic Functional Linguistics in translation research to establish a more comprehensive framework for the translation research of Systemic Functional Linguistics metaphor theory, which can better guide translation practice.

3.2.5 Systemic Functional Linguistics and the Construction of Translation Quality Assessment Model

Translation quality assessment is the core topic of applied translation theory research. German scholar Julian House takes the lead in constructing the first translation quality

---

Shanghai Translation, 2008 (1): 38-41.
[1] Chen Qing. "The Construction and Translation Strategies of Metaphors in Scientific Language" [J]. *Foreign Language Teaching*, 2012 (5): 104-108.
[2] Yang Lin. "The Cohesion Function of Discourse and Translation of Nominalization in Scientific English" [J]. *China Science and Technology Translation*, 2013 (1): 1-3.

assessment model that combines theory and empirical evidence from the perspective of Systemic Functional Linguistics, which is of epoch-making significance. However, this model "lacks parameters for analyzing and exploring the meaning/function of the text" (Si 2005)[1], which can easily lead to differences in translation assessment from person to person due to differences in evaluators' language sense, habits and intuition. In view of this, Si (2007)[2] constructs a translation quality assessment model for English-Chinese translated texts based on Systemic Functional Linguistics and text typology. This model first starts from a micro level analysis of the transitivity, mood, and thematic structure of the source text and translated clauses, analyzing and judging whether there is a deviation of ideational and interpersonal meaning from the source text in the translation. Then, based on the macro level of the entire discourse, a re-examination of the aforementioned micro level "deviation" cases is conducted from the aspects of target language characteristics, socio-cultural environment, discourse types and text functions. The "deviation" cases that have not caused damage to the quality of the translation from the macro level are excluded, and the impact weights of two different types of attribute deviation (ideational and interpersonal meaning) cases on the overall quality of the translation are determined. Yang (2008)[3] believes that this model is characterized by its completeness, systematicity, feasibility and less subjectivity. However, this model has a big defect in the evaluation of the emoticon and infection whose dominant function is interpersonal, because in order to achieve functional and meaningful equivalence to the source text, the translation of this type of text often needs to make adjustments to the textual structure of the source text, including adding, deleting, combining and so on. While the above model fails to take this situation into consideration in parameter setting, so that the type and quantity of deviation between the translation and the source text are used as the sole basis for quality assessment. In response to this flaw, the author makes a revision to the model of 2008, adding a link where the translation is equivalent at the

---

[1] Si Xianzhu. "Critique of Julian House's 'Translation Quality Assessment Model'" [J]. *Foreign Language Teaching*, 2005 (3): 79-84.
[2] Si Xianzhu. *Functional Linguistics and Translation Studies*[M]. Beijing: Peking University Press, 2007a.
[3] Yang Rufu. A Stone from Other Mountains Can Be Used to Attack Jade. Commentary on "Functional Linguistics and Translation Research - Construction of Translation Quality Evaluation Model" [J]. *Foreign Language and Foreign Language Teaching*, 2008 (11): 63-64.

micro level compared to the source text, but the main function of the text is different from the source text with the addition of a "negative equivalence"[1] in the parameters. The revised model has generally been recognized by the academic community, such as Kang and Zhang (2010)[2], Lv et al. (2010)[3] (see relevant discussions in Chapter 1 and Chapter 6).

Afterwards, Kang and Hu(2011)[4], Yin(2011)[5] construct translation quality assessment models for advertising and legal texts respectively. Inspired by this, Si once again discover the shortcomings of his previous model: a lack of genre analysis. In response to the situation of applied genre text translation, he elaborates on the viewpoint that "applied translation should pursue overall genre equivalence" and "the form and content of the translation are equally important in applied discourse translation" (Si, 2012)[6].

In addition, by comparing the translation quality assessment models of Systemic Functional Linguistics and Transformational Generative Linguistics, Li et al. (2011) find that although the assessment methods based on Transformational Generative Linguistics are relatively comprehensive, they are too complex and not highly practical; By contrast, the method of Systemic Functional Linguistics is relatively systematic by integrating macro and micro as well as qualitative and quantitative aspects. However, the operational steps are still not reasonable, and it is pointed out that this model should be set at several levels for the overall quality assessment of the translation, rather than just distinguishing between good and bad.

---

[1] Si Xianzhu. "Further Study on the Evaluation Model of Translation Discourse Quality - A Functional Linguistic Approach" [J]. *Chinese Translators Journal*, 2008 (2): 57-60.
[2] Kang Leiming, Zhang Wenhui. "Review on the Translation Quality Assessment Model of Si Xianzhu" [J]. *Journal of Heilongjiang University of Education*, 2010 (12): 148-150.
[3] Lv Gui. "Empirical and Reflection on the Translation Quality Assessment Model of Systemic Functional Linguistics" [J]. *Foreign Language Teaching*, 2010 (2): 64-69.
[4] Kang Leiming, Hu Zuoyou. "Construction of a Quality Assessment Model for Advertising C-E Translation" [J]. *Journal of Hefei University of Technology* (Social Science Edition), 2011 (4): 151-155.
[5] Yin Yan'an. "Construction of a Quality Assessment Model for Legal Text Translation from the Perspective of Functional Linguistics" [J]. *Journal of Changchun University of Technology* (Social Sciences Edition), 2011 (12): 72-74.
[6] Si Xianzhu. "On the Quality Evaluation of Applied Genre Discourse Translation - A Genre Analysis Perspective of the Systemic Functional Linguistics School" [J]. *Shandong Foreign Language Teaching*, 2012 (4): 11-16.

In summary, the main achievements in the study of translation quality assessment models guided by Systemic Functional Linguistics are the establishment of a relatively complete framework. We believe that there are still two main problems: Firstly, there is insufficient refined research on different genres and insufficient empirical research; Secondly, the current assessment model constructed within the theoretical framework of Systemic Functional Linguistics does not pay enough attention to the aesthetics or artistry of translated texts. From the perspective of "faithfulness" and "smoothness" in measuring translation quality standards, although the existing model fully pays attention to whether the translated text is "equivalent" or "faithful" to the source text in terms of ideational meaning, interpersonal meaning and textual meaning, it is vague about whether the translated text itself is smooth and beautiful, Therefore, it is difficult to assess the "smoothness","expressiveness, and elegance" that belong to the aesthetic and artistic categories of the translation. This naturally constitutes the focus and direction of future research (see Chapter 6 for details).

3.3 Review of Translation Research in Systemic Functional Linguistics: Achievements and Shortcomings

In summary, more and more translation theorists are drawing nourishment from functional linguistics and conducting translation research, and have to some extent formed the Halliday Systemic Functional Linguistic School of translation research, which has promoted the development of translation studies. However, there are still many problems and shortcomings.The main manifestation is that: translation research from the perspective of Systemic Functionalism focuses on situational meaning and its equivalence in translation, while relatively neglecting the exploration of the aesthetic and artistic aspects of translation; Second, there is a lack of innovation in research methods, resulting in many studies stopping at providing a general overview of their implications or references for translation studies, lacking depth; Third, empirical research is not sufficient and there is insufficient exploration of non-literary texts such as applied genres.

Given the broad prospects presented by Systemic Functional Linguistics in translation research, we believe that with the development, enrichment and improvement of Systemic Functional Linguistics and its various branch theories, its application in translation research will be further expanded and deepened, and new achievements will continue to emerge. The translation research framework based on Systemic Functional Linguistics will also become more comprehensive and refined. For example, *evaluation theories such as Systemic Functional Linguistics and Grammar Metaphor Theory are currently in a flourishing stage of development.* With their own development and improvement, their application in translation research will undoubtedly further enhance the descriptive and explanatory power of translation. At the same time, with the continuous expansion and innovation of research methods, from the initial qualitative research to the current combination of qualitative and quantitative research, the unity of micro and macro, and the support of a single case to the corpus, these will certainly become the accelerator and booster for the emergence of translation research achievements from this perspective.

References:

[1] Baker, M. *In Other Words: A Coursebook on Translation.* London: Routledge [M]. Beijing: Foreign Language Teaching and Research Press, 1992 / 2000.

[2] Bell, R.T. *Translation and Translating: Theory and Practice. London: Longman* [M]. Beijing: Foreign Language Teaching and Research Press, 1991: XVI.

[3] Blum-Kulka, S. *"Shifts of Cohesion and Coherence in Translation",* in L. Venuti(ed.) *The Translation Studies Reader* [J]. London: Routledge,2000:221-232.

[4] Catford, C.J. *A Linguistic Theory of Translation* [M]. London: Oxford University Press,1965: 20

[5] Halliday M. *Language as Social Semiotic: The Social Interpretation of Language and Meaning*[J]. Language in Society, 1978:39

[6] Hatim, B. & Mason, I. *The Translator as Communicator* [M]. London: Routledge, 1997:7-10.

[7] House, J.*Translation Quality Assessment* [M]. Tubingen: Gunter Narr Verlag, 1977/1981.

House, J. Translation Quality Assessment: A Model Revisited [M]. Tubingen: Gunter Narr, 1997.

[8] Munday, J. *System in Translation: A Computer-assisted Systemic Approach to the Analysis of the Translation of Garcia Marquez* [D]. University of Bradford, 1997.

[9] Munday, J. *Introducing Translation Studies* [M]. London: Routledge, 2001.

[10] Chai Tongwen."The Reproduction of Evaluation Meaning in the Target

Language: A Study of English Chinese Translators Journal Based on Evaluation Theory" [A]. Edited by Zhang Jingyuan. *Functional Linguistics and Translation Research* [C]. Beijing: Foreign Language Teaching and Research Press, 2010:192-205.

[11] Chen Mingyao."Evaluation Analysis and Translation of Attitude Resources in News Discourse" [J]. *Shanghai Translation*, 2007 (1): 23-27.

[12] Chen Qing."The Construction and Translation Strategies of Metaphors in Scientific Language" [J]. *Foreign Language Teaching*, 2012 (5): 104-108.

[13] Chen Yang."A Functional Linguistic Exploration of the Translation Research of the Three English Translations of the Analects of Confucius" [J]. *Foreign Language and Foreign Language Teaching*, 2009 (2): 49-52.

[14] Dai Fan."Discourse and Translation from the Perspective of Cultural Context"[J]. *Foreign Language Research*, 2007 (3): 77-81.

[15] Deng Yurong, Cao Zhixi."Consistency and Metaphor in English Chinese Translators Journal" [J]. *Journal of Foreign Languages*, 2010 (6): 114-116.

[16] Fu Lihua."Expression and Translation of Attitudes in Business Discourse from the Perspective of Evaluation Theory" [J]. *China Science and Technology Translation*, 2010 (1): 28-30, 23.

[17] Hu Zhuanglin, Zhu Yongsheng and Zhang Delu. *Introduction to Systemic Functional Grammar* [M]. Changsha: Hunan Education Publishing House, 1989.

[18] Huang Guowen."Introduction: About Discourse and Translation" [J]. *Foreign Language and Foreign Language Teaching*, 2002 (7): 1-2.

[19] Huang Guowen."A Functional Linguistic Approach to Translation Research" [J]. *Chinese Translators Journal*, 2004 (5): 15-19.

[20] Huang Guowen. *Linguistic Exploration of Translation Studies-Linguistic Analysis of English Translations of Ancient Poems* [M]. Shanghai: Shanghai Foreign Language Education Press, 2006.

[21] Huang Guowen."The Application of Grammar Metaphor in Translation Studies" [J]. *Chinese Translators Journal*, 2009 (1): 5-9.

[22] Huang Guowen. *Linguistic Exploration of Translation Studies-Linguistic Analysis of English Translations of Ancient Poems*[M]. Shanghai: Shanghai Foreign Language Education Press, 2006.

[23] Kang Leiming and Hu Zuoyou."Construction of a Quality Evaluation Model for Advertising C-E Translation" [J]. *Journal of Hefei University of Technology* (Social Science Edition), 2011 (4): 151-155.

[24] Kang Leiming and Zhang Wenhui."Review on the Translation Quality

Evaluation Model of Si Xianzhu" [J]. *Journal of Heilongjiang University of Education*, 2010 (12): 148-150.

[25] Li Fagen."Transitivity Process Theory and Equivalent Translation of English Chinese Semantic Functions" [J]. *Journal of Xi'an Foreign Studies University*, 2004 (2): 26-30.

[26] Li Guoqing."The Choice of Translation Strategies and the Equivalence of Cultural Context - Taking the Translation of Pun Rhetorical Advertising with Interpersonal Function as an Example" [J]. *Journal of Foreign Languages*, 2008 (6): 117-120.

[27] Li Wenping, Xu Zhibo."Comparison of System Functions and Translation Quality Assessment Models for Transformation Generation" [J]. *Journal of Chongqing Jiaotong University* (Social Sciences Edition), 2011 (6): 134-137.

[28] Liu Shizhu. "Translation Process Model under the Influence of Evaluation Theory" [J]. *Shandong Foreign Language Teaching*, 2012 (4): 24-28.

[29] Liu Xiaolin. Translation Studies from the Perspective of Evaluation: A Comparative Study of Two Translations of "Dream of the Red Chamber" [J]. *Journal of Foreign Languages*, 2010 (3): 161-163.

[30] Liu Zhuyan."The Connection between Consistency and Metaphor in Chinese-English Translation"[J]. *Journal of Tianjin University* (Social Sciences Edition), 2008 (6): 553-555.

[31] Lv Gui."Empirical and Reflection on the Translation Quality Evaluation Model of Systemic Functional Linguistics" [J]. *Foreign Language Teaching*, 2010 (2): 64-69.

[32] Qian Hong. Explanation of "Unfaithfulness" by Using Evaluation Theory-A Case Study of Translation of Perfume Advertisements" [J]. *Foreign Language*, 2007 (6): 57-63.

[33] Si Xianzhu. "Research on Translation Quality Assessment Model from the Perspective of Functional Linguistics" [J]. *Foreign Language Teaching*, 2004a (4): 52-54.

[34] Si Xianzhu."On the Systemic Functional Linguistic Model of Translation Research" [J]. *Foreign Language and Foreign Language Teaching*, 2004b (6): 45-50.

[35] Si Xianzhu."Critique of Julian House" "Translation Quality Assessment Model" [J] *Foreign Language Teaching*, 2005 (3): 79-84.

[36] Si Xianzhu. *Functional Linguistics and Translation Studies* [M]. Beijing: Peking University Press, 2007a.

[37] Si Xianzhu."On the Tension Relationship between the Hierarchy of Context and Translation" [J]. *Foreign Language and Foreign Language Teaching*, 2007b (2): 53-56.

[38] Si Xianzhu. "Further Study on the Evaluation Model of Translation Discourse

Quality-A Functional Linguistic Approach"[J]. *Chinese Translators Journal*, 2008 (2): 57-60.

[39] Si Xianzhu."On the Quality Assessment of Text Translation in Applied Genres - A Genre Analysis Perspective of Systemic Functional Linguistics School" [J]. *Shandong Foreign Language Teaching*, 2012 (4): 11-16.

[40] Si Xianzhu & Tao Yang."Ten Years of Translation Studies from the Perspective of Systemic functional linguistics in China: Review and Prospect" [J]. *China Foreign Language*, 2014 (3): 99-105.

[41] Xia Yun & Li Defeng."The Transformation of Evaluation Meaning and the Translation Effect of Novel Character Images-Taking Two Translation Versions of'Gone with the Wind'as an Example"[J]. *Foreign Language and Foreign Language Teaching*, 2009 (7): 44-47.

[42] Xie Zhijun & Wang Xianfeng. "Ideational Function, Interpersonal function and English translation of Chinese Clauses" [J]. *Journal of Tongji University* (Social Science Edition), 2006 (4): 62-67.

[43] Xu Jun."Research on Business Translation from the Perspective of Evaluation Theory" [J]. *Journal of the PLA Foreign Languages College*, 2011 (1): 81-91.

[44] Xu Jun & Xia Rong."A Comparative Study of English and Chinese Business Discourse from the Perspective of Evaluation Theory" [J]. *Foreign Language Teaching*, 2013 (3): 16-21.

[45] Xu Wu & Wu Lingjuan."Translation of Scientific Texts from the Perspective of Ideational Metaphor" [J]. *Shanghai Translation*, 2008 (1): 38-41.

[46] Yang Lin."The Discourse Cohesion Function and Translation of Nominalization in Scientific English" [J]. *China Science and Technology Translation*, 2013 (1): 1-3.

[47] Yang Rufu."A Stone from Other Mountains, Can Be Used to Attack Jade. Commentary on *Functional Linguistics and Translation Research-Construction of Translation Quality Assessment Model*" [J]. Foreign Language and Foreign Language Teaching, 2008 (11): 63-64.

[48] Yin Yan'an."Construction of Quality Assessment of Legal Texts Translation from the Perspective of Functional Linguistics" [J]. Journal of Changchun University of Science and Technology (Social Science Edition), 2011 (12): 72-74.

[49] Yu Jianping."Ideational Metaphor: An Effective Way to Realize the Stylistic Features of Scientific English Discourse" [J]. *China Science and Technology Translation*, 2006 (2): 40-43.

[50] Yu Jianping."Analysis of Several Issues in the Translation of Scientific and

Technological Papers Based on a Functional Translation Perspective" [J]. *Chinese Translators Journal*, 2007 (6): 61-64.

[51] Yu Jianping & Bai Litao."Analysis of the English Translation of" Haoliao Ge "by Using Evaluation Theory" [J]. *Journal of Xi'an Foreign Studies University*, 2007 (2): 45-48.

[52] Yu Jiying."The Significance of Evaluation and Translation Ideology - Taking the English Translation of *The True Story of Ah Q* as an Example" [J]. *Foreign Language Teaching Theory and Practice*, 2010 (2): 83-90.

[53] Zhang Xiangang."The Enlightenment of Evaluation Theory on Text Translation" [J]. *Foreign Language Teaching*, 2007 (6): 33-36.

Chapter 4 Research on Genre and Translation from Genre Perspective Translation

Starting from the concept of genre, this chapter provides an overview of genre analysis theories in different schools, with a focus on the genre theory of systemic functional linguistics and the characteristics of applied genre texts. With this as the basis, this chapter discusses several representative applied genre translation studies that this book focuses on.

4.1 Introduction to the Concept of Genre

The concept of types of discourses originates from the word "genre"[1]. The *New Oxford Dictionary of English and Chinese Interpretations* explains "genre" as "a type of artistic work such as music or literature"[2], which dates from early 19th century French and originally meant "a kind". European literary critics borrowed it to refer to the type of literary works. However, most scholars (such as Swales 2001[3], Zhang 2002a[4], 2002b[5], Yu 2003[6], 2009[7]) believe that genre research itself has a long history tracing back to Aristotle's distinction between epic, lyrical, and dramatic literary texts two thousand years ago (Aristotle 1984)[8]. Genre research is mostly concentrated in the field of literature. For

---

[1] The term 'genre' corresponds to "体裁" in Chinese. The common Chinese Translators Journals of "体裁" in existing literature also include: kind, category, style, genre, etc. This study uses the translation term "genre".
[2] The Editorial and Publishing Committee of the *New Oxford English Chinese Dictionary*, *New Oxford English Chinese Dictionary*[M] Shanghai: Shanghai Education Press, 2007:876.
[3] Swales. J. *Genre Analysis in Academic and Research Settings*[M]. Cambridge: Cambridge University Press,1990:45-60. (Reprinted by Foreign Language Teaching and Research Press, 2001).
[4] Zhang Delu. "Exploration of the Theoretical Framework for Genre Research" [J]. *Foreign Language Teaching and Research*, 2002a (5): 339-44.
[5] Zhang Delu. "Overview of Genre Research" [J]. *Foreign Languages*, 2002b (4): 13-22.
[6] Yu Hui. *Genre Analysis of Discourse—Semiotics Meaning of Abstracts of Academic Papers*[M] Zhengzhou: Henan University Press, 2003.
[7] Yu Hui. "Theoretical Tracing of the Concept of Discourse Genre" [J]. *Journal of Beijing Normal University* (Social Sciences Edition), 2006 (4): 61-66.
[8] Aristotle. Poetics[A]. In D.A. Russel & M. Winterbottom (eds.). *Ancient Literary Criticism: The Principal Texts in New Translations*[C]. Oxford: Clarendon, 1984.

example, literary works can be classified based on standards such as the medium of the text, discourse structure and style. Common literary genres include drama, novels, poetry, biographies, etc.

Since the mid-20th century, the concept of genre has gradually been introduced into different disciplinary fields. Through the creative adoption of Bakhtin (1985), the term extended from literature to non-literary discourse research, generally referring to a written or oral discourse type. Any text, from daily conversations to parliamentary speeches, has its corresponding genre category. The concept of genre was formally introduced by anthropologists into the field of linguistic research (Swales 2001/1990)[1] to study the classification of speech acts in a certain speech community. The most representative is the related description of ethnography scholar Helms. He believes that genres often overlap with speech events in communicative actions, such as humor, stories, lectures, greetings, conversations, etc."The so-called genre refers to poetry, mythology, stories, language, riddles, curses, prayers, debates, lectures, business advertisements, letters, editorials and other types"[2]. These genre types have different formal features or formal "markers", so we can identify the genre types of oral or written language discourses. However, in specific text analysis, we should pay attention to the distinction between genre and speech event. For example, a teacher's class is a speech event, but the speech event can be composed of different genres and the same genre can also function as different speech acts in different situations.

The genre in the field of literature generally refers to the artistic forms of literature, such as poetry, novels, essays, etc. The complexity and diversity of discourse and texts in non-literary fields pose great difficulties in accurately defining genres. Although it is difficult for us to define "genre" precisely, researchers in different fields have provided their own working definitions for the term "genre" based on their research questions, focus, research objectives and theoretical inheritance. Hasan (1977)[3] believes that genre is

---

[1] Swales. J. *Genre Analysis in Academic and Research Settings*[M]. Cambridge: Cambridge University Press, 1990:45-60. (Reprinted by Foreign Language Teaching and Research Press, 2001).
[2] Hymes, D. *Models of the interaction of language and social life*[A]. In Gumperz, J.J. & Hymes (eds.), *Directions in Sociolinguistics*[C]. New York: Holt, Rinehart & Winston, Inc,1972:35-71.
[3] Hasan, R. *Text in the systemic functional model*[A]. In W. Dressler (ed.). Current Trends in Text Linguistics[C]. Berlin: Walter de Gruyler,1977: 228-246.

the type of discourse, where a genre is composed of necessary and optional structural elements that can determine the discourse type of a text. The genre of Saville Troike (1982) refers to the type of communicative event, such as "joke", "story", "lecture", "greeting", "conversation", etc., which is similar to the genre definition of Heimes mentioned earlier. Swales (1990) proposes a very long working definition of "genre" which in short is the classification of human communication events with different purposes in specific social and cultural contexts. Bhatia's definition (1993)[1] is similar to Swales', who believes that genre is a recognizable communicative event with distinct internal structural features such as conventions and constraints. By combining context, form, and function, Martin (1993)[2] puts forward that that genre is a step-by-step, communicative purpose-oriented social interaction activity. Like Martin, Ventola (1995)[3] believes that genre is a recognizable step in the communication process and therefore has a conventional nature which is similar to routine-like.

Although there are various definitions of genres in the academic community, all definitions of "genre" include the following: (1) Genre is a type of discourse (oral or written) that has structural and formal representational characteristics; (2) Discourse of the same genre has similarities in communicative purposes; (3) Genre is closely related to discourse function and contextual context. The concept of "genre" has the following characteristics: stability, repeatability, and habituation, emphasizing the structural and formal conventions of genre (such as Hasan 1977[4], Swales 1990[5], Bhatia 1993[6]); Dynamicity and variability, emphasizing situational changes in genres and adapting to

---

[1] Bhatia, V. K. *Analyzing Genre: Language Use in Professional Settings*[M]. New York: Longman, 1993: 23-25; 42-43.
[2] Martin, J . R. "A Contextual theory of language" [A]. In B. Cope & M. Kalantzis (eds.). *The Powers of Literacy: A Genre Approach to Teaching Writing[C]*. Bristol, PA: Falmer Press, 1993:116- 136.
3 Ventola, E. "Generic and register qualities of texts and their realization" [A]. In P. H. Fries &M. Gregory (eds.). *Discourse in Society: Systemic Functional Perspective*[C]. New York: Ablex publishing Corporation,1995.
[4] Hasan, R. "Text in the systemic functional model" [A]. In W. Dressler (ed.). *Current Trends in Text Linguistics*[C]. Berlin: Walter de Gruyler,1977: 228-246.
[5] Swales. J. *Genre Analysis in Academic and Research Settings*[M]. Cambridge: Cambridge University Press, 1990:45-60. (Reprinted by Foreign Language Teaching and Research Press, 2001).
[6] Bhatia, V. K. *Analyzing Genre: Language Use in Professional Settings*[M]. New York: Longman, 1993: 23-25; 42-43.

certain social and cultural contexts (such as Miller 1984[1], Fang 1998[2], Kress 1987[3]); Archetypal, there may not be a clear boundary between one genre and another, but it has historical inheritance (Jamieson 1974[4]) and "family resemblance" (such as Zhang 2008[5]). Next, we will review the main theoretical schools of genre studies in linguistics and applied linguistics.

4.2 Schools of Genre Research

There are different classification criteria in genre studies, which can generally be divided into genre research in the literary field (such as Todorov 1976[6]) and genre research in non-literary fields. What's more, based on research methods, genre research can be divided into empirical research with discourse analysis as demonstration, induction and summary, and non-empirical research with pure theoretical discussion (Liang Wenhua and Qin Hongwu 2009)[7]. For another example, according to the research field, it can be divided into genre analysis in sociolinguistics, genre analysis in conversation analysis, and genre analysis in applied linguistics (Yu 2003)[8]. In terms of tracing the development of genre research, it can be divided into early research, folklore research, early 20th-century formalism, and mid-20th-century research in ethnology, anthropology, linguistics and applied linguistics (Zhang 2002a)[9]. Bhatia (1993) divides the development process of genre analysis into four stages: register analysis (surface language description), grammatical and rhetorical analysis (functional language description), interactive analysis (verbal language description), and genre analysis (explanatory language description).

---

[1] Miller C R. "Genre as social action" [J]. *Quarterly journal of speech*, 1984, 70(2): 151-167.
[2] Fang Yan. "On Language Categories" [J]. *Foreign Language*, 1998 (1): 17-22
[3] Kress, G. "Genre in a social theory of language: A reply to John Dixon" [A]. In I. Reid (ed.). *The Place of Genre in Learning: Current Debates*. Vic.: Deakin University Press, 1987: 35-45.
[4] Jamieson K M. "Antecedent genre as rhetorical constraint" [J]. *Quarterly Journal of Speech,* 1975, 61(4): 406-415.
[5] Zhang Yan. "Dynamic Genre Research from the Perspective of 'Topology' " [J]. *Rhetoric Learning*, 2008 (1): 19-24.
[6] Todorov, T. "The origin of genres" [J]. *New Literary History*,1976 (8): 159-70.
[7] Liang Wenhua, Qin Hongwu. "Overview of Research on Genre Theory in China in the Last 10 Years" [J]. *Foreign Language Teaching*, 2009 (1): 44-48.
[8] Yu Hui. *Genre Analysis of Discourse semiotics Meaning of Abstracts of Academic Papers*[M] Zhengzhou: Henan University Press, 2003.
[9] Zhang Delu. "Exploring the Theoretical Framework of Genre Research" [J]. *Foreign Language Teaching and Research*, 2002a (5): 339-44.

Genre research has gradually shifted from descriptive research at the surface level of language to explanatory research at the deeper level.

In the West, there are three main schools of genre analysis in the field of linguistics (Paltridge 1997[1], Si 2012[2]): the ESP/EAP school represented by Swales and Bhatia, the Systemic Functional Linguistic School represented by Hasan and Martin (also known as the Sydney School), and the New Rhetoric School represented by Miller. The ESP/EAP school has established a genre analysis model of moves and steps that focuses on academic and professional discourses. Based on Systemic Functional Linguistics theory and the relationship between genre, socio-cultural context and situational context, the Sydney School proposes the Generic Structural Potential theory (Hasan 1977[3]) and the Schematic Structure theory (Martin 2004)[4]. The New Rhetoric School analyzes the behaviors and purposes that can be achieved by a genre from the perspective of the social context in which the genre is formed. Its rhetoric genre research provides new dimensions and perspectives of society, history, cognition, etc. for genre analysis (Wen 2005[5]). Next is a brief overview of the genre research theories of the three schools.

4.2.1 Genre Research of Systemic Functional Linguistics School

Detailed discussion of the genre theory of the Systemic Functional Linguistics School will be provided in the third part; this section briefly elaborate on the genre theory of this school

Hassan and Martin are masters of genre theory within Systemic Functional Linguistics, but their interpretations of genre are not entirely the same. Hassan's representative achievement is the potential of genre structure. Genre is simply defined as a discourse type, and each discourse type has a universal structural formula, which is a clear

---

[1] Paltridge, B. *Genre, Frames and Writing in Research Settings*[M]. Amsterdam: John Benjamins Publishing Company, 1997.
[2] Si Xianzhu. "On the Quality Evaluation of Applied Genre Discourse Translation - A Genre Analysis Perspective of the Systemic Functional Linguistics School" [J]. *Shandong Foreign Language Teaching*, 2012 (4): 11-16.
[3] Hasan, R. Text in the systemic functional model[A]. In W. Dressler (ed.). Current Trends in Text Linguistics [C]. Berlin: Walter de Gruyler, 1977: 228-246.
[4] Martin, J. R. *English Text: System and Structure*[M]. Beijing: Peking University Press, 2004.
[5] Wen Zhisheng. "The Social Cognitive Perspective of the New Rhetoric School's Genre Study" [J]. *Journal of Tianjin International Studies University*, 2005, (6): 46-52.

configuration of a certain discourse structure (Hasan 1977)[1]. Genre structure includes essential components, optional components and repetitive components, among which essential components are the determining factors of a certain genre. The potential of genre structure is determined by contextual configuration, and situational configuration (or register) is composed of field, tenor, and mode, which are realized by specific language forms such as grammar and vocabulary. Hasan's genre structure reflects the pattern of register within the discourse, and genre and register are not "separated" and often confused as one.

Martin defines genre as a "phased, purposeful social process", which was first proposed in the article "Language, Register, and Genre" published in 1984. Martin refers to this as a working definition, which continues to develop and has become the formal definition of genre by the Sydney School from a linguistic perspective, and has been widely spread. Genre reflects conceptual forms and is an integral part of culture. He proposes a model of "ideology genre register vocabulary grammar", believing that genre reflects ideology while itself is reflected by register. In this way, Martin clearly distinguishes genre and register, which are two different levels of symbolic expression, and genre is a superior concept. Furthermore, situational context (register) is an example of culture (genre), while genre (cultural context) is the potential behind all different types of situations that arise. Cultural context is the context of meaning potential, while situational context is the context of specific examples. Just as discourse is an example of language, context is an example of culture.

Martin and his followers combine the three meta-functions and register theory to analyze various genre types and summarize the characteristics of each genre in terms of vocabulary, syntax, and macro structure (the distribution of stage and phase). The starting point of Martin's genre research is to improve the writing ability of Australian primary and secondary school students. Therefore, Martin's genre theory is practical in nature.

The genre research of Systemic Functional Linguistics inherits the essence of the detailed description of language ontology from Systemic Functional Linguistics theory, with combination of the context and function of discourse use. It not only focuses on the

---

[1] Hasan, R. *Text in the systemic functional model*[A]. In W. Dressler (ed.). Current Trends in Text Linguistics[C]. Berlin: Walter de Gruyler, 1977: 229.

macro structural layout of the genre, but also delves into the micro choice of words and sentences in the text. Therefore, Zhang[1] (2002b) commented that "Systemic Functional Linguistics studies genres from multiple perspectives, including cultural, social, situational, semantic, lexical, grammatical and phonological levels. This theoretical tradition provides theoretical guidance for this study to construct a translation quality assessment model under genre analysis from the perspectives of "schematic structure"and"manifestation style".

4.2.2 ESP/EAP School Genre Analysis

ESP and EAP are abbreviations for English for Specific Purposes and English for Academic Purpose respectively, referring to English for Special Purposes and Academic Purposes. This school believes that genre is a type of communicative event, and genre analysis is very important for these two types of English practitioners. Its research object or service object is overseas students from English-speaking countries. The ESP/EAP school is represented by Swales and Bhatia's academic and professional discourse research. They have established their own genre analysis models: Swales' genre analysis model of"moves and steps" in academic and research English; Bhatia's genre analysis model of"moves and steps"of sales discourses. Language users need to master the genre norms in their field by studying such institutional discourse, such as the writing of academic dissertations and research papers, in order to understand what discourse content a professional club member uses and how they complete their practical activities (Bhatia 1993[2]). Therefore, understanding the construction methods and language knowledge of professional discourse is crucial for both educators and learners. The contribution of this school lies in analyzing, describing and summarizing the relatively fixed content and formal characteristics of a certain professional field at the discourse level, such as academic and promotional genres. It aims to help learners master knowledge of a certain genre and successfully complete their tasks.

---

[1] Zhang Delu. "Overview of Genre Research" [J]. *Foreign Languages*, 2002b (4): 13-22.
[2] Bhatia, V. K.*Analyzing Genre: Language Use in Professional Settings*[M]. New York: Longman, 1993.

4.2.2.1 Swales' model of Moves and Steps

Swales' model contains two important concepts: moves and steps. A "move" can be considered as a superior semantic structural unit in a certain genre, and a "step" is a subordinate structural component of a move. Several "steps" form a "move". Moves are often fixed, and detailed elements can be added by the author to enrich each move (Swales 1981[1], 1990/2001[2], Dudley-Evans 1986[3]).

In 1981, Swales analyzed the introduction section of 48 scientific papers and proposed a rhetorical step of "four move" based on it (establishing the field—summarizing previous research—preparing for present research—introducing present research):

Table 1: The "Four Move" Model (Swales 1981)[4]

First move: Establishing the field
(a) Presenting the topic
(b) Stating the current research status
(c) Summarizing the main characteristics of this topic
Second move: Summarizing previous research
(a) Introducing with the researcher as the main clue
(b) Introducing without taking the researcher as the main clue
(c) Introducing based on research topic orientation
Third move: Preparing for present research
Fourth move: Introducing present research

---

[1] Swales, J. *Aspects of Article Introductions*[M]. Birmingham, UK: The University of Aston, Language Studies Unit, 1981.
[2] Swales. J. *Genre Analysis in Academic and Research Settings*[M]. Cambridge: Cambridge University Press, 1990:45-60. (Reprinted by Foreign Language Teaching and Research Press, 2001)
[3] Dudley-Evans, T. *Genre Analysis: An investigation of the introduction and discussion sections of MSc Dissertations* [A]. In M. Coulthard (ed.). Talking About Text, Discourse Analysis Monograph No. 13 [C]. University of Birmingham: English Language Research, 1986.
[4] Swales, J. *Aspects of Article Introductions*[M]. Birmingham, UK: The University of Aston, Language Studies Unit, 1981.

Using quantitative and qualitative analysis methods, Swales (1990/2001)[1] improved the 1981 model by analyzing and summarizing the introductions of some academic papers and proposed the famous "Three Move" CARS (Create A Research Space) framework. The specific content of CARS is as follows:

Table 2 CARS "Three Move" Model (Adapted from Swales 1990)[2]

First move: Establishing the field
    Step 1: Proposing the topic
    (and/or) Step 2: Summarizing the main idea
    (and/or) Step 3: Reviewing previous research findings

Second move: Identifying the gap
    Step 1A: Refuting existing arguments
    (or) Step 1B: Pointing out the gap
    (or) Step 1C: Proposing problems
    (or) Step 1D: Continuation of previous research findings

Third move: Filling the gap
    Step 1A: Overview of research objectives
    (or) Step 1B: Current research on this topic
    Step 2: Reporting main findings
    Step 3: Introducing the organization of the paper

Swales summarizes the number of occurrences of each move in these introductory texts, explores the sequence in which these moves occur and the functions of each move. The three moves are necessary semantic components of this genre, and some of the steps under each move are necessary and some are optional. However, the overall framework of the introduction to a scientific paper remains unchanged. Moves and steps have corresponding sentence structures, tenses, vocabulary and other characteristics, such as their attention to the use of passive voice in scientific English discourses and the use of

---

[1] Swales. J. *Genre Analysis in Academic and Research Settings*[M]. Cambridge: Cambridge University Press, 1990:45-60. (Reprinted by Foreign Language Teaching and Research Press, 2001).
[2] Ibid, 141.

perfect tense in biological discourses. But they do not explore further into the reasons for the occurrence of these features.

4.2.2.2 Bhatia's Seven-Move Model

Bhatia (1993)[1] advances Swales' research on move one step further. He believes that any genre analysis should start from the following seven aspects: 1) Confirming the specific genre text in a certain context; 2) Refering to existing literature; 3) Analyzing the situational context generated by the text; 4) Selecting the corpus to analyze; 5) Studying the context of conventions; 6) Making analysis at language level; 7) Seeking the opinions of experts.

Bhatia (1993)[2] summarizes characteristics of outlines of business letters and recommendation letters, and explores the inherent layout structure patterns of this genre. He finds that this type of promotional genre text presents common move characteristics in achieving the communicative purpose of "promotion". Bhatia summarizes it into seven moves, as shown in the table below:

Table 3 Seven-move model (Bhatia 1993)[3]

Move 1 Establishing credentials	Obligatory element
Move 2 Introducing the offer	Optional element
Move 3 Offering incentives	Optional element
Move 4 Enclosing documents	Optional element
Move 5 Soliciting response	Obligatory element
Move 6 Using pressure tactics	Optional element
Move 7 Ending politely	Optional element

In Bhatia's seven-move model, moves can be either necessary or optional. According to different communicative intentions, the number and order of moves are not fixed. Due to the inherent structural patterns of different genres, the parameters of moves may also change.

---

[1] Bhatia, V. K. *Analyzing Genre: Language Use in Professional Settings*[M]. New York: Longman: 1993.
[2] Ibid.
[3] Ibid, 62.

In addition to the above two genres, this school also summarizes the structures and characteristics of other common genres, such as medical research papers (Adams Smith 1984, Salager Meyer 1994, cited from Yu 2003[1]), discussion sections of research papers (summary results—research insights—future issues, cited from Swales 1990[2]), the "11 step" framework (Hopkins & Dudley Evans 1988)[3], and legal texts (Bhatia 1987[4], 1993[5]).

The genre analysis theory of the ESP/EAP school has a strong practical orientation, which utilizes the genre characteristics of specialized English discourse summarized to better guide the English learning of non-native English speakers, especially writing, in order to facilitate their discourse activities.

4.2.3 New Rhetoric School

Traditional rhetoric pays attention to the characteristics and rules embodied in the form of the text, and has given rise to the comparative rhetoric strongly influenced by structuralism. For example, Kaplan (1966)[6] summarizes the preferences of writers from different cultures in the macro structure of the text—students from American cultural backgrounds like "linear", and students from Asian countries like "circular". The New Rhetoric School aims to break the tradition of focusing only on the form of the text, and focuses more on the socio-cultural context of the text and its social action effect. The representative figures of the New Rhetoric School include Miller, Freedman, Huckin, etc.

This school takes the article "Genre as Social Action"[7] published by Miller in 1984 as its flagship work. Based on rhetoric, speech act theory, social constructivism and philosophy of language, Miller regards genre as purposeful social action, rather than just a formal means of language. The complexity and diversity of social reality determine the

---

[1] Yu Hui. *Genre Analysis of Discourse—Semiotics Meaning of Abstracts of Academic Papers*[M] Zhengzhou: Henan University Press, 200.
[2] Swales. J. *Genre Analysis in Academic and Research Settings*[M]. Cambridge: Cambridge University Press, 1990:45-60. (Reprinted by Foreign Language Teaching and Research Press, 2001)
[3] Hopkins, A. & T. Dudley-Evans.A genre-based investigations of the discussion sections in articles and dissertation" [J]. *English for Specific Purposes,*1988(7): 113-22.
[4] Bhatia, V.K. "Language of the Law" [J]. *Language Teaching,*1987(20): 227-234.
[5] Bhatia, V. K. A*nalyzing Genre: Language Use in Professional Settings*[M]. New York: Longman,1993:23-25, 42-43.
[6] Kaplan, R. B. "Cultural thought patterns in intercultural education" [J]. *Language Learning,*1966(16):1–20.
[7] Miller C R. "Genre as social action" [J]. *Quarterly journal of speech*, 1984, 70(2): 151-167.

types of genres, therefore, the types of genres are not fixed and unchanging. They are characterized by both historical inheritance (Jamieson 1975)[1] and dynamic development.

The genre theory of New Rhetoric School is mainly applied to English writing. The service purpose of the ESP/EAP school is slightly different from that of the ESP/EAP school, which studies the acquisition and development of English as a mother tongue or first language and is popular in North American university classrooms. Its research focus is on the social behavioral goals and contextual attributes that genre aims to achieve. "Genres have a series of recognizable discourse forms, which come from intrinsic dynamics"[2]. This intrinsic dynamics is the social situational attribute required to achieve a certain social behavior. Learners'learning to use a certain genre is the key to their participation in social life. Therefore, they need to master those cultural conventions under different situations through systematic learning, which is called"genre knowledge".

The New Rhetoric School is very concerned about the social motivation or intention of a particular genre, as well as the beliefs, attitudes, values, etc. displayed by members of the genre community. Therefore, the research focus of this school is not on the formal rules of genres at the linguistic level of vocabulary, syntactic structure, discourse structure, etc., but on analyzing the situational context and social behaviors that genres can achieve from the perspective of social, cultural, and historical situations formed by genres. The genre studies of the above three schools all focus on the intention of language, the function of language, and the situational nature of language use. The three share a similar genre concept, that is, "genre is a means of social communication that reflects, coordinates human understanding, and participates in world activities." They focus on how different discourse functions in different contexts and how people respond appropriately in various contexts (Bawarshi & Reiff 2010)[3]. However each of the three major schools has its own emphasis. ESP emphasizes the form and conventions of genres and uses linguistic methods to describe the genre characteristics of discourse, such as studying the structural,

---

[1] Jamieson K M. "Antecedent genre as rhetorical constraint" [J]. *Quarterly Journal of Speech*, 1975, 61(4): 406-415.

[2] Campbell, K.K. & K. H. Jamieson. *Form and in rhetorical criticism: An introduction*[A]. In Campbell & Jamieson (eds.). Form and Genre: Shaping rhetorical action [C]. Falls Church, VA: The Speech Communication Association,1978:21.

[3] Bawarshi, A. & Reiff, M.J. *Genre: An introduction to history, theory, research and pedagogy*[M]. West Lafayette, IN: Parlor Press/WAC Clearinghouse, 2010:5.

lexical and syntactic characteristics of academic and professional discourse using the "move and step" analysis model. The genre theory of the New Rhetoric School has no theoretical source of linguistic research ontology (Yu 2003)[1]. It mainly relies on the study of the acquisition and development of English as the mother tongue or the first language. The purpose of learning is to understand the social function of genre, not language itself. Furthermore, influenced by psychology and sociology, the New Rhetoric School defines genre by the social behavior that genre can accomplish. As genre as social actions are dynamic, some scholars believe that the genre is difficult to teach, which is obviously influenced by constructivism and is in sharp contrast to the traditional rhetoric school under the influence of structuralism. However, it is precisely because the New Rhetoric School overemphasizes the dynamics of genre and ignores its regularity, this study selects the genre analysis perspective of systemic functional linguistics and combines the concepts of move in ESP/EAP, so as to better explore the regularity in the translation process of applied stylistic texts and to improve the existing translation quality assessment model. The linguistic theory of genre research by the Systemic Functional Linguistics School has a profound origin, absorbing the essence of Systemic Functional Linguistics theory and emphasizing the context, structure and function of genres. This school not only focuses on the structure, rhetoric, and linguistic characteristics of discourse, but also studies the social, cultural, and situational contexts in which discourse arises. In the following section, a detailed introduction to the genre research theory of the Systemic Functional Linguistics School will be provided.

4.3 Genre Research of Systemic Functional Linguistics School

4.3.1 Introduction to Systemic Functional Linguistics Theory

The Systemic Functional Linguistics founded by Halliday takes a sociological perspective. It regards language as a social symbol, and proposes that language operates within society. Genre is the representation of the highest level in a symbolic system, which is implemented by register and in turn is implemented by the language's phonology, vocabulary, grammar and discourse semantics. Language is an extensive network of

---

[1] Yu Hui. *Genre Analysis of Discourse—Semiotics Meaning of Abstracts of Academic Papers*[M] Zhengzhou: Henan University Press, 200.

resources. When people use language, they make corresponding choices from this system network, convey experiences in this world, express attitudes and emotions or establish social relationships.

Systemic Functional Linguistics consists of two major parts: "system" and "function". The former mainly inherits the concept of Firth, that is, each system is a set of choices in a vertical aggregation relationship, and each system is a subsystem that constitutes a higher-level system. When people use language in a specific situation, they make choices in an orderly manner among countless system nodes. The grammar section of "function"mainly discusses the three major meta functions of language to solve the starting point problem of system selection. The meta functions of language include ideational function, interpersonal function and textual function. Each meta function corresponds to the corresponding semantic function and subsystem. The ideational function mainly includes the transitivity system, which expresses the speaker's understanding and reflection of the external or internal world. The transitivity system divides human activities into material, psychological, relational, behavioral, verbal and existential processes. Each process includes its own participants, environmental components, etc. Through transitivity analysis, we can understand what people have accomplished by using clauses. nterpersonal function involves the tone system, which refers to the communicative roles and social relationships established between language users. The mood system is composed of mood and residual components, where the order of the subject and finite in the mood determines the choice of mood. Textual function refers to the use of language to form sentences and convey information, hence it is also known as information function. The choice of thematic system is its main form of implementation. The order of theme and rheme reflects the differences in information transmission. Each clause possesses these three metafunctions simultaneously. People usually choose to formulate words and sentences in a certain context, so the meaning of a discourse cannot be separated from situational and cultural contexts. The situational context is reflected by the register, which includes three parts: field, tenor and mode, corresponding to the three major meta-functions. Field refers to specific events, participants, etc. that correspond to conceptual functions. The tenor refers to the relationship between participants in the register, which corresponds to interpersonal function. Mode refers to the channels or presentation methods for implementation, whether written or oral. From the definition of the three elements of register, register often determines people's specific language choices.

4.3.2 Genre Theory of Halliday and Hasan

The founder of Systemic Functional Linguistics theory, Halliday, has never published any articles or monographs specifically on "genre". We can only find a few references to genre in his writings. As mentioned by Halliday&Hasan in 1976[1], mode is a function of discourse, including language channels and genres, or rhetorical devices such as narration, preaching, persuasion and communication. In his book *Language as a Social Semiotic*, Halliday pointed out that "the language format can roughly cover the channels, tone, and genre proposed by Hymes" (Halliday 1978)[2], which means that Halliday attributed "genre" to the language format within the three variables of register. When discussing the correspondence between the three variables of register and the three meta-functions, Halliday compared the register variables with the eight major discourse components[3] of Hymes, and continued to say that "the language style includes Hymes' instrumental and genre" (Halliday 1978)[4]. Halliday's classification is related to the definition of genre by Hymes mentioned earlier, which means "genre refers to poem, myth, story, words, riddle, curse, prayer, debate, lecture, business advertisement, letter, editorial and other types"[5]. Analyzing discourse into a speech act is equivalent to analyzing discourse into a certain genre. The concept of "genre" means that it is possible for us to identify the formal features or formal "markers" of traditional genres[6]. Hymes' genre focuses on the formal characteristics of discourse in various styles, which is consistent

---

[1] Halliday, M.A.K. & R. Hasan. *Cohesion in English*[M]. London: Longman,1976:22.
[2] Halliday, M.A.K. *Language as Social Semiotic: The Social Interpretation of Language and Meaning* [M]. London: Edward Arnold,1978:62.
[3] The eight major discourse components of Hymes are: form and content, setting, participants, ends (intent and effect), key, medium, genre and interactional norms (Hymes 1972: 59-65). Halliday (1978) proposed that field corresponds to setting and ends, tenor corresponds to participants and key, and mode corresponds to instrumentality and gene.
[4] Halliday, M.A.K. *Language as Social Semiotic: The Social Interpretation of Language and Meaning* [M]. London: Edward Arnold,1978:62.
[5] Hymes, D. 1972. "Models of the interaction of language and social life" [A]. In Gumperz, J.J. & Hymes (eds.), *Directions in Sociolinguistics* [C]. New York: Holt, Rinehart & Winston, Inc,1972:65.
[6] Ibid.

with Halliday's stylistic connotations. From this perspective, it is reasonable to attribute genre to mode. Halliday understands genre from a general concept, and genre structure is only one aspect of discourse characteristics. Therefore, genre itself is not Halliday's focus. In an interview twenty years later, he proposed that establishing a genre model is related to what needs to be done, while his focus is on establishing a functional grammar system of language.

Hasan's representative achievement in genre research is the genre structure potential. Genre can be simply defined as a discourse type, and each discourse type has a universal structural formula that divides a discourse structure into clear and distinct configurations (Hasan 1977)[1]. Language is only a formal system, and there is no way to directly predict the "formula" of a certain genre. The control lies in the context. The overall effect formed by the special values of the various elements of context, namely the three variables of register (field, mode, and tenor), is called context configuration. Context configuration is directly related to the genre structure of a certain text, or can predict the structural pattern of a genre, namely genre structure potential (GSP) (Halliday&Hasan 1989)[2]. Genre structure potential is an abstract category that encompasses all discourse structures within a certain genre, including necessary and optional structural components and their sequential structures (Hasan 1996)[3]. From Hassan's explanation of contextual typology, the concept of register serves as a bridge between genre structure and context. Although Hassan also believes that the genre of a text is not determined solely by one of the three variables of register, in practical operations, such as in the analysis of genre structure in children's fairy tales, only the necessary structural components play a crucial role in determining which genre the text belongs to. These essential components are mainly determined by the discourse field, indicating a close connection between discourse field, discourse structure and genre is very close (Martin 2004)[4].Register and genre are at the same level, and the overall structure of different types of discourse is the focus of Hasan's

---

[1] Hasan, R. "Text in the systemic functional model" [A]. In W. Dressler (ed.). *Current Trends in Text Linguistics*[C]. Berlin: Walter de Gruyler,1977:229.
[2] Halliday, M.A.K. & R. Hasan. *Language, Context and Text: Aspects of Language in a Social-semiotic Perspectives*[M]. Oxford: Oxford University Press, 1989.
[3] Hasan, R."The nursery tale as a genre"[A]. C. Cloran, D. Butt & G. Williams (eds.)*Ways of Saying: Ways of Meaning*[C]. London: Cassell, 1996:53.
[4] Martin, J.R. *English Text: System and Structure*[M]. Beijing: Peking University Press,2004:505.

genre research. However, Hassan did not develop his genre structure potential in a systematic/structural direction, which is a deficiency of Hasan's theory compared to Martin's genre research.

Hasan's genre research took a step forward by proposing the theory of establishing the potential for genre structure. Her research focus, like that of Michel and Lapov, is on the step distribution of discourse structure. Hasan believes that genre structure potential is a concrete manifestation of the discourse scope, discourse mode and discourse tone formed in a specific context, which includes all discourse patterns and structures that may appear in a certain genre. The structure of a certain genre has both obligatory and optional features. Obligatory features define the framework of genres, enabling people to identify differences between different genres. Selective features allow language users to transform language forms within a specific genre framework.

The construction of the genre structure potential (GSP) model plays a crucial role in describing the relationships between various variables within a genre. It was first proposed by Hasan in 1984, and the GSP model mainly describes the following structural characteristics of a text: First, which components must appear; Second, which components can appear; Third, the location where the component must appear; Fourth, the location where components can appear; Fifth, the frequency at which each component can appear. In short, the purpose of genre structure potential is to study which structural components are obligatory and which are optional. The existence, sequential arrangement, and recursion of these components constitute the macro structure of a certain genre, such as the necessary semantic components and macro discourse layout of various applied text genres discussed in this research. After GSP was proposed, researchers followed suit and gradually summarized the structural components of different genres.

Hasan (1996)[1] analyzed the potential of purchasing genre structures. The details are as follows: [(Greeting)· (Sale Initiation) ^] [⁻(Sale Enquiry·) ⁻ {Sale Request ^ Sale Compliance} ^ Sale ^] Purchase^ Purchase Closure (^ Finish). This is a linear description of the schematic structure of this genre. The elements in parentheses are optional. All other elements outside the parentheses are obligatory. The symbol ^ indicates that element

---

[1] Hasan, R."The nursery tale as a genre"[A]. C. Cloran, D. Butt & G. Williams (eds.)*Ways of Saying: Ways of Meaning*[C]. London: Cassell, 1996.

X must appear before element Y, that is, in a fixed order. The symbol ⌐ appearing in front of a program indicates that the element can appear more than once. The small dot in front of an element indicates that it has no sequential order, but can only be adjusted within square brackets. The components enclosed in curly braces are recursive sequences as a whole. Therefore, SR ^ SC can appear more than once, but can only appear inside curly braces.

Eggins (1994)[1] concluded that the structural potential of commercial transaction genres can be expressed as: (Sales Initiation) ^ { Sales Request ^ Sales Compliance ^ Purchase ^ (Price) } ^ Payment ^(Thanks) ^(Change) ^Purchase Closure. Namely: 1)All texts belonging to this genre must include the obligatory elements of Sales Request, Sales, Compliance, Purchase, Payment, Purchase, and Closure. 2)The components within parentheses are not obligatory and serve as the basis for discourse diversification; 3)All components within the curly braces can be repeated; 4)All components are arranged in a certain order, and their positions cannot be reversed from each other.

There are also scholars in China who use Hasan's GSP model to analyze the structural configurations of various genres. For example, Yu Hui analyzed the genre characteristics in English academic paper abstracts in his doctoral thesis published in 2003; Fang Yan applied genre analysis to the writing of English textbooks for primary and secondary schools.

Hasan's genre analysis model has had a widespread impact, but it also has its shortcomings. For example, she did not treat genre as an independent system, and genre structure is only one of the textual factors, which is one or several aspects of the register. In the discussion, she occasionally juxtaposed genre and register or style (Halliday&Hasan 1976)[2], which did not seem to strictly distinguish these terms. Martin's genre theory is based on such theoretical loopholes.

4.3.3 Martin's Genre Theory

The vigorous development of Systemic Functional Linguistics in Australia has given

---

[1] Eggins, S. *An Introduction to Systemic- Functional Linguistics*[M]. London: Pinter,1994:40.
[2] Halliday, M.A.K. & R. Hasan. *Cohesion in English*[M]. London: Longman，1976.

rise to the "Sydney School"[1], and one of the biggest contributions of the Sydney School to Systemic Functional Linguistics is genre research, which is based on the combination of genre research with teaching practice. (Such as: Martin 1984a[2], 1984b[3], Martin & Rothery 1984[4], Martin & Rose 2008[5]). Genre is the coordination principle and starting point of discourse analysis, and genre research has created the Sydney School. Martin is a leading figure and master of this school. His genre definition, genre model, genre system and genre relationship have broadened the theoretical framework of Systemic Functional Linguistics, established a series of discourse system networks (Wang et al., 2010)[6], which also have opened up a new perspective for us to understand the relationship between language and culture in social practice.

Martin defined genre as "a phased, purposeful social process". Genre has three major attributes: phased, purposeful, and social. These three attributes come together to define a certain genre. Genre is also considered as a repetitive configuration of meaning that plays a role in a certain culture (Martin & Rose 2008)[7], which is Martin's emphasis on genre intention. These two definitions complement each other and jointly construct Martin's genre view from social and cultural perspectives.

First, 'staging' reflects the step-by-step nature of discourse structure, similar to the moves and steps in ESP/EAP. The terms adopted by Martin are stage and phase, which are recurrent local patterns, and genre is a type of overall schematic structure that recurs. Martin once used a vivid metaphor -"how a text grows"- to illustrate the dynamic step-by-step nature of discourse. A discourse is usually composed of a series of small sentences, forming different phases, and then forming a stage where each discourse

---

[1] The term 'Sydney School' was proposed by Green and Lee in 1994, see Green & Lee 1994 (Writing Geography Lessons: Literacy, identity and schooling 207-24. Freedman and Medway). But in fact, the genre model they proposed was widely used and developed in major universities in Sydney, Australia before 1994.

[2] Martin, J.R. "Language, Register and Genre" [A]. In F. Christie, (ed.). *Children Writing: Reader*[C]. Geelong, Vic.Deakin University Press, 1984a:21-30.

[3] Martin, J.R. "Types of Writing in Infants and Primary School" [A].In L. Unsworth, (ed.). *Reading, Writing, Spelling. Sydney* [C] Macarthur Institute of Higher Education, 1984b:34-55. (Republished by Shanghai Jiaotong University Press 2012).

[4] Martin, J.R. & J. Rothery. Choice of Genre in a Suburban Primary School. Paper presented at *Annual Conference of the Applied Linguistics Association of Australia*, Alice Springs, Northern Territory,1984.

[5] Martin, J.R. & D. Rose. *Genre Relations: Mapping Culture* [M]. London: Equinox Publishing Ltd, 2008.

[6] Wang Zhenhua, Zhang Daqun and Zhang Xiangang."Marti's Study of Text Semantics"[J]. *Contemporary Foreign Language Research*, 2010 (10): 43-49.

[7] Martin, J.R. & D. Rose. *Genre Relations: Mapping Culture*[M]. London: Equinox Publishing Ltd, 2008: 206.

exhibits its unique schematic structure. If this meaning structure repeatedly appears, we can use it as one of the criteria for distinguishing a certain genre. Genre is an intentional activity limited by culture, and we can identify it through different stages and schematic structures, which is similar to Hasan's genre structure potential. Second, "purposefulness" embodies the core of Martin's genre view, which is that the discourse is intended. Martin extracted intention from the register and placed it in an implicit symbolic layer, which is represented by language and register, and the genre took on its content layer. This is an important prerequisite for Martin's genre research, that is, intention is placed within the scope of the genre. Martin believed that this separation could enhance the predictability between the three metafunctions and the three variables of register. Third, the genre is social, processive and cultural. Martin's understanding of genres was based on his understanding of language. He "approached the relationship between social culture, language structure and meaning from a social and cultural perspective"[1]. This definition is also inseparable from the emphasis on meaning in Systemic Functional Linguistics, as meaning arises from the practical process of social culture. Such genre theory can provide a more comprehensive perspective for contextual analysis and be in line with research traditions such as literature and culture (Halliday & Martin 1993)[2].

Martin believes that genre is a symbolic layer that transcends language and register. The level of context includes three aspects: ideology, genre, and register. The relationship between the three is realization, with register corresponding to situational context, genre corresponding to cultural context[3], and ideology being the highest level of context (Martin & Rose 2008)[4]. Martin also distinguishes three levels of semiotics: language, register and genre, and genre is an independent semiotic level: 1. Distinguish between intention and content; 2. Place the intention at the genre level; 3. Extract the genre from the register. These three points were not discussed in the genre studies of Halliday and Hasan.

Discourse intention is the starting point of Martin's genre theory. From his discussion on genre types and genre relationships, the role of discourse intention is indispensable. For example, in the subclassification of story genres, stories can be divided into recitations, anecdotes, illustrations, observations and narrations, and the interpretations for these five sub genres of stories are as follows: Recitations correspond to

---

[1] Zhu Yongsheng. "Ideology in Discourse and the Social Responsibility of Linguists - On Martin's Related Theory and Its Application" [J]. *Contemporary Foreign Language Research*, 2010 (10): 25-28.
[2] Halliday, M.A.K. & J.R. Martin. *Writing Science: Literacy and Discursive Power*[M]. London: Falmer, 1993.
[3] When Martin gave a lecture at Peking University in December 2012, he proposed that language categories include culture and ideology, with language categories being the highest level.
[4] Martin, J.R. & D. Rose. *Genre Relations: Mapping Culture*[M]. London: Equinox Publishing Ltd, 2008.

"recording personal experiences", anecdotes correspond to "reaction to events", illustrations correspond to "explanatory events", observations correspond to "comments on events", and narrations correspond to "solving complex plots". These interpretations are actually intended to describe the discourse purpose of these sub-genres. Before elaborating on each genre, Martin indicates the purpose of that genre. Therefore, Martin mentions that the intention of discourse is also one of the criteria for further distinguishing between genres and subgenres. Martin separates genre from the register, making it an independent symbolic layer and expressing it in terms of language and register. Genre thus becomes a higher semantic level spanning the three variables of register. As shown in the following figure:

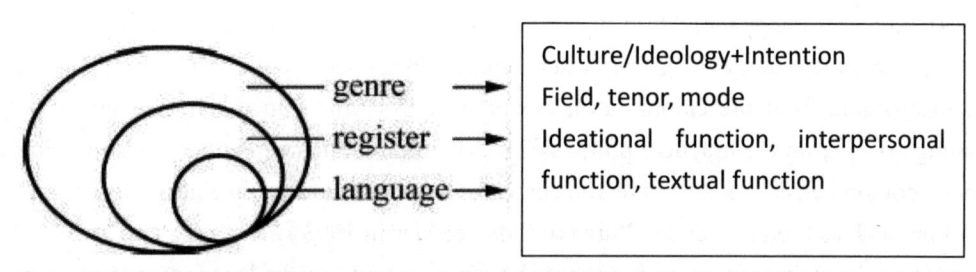

Figure 1: Three levels of language, register, and genre (cited from Xiao Lin and Si Xianzhu in 2014)[1]

The figure above distinguishes three levels of semiotics: language, register and genre (i.e. genre). Genre becomes an independent semiotic level beyond register and language, including culture and ideology. Intention determines the text type. Due to the inability of any of the three variables of register to control discourse intention, discourse intention is assumed by genre. The three major metafunctions in systemic functional grammar are the organizational levels of language, while the three variables of register are the organizational levels of situational context. The three variables of register closely correspond to the three major meta-functions, namely field corresponding to ideational function, tenor corresponding to interpersonal function, and pattern corresponding to textual function. Martin believes that genre cannot have a one-to-one correspondence with metafunctions, as it focuses on the overall effects of the three variables of register. A

---

[1] Xiao Lin, Si Xianzhu. "Further Exploration of Martin's Linguistic View" [J]. *Contemporary Foreign Language Research*, 2014 (3): 5-8. The word 'genre' in the original text has been translated as '语类' in Chinese.

certain genre can exert influence on the three metafunctions at the same time, for example, the story genre pays attention to process (empirical function), inclines to use the general present tense or the general past tense (interpersonal function), and tends to use conjunctions (textual function) to express time, which means that "the potential of grammatical meaning is limited by the actual social process (genre)"[1]. On the other hand, no metafunction can be equal to genre alone, and no register variable can achieve genre alone. The implementation of genre is scattered among the three major metafunctions. Furthermore, although meta-functions can achieve various meanings of language, there is no meta-function that can encompasses the intention of a particular chapter. Genre has intention, allowing the three variables of register to predict the discourse composition of the three major meta-functions to the greatest extent possible, thus also making the one-to-one correspondence between register and language closer. It is precisely because of the relationship between genre, register, and meaning that Li and Lu evaluate that "genre research cannot only reveal the relationship between expression form, meaning, and context...People can predict possible forms of expression based on specific contexts, and can also infer the language category and context they belong to based on discourse examples"[2].

Domestic articles exploring Martin's genre research mainly focus on applying its theoretical framework to analyze various discourses. Wang (2012)[3] analyzed and discussed the meaning of writing in the Constitution of the People's Republic of China, starting from the "phases" and "purpose orientation" in Martin's genre definition, and established a genre structure model of the Constitution: summarizing^qualitative^prescriptive. By using assessment theory, Tang (2004)[4] analyzed 10 academic book reviews, summarized the genre structure of academic book reviews, and pointed out that the genre structure of book reviews may exhibit various variations while adhering to

---

[1] Martin, J.R. Genre Studies[A] (vol.3). In Works of J. R. Martin[C], edited by Wang Zhenhua. Shanghai: Shanghai Jiao Tong University Press, 2012: 260.
[2] Li Zhanzi, Lu Danyun. "Multimodal semiotics: Theoretical Basis, Research Approaches and Development Prospects" [J]. *Foreign Language Research*, 2012 (2): 1-8.
[3] Wang Zhenhua. "A Genre Study of the Constitution" [J]. *Journal of Guangdong University of Foreign Studies and Economics*, 2012 (3): 49-54.
[4] Tang Liping. "Assessment and Analysis of the Genre Structure of Academic Book Reviews" [J]. *Foreign Languages*, 2004 (3): 35-43.

systematicity and tradition. Chai (2012)[1] used quantitative and qualitative methods to analyze 49 texts of acknowledgment and summarized the structural patterns of this subgenre: review ^ acknowledgment ^ conclusion ^ signature.

Wang (2012)[2] pointed out in a comparison between Swales and Martin's genre theory that Martin places more emphasis on the theoretical construction of genres. Martin's research on genre began with teaching practice in primary and secondary schools. Afterwards, he theoretically explored the definition of genre, its position within the framework of Systemic Functional Linguistics, genre types and classifications, and the relationship between genre and socio-culture, establishing an increasingly comprehensive system of genre theory. Martin's research on genre is inseparable from the emphasis on register, metafunction and meaning potential in Systemic Functional Linguistics. Martin & Rose (2008)[3] also concluded that Martin's genre analysis is based on the perspective of functional linguistics and language is the ideological form of social action.

The overall theoretical framework of this topic is Systemic Functional Linguistics. In the analysis of specific clauses, that is, in terms of language implementation methods, we adopt Halliday's systemic functional grammar analysis model, such as transitivity system, mood system and thematic system. In terms of the macrostructure of the discourse, we draw inspiration from Hasan's Genre Structure Potential and summarize the necessary and optional components of each genre after text analysis. In the analysis of optional and required components, we also borrow the concept of movement from the ESP/EAP school to better clarify the order and quantity of each component, and further derive the distribution tendencies of Chinese and English discourses.

4.4 Research on Three Applied Genres Texts and Their Translation

What is an applied genre? According to Bakhtin (1985)[4], genres can be divided into two categories: primary genres and secondary genres. Primary genres mainly include

---

[1] Chai Tongwen. "Research on the Generic Structure and Functional Variants of Acknowledgement Texts" [J]. *Foreign Language Teaching*, 2012 (6): 24-34.
[2] Wang Zhenhua. "A Genre Study of the Constitution" [J]. *Journal of Guangdong University of Foreign Studies and Economics*, 2012 (3): 49-54.
[3] Martin, J.R. & D. Rose. *Genre Relations: Mapping Culture*[M]. London: Equinox Publishing Ltd, 2008.
[4] Bakhtin, M. M. *The Formal Method in Literary Scholarship*. (trans. by A.J. Wehrle)[M]. Cambridge, Mass.: Harvard University Press, 1985/1928.

practical genres such as letters, diaries, notes, daily stories, and spoken language. Secondary genres include various complex types, such as literary discourses and technological discourses. Applied genres belong to primary genres distinguished by Bakhtin. Newmark (1988) classified texts into three types based on the function of language: literary works (poetry, novels, dramas, etc.), autobiographies, political speeches, personal letters, etc., which belong to the expressive texts; Textbooks, reports, papers, etc. with themes such as science and technology, business, and economics belong to informational texts; Operative texts refers to text that can affect readers and provide them with information, such as brochures and advertisements. Applied texts generally belong to the categories of informational function and operative function, mainly used to convey information (such as news discourses) and promotion (advertising discourses). So, generally speaking, apart from literary genres, texts used to achieve social behavior in real-life situations can be referred to as applied genres.

Applied genres, due to their obvious communicative purposes, generally have significant genre markers. The genres and types of applied texts are diverse. Similarly, there are also many types of applied genre translation. For example, according to content, there are legal translation, technology translation, tourism translation, academic translation, advertisement translation, etc. The classification principles and methods of applied genres vary, and each genre has its own regular text structure and language usage. Therefore, genre analysis of texts directly affects the selection and application of translation methods. The types of applied genres explored in this book include: corporate profiles, sports news reports, and museum introductions. So the following focuses on the characteristics of these application genres and their translations.

4.4.1 Corporate Profiles and Translation

As an applied genre, the corporate profile contains content about corporate culture and basic information, and its communicative purposes are primarily to inform potential consumers of relevant information about the company, such as products, services, and others; attract more consumers' attention and meet their needs. Among them, the most crucial purpose is to persuade consumers to purchase the company's products or services.

Regarding genres such as corporate profiles, Zhang (2010)[1] mainly used Swales'method to conduct genre analysis of corporate profiles from the perspective of cross-cultural communication. Ren (2009)[2] focused on the connections between vocabulary, the degree of coherence between sentences, and the study of subjects. Scholars such as Bliss (2005)[3], Hackett (2003)[4] and Zhang (2003)[5] mainly study the lexical and syntactic characteristics of this genre, without rising to an abstract socio-cultural level.

With the rapid development of China's economy and society, many domestic companies and brands have entered the international market. As a medium for transmitting information between companies and consumers, corporate profiles play a crucial role in establishing a company's image and developing its business. From a consumer perspective, corporate profiles can help them quickly and comprehensively understand the company's culture, products, services and other information. Therefore, high-quality translation of corporate profiles undoubtedly contributes to a company's development in the international market, and its significance cannot be underestimated. But how do we translate this type of text to achieve its intended function and purpose?

ALiterature review has found that most studies are limited to specific translation strategies and translation errors. Tang (1999)[6] proposed the strategies of "deletion" and "addition" in the translation of corporate profiles. Xu (2003)[7] elaborated on the restructuring of structure, information equivalence and smooth discourse coherence in the translation of corporate profiles. Xu and Xu (2005)[8] focused on spelling, punctuation,

---

[1] Zhang Xiaojuan. *A Genre Comparative Study of Chinese and American Enterprise Introduction Texts from a Cross Cultural Perspective*[D]. Guangzhou: Guangdong University of Foreign Studies, 2010.
[2] Ren Siwei. *Comparative Analysis of Genres of Chinese and English Enterprise Introduction*[D]. Changchun: Northeast Normal University, 2009.
[3] Bliss, A. How to write a company profile[OL]. 2005. http:// www.sideroad.com/public relations/write-company-profile.html.
[4] Hackett,A.How to develop an effective company profile--and why[OL].2003.http://ezinearticles.com/?how-to-develop-an-effective-company-and-why&id=1952.
[5] Milton, Zhang. Your Company Profile: a Step by Step Guide[OL]. 2003.http://resources.alibaba.com/article/155/Your_company_profile_a_step_by_step_guide.htm.
[6] Tang Fuhua. "Translation Techniques for Enterprise Introduction" [J]. *Journal of Huizhou University*, 1993 (3): 118-120.
[7] Xu Qin, Wu Ying. "Exploration of Translation of Economic and Trade Publicity Materials" [J]. Chinese Translators Journal, 2003 (5): 75-80.
[8] Xu Fangfang, Xu Xin. "Analysis and Exploration of the English Translation of 'Company Introduction' " [J]. *Journal of Zhejiang University of Education*, 2005 (1): 41-46.

grammar and logical errors and pointed out that these errors are the reasons for low translation quality.

Other studies have a relatively clear theoretical awareness. Wen (2006)[1] applied relevance theory to translation practice of corporate profiles. Jia (2004)[2] used functional theory to assess translation quality, placing the ultimate goal of corporate profiles in a prominent position, while also fully considering factors such as culture and ideology. Xiong (2000)[3] applied the register theory of Systemic Functional Linguistics to analyze the linguistic characteristics and similarities and differences between Chinese and English corporate profiles. Based on the Skopos Theory of the German Functional School, Zhu (2012)[4] analyzed the problems in the translation of corporate profiles and proposed that the translation of corporate profiles must be based on the cultural background of the target language, with flexible selection of various translation techniques to make the translation easier for target language readers to accept.

In existing research, however, there has been a lack of a systematic description of the structure and linguistic features of generic texts such as corporate profiles, a lack of analysis of similarities and differences between English and Chinese corporate profiles, and a lack of discussion on how to determine translation strategies and improve translation quality from the perspective of how to maximize and demonstrate the vocative function of these texts in the target language.

4.4.2 News Discourse, Sports News and the Translation

The main function of news is to accurately convey information, which can be divided into political, military, economic, scientific, cultural and educational, and sports categories according to their content. According to its stylistic characteristics, it can be

---

[1] Wen Hong. "Application of Relevance Theory in the Translation of Economic and Trade Foreign Publicity Materials" [J]. *Journal of Guangdong Normal University of Technology*, 2006 (3): 89-91.
[2] Jia Wenbo. *Functional Theory of Applied Translation*[M]. Beijing: China Foreign Translation Publishing Company, 2004
[3] Xiong Linglin. "Translation of corporate profiles for the Purpose of External Propaganda" [J]. *Science and Technology Information (Academic Research)*, 2007. (2): 29-30.
[4] Zhu Minhua. "The Chinese and English Translation of corporate profiles From the Perspective of Functional Skopos Theory: Taking the Website Introductions of Famous Chinese Home Appliance Enterprises as an Example" [J]. *Jiangsu Business Journal*, 2012 (2): 139-142.

divided into dynamic news, communication, close-up, comments, editorials, announcements, etc. Wu and He (2008)[1] summarized that this type of discourse has the characteristics of accurate and clear vocabulary, a tendency to use words and frequent occurrence of new words. In terms of sentence structure, the present tense, the active voice and the extended simple sentence are often adopted. The macrostructure of a discourse usually includes three parts: title, introduction and the main text. As a genre, news is a major category, and discussions in the academic community on news translation mainly focus on a certain subcategory, such as sports news.

The focus of sports news is the reporting of sports activities, which is an important way of news practice. Since the 1990s, with the development of China's social-economy and culture, especially the vigorous development of sports, people's attention to and love for sports events have become an indispensable part of social life. Watching sports news has become a hot spot for Chinese people after dinner. Why has sports news, as a applied genre, developed so rapidly? This is first and foremost because sports news is the reflection of a humanistic spirit that disseminates human sports, fitness activities and related information, advocating for humanity to challenge its limits, constantly overcome itself, surpass itself, and pursue its own perfection and beauty. It is undoubtedly closely related to the competitive, entertaining, and emotional characteristics of its reported content.

With the increasing international exchange, sports news translation has become an important part of sports news practice. From a domestic perspective, the international dissemination of sports news in China is largely translated directly from domestic Chinese reports, and a large amount of international sports news is directly translated into Chinese from international news. The translation of sports news is not a simple process of meaning transmission. First, any news discourses, including sports news discourses, will convey specific news event information while also expressing certain attitudes and positions; Second, due to cultural differences, the expression of meaning in news discourse inevitably chooses different presentation methods. Meanwhile, sports news has its own characteristics, such as paying more attention to the development of events and preferring

---

[1] Wu Feng, He Qingji, ed. *Translation of Practical Style: Theory and Practice*[M]. Zhejiang University Press, 2008.

the use of verbs. Domestic journalists have gradually realized that in the process of news translation, they cannot mechanically pursue literal translation word by word, but must reconstruct the translation according to the writing habits of the target language, resulting in news compilation. In the practice of sports news translation, translators often adopt the form of compilation to adjust the structural arrangement and language use of sports news translations, making them more aligned with the habits of the target language. However, there are still many problems that cannot be ignored.

In terms of domestic research on sports news translation, the theoretical perspective is quite broad, covering topics such as functional equivalence theory, communication theory and Skopos, especially the theory of register and context, which is widely applied to sports news translation research. Yu and Su (2002) [1] proposed that sports news translation is usually limited by the social context of the target language culture. Therefore, translators should fully consider the influence the social register of the target language culture during the translation or compilation process. Wu (2004)[2] pointed out that due to the effectiveness, immediacy, and differences between different languages and cultures of news, the traditional translation standards of "faithfulness, expressiveness, and elegance" cannot be fully applicable to sports news translation. In order to better achieve the communicative purpose of news translation, translators sometimes need to make adjustments to the content and style of the source text. Zhuang[3] (2005) emphasized that sports news translation must achieve functional equivalence in communicative purposes. Liao (2006)[4] proposed specific standards for the translation of sports news headlines. Chen (2001)[5] proposed that different translation strategies and standards should be adopted for different news leads.

While conveying ideational meaning, any form of discourse is also an expression of

---

[1] Yu Fuqing, Su Xuelei. "Research on News Translation Based on Register Theory" [J]. *News enthusiasts*, 2010 (22): 132-133.
[2] Wu Zixuan. "The Magnitude of 'Xin' in Chinese English Translation of Television News" [J]. *Chinese Translators Journal*, 2004 (6): 29-32
[3] Zhuang Qimin. "On the Principle of 'Functional Equivalence' in News Vocabulary Translation" [J]. *Shanghai Translation*, 2005 (3): 32-34.
[4] Liao Zhiqin. "English News Headlines and Their Translation Strategies" [J]. *Chinese Science and Technology Translation*, 2006 (2): 44-47.
[5] Chen Mingyao. "On Equivalence Standards and Translation of News Leads" [J]. *Shanghai Science and Technology Translation*, 2001 (2): 11-14.

interpersonal meaning, and sports news discourse is a transmission of values as well. For example, in reports about award-winning champions delivering post-competition speeches, athletes from China and the United States exhibit significant differences in their language. Therefore, in specific translation practice, the logical stance and value expression behind sports news should be considered (Cheng Zhenqiu, 2003)[1]. Qian and Wang (2006)[2] challenged the traditional"faithfulness"standard of translation and believed that due to differences in culture, language coding and thinking habits, sports news should not be simply translated, but must be compiled.

However, domestic scholars'research on sports news translation mainly focuses on the translation of specific vocabulary, phrases, clauses, titles and introductions. Xiao (2004)[3] analyzed the characteristics of the use of compound words in news and proposed three translation strategies for compound words. He, Liu (2007)[4], and Cao (2008) analyzed some methods and techniques for translating sports news slogans. Jia (2008)[5] analyzed the differences between Chinese and English news leads from the perspectives of length, grammar and news sources, and proposed three translation strategies for news leads: combination and splitting, information reconstruction, and the adjustment of news source position.

Although genre analysis is widely used in the study of English texts for specific purposes, it is basically a writing guide for a certain type of genre text, and there are few studies on genre reconstruction in the process of sports news translation from the perspective of genre analysis. In addition, many scholars mentioned above have used different theories to conduct research on sports news translation based on typical cases, lacking empirical research based on a large amount of corpus, and the credibility of

---

[1] Cheng Zhenqiu. "Translation of Political Articles Should Focus on Politics" [J]. *Chinese Translators Journal*, 2003 (3): 18-22.
[2] Qian Yeping, Wang Yinquan. "From the Perspective of Functional Translation Theory, the C-E Translation of Soft news" [J]. *Journal of Beijing Second Foreign Language College (Foreign Language Edition)*, 2006 (6): 11-14.
[3] Xiao Aiping. "Translation of Compound Words in English Newspapers and Periodicals" [J]. *Journal of Shanghai Electrical Engineering College (1)*, 2004:65-67.
[4] He Mingfang, Liu Hongquan. "Analysis of Translation of Sports News Headlines" [J]. *Exam Weekly*, 2007 (3): 93.
[5] Jia Hui. "Ideology and the Translation of Chinese Words in Newsweek" [J]. *Shanghai Translation*, 2008 (2): 27-31.

research conclusions is not high.

To address and make up for the aforementioned research shortcomings, this book proposes to establish three parallel corpora, each containing 40 English sports news, Chinese sports news, and the English translation of Chinese sports news. Based on the genre analysis theory of Systemic Functional Linguistics, the data in the corpora are analyzed on two levels: schematic structure and presentation style, and similarities and differences are found and then discussed. In order to maximize the operative purpose of sports news texts in the target language cultural environment and improve the quality of translation - to achieve smooth and beautiful language, why and how manipulation must be applied at the generic level when translating this genre to verify the quality assessment model of applied genre discourse constructed in Chapter 6.

4.4.3 Tourism Text, Museum Introduction and Translation

The tourism text is an informative and vocative text type with many subcategories, such as tourism materials including scenic spot introductions, promotional advertisements, billboards, folk customs, style albums, and couplets of historical sites. Wu and He (2008)[1] summarized that the vocabulary characteristics of tourism genres are their "richness" (involving various fields such as culture, religion, history, geography, folk customs, etc.), as well as a large number of specific cultural professional names (such as personal names and place names). There are significant differences in syntax between Chinese and English, such as the emphasis on sentence coherence in Chinese, while the emphasis on flexible and varied sentence structures in English. In terms of discourse, Chinese tends to use induction while English tends to use deduction.

Museum introduction is a subcategory under the tourism genre, which is an educational activity that connects tourists with museum culture (Kang, 2011)[2] Museum introductions are a type of cultural communication event, and language is its carrier. Swales (1990)[3] pointed out that for museum introductions, authors and editors, in order to

---

[1] Wu Feng, He Qingji. *Translation of Practical Style: Theory and Practice*[M]. Zhejiang University Press. 2008.
[2] Kang Yanyan. "A Study on the Translation Process of Museum Commentaries from the Perspective of Relevance Adaptation" [J]. *Business Culture,* 2011 (9): 6-10.
[3] Swales. J. Genre. *Analysis in Academic and Research Settings*[M]. Cambridge: Cambridge University Press. 1990:45. (Reprinted by Foreign Language Teaching and Research Press, 2001).

write a specific type of museum introductions, they must follow some long-standing habitual expressions about the structure and linguistic features of such specific texts rather than highlighting their personal writing style.

Regarding the translation research of museum introductions, Li (2009)[1] summarized some word and sentence features in museum introductions, and proposed to develop corresponding translation strategies to achieve consistency with the source text. Xu and Yang (2013)[2] pointed out that the lack of cultural factors can lead to some mistranslations. Taking the name of the items in the collection of Shanxi Museum as an example. In the translation of the Jin Marquis style display board,"Jin Marquis" is translated as "Princes of Jin" in the title, and "Jin of Marquis" in the content. "Marquis" refers to a royal title, while "prince" is equivalent to the emperor of the Zhou Dynasty. Obviously, using "Marquis" here is more appropriate. This is a typical case of the lack of traditional cultural knowledge. Xu (2013)[3] summarized the addition and deletion in the translation of cultural allusions. Guided by the theory of cross-cultural communication, Dou (2009)[4] elaborated on the translation principles and methods of cultural relics in the introduction of Chinese museums. Zheng (2011)[5], guided by Skopos theory, pointed out that translation should follow the equivalence of "information function" and "appellation function". Ren (2012)[6] introduced translation research to museums under the guidance of functional equivalence theory, pointing out that the accuracy of translation is closely related to culture, ideology, and way of thinking.

It is not difficult to see that existing research mainly focuses on some words, phrases, or sentences, lacking research from a generic perspective at a macro level. In addition, the

---

[1] Li Fang. "Strategies for Translating Commentaries from Chinese Museums into English" [J]. *Chinese Translators Journal*, 2009 (3): 74-77.
[2] Xu Huijing, Yang Jing. "A Study on Translation of Museum Texts from a Cultural Perspective" [J]. *Chinese Extracurricular Education. Higher Education,* 2013 (1): 32.
[3] Xu Li. "Analysis of the Current Situation of Text Research in Domestic Museums" [J]. *Overseas English*, 2013 (1): 148-149.
[4] Dou Hongli. *The Study on the English Translation System of Chinese Museum Texts - Taking Henan Museum as an Example*[D]. Henan: Henan University, 2006.
[5] Zheng Jia. "Translation of Museum Commentaries from the Perspective of Skopos Theory: A Case Study of the Museum of Chinese Characters" [J]. *Journal of Graduate Studies at Central China Normal University*, 2011 (1): 87-90.
[6] Ren Ning. "On the English Translation of Museum Commentaries from the Perspective of German Functional Theory" [J]. *Journal of Taiyuan City Vocational and Technical College*, 2012 (7):183-184.

corpus used only includes a few typical cases, and the research results lack persuasiveness and scientificity.

Various tourism introductions aim to "promote tourism products, stimulate potential consumers, and even persuade them to purchase products." (Zhang, 2010)[1] For the English translation of Chinese museum introductions, if it is only a word-for-word, sentence-for-sentence mechanical translation without considering the layout and language characteristics of the genres created by English-speaking countries, it is difficult to fully utilize the "vocative" function of this genre. In China, among the websites that promote Chinese culture to Western tourists, China Culture Network should be the most influential one. It is extremely important to translate the content of China Culture Network is arguably into English for the communication of Chinese culture. In view of this, this study intends to evaluate the translation quality of some Chinese museums' translated texts on the website, to provide suggestions on how to improve them.

4.5 Genre Analysis Models of This Book

In general, research on applied text translation based on genre analysis is relatively limited both domestically and internationally. Internationally, a few researchers have specifically mentioned genre analysis in translation. Reiss (2000)[2] first examined the relationship between genre and translation, but her main focus is on the classification of discourse types and translation standards for different discourse types, without conducting a comprehensive genre analysis of specific texts during the translation process. Bhatia (1987) explored legal translation based on his own genre analysis model, proposing that legal translation should maintain genre consistency with the source text and conform to the genre norms commonly accepted by target language readers. Schäffner (1998)[3] and Nord (1997)[4] used applied discourse translation as an example to analyze genre analysis of parallel texts (i.e. texts of the same genre as the original text in the target language),

---

[1] Zhang Weijing. *Genre Analysis of English Scenic Spots Introduction Text from the Perspective of System Functionality*[D]. Chongqing: Chongqing University, 2010.
[2] Reiss, C. *Translation Criticism: The Potentials and Limitations*[M]. Manchester, UK: St Jerome Publishing,2000.
[3] Schäffner, C. *Translation and Quality*[M].Clevedon:Multilingual Matters Limited,1998.
[4] Nord, C. *Translating as a Purposeful Activity: Functionalist Approaches Explained*[M]. Manchester: St Jerome   Publishing,1997.

which can obtain genre norms and structures for effective translation. However, they do not provide detailed explanations on how to obtain this information through genre analysis of parallel texts.

Based on the significance of genre analysis in applied genre text translation and the shortcomings of existing research, and based on the empirical needs of constructing a quality evaluation model for applied genre text translation, this book is guided by Systemic Functional Linguistics and its genre analysis theory to reflect the schematic structure, discourse structure potential (GSP), and characteristics of moves of the genre structure. Taking the process types (transitivity system), mood system, and thematic system that reflect the linguistic features of generic discourses, namely the realization pattern, as parameters, this study conducts a genre feature analysis and comparison of English, Chinese, and Chinese English translations of three types of applied generic texts in the self-built corpus (see Chapter 5 for details) - corporate profiles, sports news, and museum introductions. Starting from this, evaluation and improvement suggestions for the quality of English translation texts of certain Chinese genres will be made to achieve empirical testing of the translation quality assessment model constructed in Chapter 6.

References:

[1] Aristotle. Poetics [A]. *In D.A. Russel & M. Winterbottom (eds.). Ancient Literary Criticism: The Principal Texts in New Translations* [C]. Oxford: Clarendon, 1984.

[2] Bakhtin, M. M. *The Formal Method in Literary Scholarship.* (trans. by A.J. Wehrle) [M]. Cambridge, Mass.: Harvard University Press, 1985/1928.

[3] Bawarshi, A. & Reiff, M.J. *Genre: An introduction to history, theory, research and pedagogy.* [M]West Lafayette, IN: Parlor Press/WAC Clearinghouse, 2010.

[4] Bhatia, V. K. *Analyzing Genre: Language Use in Professional Settings* [M]. New York: Longman,1993.

[5] Bhatia, V.K. *Language of the Law* [J]. Language Teaching,1987(20): 227-234.

[6] Bliss, A. How to write a company profile [OL]. 2005. http://www.sideroad.com/public relations/write-company-profile.html.

[7] Campbell, K.K. & K. H. Jamieson. *Form and in rhetorical criticism: An introduction.* [A]In Campbell &Jamieson (eds.). Form and Genre: Shaping rhetorical action [C]. Falls Church, VA: The Speech Communication Association,1978:21.

[8] Dudley-Evans, T. *Genre Analysis: An investigation of the introduction and discussion sections of MSc Dissertations* [A]. In M. Coulthard (ed.). Talking About Text, Discourse Analysis Monograph No. 13 [C]. University of Birmingham: English Language Research,1986.

[9] Eggins, S. *An Introduction to Systemic- Functional Linguistics* [M]. London:

Pinter,1994.

[10] Hackett,A.How to develop an effective company profile--and why [OL].2003.http://ezinearticles.com/?how-to-develop-an-effective-company-and-why&id= 1952.

[11] Hopkins, A. & T. Dudley-Evans. *A genre-based investigations of the discussion sections in articles and dissertation* [J]. English for Specific Purposes,1988(7): 113-22.

[12] Milton, Zhang. Your Company Profile: a Step by Step Guide[OL]. 2003.http://resources.alibaba.com/article/155/Your_company_profile_a_step_by_step_guide.htm.

[13] Martin, J.R. Language, *Register and Genre* [A]. In F. Christie, (ed.). Children Writing: Reader [C]. Geelong, Vic.Deakin University Press, 1984a:21-30.

[14] Martin, J.R. & J. *Rothery. Choice of Genre in a Suburban Primary School*. Paper presented at *Annual Conference of the Applied Linguistics Association of Australia*, Alice Springs, Northern Territory,1984.

[15] Martin, J.R. *Types of Writing in Infants and Primary School* [A].In L. Unsworth, (ed.). Reading, Writing, Spelling. Sydney [C] Macarthur Institute of Higher Education, 1984b:34-55. (Republished by Shanghai Jiaotong University Press 2012).

[16] Martin, J . R. *A Contextual theory of language* [A]. In B. Cope & M. Kalantzis (eds.). The Powers of Literacy: A Genre Approach to Teaching Writing [C]. Bristol, PA: Falmer Press, 1993:116- 136.

[17] Martin, J.R. *English Text: System and Structure* [M]. Beijing: Peking University Press,2004.

[18] Martin, J.R. & D. Rose. *Genre Relations: Mapping Culture* [M]. London: Equinox Publishing Ltd，2008.

[19] Martin, J.R. *Genre Studies* [A] (vol.3). In Works of J. R. Martin [C], edited by Wang Zhenhua. Shanghai: Shanghai Jiao Tong University Press，2012.

[20] Miller C R. *Genre as social action* [J]. Quarterly journal of speech, 1984, 70(2): 151-167.

[21] Newmark, P. *A Textbook of Translation* [M]. New York: Prentice Hall,1988.

[22] Nord, C. *Translating as a Purposeful Activity: Functionalist Approaches Explained* [M]. Manchester: St Jerome   Publishing,1997

[23] Halliday, M.A.K. & R. Hasan. *Cohesion in English* [M]. London: Longman，1976.

[24] Halliday, M.A.K. *Language as Social Semiotic: The Social Interpretation of Language and Meaning* [M]. London: Edward Arnold,1978.

[25] Halliday, M.A.K. & R. Hasan. *Language, Context and Text: Aspects of Language in a Social-semiotic Perspectives* [M]. Oxford: Oxford University Press，1989.

[26] Halliday, M.A.K. & J.R. Martin. Writing Science: Literacy and Discursive Power [M]. London: Falmer，1993.

[27] Hasan, R. *Text in the systemic functional mode*l [A]. In W. Dressler (ed.). Current Trends in Text Linguistics [C]. Berlin: Walter de Gruyler,1977.

[28] Hasan, R. *The nursery tale as a genre* [A]. C. Cloran, D. Butt & G. Williams (eds.)Ways of Saying: Ways of Meaning [C]. London: Cassell, 1996:53.

[29] Hymes, D. 1972. *Models of the interaction of language and social life* [A]. In Gumperz, J.J. & Hymes (eds.), Directions in Sociolinguistics [C]. New York: Holt,

Rinehart & Winston, Inc,1972:65.

[30] Jamieson K M. *Antecedent genre as rhetorical constraint* [J]. Quarterly Journal of Speech, 1975, 61(4): 406-415.

[31] Kaplan, R. B. *Cultural thought patterns in intercultural education* [J]. Language Learning,1966(16):1–20.

[32] Kress, G. *Genre in a social theory of language: A reply to John Dixon* [A]. In I. Reid (ed.). The Place of Genre in Learning: Current Debates [A]. Vic.: Deakin University Press, 1987: 35-45.

[33] Paltridge, B. Genre, Frames and Writing in Research Settings [M]. Amsterdam: John Benjamins Publishing Company, 1997.

[34] Reiss, C. *Translation Criticism: The Potentials and Limitations* [M]. Manchester, UK: St Jerome Publishing,2000.

[35] Saville-Troike, M. *The Ethnography of Communication* [M].Oxford: Basil Blackwell,1982.

[36] Swales, J. *Aspects of Article Introductions* [M]. Birmingham, UK: The University of Aston, Language Studies Unit, .1981.

[37] Swales. J. Genre. *Analysis in Academic and Research Settings* [M]. Cambridge: Cambridge University Press. 1990:45. (Reprinted by Foreign Language Teaching and Research Press, 2001)

[38] Schäffner, C. *Translation and Quality*[M].Clevedon:Multilingual Matters Limited,1998.

[39] Todorov, T. *The origin of genres* [J]. New Literary History,1976 (8): 159-70.

[40] Ventola, E. *Generic and register qualities of texts and their realization* [A]. In P. H. Fries &M. Gregory (eds.). Discourse in Society: Systemic Functional Perspective [C]. New York: Ablex publishing Corporation,1995.

[41] Chai Tongwen."Research on the generic structure and functional variants of academic acknowledgements" [J]. *Foreign Language Teaching*, 2012 (6): 24-34.

[42] Cao Qiaohui."On the Translation of English Sports News Headlines" [J]. *Southern Forum*, 2006 (6): 61-62.

[43] Chen Mingyao."On Equivalence Standards and Translation of News Leads" [J]. *Shanghai Science and Technology Translation*, 2001 (2): 11-14.

[44] Cheng Zhenqiu. "Translation of Political Articles Should Focus On Politics" [J]. *Chinese Translators Journal*, 2003 (3): 18-22.

[45] Dou Hongli. *A Study on the English Translation System of Chinese Museum Texts - Taking Henan Museum as an Example* [D]. Henan: Henan University, 2006.

[46] Fang Yan. "On Language Categories" [J]. *Foreign Language*, 1998 (1): 17-22.

[47]He Mingfang, Liu Hongquan."Analysis of Translation of Sports News Headlines" [J]. *Exam Weekly*, 2007 (3): 93.

[48] Jia Hui."Ideology and the Translation of Chinese Words in American Newsweek" [J]. *Shanghai Translation*, 2008 (2):27-31.

[49] Jia Wenbo. *Functional Theory of Applied Translation* [M]. Beijing: China

Foreign Translation Publishing Company, 2004.

[50] Kang Yanyan."A Study on the Translation Process of Museum Commentaries from the Perspective of Relevance Adaptation" [J]. *Business Culture,* 2011 (9): 6-10.

[51]Ren Siwei. *Comparative Analysis of Genres of Chinese and English Enterprise Introduction* [D]. Changchun: Northeast Normal University, 2009.

[52] Li Fang. Strategies for Translating Commentaries from Chinese Museums into English [J]. *Chinese Translators Journal*, 2009 (3): 74-77.

[53] Li Zhanzi, Lu Danyun. Multimodal semiotics: Theoretical Basis, Research Approaches and Development Prospects [J]. *Foreign Language Research*, 2012 (2): 1-8.

[54] Liang Wenhua, Qin Hongwu. *Overview of Research on Genre Theory in China in the Last 10 Years* [J]. Foreign Language Teaching, 2009 (1): 44-48.

[55] Liao Zhiqin."English News Headlines and Their Translation Strategies" [J]. *Chinese Science and Technology Translation*, 2006 (2): 44-47.

[56] Lu Shan. *Genre Analysis of corporate profiles in the Chinese and American Cosmetics Industry* [D]. Chongqing: Chongqing University, 2008.

[57] Qian Yeping, Wang Yinquan. The C-E Translation of Soft News From the Perspective of Functional Translation Theory [J]. *Journal of Beijing International Studies University*(Foreign Language Edition), 2006 (6): 11-14.

[58] Ren Ning. "On the English Translation of Museum Commentaries from the Perspective of German Functional Theory" [J]. *Journal of Taiyuan City Vocational and Technical College*, 2012 (7):183-184.

[59] Si Xianzhu."On the Quality Assessment of Applied Genre Discourse Translation - A Genre Analysis Perspective of the Systemic Functional Linguistics School" [J]. Shandong Foreign Language Teaching, 2012 (4): 11-16.

[60] Tang Fuhua."Translation Techniques for Enterprise Introduction" [J]. *Journal of Huizhou University*, 1993 (3): 118-120.

[61] Tang Liping. "Evaluation and Analysis of the Genre Structure of Academic Book Reviews" [J]. *Foreign Languages*, 2004 (3): 35-43.

[62] Wang Zhenhua."A Genre Study of the Constitution" [J]. *Journal of Guangdong University of Foreign Studies and Economics*, 2012 (3): 49-54.

[63] Wang Zhenhua, Zhang Daqun and Zhang Xiangang."Martin's Study of Text Semantics" [J]. *Contemporary Foreign Language Research*, 2010 (10): 43-49.

[64] Wen Hong."Application of Relevance Theory in the Translation of Economic and Trade Foreign Publicity Materials" [J]. Journal of Guangdong Normal University of Technology, 2006 (3): 89-91.

[65] Wu Feng, He Qingji. *Translation of Practical Writing: Theory and Practice* [M]. Zhejiang University Press. 2008.

[66] Wen Zhisheng. "The Social Cognitive Perspective of the New Rhetoric School's Genre Study" [J]. *Journal of Tianjin International Studies University,* 2005 (6): 46-52.

[67] Xiao Aiping. "Translation of Compound Words in English Newspapers and Periodicals" [J]. *Journal of Shanghai Electrical Engineering College*, 2004 (1): 65-67.

[68] Xiao Lin, Si Xianzhu."Further Exploration of Martin's Genre View" [J]. *Contemporary Foreign Language Research*, 2014 (3): 5-8.

[69] The Editorial and Publishing Committee of the New Oxford English Chinese Dictionary. *New Oxford Dictionary of English and Chinese Translators Journal* [M]. Shanghai: Shanghai Education Press, 2007:876.

[70] Xu Fangfang, Xu Xin."Analysis and Exploration of the English Translation of 'Company Introduction'" [J]. *Journal of Zhejiang University of Education*, 2005 (1): 41-46.

[71] Xu Huijing, Yang Jing. "A Study on Translation of Museum Texts from a Cultural Perspective" [J]. *Chinese Extracurricular Education. Higher Education*, 2013 (1): 32.

[72] Xu Li. "Analysis of the Current Situation of Text Research in Domestic Museums" [J]. *Overseas English*, 2013 (1): 148-149.

[73] Xiong Linglin."Translation of Enterprise Introduction for the Purpose of External Propaganda" [J]. *Science and Technology Information (Academic Research)*, 2007. (2): 29-30.

[74] Xu Qin, Wu Ying."Exploration of Translation of Economic and Trade Publicity Materials" [J]. *Chinese Translators Journal*, 2003 (5): 75-80.

[75] Wu Zixuan."The Degree of 'Faithfulness' in Chinese English Translation of Television News" [J]. *Chinese Translators Journal*, 2004 (6): 29-32.

[76] Yu Fuqing, Su Xuelei."Research on News Translation Based on Register Theory" [J]. *News enthusiasts*, 2010 (22): 132-133.

[77] Yu Hui. *Genre Analysis of Discourse semiotics Meaning of Abstracts of Academic Papers* [M] Zhengzhou: Henan University Press, 2003.

[78] Yu Hui. "Theoretical Tracing of the Concept of Discourse Genre" [J]. *Journal of Beijing Normal University* (Social Sciences Edition), 2006 (4): 61-66.

[79] Zhang Delu."Exploration of the Theoretical Framework for Genre Research" [J]. *Foreign Language Teaching and Research*, 2002a (5): 339-44.

[80] hang Delu. "Overview of Genre Research" [J]. *Foreign Languages*, 2002b (4):

13-22.

[81] Zhang Weijing. *Genre Analysis of English Scenic Spots Introduction Text from the Perspective of System Functionality* [D]. Chongqing: Chongqing University, 2010.

[82] Zhang Xiaojuan. *A Genre Comparative Study of Chinese and American Enterprise Introduction Texts from a Cross Cultural Perspective* [D]. Guangzhou: Guangdong University of Foreign Studies, 2010.

[83] Zhang Yan."Dynamic Genre Research from the Perspective of 'Topology' " [J]. *Rhetoric Learning*, 2008 (1): 19-24.

[84] Zheng Jia."Translation of Museum Commentaries from the Perspective of Skopos Theory: A Case Study of the Museum of Chinese Characters" [J]. *Journal of Graduate Studies at Central China Normal University*, 2011 (1): 87-90.

[85] Zhu Minhua."The Translation of corporate profiles From Chinese to English From the Perspective of Functional Skopos Theory: Taking the Website Introductions of Famous Chinese Home Appliance Enterprises as an Example" [J]. *Jiangsu Business Journal*, 2012 (2): 139-142.

[86] Zhu Yongsheng."Ideology in Discourse and the Social Responsibility of Linguists - On Martin's Related Theory and Its Application" [J]. *Contemporary Foreign Language Research*, 2010 (10): 25-28.

Chapter 5 Construction of a Quality Assessment Model for Translation of Applied Genre Discourses

This chapter reviews the ideas, procedures, and parameters of the predecessor of this study,"Functional Linguistics and Translation Studies — Construction of Translation Quality Evaluation Model", discusses the development and achievements of the original model, analyzes the existing shortcomings, and elaborates on the translation quality evaluation standards and the translation objectives and characteristics of applied genre texts. On this basis, the discussion focuses on how to inherit the effective parts of the original model and integrate genre analysis into the translation assessment parameter system, ultimately constructing a new translation quality assessment model.

5.1 Construction and Development of Original Translation Quality Assessment Model

1. Construction of the Original Translation Quality Assessment Model: Concepts, Procedures, and Parameters

People's understanding and judgment of translation quality are closely related to the translation standards they adhere to, and translation standards are closely related to people's understanding of the essence of translation. Therefore, when discussing translation quality, it is necessary to first clarify the essence of translation.

What is the essence of translation? Based on the differences in researchers' cognition and perspectives, the answer to this question varies from person to person. From the perspective of Systemic Functional Linguistics, language has three metafunctions: ideational function, interpersonal function and textual function. Correspondingly, the existing forms of language use—discourse, parole and text—have three meanings carried by the above functions: ideational meaning, interpersonal meaning and textual meaning. Therefore, the essence of translation lies in the fact that "meaning"remains unchanged when transferred from one language to another. "Translation is the use of semantic and pragmatic equivalence in the target language to replace the source text."[1] "Translation

---

[1] House, J. *Translation Quality Assessment*[M] .Tubingen: Gunter Narr Verlag,1977:30.

generally seeks equivalence in meaning between the source text and the translated text. Translation should seek to have the same meaning and function in discourses of two languages within the same overall situational context." "The equivalence relationship in translation cannot be based solely on one meaning (usually ideational meaning); while seeking ideational equivalence in discourse between two languages, it is also necessary to seek equivalence in interpersonal meanings such as the speaker's attitude, motivation, judgment and role, as well as in discourse meanings such as medium, channel and rhetorical device. In general, a good translation needs to be equivalent to the source text in all three senses."[1]

Therefore, based on the explanation of the essence and standards of translation in Systemic Functional Linguistics, assessing the quality of translated discourse is to examine whether the translation is equivalent to the source text in the three meanings or functions mentioned above.

However, from the perspective of constructing translation assessment models, this does not necessarily mean that the three classifications of language function in Systemic Functional Linguistics and the three segmentation of meaning carried by language (represented by discourse) should be listed in parallel as the three parameters for examining translation quality. This is because, although the meaning (ideational and interpersonal) that people use language to express cannot be separated from the "intermediary" of textual meaning, the latter's role is after all to organize the ideational and interpersonal meanings expressed in language, and its role is to assist in the realization of the first two meanings, and it does not itself represent "content", so it is not at the same level as the first two meanings. From the perspective of expressing non-linguistic content, any discourse (parole, text) and its components, such as clauses, only express two functions/meanings. In view of this, the judgment of translation quality depends only on whether the ideational meaning/function and interpersonal meaning/function of the translated text are equivalent to the source text. In other words, in terms of setting parameters for the evaluation model, only two items are needed:

---

[1] Hu Zhuanglin, Zhu Yongsheng and Zhang Delu. *Introduction to Systemic Functional Grammar*[M]. Changsha: Hunan Education Publishing House, 1989:188.

ideational and interpersonal meaning. (House 1977[1],1997[2];Si 2007a[3],2008[4]) However, it must be emphasized that it is impossible for the translated text to achieve equivalence in both the ideational and interpersonal meanings with the source text without the simultaneous equivalence at the organizational level, namely the equivalence in the textual meaning.

Based on this, when conducting translation discourse quality assessment, the discourse on the relationship between form and function/meaning in Systemic Functional Linguistics (Thompson 1996/2000[5]; Sii 2005[6], 2007b[7]) is to explore the ideational and interpersonal meanings of the source and translated texts by analyzing the transitivity and mood (including modality) systems that respectively reflect ideational and interpersonal meanings, as well as the vocabulary grammar systems (such as themes) that reflect textual function and assist in the realization of linguistic ideas and interpersonal meanings. Whether the translation deviates from the source text in these two parameters can thus be decided.

That is to say, to construct a translation quality assessment model, on the one hand, only two parameters of ideational and interpersonal meaning need to be established. On the other hand, when examining whether the translation is equivalent to the source text in these two parameters, it is necessary to examine whether the textual function of assisting in expressing language ideas and interpersonal meanings as well as the vocabulary grammar system that reflects this function are appropriate, because the textual function that reflects information organization, whether at the micro or macro level, has an impact on the expression of ideas and interpersonal meanings.

Specifically, the procedure and parameters on which a translation quality assessment model is based are as follows:

According to the speech act framework of Systemic Functional Linguistics on language use and its form, function, and situational interaction (Si 2007b), the first step

---

[1] House, J. *Translation Quality Assessment* [M]. Tubingen: Gunter Narr Verlag, 1977.
[2] House, J. *Translation Quality Assessment: A Model Revisited* [M]. Tubingen: Gunter Narr Verlag,1997.
[3] Si Xianzhu. *Functional Linguistics and Translation Studies - Construction of Translation Quality Assessment Model*[M]. Peking University Press, 2007a.
[4] Si Xianzhu. "Further Study on the Evaluation Model of Translation Discourse Quality: A Functional Linguistic Approach" [J]. *Chinese Translators Journal*, 2008 (2): 57-60.
[5] Thompson, G. *Introducing Functional Grammar*[M]. London: Arnold,1996.
[6] Si Xianzhu. "Speech Act Framework Theory and Translation Quality Assessment" [J]. *Foreign Language Research*, 2005 (5): 54-58.
[7] Si Xianzhu. "The Framework of Speech Act and the Interaction between Its Forms, Functions and Situations" [J]. *Journal of Foreign Language*, 2007b (6): 57-60.

starts from the cognitive perspective of the organic combination of the overall meaning/function of a discourse, which is composed of its basic constituent units—the meaning/function of clauses. At the micr- clause level, the three meanings of the clause —ideational, interpersonal, and textual—are directly influenced by the register reflecting the situational context—field, tenor, and mode. Then, starting from the corresponding vocabulary grammar system in the language that reflects these three meanings, this project analyzes the transitivity, mood (including modality) and theme of clauses in the source and translated texts to reveal and describe their ideational and interpersonal meanings, and based on this, and to further determine whether or where the translation has "deviated" from the source text.

The second step, from a macro perspective, is to re-examine the various "deviated" cases discovered and described at the micro level from the perspective of form, function, and situational interaction of the target language, as well as the characteristics of the target language form, translation scenarios and requirements, and purposes, all of which aim to eliminate the "deviations" that do not constitute the overall quality of the translation from this perspective.

Next, in the third step, based on the value judgment in the second step, the statistical quantities in the first step are revised. Only by adjusting the "deviated" cases can we determine to what extent the translation is "equivalent" or "faithful" to the source text.

Finally, when evaluating the overall quality of the translation, it is also necessary to consider the type of discourse being translated, and determine the corresponding weights of different types of meaning deviations—ideas, interpersonal relationships, and their impact on the quality of the translation based on different discourse types. This model is illustrated as follows:

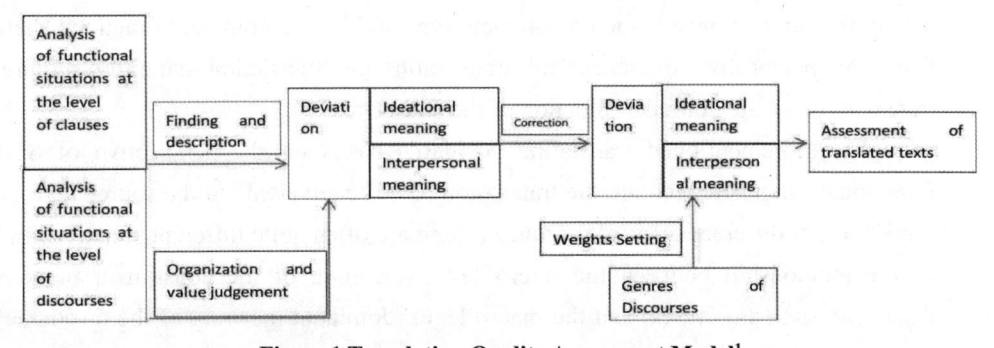

Figure 1 Translation Quality Assessment Model[1]

---

[1] Si Xianzhu. *Functional Linguistics and Translation Studies - Construction of Translation Quality Evaluation Model*[M]. Peking University Press, 2007a: 192.

For this model, we have conducted an actual assessment of the translation quality of popular science papers, novels, and advertisements representing three types of discourse: information, expression, and infection (Si 2007a)[1]. We have found that in the actual translation quality assessment, we can strengthen certain steps based on different discourse types, and weaken or even omit other steps. For the assessment of operative texts such as advertising translations, the second step in the assessment model needs to be strengthened; on the other hand, the assessment of information texts such as popular science is the opposite, strengthening the first step and weakening the second step.

2. Revision and Development of the Original Model

Judging the quality of a translation based on the aforementioned model is both descriptive—where the translation deviates from the source text, and illustrative—why some parts of the translation do not correspond to the source text, which is deviation. In the second and third steps of this model, the deviations described at the micro level are sorted out from the perspective of the relationship between the whole and the parts, as well as the impact of internal and external factors on the discourse (wording). In this way, the "deviations" (referred to as positive deviations) that do not have a negative impact on the overall quality of the translation are eliminated, thus breaking away from the static perspective of the text. However, due to the fact that the assessment of translation quality is entirely based on the statistical analysis of "deviation" cases, for translation texts that are constrained by micro level "functional equivalence", especially for emoticons and infectious translations whose dominant function belongs to the interpersonal function/meaning category, the quality assessment of the translation made according to the above model is often difficult to be convincing.

Why is this so? This is because translation deals with specific discourses, and as an actual discourse, it must belong to a certain type and have a dominant function. Therefore, from the perspective of successful translation, the translation naturally requires the transmission of the dominant function of the source text.

The aforementioned translation standards based on the perspective of Systemic Functional Linguistics require the translation to be "equivalent" to the source text. For the translation of different types of discourse, there are often quite different situations in terms of the relationship between the micro level (meaning of the constituent parts of the discourse, such as clauses) and the macro level (dominant meaning of the discourse). For informational discourse, generally speaking, as long as the equivalence transformation of the aforementioned three language functions is achieved in the micro part of the

---

[1] Ibid.

constituent discourse, the entire translated discourse basically achieves equivalence of the dominant function/meaning of the source discourse, that is, the micro and macro aspects are basically unified. However, for the translation of vocative texts, in order to achieve equivalence in the dominant function of the source text—the same or similar post discourse effects—what House calls "cultural filtering" is often implemented—in the translation, adjustments are made to the textual structure, expression, and other aspects of the source text—addition, deletion, combination, and change of expression. This is also known as genre-level adaptation and adjustment. As a result, the translation often fails to maintain consistency with the source text at the micro level, such as the language function/meaning level of phrases and clauses (Si, 2007a)[1]:

西苑饭店

西苑饭店是一座具有国际四星级水准的大型涉外饭店，位于北京三里河路，与进出口谈判大楼、北京图书馆、首都体育馆等相毗邻，环境优美，交通便利。

饭店共有客房 1300 余套，房间舒适、宁静，配有全套现代化设施。饭店共设餐厅酒吧 12 个，中餐经营粤、鲁、川、淮扬及穆斯林风味菜肴；西餐主要经营俄式、法式及英式大菜。饭店还设有传真、电传、国际直拨电话等现代通信设施及各种综合服务设施和娱乐设施，为每位宾客提供尽善尽美的服务。

西苑饭店欢迎您的光临。

The first version of translation:

Xi Yuan Hotel

Xi Yuan Hotel, located at Sanlihe Road in Beijing, adjacent to the Import & Export Negotiation Building, Beijing Library, the Capital Gymnasium, is a four-star hotel, with an elegant environment and convenient transportation.

Xi Yuan Hotel boasts 1,300 well-equipped guest rooms and suites. There are altogether 12 restaurants and bars. The Chinese restaurants offer Cantonese, Shandong, Sichuan, Huaiyang and Xinjiang Moslem cuisine. The Western restaurants features Russian, French and British dishes. The hotel is equipped with modern communication appliances such as fax, telex and IDD, as well as a full set of comprehensive service and

---

[1] Si Xianzhu. *Functional Linguistics and Translation Studies - Construction of Translation Quality Evaluation Model* [M]. Peking University Press, 2007a: 173-175.

recreational facilities available, to ensure that every guest receives sound service.

Sincerely welcome to Xi Yuan Hotel.

We know that the main function of operative discourse, including advertisements, is to "be vocative" and focus on the effects on readers, rather than "focusing on content". Therefore, the original translation quality assessment model introduces text type parameters in parameter settings, which means that the assessment of translation quality for this type of text should focus on the parameters of interpersonal meaning. From this point of view, it is not difficult to find that although the translation of "Xiyuan Hotel" provided above has almost no defect in expressing the ideational meaning of the source text at the micro clause level, since there is no use of the second person in any place but simple statement of the facts from the perspective of an outsider, that is, the third person. In the eyes of people from the U.S. and Britain who are accustomed to advertisements which highlight "people-oriented" mindset and emphasize the interpersonal meaning of interaction, this advertisement (translated in English) gives people a feeling of being outside, and it is difficult to achieve the original intention of attracting foreign guests to stay. In view of this, in order to put into action the afterword power of the advertisement on native English speakers after it is translated into English, it is necessary to reorganize the discourse during translation based on the characteristics of the English advertisement and the appropriate emphasis on interpersonal meaning. Translation 2 is based on this consideration:

Xiyuan Hotel

Luxuriance, Convenience and Reassurance

The four-star Xiyuan hotel boasts of easy transportation, quiet and elegant environment as well as first class service.

Located at Sanlihc Road and adjacent to the Negotiation Building, the Beijing Library and the Capital Gymnasium, Xiyuan Hotel is within your easy reach.

In any of the 1,300 guest rooms and suites, you can enjoy the opulent comfort of the modern facilities and courtesy service.

The 12 restaurants and bars offer you both Chinese food including Cantonese, Shangdong, Sichuan, Huaiyang and Moslem cuisine, and western food featuring Russian, French and British dishes.

The up-to-date communication facilities, the recreational applicances and other comprehensive services are sure to win your appreciation.

When in Beijing, make your choice Xiyuan Hotel.

Xiyuan Hotel: Service is all and all is for you.

In the second translation, by using the second person (eg. Xiyuan Hotel is within your easy reach. You can enjoy the opulent comfort of the modern facilities and courtesy service…are sure to win your appreciation. Service is all and all is for you.), the translator greatly narrows the distance between "me" (the hotel operator) and potential guests, making it appear friendly and inviting. Compared with the original translation, it can better achieve the main function of this interpersonal oriented type—infectious function, and attract guests to stay. In other words, compared to the original translation with respect to the first part of the assessment model, although there are many deviation cases at the micro level such as clauses, Translation 2 is better than the original translation in achieving the main function of the source text—the infectious function.

We know that the difference between the two texts is mainly due to their different ideational meanings. If the ideational meanings of two or more texts are the same or similar, they are the same type of discourse, while on the contrary, they belong to different discourse types. The translation should be consistent with or identical to the source text in terms of ideational meaning. If the translation is different from the source text in this regard, the translation cannot be considered as a translation of the source text. They are actually just two different texts expressed in two different languages.

The ideational meaning and discourse scope reflected in a discourse remain relatively unchanged, while the interpersonal meaning and corresponding discourse tone are the most susceptible to change. This is because the participants of the discourse are constant variables, and if the interpersonal meaning of the discourse changes, the mood, modality and evaluation system of the discourse will change. The mood of the discourse is the main factor affecting the choice of discourse theme. Therefore, the mood of the discourse and the changes in modality and evaluation system will directly affect the textual meaning and discourse style of the text. Different translators will inevitably have different textual meanings and discourse styles reflected in their translations.

Therefore, from the perspective of translation quality assessment, if the equivalence requirements of the translated text can be unified at both the micro level (ideational and interpersonal function of phrases and clauses) and the macro level (dominant function of the text), such as the translation of some informational texts, then translation quality assessment is relatively simple in using the procedures and parameters of the original assessment model to examine whether there are or how many "deviation" cases in the translation and determine its quality. Based on the above reasons, however, for the evaluation of translation quality, including some infectious texts , simply using "deviation" as the observation point is not enough. The original assessment model uses statistical analysis of the types and quantities of deviations from the source text as the sole basis for determining the quality of the translation, the design of which is severely flawed. To evaluate the quality of such translations, while examining the types and quantities of "deviations", it is also necessary to pay high attention to the micro dimensions (such as the meaning/function of clauses and words) to ensure "faithfulness", while the observation of "false equivalence" from the perspective of the dominant function of discourse is a failure. In other words, a value judgment should be made based on the positive and negative correlation between"equivalence"and the transmission of the entire topic. As the original model indicates, when discussing the situation of "deviation", not all "deviations" have a negative impact on the translation, and not all "equivalence" helps to achieve the equivalent transmission of the original function in the translation. For translated texts, including some vocative ones, there are indeed some translations that are"equivalent"to the source text at the micro level, such as clauses. However, at the macro level, it often means that the dominant function of the translated text is "not equivalent" to the source text, which is known as "equivalence in small areas and inequality in large areas", such as the first translation of "Xiyuan Hotel" mentioned earlier. Therefore, in order to evaluate the quality of translations more comprehensively and scientifically, it is necessary to make revisions to the original assessment model both in terms of program and parameters.

In terms of procedure, it needs to be revised to add a link where the translation is functionally/meaningfully equivalent to the original text at the micro level, such as clause level, but the main function of the text is considered to be contrary to the original function; In terms of parameters, it is to add "negative equivalence", which refers to the aforementioned "equivalent at micro level but not at macro level" or "false equivalence". (As for the situation of "equivalence" at the discourse level and "deviation" at the micro level, it has already been reflected and resolved in the "deviation" link of the original model—not recorded as deviation cases that affect the quality of the translation.) Due to our perspective on assessing translation quality starting from negative impacts and considering simplification, when constructing a translation quality assessment model, we only need to pay attention to the situations of "deviation" and "negative equivalence". In this way, the modified evaluation model process is (Si, 2008)[1]:

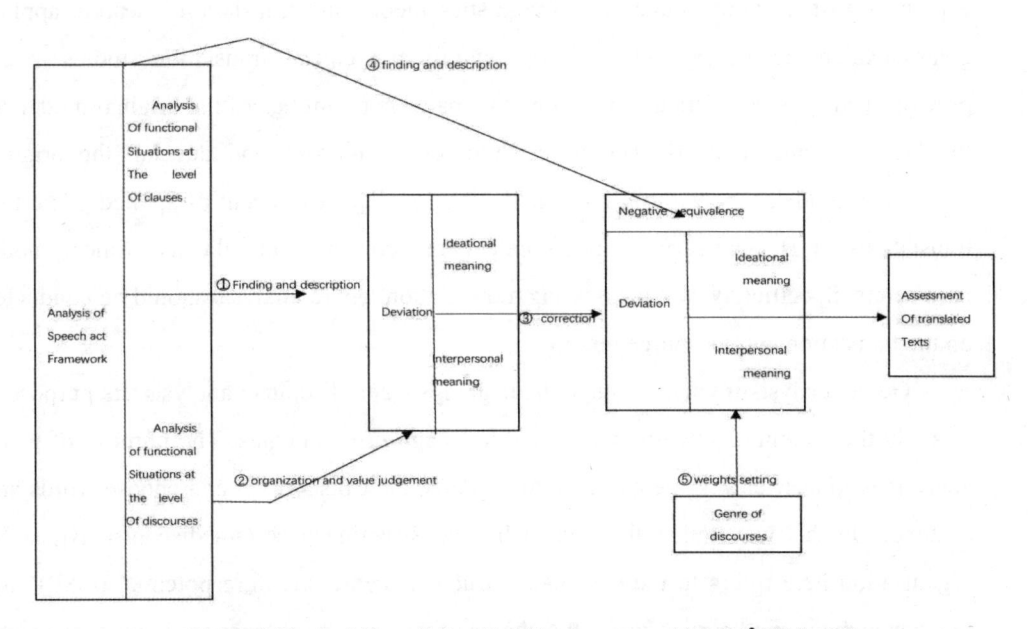

Figure 2 Revised Translation Quality Assessment Model[2](Ibid: 193)

5.2 Construction of A Quality Assessment Model for Applied Discourse Translation

As some comments have stated, according to the explanation of the original

---

[1] Si Xianzhu. "Further Study on the Translation Text Quality Assessment Model - Functional Linguistics Path" [J]. *Chinese Translators Journal*, 2008 (2): 57-60.
[2] Si Xianzhu. *Functional Linguistics and Translation Studies - Construction of Translation Quality Evaluation Model*[M]. Peking University Press, 2007a: 192.

translation quality assessment model and its revision and development in the previous section, this model has high academic value and status: "Professor Si Xianzhu is the first scholar in China to systematically conduct translation quality evaluation research and publish the results in books. He constructs a discourse-based translation quality assessment model guided by the theories of Functional Linguistics and text typology. His research is groundbreaking in China."[1] "Due to its completeness, systematicity, operability and less subjectivity, it has distinct characteristics. Compared to the translation and review of foreign translation quality evaluation models, this independently created model is the first in China and is undoubtedly a huge progress in academic research."[2] However, through the analysis of the shortcomings of the original model and the explanation of Systemic Functional Linguistics theory and translation research, applied genre text characteristics, genre theory schools and corpus translation studies in the previous text, it is not difficult to see that the main shortcomings of the original model are the lack of genre analysis. Therefore, in order to improve and develop the original assessment model, especially in constructing the quality assessment of applied genre text translations, it is necessary to incorporate genre concepts into the assessment model parameters. Specifically, when assessing a translation, genre analysis should be conducted on the translation and its source text.

Genre analysis involves both stylistic analysis and discourse analysis. Its purpose is to study the communicative purposes and language use strategies. The purpose of genre analysis is to answer why people tend to organize their discourses and choose words and sentences in this way rather than that when constructing a certain discourse type. The organization here refers to the schematic structure, genre structure potential (GSP), and move-step mentioned earlier, while the choice of words and sentences belongs to the same category as the aforementioned stylistic and linguistic features, matching methods, and stylistic markers. In view of this, we believe that in order to determine the quality of a translation about whether it is excellent or inferior, in addition to the ideational and interpersonal meaning that the original model focuses on from the perspective of the

---

[1] Kang Leiming, Zhang Wenhui. "Review on the Translation Quality Assessment Model of Si Xianzhu" [J]. *Journal of Heilongjiang University of Education*, 2010 (12): 148-150.
[2] Lin Changyang. "On the Probability Tool in Translation Quality Assessment: Reflections on the Assessment Model of Si Xianzhu" [J]. *China Electric Power Education*, 2010 (34): 109-113.

register (situational context), it also depends on whether it is equivalent or similar in the cultural context—genre, that is, to what extent the dimensions of the genre schematic structure and manifestation style are equivalent or similar. Namely, genre equivalence.

So, in translation practice, how to achieve genre equivalence between the translation and the source text? We believe that to achieve the communicative purpose of the translation and achieve genre equivalence between the translation and the source text, at the level of genre planning and organization, translators can identify the discourse structure of the target language by analyzing parallel texts of the same genre as the source text, clarify the differences between the source text and the translation in this regard, and make corresponding adjustments to the translated text; at the level of style, translators can also analyze target language texts of the same genre as the source text to identify the language characteristics and matching methods of this genre in the target language society, in order to guide the choice of words and sentences in the construction of the translated text. From this, it is not difficult to see that this is a top—down translation perspective and strategy based on the overall discourse. From the perspective of constructing a translation quality assessment model, it is evident that this is also at the overall discourse level, examining whether the textual organization of the translation is equivalent or deviated from the same type of text in the target language from the perspective of genre structure. In terms of expression style, whether the word—grammar structural features that express the ideational meaning, interpersonal meaning and textual meaning of the discourse are similar to or deviated from the same type of text in the target language is examined.

The setting of genre analysis parameters (schematic structure and presentation style) not only pays attention to the natural, smooth, and aesthetic aspects of the translated text in the target language system in terms of structure but also in terms of linguistic features. From the perspective of translation quality assessment, it examines the issue of "expressiveness and elegance" required by traditional translation standards to measure translation quality. If we consider the traditional translation standard of the three characteristics "faithfulness, expressiveness, and elegance", it is obvious that the original assessment model only focuses on the "faithfulness" of the translated text relative to the source text, while the requirements for "expressiveness, and elegance" of the translated work are missing in both parameter and link settings, and not enough attention is given.

This should be regarded as a serious defect of the original model. In other words, the setting of genre analysis parameters addresses the aforementioned shortcomings of the original model.

Of course, it should be affirmed that the original model has given sufficient attention to whether or to what extent the translated text is "equivalent" and "faithful" in terms of ideational and interpersonal meaning compared to the source text. For 'meaning-based' translation, the success of the translation quality assessment model largely depends on whether and to what extent the parameters set in the model can actually evaluate. It is gratifying that the original model has effectively solved this problem, which is the biggest success of the original model. Since it can be incorporated into the new model, improvements need to be made.

The improvement is that the expression of "false equivalence" in the original assessment model, the so-called "equivalence at the micro level but not the macro level", is not accurate, because "equivalence" mainly refers to the faithfulness of the translation relative to the source text at the semantic and functional levels, which is the traditional translation standard of "faithfulness, expressiveness, and elegance". However, the phenomenon of "false equivalence" involved in the original assessment model refers to the issue of whether the meaning carried by the source text is sufficiently and appropriately expressed in the translation. Therefore, it refers to the structure of the source text with a strong translation tone, and does not mainly focus on "faithfulness" but belongs to the categories of "expressiveness" and "elegance". For instance:

八月一日第AG-3号合同项下的10万吨小麦,原定于十月底以前交货。你方在合同中保证提前交货,并且以此作为签订合同的条件。但是,这批小麦迄今尚未装运。对此,我们深表遗憾。

If translated directly into Chinese, the translated text may look like this:

The 100,000 tons of wheat under Contract No. AG-3 of August 1 is scheduled to be delivered by the end of October. You have guaranteed an early delivery in the Contract and it is on this understanding that we signed the contract. Up to now, however, the shipment has not yet been made. We very much regret for that.

This kind of translation, due to its complete adherence to the original structure, can be said to be "faithful" or "equivalent" at the micro clause level; However, from the perspective of the entire English writing, there is a loose structure, weak logic, and lack of prominent semantics, which makes people feel confused and not be able to get the point. Therefore, although the translated text can barely be said to be faithful to the source text in terms of meaning transmission, the problem is that the translated text shows a strong translation tone due to being limited to the original structure, which is not smooth, let alone beautiful, that is, the so-called "faithful but not beautiful". While if translated as:

We very much regret that the 100000 tons of wheat under Contract No. AG-3 of August 1, scheduled to be delivered by the end of October, is up to this moment not dispatched, in spite of fact that you have guaranteed an early delivery in the Contract, which was actually signed on this understanding.

This translation is both faithful and smooth.

Therefore, we believe that the "negative equivalence" or "false equivalence" that reflects the phenomenon of "equivalence at the micro level but not the macro level" in the assessment model parameters should be modified to"mechanically corresponding, stiff and rough", that is,"not smooth".

On the other hand, whether it is the original wording of "equivalence at the micro level but not the macro level"or the modified expression of"not smooth", in order to become an effective parameter in the evaluation model, it must be practical. However, the original model has almost no way to judge such "false equivalence" , "It is true that the structural characteristics of articles such as those in English and Chinese, as well as the differences in thinking patterns and aesthetic concepts reflected by the two ethnic groups, can be perceived by people who are very familiar with them."[1] "The factors involved are very complex."[2] In fact, based on the aforementioned explanation of genre and corpus translation studies, the evaluation of whether a translation is "mechanically corresponding, stiff or rough" or "not smooth" can be fully grasped by analyzing and summarizing the schematic structure and linguistic features of similar genre texts in the target language. In fact, the empirical research section in the latter half of this book mainly discusses how to establish a corpus of English, Chinese, and Chinese-English translations of several applied

---

[1] Si Xianzhu. *Functional Linguistics and Translation Studies - Construction of Translation Quality Evaluation Model*[M]. Peking University Press, 2007a: 188.
[2] Ibid :194.

genres and analyze their genres to grasp their structure and language features, thus providing tools for us to identify "irregularities" in translations when evaluating translation quality.

In addition, the original model's elaboration of the speech act framework and its context, function and form relations are basically limited to the situational context, that is, the register level, to discuss the equivalence and appropriateness of the translation to the original meaning expression. This is necessary, but it ignores the cultural context, that is, the equivalence and appropriateness of the translation to the original at the genre level. According to our research[1], genre is an independent symbolic layer that transcends register and language. The three major meta-functions in systemic functional linguistics are the organizational levels of language, while the three variables of register are the organizational levels of situational context. The three variables of register closely correspond to three major metafunctions, namely field corresponds to ideational function, tenor corresponds to interpersonal function, and mode corresponds to textual function. However, none of these meta-functions can cover the intention of a particular discourse. Genre has intentions, but cannot generate a one-to-one correspondence with meta-functions. It focuses on the overall effects of the three variables of register. That is to say, the implementation of genres is spread among the three major meta-functions. So, from the perspective of translation, if the translated work is not equivalent or similar in genre to the source text, its quality cannot be satisfactory. Therefore, from the perspective of improving the original model and enhancing operability, it is necessary to change the situational, functional and formal expressions at the micro level of clauses to register analysis, and modify the "situational, functional and formal analysis at the macro level" to "genre analysis", which not only focuses on the impact of situational and cultural context on the meaning and language form of the translation, but also makes it more accessible and understandable. Of course, both "register analysis" and "genre analysis" are essentially speech act frameworks that reflect the context, functions, formal relations and laws involved in speech communication and behavior.

In this way, the assessment of the translation quality of applied genre discourse can be divided into two stages:

---

[1] Xiao Lin, Si Xianzhu. "Further Exploration of Martin's Linguistic Category View" [J]. *Contemporary Foreign Language Studies*, 2014 (3): 7-11.

In the first stage, assessing the function and significance of the translated work relative to the source work is related to "faithfulness" and "equivalence", as shown in the diagram:

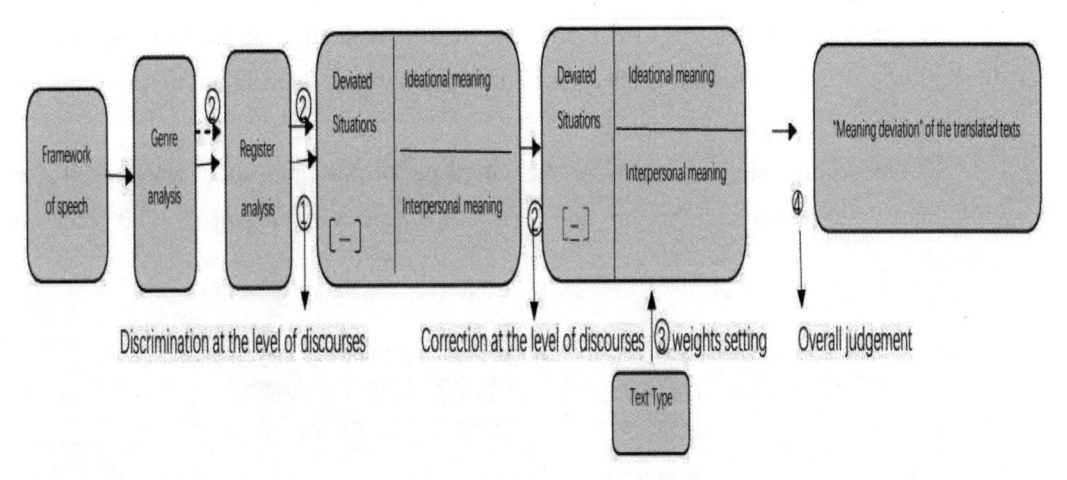

```
[Framework of speech] → [Genre analysis] ⇢② [Register analysis] →② [Deviated Situations / Ideational meaning / Interpersonal meaning [-]] ① →② [Deviated Situations / Ideational meaning / Interpersonal meaning [-]] ④ → ["Meaning deviation" of the translated texts]

↓                                    ↓                              ↓
Discrimination at the level of discourses    Correction at the level of discourses  ③ weights setting    Overall judgement
                                             ↑
                                          Text Type
```

Flow Chart 1 of Translation Quality Assessment Model

That is, the first step is to start from the cognition of the organic combination of the overall meaning/function of the discourse, which is its basic constituent unit—the meaning/function of the clause. At the clause level, from the perspective of context, function and formal interaction, starting the one-to-one correspondence between field, tenor, and mode of the register, the three meanings of the clause—ideational, interpersonal and textual and the vocabulary—grammar system of the language that reflects these three meanings—transitivity, mood (including modality) and theme, the source and translated texts are analyzed, their ideational and interpersonal meanings are revealed and described, and whether or where the translation has deviated from the source text is determined.

The second step is to re-examine the various "deviation" cases discovered and described in the first step from the perspective of genre, standing at the height of the entire discourse, as well as from the perspectives of form, function, and situational interaction, and to exclude "deviation" cases that do not constitute the overall quality of the translation from this perspective. As mentioned earlier, the role of genre in discourse is generally mediated through register, so dashed lines are used here to connect: On the one hand, it indicates that genre functions through register; On the other hand, unlike the first step, the second step mainly assesses deviation situations at the genre level beyond the register.

The third step is to determine the corresponding weights of different types of meaning deviations—ideational and interpersonal—on the quality of the translated text based on the type of text being translated.

Finally, the fourth step is to complete the quality evaluation of the first stage of the translation: that is, to what extent the translation is faithful to the original text in terms of ideational and interpersonal meanings.

In the second stage, evaluating the language of the translated work itself for smoothness and elegance, focusing on "expressiveness and elegance". The diagram shows:

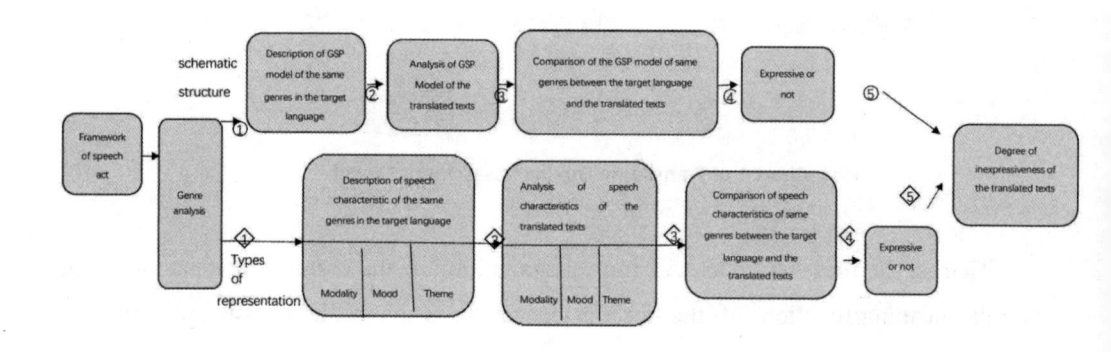

Flow Chart 2 of Translation Quality Assessment Model

That is, under the guidance of the speech act framework, it starts from the schematic structure and embodiment style of the two dimensions of genre analysis. Firstly, the first step is to identify the GSP patterns and linguistic features of the translated and target language (target language) texts of the same genre in the translation assessment. Then, the second step is to analyze the GSP patterns and linguistic features of the assessment object—the translated text. On this basis, the third step is to compare the translation with similar genres of the target language in terms of schematic structure and linguistic features. The fourth step is to evaluate whether the translated text is "smooth"based on the schematic structure and linguistic features of similar genres of the target language. Finally, the fifth step is to make an evaluation conclusion on the overall degree of "accessibility" and "smoothness" of the translation.

In this way, by combining the first and second stages, the overall evaluation of the translation quality can be completed from two aspects: "faithfulness" and "smoothness". The diagram shows:

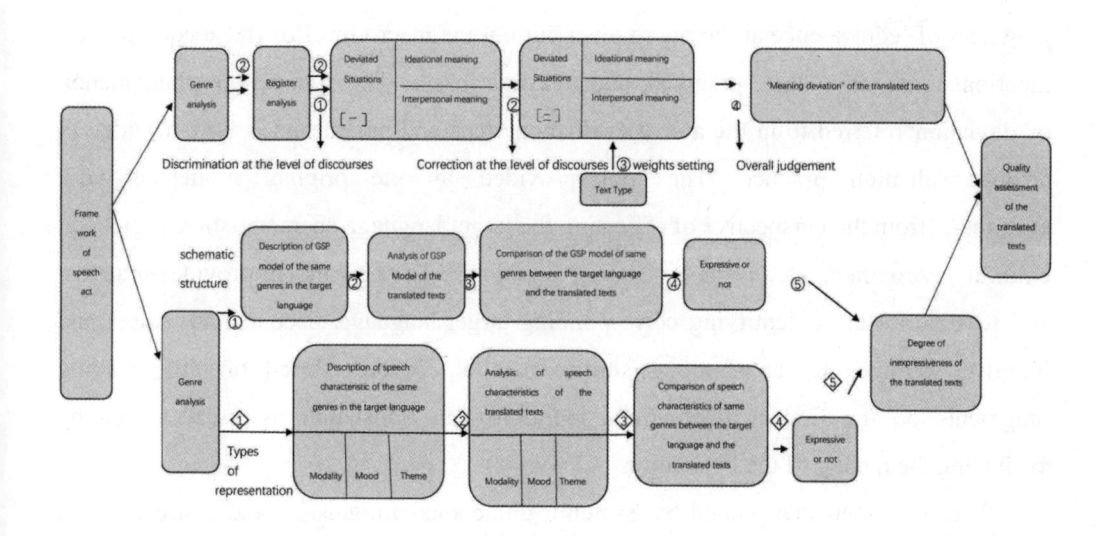

Overview of Translation Quality Assessment Model Process

Compared to the original model, this translation quality assessment model has the advantages of improvement. In addition to the two major shortcomings mentioned earlier, which are making up for the lack of genre parameters and the lack of evaluation of smooth and beautiful translations, it also improves operability. Why is that? Because regardless of either the elimination of the so-called "positive deviation" of the original model, "the second step is, standing at the height of the entire discourse at the macro level, from the perspective of form, function and situational interaction as well as from the perspective of reflecting the target language characteristics, social and cultural environment of the translation situation, to re-examine the various" deviation "cases discovered and described at the micro level, and exclude 'deviation' cases that have not caused harm to the quality of the translation from a macro perspective"; or "In terms of procedure, what needs to be corrected is to increase the equivalence between the translation and the source text. Although the translation is equivalent at the micro level, such as the function/meaning of a small sentence, the main function of the text is considered to be contrary to the function of the source text. In terms of parameters, the addition of 'negative equivalence', that is, the judgment of 'equivalence at the micro level but not the macro level' or 'false equivalence' mentioned earlier"[1] lack practical and feasible basis. The translation phenomenon or "deviation" referred to in the above evaluation steps and parameters is how to judge in actual evaluation practice. The tool provided by the original model is very abstract—"from the perspective of reflecting the target language characteristics, social and cultural environment, etc. of the translation situation"[2]. The new model provides practical and feasible means—identifying corresponding target language discourse structures and linguistic features by constructing similar parallel corpora. Based on this, making judgments on the first two situations mentioned in translation assessment, thereby evaluating the quality of the translation.

It can be seen that guided by Systemic Functional Linguistics and genre analysis theory, the new model addresses the shortcomings of the original model and constructs an applied genre translation quality assessment model by using corpus translation studies as a methodology. However, apart from its inheritance of the original model which determines whether the quality of the translation is "faithful" to the source text, the above model has been empirically tested during the construction of the original model (Si 2007a)[3]. Although the empirical evidence is still insufficient, the parameters aimed at evaluating the smoothness of the translation, such as genre analysis paths and tools, have not yet been tested. Therefore, the latter part of this book is to conduct empirical research on the second stage of the aforementioned model, which is how to use genre analysis tools

---

[1] Si Xianzhu. *Functional Linguistics and Translation Studies - Construction of Translation Quality Assessment Model* [M]. Peking University Press, 2007a: 188.
[2] Si Xianzhu. *Functional Linguistics and Translation Studies - Construction of Translation Quality Assessment Model* [M]. Peking University Press, 2007a: 137.
[3] Ibid, 140-180.

to evaluate the translation quality of practical genre discourse. Specifically, the acceptability and appropriateness of the translated text in the target language environment, which is the focus of traditional translation theory on "smoothness and elegance". To effectively use genre analysis paths or tools to evaluate whether a translated text of a given genre is "expressive and elegant", the prerequisite is to have a clear understanding of the schematic structure and stylistic features of similar genres of text in the target language. So the main content of the second part of this book is to discuss how to construct a corpus to understand the above characteristics of several applied genres of text, and to grasp the structure and linguistic features of the given genres of text in the source and target languages involved in translation by analyzing the texts in the corpus. Of course, it should be pointed out again that the revised new model mentioned above, like the original model, is a translation quality assessment model developed based on the translation perspective of systemic functional linguistics, which inevitably presupposes a "bystander" or "blind eye" to some factors, and is therefore descriptive rather than prescriptive; This kind of assessment is just the author's viewpoint which is not exclusive and does not exclude translation assessment from other perspectives. It is complementary to each other's assessment from other perspectives.

References:

[1] House, J. *Translation Quality Assessment* [M] .Tubingen: Gunter Narr Verlag,1977.

[2] House, J. *Translation Quality Assessment: A Model Revisited* [M]. Tubingen: Gunter Narr Verlag,1997.

[3] Thompson, G. *Introducing Functional Grammar* [M]. London: Arnold,1996.

[4] Hu Zhuanglin, Zhu Yongsheng and Zhang Delu. *Introduction to Systemic Functional Grammar* [M]. Changsha: Hunan Education Publishing House, 1989.

[5] Si Xianzhu."Speech Act Framework Theory and Translation Quality Assessment" [J]. *Foreign Language Research*, 2005 (5): 54-58.

[6] Si Xianzhu. *Functional Linguistics and Translation Studies - Construction of Translation Quality Assessment Model* [M]. Peking University Press, 2007a.

[7] Si Xianzhu."The Framework of speech act and the Interaction between Its Forms, Functions and Situations" [J]. The Journal of Foreign Language, 2007b (6): 57-60.

[8] Si Xianzhu."Further Study on the Quality Assessment Model of Translation Discourse: A Functional Linguistic Approach" [J]. Chinese Translators Journal, 2008 (2): 57-60.

[9] Kang Leiming, Zhang Wenhui."Review on the Translation Quality Assessment Model of Si Xianzhu" [J]. Journal of Heilongjiang University of Education, 2010 (12): 148-150.

[10] Lin Changyang. "On the Probability Tool in Translation Quality Evaluation: Reflections on the Assessment Model of Si Xianzhu" [J]. *China Electric Power Education*, 2010 (34): 109-113.

[11] Xiao Lin, Si Xianzhu."Further Exploration of Martin's Linguistic Category View" [J].*Contemporary Foreign Language Research*, 2014 (3): 7-11.

Part II Empirical Study

Chapter 6 Research on the Translation Quality of The Genre of Enterprise Profiles

This chapter introduces the content, steps, and methods of constructing a corpus of three types of corporate profiles (English corporate profiles, Chinese corporate profiles, and English translation of Chinese corporate profiles). Based on this, firstly, from the perspective of schematic structure, the GSP model is summarized by analyzing and screening all text components in the three corpora; Secondly, to analyze the lexical and grammatical characteristics (reflecting styles) of this genre of text in the three corpora by starting from the transitivity system, mood system, and thematic system; Then, by comparing the three types of corporate profiles included in the corpus from the dimensions of schematic structure and style that reflect the characteristics of discourse genres, commonalities and differences are found; Finally, starting from the second stage of the translation quality evaluation model constructed in Chapter 6, which judges and measures whether the translation is smooth and unobstructed parameters, and using the characteristics of the English corporate profiles as a benchmark, this paper evaluates and proposes improvement suggestions for the quality of the English translation text of the Chinese corporate profiles, achieving empirical analysis of the translation quality assessment model constructed in Chapter 6.

By selecting translations of corporate profiles, sports news and museum introductions as the research objects, this chapter as well as Chapters 7 and 8 use genre equivalence as the research material to build a practical text analogy corpus for the above three themes. In order to objectively analyze the differences in structure and rhetoric among the native English texts, native Chinese texts, and domestic English translation or compiled texts of the three practical texts on the above-mentioned themes, the analog corpus for each theme constructed includes three corpora: native English corpus, native Chinese corpus, and translated English corpus for that theme. We use an analogical corpus of these themes to compare the translated language with the source language, as well as to compare the translated content with the non-translated part of the target language. Based on this, we assess the translation quality of practical texts for these three themes and validate the constructed applied genre translation quality assessment model.

6.1 Construction of a Corporate Profile Genre Corpus

Based on research needs, we select a total of 120 corporate profiles from the official websites of Chinese and English companies involved in four different types of industries closely related to everyday life, namely food, beverage, clothing and home appliances, which are divided into English, Chinese, and English translations of Chinese。 According to the principles of type and correspondence (for example, after selecting the introduction of the English local dairy ice cream type of company Baskin Robbins as the corpus, the Chinese local corpus must be the same, i.e. "Feihe Dairy"), three analogical corpora, namely the native English corpus, the native Chinese corpus, and the English translation of Chinese corpus with 79105, 37302, and 105786 characters respectively are established.

6.1.1 About GSP Model

According to genre research, different genres have different schematic structures. A specific genre has its unique schematic structure and presentation style.

According to Hasan's explanation of the GSP model, this concept summarizes how to analyze and distinguish the differences between genres from a structural perspective. It mainly explores which structures are necessary components (factors) in a given genre? Which are selective? What is the order in which these factors appear and their recursion? That is:

1. Which factors are necessary to appear?
2. Which factors can appear?
3. If they must appear, where do they appear?
4. If they can appear, where should they appear?
5. How often do these factors appear?

Questions 1 and 2 are related to necessary and selective factors. Questions 3 and 4 are about the location and recursion of these factors. We can determine the type of a genre by observing its necessary factors, which can help people identify the differences between different genres; Selective features allow language users to transform language forms within a specific genre framework.

For example, the behavior of trading can be expressed in the following GSP model:

[(G). (SI) ^] [(SE.) {SR^SC} ^S^] P^PC (^F)

Connotations of characters:
G=greeting   SI=sale initiation   SE=sale enquiry
SR=sale request   SC=sale compliance   S=sale
P=purchase   PC=purchase closure   F=finis

Factors not enclosed in parentheses are necessary elements.
(X)   X is a selective element
[X.Y]   X and Y can exchange positions, and they must appear bundled together
X^Y   X must appear in front of Y (fixed position)
. X   X can be swapped with the previous elements
⌒   This element can recur
{X^Y}   X and Y, as a fixed order, must appear together
X
※   The X element can appear in any position

Quoted from: Halliday & Hasan(1985: 64-65) [1]

Customer: May I take a look at this skirt?   SR Purchase requirement
Salesperson: Okay, what else do you need?   SC Seller's affirmation
Customer: No, thank you.   G Greeting
Salesperson: Fifty dollars.   S Sale
The customer gives $50 to the salesperson   P Purchase
Salesperson: Okay, thank you.   F End

---

[1] Halliday, M. A. K. & Hasan, R. *Language, Context and Text: Aspects of Language in a Social-Semiotic Perspective* [M]. Victoria: Deakin University Press,1985: 64-65.

The main content represented by the GSP model can be expressed as follows:

(1) Which structures are necessary factors, which are optional factors, and the order between these elements;

(2) Each specific genre contains its unique GSP model, which includes necessary elements, optional factors, the order of elements, and the frequency of occurrence;

(3) Necessary elements play a decisive role in genre division, while optional elements only add diversity of forms between the same genres;

(4) A complete GSP model can fully reflect necessary and optional elements, and can clearly display the order and recursion between these elements.

In other words, the GSP model of a genre is a fundamental description of the structural characteristics of that genre, so the exploration path of the structural characteristics of the genre in this book is to analyze the GSP model that reflects the structural characteristics of the discourse.

6.1.2 Constructing Corpus: Content, Steps and Methods

According to the description of constructing an enterprise profile corpus in Chapter 5, based on research needs, we have established three parallel corpora for a total of 120 corpus, including 40 native English corporate profiles from English speaking countries and 40 Chinese corporate profiles, 40 translated versions corresponding to Chinese corporate profiles (referred to as English translations of Chinese corporate profiles).

The data in the corpus are arranged in order of food, beverage, clothing, and household appliances, labeled as Text 1 to Text 40, with the following titles (see the appendix for specific corpus content):

Table 1 List of Corpus for Genre Text of Three Types of Corporate Profiles

编号	英文企业简介	中文企业简介	中文企业简介英译
1	About DOVE BAR	光明乳业	About Bright Dairy
2	About Northfield	关于伊利	About Yili
3	About Baskin-Robbins	关于飞鹤	About Feihe
4	About Bruster	关于恰恰	About Qiaqia
5	About Ciao Bella Gelato Company	关于雨润	About Yurun
6	About Carvel	关于统一	About Uni-President
7	About Cold Stone Creamery	维维介绍	About VV

8	About Ice Cream Farm	关于娃哈哈	About Wahaha
9	About Hjem-IS	关于安踏	About Anta
10	About Friendly	关于报喜鸟	About Baoxiniao
11	About LEDO	关于以纯	About Yichun
12	About Tofutti	关于歌莉娅	About GOELIA
13	About Turkey Hill Minit Markets	关于鸿星尔克	About Hongxing China
14	About Whitey	关于九牧王	About JOEONE
15	About Canada Dry	关于美特斯邦威	About Metersbonwe
16	About 7UP	关于太和	About Tahan
17	About PepsiCo	关于西域骆驼	About Vancamel
18	About Brooks	关于雅戈尔	About Youngor
19	About Saucony	关于庄吉	About Judger
20	About New Balance	关于上海家化	About domestic cosmetics industry
21	About Embry	关于太平鸟	About Peacebird
22	About Converse	关于纵横 2000	About G2000 Group
23	About Brooks Brothers	关于 TCL	About TCL
24	About Lotto Sport	关于爱仕达	About ASD
25	About ISSEY MIYAKE INC.	关于奥克斯	About AUX
26	About Ottavio Missoni	关于澳柯玛	About Aucma
27	About H & M	关于创维	About Skyworth
28	About Reebok	关于春兰	About ChunLan
29	About paradox	关于格力	About Gree Corporation
30	About Levi	关于小熊	About Guangdong Bear
31	About AGE	关于海尔	About Haier
32	A world made simpler by Xerox	关于美菱	About Meling
33	About A. O. Smith	关于康佳	About KONKA

34	About ABB	关于联想	About Lenovo
35	About Bompani	关于美的	About Midea
36	OSRAM profile	关于魅族	About Meizu
37	About Fagor Electro domesticos	关于奔腾	About Povos
38	Electrolux profile	关于帅康	About Sacon
39	About SMEG	关于万利达	About Wanlida Group
40	About Royal Philips Electronics	关于长虹	About ChangHong

Then, we conduct genre analysis on 120 corora from the aforementioned database, with the specific steps as follows:

(1) By analyzing and distinguishing all the components of the text in the three corpora, which parts are necessary and optional as well as their order and recursion are determined, the GSP pattern is summarized;

(2) Starting from the transitivity system, mood system, and thematic system that reflect the style of genre expression, the grammatical and lexical characteristics of this genre in three corpora are analyzed;

(3) By comparing the GSP model and lexical grammar levels of texts from three corpora, commonalities and differences are found;

(4) Finally, starting from the smooth and unobstructed parameters used in the translation quality assessment model to measure the quality of translations, this paper evaluates and proposes improvement suggestions for the quality of English translated texts of Chinese enterprise introduction genres based on the text structure and linguistic dimensions that reflect the characteristics of English enterprise enterprise genres, making empirical analysis of the aforementioned constructed translation quality assessment model.

6.2 Corpus Based Discourse Schematic Structure of Corporate Profiles

6.2.1 Composition of the Genre Structure of Corporate Profiles

According to Nwogu, K. N (1997), if there is a necessary connection between the discourse function of a particular genre of text and its language use characteristics, then that segment is a move of the text.

In order to draw the GSP model for English, Chinese, and Chinese-English translation of corporate profiles, we need to understand the structural components of discourse in such genres as corporate profiles, namely moves. Next, we will randomly select a company profile from each of the three corpora mentioned above, and conduct a schematic structure analysis to identify and count the structural components of this genre, explaining how to conduct genre structure analysis. Then, following the same method, to complete the analysis, screening, and statistics of all remaining corpora in the three corpora.

After completing the structural analysis of all data in the corpora, based on their different communicative purposes in the text, genres such as corporate profiles can generally be abstracted in 12 steps (structural components), namely: I: Identification, BI: Company's Basic Information, CA: Company's Achievements, EP: Evaluation and Position, CLS: Company's Location and Supply Scope, CF: Company's Future, CIC: Company's Ideas and Concepts, Company's Commitment and Insurance (CPI), Leadership and Staff (LS), Entrepreneurship History (EH), Founder and Founder's Story (FS), and Social Activities (SA) in which the company participates. Of course, it is in a collective sense. When it comes to a specific enterprise profile case, as shown in the following text, it rarely includes all the structural components mentioned above but only includes certain parts of it.

The names and functions of these 12 structural components are:

Identification (I): Provide the name of the relevant company.

Basic Information (BI): Introduce the basic information of relevant companies, including their main production and sales areas, products or services.

Company's Achievements (CA): Describe the achievements and development of the company.

Evaluation and Position (EP): The honors obtained by the company and its position in similar industries.

Company's Location and Supply Scope (CLS): List the company and branch addresses, as well as the company's scope of supply.

Company's Future (CF): Describe the company's future development plans.

Company's Ideas and Concepts (CIC): Introduce the company's business or development philosophy.

Company's Commitment and Insurance (CPI): The company promises and guarantees the quality of its products and services to consumers.

Leadership and Staff (LS): Introduce the situation of company leaders and employees.

Entrepreneurship History (EH): Background, purpose, and success opportunities related to the establishment of the company.

Founder and Founder's Story (FS): About founders and their entrepreneurial stories.

Social Activities (SA): The social activities or public welfare activities that the company participates in.

6.2.2 The GSP Model of English Corporate Profile Texts

Based on the structural components of the genre of corporate profiles summarized earlier, the following analysis randomly selects a case (Text 6) from an English corpus for structural analysis.

(I) ABOUT CARVEL （www.carvel.com.cn）

(BI) Carvel provides an affordable ice cream experience and family fun for everyone by offering a variety of fresh made cakes, novelties and fountain ice cream products. (EP)This all-American favorite is the nation's first retail ice cream franchise, and has become one of the best-loved and most recognized names in its industry. Carvel is not only one of our country's most beloved icons, but also representing the all-American dream with the most all-American of foods.

(CA) Carvel has been making ice cream fresh daily for over 75 years and is home of the original all ice cream cake. Today, Carvel-lovers still seek out our creamy, crunchy treats in more than 500 Carvel stores and over 8,500 supermarkets nationwide.

(FS) Tom Carvel was the personification of the American dream. Once known as the "patriarch of the world's biggest mom and pop ice cream parlor," he was a man who wasn't afraid of hard work and did what it took to make his "rags to riches" story come true. He had an engaging manner, twinkling blue eyes, neatly trimmed handlebar mustache, and a friendly face. But he was a tough and honest businessman who demanded only the best from those who worked with him.

Athanassios Karvelas (1906-1990) was brought to the United States as a child from his native Greece. At the age of 26, after a variety of careers that ranged from a drummer in a Dixieland band to an auto test driver for Studebakers, Carvel was incorrectly diagnosed with fatal tuberculosis and fled to the country air of Westchester, New York. Borrowing $15 from his future wife Agnes, Tom began selling ice cream from his battered truck. Memorial Day weekend of 1934, Tom's truck suffered a flat tire so he pulled his trailer into a parking lot next to a pottery store and began selling his melting ice cream to vacationers driving by. Within two days, Tom had sold his entire supply of ice cream, and realized that he could make a lot more money working from a fixed location. (EH) The generous potter allowed Tom to hook into his store's electricity, and Tom opened for business. Two years later, Tom bought the pottery store, converted it into a roadside stand, and permanently established himself as the first retailer to develop and market soft ice cream. With the coming of World War II, Carvel was sent to Fort Bragg, N.C. where he served as a refrigeration consultant and concessionaire.

(CIC) Often referred to as the "father of franchising," many of Carvel's marketing concepts have been emulated not only in franchising, but in almost every industry. Like our delicious products themselves, Carvel is all about making people happy from our franchisees and owners, to our associates, consumers, and each community we serve. Everything we do is focused on getting people to smile, inside and out.

(CPI) To do this, we need the best associates in the business. We believe that all of our associates are leaders, and we strive to continually enhance their abilities so that they can make the most of their careers. (CF)We've built a diverse culture that recognizes great efforts, rewards outstanding leadership, and provides a work/life balance that is imperative to all of us. We empower them to make decisions, encourage them to take risks, and promise open and honest communication.

So, join us in our pursuit of happiness.

The basic structure of Text 6 can be summarized as follows:
I^BI^EP^CA^FS^EH^ CIC^CPI^CF

This company profile starts with the company name, starting with the company name CARVEL, followed by an introduction to CARVEL's position in the ice cream industry—not only being the first ice cream retailer in the United States, but also the most famous brand name in the ice cream industry; Not only is it loved by customers in this city, but it has also won praise from consumers all over the United States; Then, the introduction of the development and achievements of CARVEL in recent years, pointing out that the variety of products is constantly increasing; Next, the entrepreneurial story of Tom Carvel, the founder of CARVEL Ice Cream Company; Subsequently, the development status of CARVEL company and how to seize opportunities to acquire current achievements; Finally, the company's business philosophy is introduced, ensuring superior quality to consumers, and we sincerely invite consumers to learn more about CARVEL company, showcasing the company's future development trend and attracting consumers to further understand CARVEL company.

Using the same method to analyze the remaining English corporate profiles in the corpus, their structural components and order are shown in the table below:

Table 2 schematic structure of Texts of English corporate profiles

Number	Structural components and their order
1	I^FS^EH^CA^EP^BI^EH^CPI
2	I^BI^CLS^CA
3	I^EP^BI^CA^EH^FS^EH^CPI^CF^CA
4	I^BI^EH^CA^EH^CF
5	I^BI^FS^CA^CIC^CPI
6	I^BI^EP^CA^FS^EH^CIC^CPI^CF
7	I^BI^FS^CA^CPI^CF
8	I^BI^CPI^CLS^FS^LS
9	I^BI^CLS^CPI^CIC
10	I^BI^CLS^FS^CA
11	I^BI^CPI^CIC^EP^FS^CA^FS
12	I^BI^CPI^CF
13	I^BI^EP^CA^FS^CA
14	I^BI^FS^CA^CIC^CF
15	I^BI^FS^CA^EH
16	I^BI^CA^CLS^CIC
17	I^BI^EP^CIC^CF
18	I^BI^CA^CIC^CPI^CF
19	I^BI^CIC^CA^FS^CF^CA^CPI
20	I^EP^CA^FS^CA^CPI^CIC^CF
21	I^BI^CA^FS^EH^CF
22	I^BI^EP^CA^FS^CIC^CPI^CF
23	I^BI^CIC^CPI^CA^CF
24	I^BI^CA^EH^CF
25	I^BI^CA^CIC^CPI^EH^CA^CF
26	I^BI^CLS^EH^CA^CF
27	I^BI^FS^CA^EH
28	I^BI^FS^EH^CA^EH
29	I^BI^FS^CA^EH^CA^CPI

30	I^BI^CA^EH^CA^CF
31	I^BI^CA^LS
32	I^BI^CIC^CPI^CF
33	I^BI^CA^EH^CA^CLS^CF
34	I^BI^FS^EP^CIC^CF
35	I^BI^CLS^CA^CPI^CA
36	I^BI^FS^CA^EH^CA
37	I^BI^FS^EH^CA
38	I^BI^CA^CLS^CF
39	I^BI^CIC^CPI^CA^FS^EH
40	I^BI^CA^EH^CA^CF

The distribution of each structural component is as follows:

Table 3 Distribution of Structural Components in Texts of English corporate profiles

No.	I	BI	CA	EP	CLS	CF	CIC	CPI	LS	EH	FS	SA
1	√	√	√	√				√		√	√	
2	√	√	√		√							
3	√	√	√	√		√		√		√	√	
4	√	√	√			√				√		
5	√	√	√				√	√			√	
6	√	√	√	√		√	√	√		√	√	
7	√	√	√			√		√			√	
8	√	√			√			√	√		√	
9	√	√			√		√	√				
10	√	√	√		√						√	
11	√	√	√	√			√	√			√	
12	√	√				√		√				
13	√	√	√	√							√	
14	√	√	√			√	√				√	
15	√	√	√							√	√	
16	√	√	√		√		√					
17	√	√		√		√	√					
18	√	√	√			√	√	√				
19	√	√	√			√	√	√			√	

	I	BI	CA	EP	CLS	CF	CIC	CPI	LS	EH	FS	SA
20	√		√	√		√	√	√			√	
21	√	√	√			√				√	√	
22	√	√	√	√		√	√	√			√	
23	√	√	√			√	√	√				
24	√	√	√			√				√		
25	√	√	√			√	√	√		√		
26	√	√	√		√	√				√		
27	√	√	√							√	√	
28	√	√	√							√	√	
29	√	√	√					√		√	√	
30	√	√	√		√					√		
31	√	√	√						√			
32	√	√				√	√	√				
33	√	√	√		√	√				√		
34	√	√		√		√	√				√	
35	√	√	√		√			√				
36	√	√	√							√	√	
37	√	√	√							√	√	
38	√	√	√		√	√						
39	√	√	√					√	√	√	√	
40	√	√	√			√				√		

The frequency of occurrence of each structural component in the corpus is shown in Table 4 after statistical analysis.

Table 4 Frequency of Structural Elements in Texts of English Enterprise Profile

	I	BI	CA	EP	CLS	CF	CIC	CPI	LS	EH	FS	SA
Total	40	39	34	9	9	21	16	19	2	19	21	0
%	100	97.5	85	22.5	22.5	52.5	40	47.5	5	47.5	52.5	0

Through the analysis of the above three tables, it can be found that the frequency of the company name (I), basic information (BI), achievements (CA), future development (CF) and founder's entrepreneurial story (FS) is more than 50%. Therefore, these five items can be regarded as essential components of the English company profiles. Almost all English company profiles have these five items, while the occurrence rate of other components is less than 50%, which are called optional components.

Although the order of necessary and selective components in a company profile is sometimes complex and flexible, there are still rules to follow. For example, components I and BI must appear in the company profile, and the position of component I must appear before the BI component, while the necessary component CA usually appears at the same time as the FS component. The positions of the two components are usually flexible and interchangeable. These two components together explain how the company has developed to its current scale, what kind of effort the founder has injected, and these difficult entrepreneurial stories can impress consumers, enhance consumers'trust in the company and deepen their understanding of the company. The CA component can appear repeatedly in the company profile over time. The components CIC and CPI often appear as a whole, indicating the company's business philosophy and ensuring the quality of products or services to consumers. These two components, as a whole, have a relatively flexible position in the company profile. The CF component usually appears in the last part of the company profile, mainly to attract more consumers'attention. The positions where the selective components EP, CLS, LS, and EH appear are relatively flexible.

In this way, we can derive the GSP model for English company profiles as follows:

I^ EP. BI (LS) (FS) ^ CIC^ CA (CLS) (CPI) (SA) ^ CF

From the above pattern, it can be seen that I, EP, BI, CIC, CA, and CF are all necessary components, while others are optional. The position of I is always at the forefront of the pattern, and the positions of EP and BI can be interchanged, which is relatively flexible, and BI can appear repeatedly. CA always appears after CIC, and the author of the company profile wants to demonstrate through describing the company's recent performance and development that these achievements are mainly attributed to adhering to the correct business philosophy, benefiting from the care of leaders and the efforts of employees. The positions of LS, FS, CLS, CPI, and SA are relatively flexible, and CF is always located at the end of the company profile.

6.2.3 GSP Model for English Translation of Chinese Corporate Profiles

The following is an analysis of the schematic structure of Text 1 in the English translation corpus of Chinese corporate profiles.

(I) Bright Diary (translated version) (http://en.brightdairy.com/about-intor.php)

(BI) Bright Dairy & Food Co., Ltd is a listed joint-stock enterprise specializing in the development, production and sales of milk and dairy products, the rearing and fostering of milk cows and bulls, logistic distribution, the development, production and sales of health and nutrition products. The company boasts a world-class dairy product research and development center, dairy product processing facilities, and advanced dairy product processing techniques, and has developed various product series including pasteurized milk, fresh milk, and yogurt, ultra-high heat pasteurized milk, milk powder, butter and cheese, and fruit juices. It is one of the largest dairy production and sales companies in China.

(EP) As a leading enterprise of agricultural industrialization in China, Bright Dairy & Food Co., (CIC) Ltd has always committed to the corporate mission of "to innovate life and share health", and has continued to blaze new trails with pioneering creativity in the industry, thereby scoring remarkable achievement in building the Chinese top brand in the fresh product sector. (CA) In 2000, the "Bright" series of products received the title of exclusively designated dairy products for the Chinese delegation for the 27th Olympic Games. In 2001, it was included in "China's Top 50 Most Respected Enterprises". From 2002 till now, it was included in "Shanghai's Top 100 Enterprises" and was ranked higher every year; it was successively included in "China's Top 500 Enterprises" chosen through public appraisal organized by the China Enterprise Confederation and China Enterprise Directors Association. In 2004, Bright Dairy was included in "2004 Top 20 Listed Companies with the Strongest Leadership in China" in the 2004 Report on the Leadership of China's Securities Market issued by Fortune China, a well-known publication. From 2005 to now, it was successively rated as a national AAA①-grade creditworthy enterprise by the Chinese Academy of International Trade and Economic Cooperation of the Ministry of Commerce. In 2006, it received the title of "Excellent Independent Innovation Products" at the annual meeting on competitiveness organized by the Chinese Academy of Social Sciences and China Business Journal. In January 2007, it was chosen as China's brand with the strongest market competitiveness of 2006 by the Ministry of Commerce of the People's Republic of China. In September 2007, it received the title of "China's Top 10 Safe Food Enterprises" jointly granted by the Ministry of Health, the Ministry of Agriculture, the Ministry of Public Security, the State Administration for Industry and Commerce, the State Food and Drug Administration, etc. and became the only Chinese liquid dairy enterprise to receive this title. In October 2007, it passed the reappraisal by the "Shanghai Quality Gold Award" appraisal group and won the "Shanghai Quality Gold Award" again. In 2009, it received the title of "Confidence 2009—Top 20 Companies with Happy Competitiveness" from the Chinese Academy of International Trade and Economic Cooperation under the Ministry of Commerce again, and the Room Temperature Division received the "Confident Team" Single Award of "Confidence 2009 — Investigation of Happy Competitiveness of Companies". In September 2009, it received the "60 Years of Glory—China's Intelligent Sci-Tech Development" Outstanding Contribution Award at the "2009 Chinese and Foreign Sci-Tech Top 100 Summit Forum and Ceremony of Conferring Outstanding Sci-Tech Contribution Awards". In October 2009, it was chosen as "the Brand Most Loved/Trusted by China's Female Consumers" by Women of China Magazine Publishing House. On November 21, 2009, it received "the 60th Anniversary of the Founding of the People's Republic of China – Entities with Outstanding Contributions to China's Food Industry" Award and the title of "2009 Top 10 Safe Food Enterprises" for its contributions to the industry in terms of science and technology at the 7th China Food Security Annual Conference held under the joint support of seven ministries and commissions including the National Development and Reform Commission, the Ministry of Agriculture, the General Administration of Quality Supervision, Inspection and Quarantine of the People's Republic of China, the State Administration for Industry and Commerce, the State Food and Drug Administration, etc. Bright Dairy was the only enterprise and individual in the dairy industry to receive the above honor. In 2009, it received the honor of "the 5th Ceremony for China's Best Brand Building Cases" at "China Brand Value Management Forum and the 5th Ceremony of Conferring Awards for China's Best Brand Building Cases". In 2009, it received the "China Medium Innovation Marketing Award" at the 16th China International Advertising Festival for the case of marketing cooperation with Sina, which became the model of diversified marketing integrating China's fast consumables and the Internet

(CPI) The "Bright" brand has undergone more than 50 years of history. All of the Bright employees are committed to providing consumers with safe, fresh, nutritious and healthy dairy products. (EP)Currently, Bright's market share of fresh milk, yoghurt, and cheese all ranks first in China.

Through analysis, its schematic structure is as follows: **I^BI^EP^CIC^CA^CPI^EP**, which is exactly the same as its source Chinese.

Structural analysis is conducted on English translation texts of the remaining Chinese enterprise profiles using the same method. The following table shows that their structural composition and order are consistent with their corresponding source Chinese texts.

Table 8 schematic structure of English Translation of Chinese corporate profiles

No.	Structural Components and Their Order
1	I^BI^EP^CIC^CA^CPI^BI
2	I^EP^BI^CA^CIC^CA^CPI^CF
3	I^CIC^CLS^EP^CA^BI^LS^CA^CPI^BI^CF
4	I^BI^CIC^CA^CPI^CA^CIC^CF
5	I^BI^CA^LS^CA^EP^BI
6	I^FS^CIC^CPI^CF
7	I^BI^EP^CA^CIC^CA^CLS^LS^CPI
8	I^BI^FS^CA^EP^CLS^LS
9	I^EP^LS^CIC^CA^CLS^**SA**^CA
10	I^BI^CLS^LS^CA^BI^CA^CIC^CPI^CF
11	I^CLS^BI^CA^CIC
12	I^CLS^CIC^BI^CIC^CA^LS^CA
13	I^CIC^BI^CLS^EP^CIC^CA^**SA**^CPI^CF
14	I^EP^CA^CIC^CPI^CA^SA^CF
15	I^BI^CA^CLS^LS^CA^CF^CIC
16	I^BI^CLS^BI^CIC^CA^CF
17	I^BI^CIC^BI^CLS^CA^CF
18	I^BI^LS^CA^EP^CIC^CF
19	I^CA^BI^LS^CPI^CIC^CF
20	I^BI^CPI^EP^CA^CF
21	I^BI^EP^BI^CIC^CA
22	I^BI^LS^CIC^CA^SA^CF
23	I^BI^EP^CA^CIC^CPI^CF
24	I^EP^BI^LS^CA^CIC^CPI^CLS
25	I^EP^BI^CA^CF
26	I^BI^LS^FS^CIC^CA^SA
27	I^BI^CIC^CF
28	I^BI^CA^EP^SA
29	I^EP^BI^FS^CIC^CF

No.	
30	I^BI^CA^CPI^CF
31	I^BI^CLS^CIC^CPI^SA
32	I^BI^CIC^CA^CF
33	I^BI^EP^CLS^CA
34	I^BI^EP^CIC^CA^CLS
35	I^BI^CA^EP^CA^CF
36	I^BI^EP^BI^CA^BI^CA
37	I^EP^BI^CA^CF
38	I^BI^CIC^CLS
39	I^EP^BI^CA^CPI
40	I^EP^BI^CIC^CPI^SA^CF

The distribution of all text structure components in the English translation of Chinese corporate profile corpus is as follows.

Table 9 Distribution of Structural Components in the English Translation of Chinese Corporate Profiles

No.	I	BI	CA	EP	CLS	CF	CIC	CPI	LS	EH	FS	SA
1	√	√	√	√			√	√				
2	√	√	√	√		√	√	√				
3	√	√	√	√	√	√	√	√	√			
4	√	√	√			√	√	√				
5	√	√	√	√					√			
6	√					√	√	√			√	
7	√	√	√	√	√		√	√	√			
8	√	√	√	√	√				√		√	
9	√		√	√	√		√		√			√
10	√	√	√		√	√	√	√	√			
11	√	√	√		√		√					
12	√	√	√		√		√		√			
13	√	√	√		√	√	√		√			
14	√		√	√		√	√	√				√
15	√	√	√		√	√	√		√			
16	√	√	√		√	√	√					
17	√	√	√		√	√	√					

#	I	BI	CA	EP	CLS	CF	CIC	CPI	LS	EH	FS	SA
18	✓	✓	✓	✓		✓	✓		✓			
19	✓	✓	✓		✓	✓	✓	✓				
20	✓	✓	✓	✓		✓		✓				
21	✓	✓	✓	✓			✓					
22	✓	✓	✓				✓	✓	✓			✓
23	✓	✓	✓	✓		✓	✓	✓				
24	✓	✓	✓	✓	✓		✓	✓	✓			
25	✓	✓	✓	✓		✓						
26	✓	✓	✓				✓		✓		✓	✓
27	✓	✓				✓	✓					
28	✓	✓	✓	✓								✓
29	✓	✓		✓		✓	✓				✓	
30	✓	✓	✓			✓		✓				
31	✓	✓			✓		✓	✓				✓
32	✓	✓	✓			✓	✓					
33	✓	✓	✓	✓	✓							
34	✓	✓	✓	✓	✓		✓					
35	✓	✓	✓	✓		✓						
36	✓	✓	✓	✓								
37	✓	✓	✓	✓		✓						
38	✓	✓			✓		✓					
39	✓	✓	✓	✓				✓				
40	✓	✓		✓		✓	✓	✓				✓

After describing the structural features of the texts mentioned above, we calculated the frequency of each step appearing in the corpus as follows:

Table 10 Frequency of Structural Elements inEnglish Translation of Chinese corporate profiles

	I	BI	CA	EP	CLS	CF	CIC	CPI	LS	EH	FS	SA
Total	40	37	34	23	17	22	29	17	13	0	4	7
%	100	92.5	85	57.5	42.5	55	72.5	42.5	32.5	0	10	17.5

Through analysis, it is found that the English translation of the company profiles and its corresponding Chinese company profiles are identical in terms of GSP model parameters such as structural element composition, distribution and arrangement, namely:

$$\text{I}^\wedge \text{ EP. BI (LS) (FS)} \wedge \text{CIC}^\wedge \text{ CA (CLS) (CPI) (SA)} \wedge \text{CF}$$
※ ※　　　　　　※ ※ ※

It is a gradual translation of the structural elements of the source text.

6.3 Corpus-based Discourse Features of Corporate Profiles

Michael Halliday believes that the nature of language determines people's requirements for language, that is, the functions that language must complete. He abstractly summarizes these functions a"metafunctions". This is a common characteristic of various languages.

The pure rational function of language includes three aspects: first, ideational function, which includes two parts: experiential function and logical function. The experiential function is mainly reflected through the transitivity system and voice system. The logical function is the mechanism that represents the relationship between clauses. The second is interpersonal function, which is expressed by the mood system, modality system and key system. The third is textual function, which includes theme system, information system, and coherence system. According to discourse typology theory, although these three metafunctions coexist in adult language, the functions emphasized in different discourses may vary accordingly.

Ideational function is mainly achieved through the transitivity system, interpersonal function is mainly achieved through the mood system and modality system, and discourse function is mainly reflected by the thematic system.

1)Transitivity system

The transitivity system includes three components: participant, process and circumstance. The process is the core component of the transitivity system. Human activities and natural processes include material process, psychological process, relational process, behavioral process, verbal process, and existential process.

These six process are shown in Table 11:

Table 11 List of Process Types

Process type	Category meaning	Participants, directly involved	Participants, obliquely involved
Material	doing:	Actor	Recipient

process: Action Event	doing happening	Goal	Client Scope Initiator Attribute
Behavioral process	Behaving	Behaver	Behaviour
Mental process: Perception Cognition Desideration Emotion	Sensing: Seeing Thinking Wanting Feeling	Senser) Phenomenon	
Verbal process	Saying	Sayer Target	Receiver Verbiage
Relational process: Attribution Identification	Being: Attributing Identifying	Carrier Attribute Identified Identifier Token Value	Attributor Beneficiary Assigner
Existential process	Existing	Existent	

2) Mood System and Modal System

As a communication tool, language inevitably involves mutual dialogue among language users. The essence of dialogue is the communicative role of language users, whether giving or requesting. The exchange of goods, services or messages are expressed as suggestions and statements, respectively. The combination of these four factors provides four main language functions: offer, statement, command and question.

The above four speech functions are implemented by the tone system. Mood consists of two components: subject and finite element, whose appearance and word order determine the choice of mood; The parts outside the tone are called residue. The relationship between speech function and mood is shown in Table 12:

Table 12　Speech Function and Mood

Speech function	Typical clause mood	Non-typical clause mood
Command	Imperative	Modulated interrogative Declarative
Offer	Modulated interrogative	Imperative declarative
Statement	Declarative	Tagged declarative
Question	Interrogative	Modulated declarative

　　Modality represents the estimation of language users' understanding of things. Michael Halliday uses modalisation and modulation to explain the modality system. The distinction between modalisation and modulation is shown in Table 13:

Table 13 Modalisation and Modulation

Types of modality	The content of exchange	Emphasis
Modalisation	Propositions	Probability or frequency
Modulation	Proposals	Obligation or inclination

3) Theme system

　　One function of language is to transfer information. As far as the clause is concerned, it is implemented by the "theme" in the clause. Theme is the starting point for language users to organize information, and clauses are unfolded according to this theme. The unfolded part is called "rheme". Theme and rheme form a thematic structure. Themes are divided into single themes and multiple themes, as shown in Table 14.

able 14 Types of Theme

Types of theme	Specific types of each theme
Experiential theme	Participant Circumstance Process
Textual theme	Continuative Conjunction Conjunctive adjunct
Interpersonal theme	Modal or comment adjunct Vocative Finite verbal operator

　　This section will use the transitivity system, mood system and thematic system, which reflect the ideational function, interpersonal function, and textual function of language, as analytical tools to conduct a lexical and grammatical analysis of the linguistic features—expression styles—of English, Chinese, and English translation of Chinese texts in the enterprise profile corpus.

6.3.1 Verbal Features of English Corporate Profiles
1) Transitivity system

As mentioned earlier, the transitivity system includes three components: participant, process and circumstance. Among them, process is the core component of the transitivity system. Therefore, the transitivity analysis of text below focuses on process, which is called process analysis.

Take Text 10 in this corpus as an example.

About Friendlys (http://www.friendlys.com)

(1) We are a company founded on ice cream but built around families.

(2) We opened our first Friendly's Ice Cream Shop in Springfield, Massachusetts in 1935.

(3) Friendly's is a place where hungry people can sit together, eat together, joke together and debate about who has the best way to eat an ice cream sundae, where sons can find out why lefty pitchers are harder to hit and where families can meet up to get an extra fifteen minutes of talk time over our famous ice cream.

(4) We are committed to quality in everything we do, from our made to order Friendly's Big to our signature SuperMelt Sandwiches every meal with classic comfort foods and delicious new dishes that you can only find at Friendly's.

(5) And we end every meal with unbelievable homemade ice cream in limitless sizes, shapes, and flavors.

(6) For over 70 years, we've built a place that brings you a friendly staff, reasonable prices, and a thousand sweet ways to end your day. (7)That's why we truly are the one place where Ice Cream Makes the Meal.

The analysis of the process of the above text is as follows:

Table 15 Process Type Analysis of Text 10

Sentence Number	Process Number	Process Type	Verbs Involved
(1)	1	Relational process	are
	2	Material process	(was)founded
	3	Material process	(was) built
(2)	4	Material process	opened
(3)	5	Relational process	is
	6	Behavioral process	sit
	7	Behavioral process	eat
	8	Verbal process	joke
	9	Verbal process	debate
	10	Relational process	has
	11	Material process	find
	12	Relational process	are
	13	Material process	meet
(4)	14	Mental process	are committed to
	15	Material process	do
	16	Material process	find
(5)	17	Behavioral process	end
(6)	18	Material process	have built
	19	Material process	brings
(7)	20	Relational process	is

Through the above analysis of the remaining text, the distribution of the six process types in all corporate profiles in the library is as follows:

Table 16 Distribution of Process Types in All Texts of English corporate profiles

Text No.	Relational process	Material process	Mental process	Behavioral process	Verbal process	Existential process	Total
1	3	10	4	3	0	0	20
2	4	3	2	0	0	0	9
3	18	29	15	10	1	6	79
4	1	7	2	3	0	0	13

5	4	15	12	10	0	1		42
6	9	24	17	11	1	0		62
7	3	13	4	5	0	0		25
8	4	12	5	7	0	0		28
9	8	10	2	2	0	0		22
10	6	10	1	3	2	0		22
11	11	7	3	4	1	3		29
12	1	3	1	0	0	3		7
13	9	20	0	8	0	0		37
14	4	15	1	7	0	0		27
15	3	18	6	3	2	0		32
16	3	8	2	3	0	0		16
17	3	11	0	2	0	0		16
18	5	22	2	13	0	1		43
19	3	13	5	7	0	2		30
20	4	8	1	3	0	1		17
21	4	9	2	5	1	0		21
22	9	15	4	10	0	0		38
23	7	20	3	5	0	2		37
24	5	15	2	3	1	0		26
25	7	19	1	5	2	1		25
26	5	14	1	3	0	0		23
27	3	15	0	5	0	1		24
28	7	19	0	3	0	2		31
29	5	20	1	3	0	0		29
30	7	25	2	5	1	0		40
31	3	10	0	2	0	3		18
32	5	17	0	3	0	0		25
33	4	12	1	3	0	1		21
34	6	13	0	2	0	0		21
35	5	17	1	3	1	2		29
36	3	16	0	1	0	0		20
37	5	19	1	3	0	0		28
38	7	21	0	4	0	0		32
39	5	26	1	2	0	3		34
40	4	15	1	2	0	2		24

The distribution ratios of different types of processes are:

Table 17 Distribution Ratio of Different Process Types

	Relational process	Material process	Mental process	Behavioral process	Verbal process	Existential process	Total
Total	212	595	106	176	13	34	1136
%	18.7	52.3	9.3	15.5	1.2	3.0	100

From the data in the above table, it can be seen that material processes are the most commonly used in corporate profiles, accounting for more than half of the entire process type, namely 52.3%. The content expressed in material processes is mostly "doing", which refers to how the enterprise has developed and what efforts have been made in recent years. The company profile uses this process to inform consumers of the company's recent situation, basic information, basic product services, and stories of entrepreneurs. For example:

By the late 70s over one million DOVE BAR **were sold** in a single year by street vendors to eager children and adults. (Text 1)

Baskin-Robbins **was founded** in 1945 by two ice cream enthusiasts whose passion led to the creation of more than 1,000 ice cream flavors and a wide variety of delicious treats. (Text 3)

Carvel **provides** an affordable ice cream experience and family fun for everyone by offering a variety of fresh made cakes, novelties and fountain ice cream products.(Text 6)

The second most commonly used process is the relational process, which accounts for 18.7% of the total process. The relational process mainly represents a type of ownership relationship, which can be used to describe the characteristics and attributes of products and services, as well as to describe the subsidiaries, sub-brands, etc. under a brand. For example:

Northfield, Ill.-based Kraft Foods Inc. (NYSE: KFT) **is** a global snacks powerhouse with an unrivaled portfolio of brands people love. (Text 2)

Named the top ice cream and frozen dessert franchise in the United States by Entrepreneur magazine's 31st annual Franchise 500 ranking, Baskin-Robbins **is** the world's largest chain of ice cream specialty shops. (Text 3)

The production unit **is** possibly the biggest in the North West. (Text 8)

The behavioral process also accounts for a certain percentage in the English company profile, which is 15.5%. Behavioral process is a process that lies between material and mental processes. For example:

This concept eventually **grew** into Baskin-Robbins.（Text 3）

With this over-arching branding, Baskin-Robbins'iconic pink spoons were created with the belief that people should **be able to** try any of their many flavors without cost.（Text 3）

He eventually quit school, **raised** $25,000 from family.（Text 3）

Overall, the most commonly used in corporate profiles are material and relational processes, as well as a small number of behavioral processes. However, when a company profile is used to establish a closer relationship with potential consumers, it often involves verbal processes, attempting to engage in a conversation with consumers and to be friendly and natural.

2) Mood System

Mood contains two elements: the subject and the finite. The subject, the finite and their word order determine the mood type. Therefore, our mood analysis of the text focuses on the mood analysis of the sentence, the subject and the finite of the clause, and the tense attached to the finite. Take text 4 as an example:

Bruster(http://www.brustersicecream.com/aboutus.asp)

(1) [1] Bruster was founded in 1989 by a man [2]whose passion for extraordinary ice cream and stellar customer service runs deep.

(2) [3] Born into the restaurant business, [4] Bruce Reed opened his first Bruster's in Bridgewater, Pennsylvania,after perfecting his recipe for rich, creamy homemade ice cream.

(3) [5] People came from miles around to enjoy the skillfully prepared desserts [6] that Bruce created right in that first store.

(4) [7] It got to [8]where he had to expand to keep up with the growing demand for his ice creams.

(5) [9] Before long, Bruster became one of the fastest expanding ice cream stores in the country [10]and Bruce regretfully all but stopped wearing his apron to work.

(6) [11] While we've come a long way from those early days, [12] we adhere to the guiding principles [13]that have made Bruster's the revered brand [14] that it is today.

(7) [15] For example, we continue to make all our desserts, such as our cakes, pies, and waffle cones, as well as our ice creams, right in the store [16]where they're served.

(8) [17] Most importantly, we've never lost sight of the reason [18]Bruce started serving ice cream in the first place: to make our customers happy.

(9) [19] Come treat you to the extraordinary taste of Bruster's ice cream today.

Table 18 Analysis of Mood System in Text 4

Sentence No.	Clause No.	Subject	Finite	Tense	Mood type
(1)	[1]	Bruster	was	Past tense	Indicative mood
	[2]	Passion	runs	Present tense	Indicative mood
(2)	[3]	Bruce Reed	(was)	Past tense	Indicative mood
	[4]	Bruce Reed	opened	Past tense	Indicative mood
(3)	[5]	People	came	Past tense	Indicative mood
	[6]	Bruce	created	Past tense	Indicative mood
(4)	[7]	It	got	Past tense	Indicative mood
	[8]	He	had	Past tense	Indicative mood
(5)	[9]	Bruster	became	Past tense	Indicative mood
	[10]	Bruce	stopped	Past tense	Indicative mood

(6)	[11]	We	have come	Present perfect tense	Indicative mood
	[12]	We	adhere	Present tense	Indicative mood
	[13]	That	have made	Present tense	Indicative mood
	[14]	That	is	Present perfect tense	Indicative mood
				Present tense	
(7)	[15]	We	continue	Present tense	Indicative mood
	[16]	they	are	Present tense	Indicative mood
(8)	[17]	We	have lost	Present perfect tense	Indicative mood
	[18]	Bruce	started	Past tense	Indicative mood
(9)	[19]	(you)	come	Present tense	Imperative mood

According to the above analysis, only one of all 19 is an imperative clause, the other clauses are in the declarative mood. The imperative mood aims to persuade consumers to buy products and services or learn more about the company's products and services, while the main function of indicative mood is to provide information. The past tense mainly describes the entrepreneurship and development of enterprises, while the present tense mainly introduces the current situation of companies. The subject "we" expresses the willingness that employees and leaders as a whole are dedicated to serving consumers.

By analyzing the mood of the remaining texts in the English enterprise profile corpus, the results are as follows:

Table 19 Analysis of the Mood System in All Texts of English Enterprise Introduction

Text No.	Number of clauses	Type of mood			Subject			Tense		
		Indicative	Imperative	Interrogative	First person	Second person	Third person	Past tense	Present tense	Future tense
1	28	28	0	0	0	0	28	5	23	0

2	10	10	0	0	0	0	10	4	6	0
3	82	77	5	0	5	5	72	35	46	1
4	19	18	1	0	4	1	15	11	8	0
5	45	45	0	0	1	0	44	20	25	0
6	42	41	1	0	8	1	33	28	14	0
7	30	30	0	0	2	0	28	17	13	0
8	28	28	0	0	0	0	28	12	16	0
9	41	41	0	0	3	0	38	25	15	1
10	29	28	1	0	1	0	28	19	10	0
11	31	30	0	1	4	0	27	17	14	0
12	27	27	0	0	3	0	24	17	9	1
13	30	29	1	0	3	1	26	7	23	0
14	29	29	0	0	3	0	26	8	20	1
15	33	33	0	0	4	0	29	9	24	0
16	28	27	1	0	5	1	22	20	7	1
17	30	29	0	1	3	0	27	10	20	0
18	37	37	0	0	4	0	33	20	16	1
19	35	35	0	0	3	0	32	15	18	2
20	23	22	1	0	2	1	20	15	8	0
21	27	26	1	0	4	1	22	10	17	0
22	35	33	2	0	3	2	30	20	14	1
23	37	36	1	0	4	1	32	18	17	2
24	31	31	0	0	3	0	28	10	21	0
25	27	24	3	0	5	3	19	17	10	0
26	35	33	2	0	3	2	30	15	19	1
27	26	25	1	0	3	1	22	6	20	0
28	21	20	0	1	3	0	18	7	13	1
29	23	20	3	0	3	3	17	13	10	0
30	19	19	0	0	1	0	18	10	7	2
31	24	24	0	0	0	0	24	10	13	1
32	30	29	1	0	3	1	26	13	17	0
33	31	30	1	0	2	1	28	18	13	0

34	33	33	0	0	2	0	31	15	18	0
35	35	32	3	0	1	3	31	14	21	0
36	33	31	1	1	2	1	30	23	10	0
37	37	35	2	0	2	2	33	20	15	2
38	39	39	0	0	5	0	34	16	21	2
39	31	30	1	0	0	1	30	17	13	1
40	22	22	0	0	0	0	22	10	12	0

The distribution ratio of the three types of mood and their related person and tense parameters in the corpus of English corporate profiles is as follows:

Table 20 Analysis and Statistics of Mood System

	Total number of clauses	Type of mood			Subject			Tense		
		Indicative mood	Imperative mood	Interrogative mood	First person	Second person	Third person	Past tense	Present tense	Future tense
Total number	1253	1216	33	4	107	32	1115	596	637	21
%	100	97	2.7	0.3	8.5	2.6	88.9	47.5	50.8	1.7

By analyzing the above table, it is found that:

Mood type: there are 1253 clauses in the corpus, 1216 of which are declarative, 33 are imperative and 4 are interrogative.

The declarative mood is most commonly used in English corporate profiles, up to 97%, mainly introducing information about the company's products and services.

Imperative mood accounts for 2.7%, mainly used to persuade consumers to buy products or services, or to invite consumers to learn more about corporate culture and the company's products and services. For example:

Join us in our pursuit of happiness. (Text 6)

Keep up with college and community events here. **Visit** our blog to connect stay current on news and events both in the community and on campus. (Text 18)

The interrogative tone is rarely used in English company profiles, accounting for only 0.3%. Generally, self questioning and self answering are used to arouse consumer interest. For example:

Do you want to learn more about our company? Please click the website.(Text 6)

Has It Really Been That Long? (Text 7)

Subject choice: The third person pronoun accounts for the majority, 88.9%. The second person is the least, accounting for 2.6%, while the first person is in the middle, accounting for 8.5%. From the content referred to by these personal pronouns, the first person often uses the plural "we" which refer to employees and leaders as a whole, representing the entire company. The second person "you" mainly refers to consumers and potential consumers. The third-person pronoun refers to the company, the founder or employees, and leaders. For example:

We're one of the world's most recognizable brands of ice cream treats and the world's largest ice cream specialty chain. (Text 3)

You might be surprised where in the world you'll find us. We're one of the world's most recognizable brands of ice cream treats and the world's largest ice cream specialty chain! (Text 3)

Witnessing his son racing down the street after an ice cream truck, **the Chicago candy store owner** developed the DOVEBAR out of concern for his children's safety. (Text 1)

They started out in separate ventures at the advice of Irv's father. They had six stores between them. This concept eventually grew into Baskin-Robbins. (Text 3)

Tense: Present tense accounts for the most, up to 50.8%. The frequency of the use of past tense and present tense is basically the same, accounting for 47.5%. The percentage of future tense is the least, accounting for about 1.7%. From the content described by these tenses, the present tense is mainly used to describe the company's current situation or basic information such as product services, while the past tense mainly describes the company's entrepreneurial story and development history, and the future tense introduces the company's bright prospects and future to consumers. For example:

1980 ,Tom and Margaret Fell **moved** (past tense) to Drumlin Hall Farm with their two sons Jonathan and Graeme.(Text 8)

Cheshire Farm Ice Cream also **supplies** (present tense)over 900 pubs, restaurants, hotels, retail outlets throughout the North-West And nationwide through local wholesalers. (Text 8)

No matter where you are in the world, you **will**(future tense) find unparalleled quality and variety at every shop.(Text 3)

2) Modality System

As mentioned earlier, the interpersonal function of language is not only realized by the mood system, but also reflected by the modality system, which is divided into two parts: modalisation and modulation. When discussing possibility or frequency, the modalisation system is used; When discussing intentions, the modulation system is used. Table 21 shows a list of commonly used modal verb in Chinese and English modality systems.

Table 21 List of Chinese and English Modality Systems

Modal verb	Low	Middle	High	低	中	高
Affirmative	can, may, could	will, would, should	must, need, has to, need to	可能，可，能，能够	愿意，希望，要，想要	应，应该，必须，务必，应当
Negative	can't, may not, couldn't	will not, would not, should not	mustn't, needn't to, has not to	可能不，不会，无须，不能够	不愿意，不乐意，不想，不肯	不可能，不能，犯不着

The following table is the analysis and statistics on the use of modal verbs in the corpus of English corporate profiles.

Table 22 Distribution of Modal Verbs in English corporate profiles

Text No.	should	might(may)	could(can)	must	need	will(would)
1			√			
2			√			√
3	√					
4			√			

5						
6			√			
7			√			
8			√			√
9						
10			√			
11						
12			√			
13						
14			√			√
15						
16			√			
17						
18			√			
19						
20			√			
21						
22			√			
23						
24						√
25						
26						
27			√			√
28						
29						√
30			√			
31			√			
32			√			
33						
34						
35						√
36						
37						√
38			√			

39		√					
40							√

The frequency of use is as follows:

Table 23 Frequency of Modal Verbs Used in English corporate profiles

	Low		Middle		High		Sum
	might(may)	could(can)	should	will(would)	must	need	
Total	0	18	1	9	0	0	28
%	0	64.3	3.6	32.1	0	0	100

It can be seen from the above table that modal verbs are seldom used in English corporate profiles, with the highest frequency of "could(can)" and "will(would)".

3) Theme System

The textual function of language is realized by the theme system. As for clauses, from the perspective of information organization, they are divided into two parts: "theme" refers to known information, and clauses revolve around the theme; the expanded part is called "rheme" and refers to new information. Theme and rheme form a thematic structure. Theme is divided into single theme and multiple theme, including experiential theme, interpersonal theme, and textual theme. According to the relationship between theme and subject, theme can be further divided into marked theme and unmarked theme. The following is a random analysis of the thematic distribution of Text 24.

About Lotto Sport(http://www.lottosport.com/choose-country)

(1) [1] In June 1999 the Company was taken over by a group of local business people [2]who were already very active in the sports segment.

(2) [3] It was headed by Andrea Tomat, [4]who took on the role of President and CEO of the new company, [5]which was renamed Lotto Sport Italia S.P.A.

(3) [6] The new ownership's objective was to exploit the brand's strengths – dynamism, innovation, quality, Italian design and a real passion for sport – combined with its increasingly painstaking and effective customer service.

(4) [7] Today, the performance segment has been strengthened, in line with the new corporate mission.

(5) [8] Special focus is given to footwear and technical clothing for football and tennis, also supporting the brand's worldwide leadership with products [9]that are right on the cutting edge in terms of innovation and design.

(6) [10] In parallel, based on production, technical and stylistic know-how, an idea has been developed for men's and women's leisure clothing and footwear with a sport-inspired image and taste in terms of the selection of fabrics, colors and styles.

(7) [11] Technical underwear, home textiles, stationery, body care products, socks, eyewear and watches with Lotto branding are also manufactured and distributed under license by third-party companies.

Table 24 Theme Analysis of Text 24

Sentence No.	Clause No.	Theme System			Marked	Unmarked
		Textual theme	Interpersonal theme	Experiential theme		
(1)	[1]			In June 1999	√	
	[2]			who		√
(2)	[3]			It		√
	[4]			who		√
	[5]			which		√
(3)	[6]			The new ownership's objective		√
(4)	[7]			Today	√	
(5)	[8]			Special focus		√
	[9]			that		√
(6)	[10]	In parallel		Based on production, technical and stylistic know-how	√	

| (7) | [11] | | | Technical underwear, home textiles, stationery, body care products, socks, eyewear and watches with Lotto branding | | √ |

From the table, it can be seen that this English enterprise profile has a total of 11 thematic combinations, of which only 1 is a multiple theme and the rest are all single themes. There are three marked themes, with the remaining being unmarked themes.

The thematic analysis of all texts in the corpus is completed, and the thematic distribution is shown in the table below.

Table 25 Distribution of the Theme of English corporate profiles

Text No.	Multiple Theme	Single Theme	Marked Theme	Unmarked Theme
1	3	13	2	14
2	2	11	1	12
3	1	10	2	9
4	3	15	2	16
5	2	7	1	8
6	5	14	3	16
7	3	11	2	12
8	3	8	2	9
9	3	5	3	5
10	2	14	1	15
11	4	31	2	33
12	4	6	3	7
13	3	11	1	13
14	2	15	1	16
15	3	17	3	17
16	3	16	2	17

17	1	12	3	10
18	4	11	2	13
19	2	15	1	16
20	5	17	3	19
21	3	15	1	17
22	2	9	3	8
23	4	12	3	13
24	1	10	2	9
25	6	13	6	13
26	3	18	4	17
27	5	20	4	21
28	4	17	2	19
29	5	12	4	13
30	7	21	3	25
31	6	23	5	24
32	2	15	3	14
33	4	17	5	16
34	2	18	5	15
35	3	12	5	10
36	4	15	3	16
37	3	8	2	9
38	6	17	2	21
39	5	10	2	13
40	7	11	4	14
Total	140	552	108	584
%	20	80	15.6	84.4

From the above table, it can be seen that the single theme accounts for nearly 80% of the total number, while the multiple theme accounts for 20%. Among multiple themes, the subject is "textual theme+experiential theme". The marked theme accounts for 15.6% of the total, mainly involving the company's location and development status at different time periods. For example:

In the UK, Cream Carvel attract the more and more consumers. (Text 6)

In the 1960s, the branches of the company were established in other countries. (Text 12)

6.3.2 Verbal Features of Chinese Corporate Profiles
1) Transitivity system
Taking Text 3 as an example.

飞鹤乳业(http://www.feihe.com/)

(1)始**建**于1962年的飞鹤乳业，**专注**于婴幼儿奶粉行业50年，以全产业链模式，**创**优质产品、优质服务，**给予**中国宝宝有保障的爱。

(2)飞鹤乳业从美丽的"鹤城"齐齐哈尔**起飞**，迄今已**有**50年专业乳品制造历史。

(3)作为中国最早的奶粉生产企业之一，飞鹤乳业**打造**了一条从奶源到终端，完全自主掌控的全产业链，**成为**我国唯一拥有全产业链的婴幼儿奶粉企业。

(4)从**立足**于黑龙江，到**成为**遍及全国的知名品牌，飞鹤乳业**精进**不已，在资本市场也曾**激起**千层浪。

(5)2003年，飞鹤乳业正式**登陆**美国纳斯达克，**成为**中国第一家在美国上市的乳品企业。

(6)2009年，飞鹤乳业又成功**转战**纽交所主板，再次**成为**第一家且唯一一家在纽交所主板上市的中国乳企。

(7)上市后的飞鹤乳业，业务及品牌**发展**迅猛。

(8)目前，飞鹤**拥有**北京飞鹤生物科技公司、飞鹤克东分公司、飞鹤拜泉分公司、飞鹤甘南分公司、飞鹤齐市分公司、山西飞鹤三泰生物科技有限公司、飞鹤大豆科技公司、飞鹤廊坊分公司等8家子公司；

(9)在全国省会级城市**设有**24个销售分公司，6380多个销售网点；

(10)现**有**生产员工6000人，市场销售人员10000余人；

(11)**荣揽**"亚洲500强""中国驰名商标""中国名牌""中国著名畅销品牌"等多项殊荣。

(12)自身茁壮成长的同时，飞鹤乳业也在通过全产业链建设，**推动**行业发展。

(13)飞鹤全产业链**依托**得天独厚的自然资源，**实现**了从饲草种植、奶牛养殖、生产加工到终端销售及消费者服务的自主掌控，**确保**了最新鲜的奶源、最优质的原料、最先进的工艺、最专业的服务。

(14)**依托**北纬47度黄金奶源带的天赋资源，飞鹤以天然牧草精心**养护**名种荷斯坦奶牛，**撷取**100%原生态牧场奶，从源头**奠定**奶粉的金牌品质。

(15)在国际化样板工厂，通过2小时生态圈、湿法工艺等领先的生产管理和严格苛刻的检验程序层层**把关**,飞鹤**打造**了国际一流的生产和品控体系,**保障**了奶粉新鲜营养、安全如一。

(16)**汇聚**全球战略合作伙伴专业力量,飞鹤**成立**妈妈宝宝营养研究中心,**采用**全球顶级乳品原料,**开发**了最适合中国宝宝营养需求的科学配方。

(17)通过**开设** 400 服务热线、全国孕婴讲座,飞鹤为妈妈**提供**最贴心的服务,全程**护航**中国母婴。

(18)有专家**认为**,经过深耕细作,飞鹤的全产业链不仅**确保**了企业自身在三聚氰胺等奶粉安全事故中能**独善其身**,更为中国乳企**开创**了最佳的发展模式。

(19)2011 年,始终**专注**于研发的飞鹤乳业**承担**了国家 863 项目、科技部十二五项目,其科研实力**有目共睹**,**得到**业界肯定。

(20)目前,飞鹤**开发**了奶粉、豆奶粉、米粉、核桃粉、保健休闲食品等十大系列,近百种产品。

(21)其中,星飞帆**成为**国内第一款实现全面母乳化的配方奶粉,**引领**奶粉市场**步入**超高端阶段。

(22)长期以来,飞鹤乳业一直**致力**于为消费者**提供**安全优质的产品,使一"贯"好奶粉**有口皆碑**,同时,飞鹤也**不忘**践行企业社会责任,**引领**民族乳业发展,让爱与责任**同行** 50 年。

Table 26 Analysis of Types of Process in Text 3

Sentence No.	Process No.	Process Type	Process Verb
(1)	1	Material process	建
	2	Mental process	专注
	3	Material process	创
	4	Material process	给予
(2)	5	Material process	起飞
	6	Relational process	有
(3)	7	Material process	打造
	8	Relational process	成为
(4)	9	Material process	立足
	11	Relational process	成为
	12	Material process	精进
	13	Material process	激起
(5)	14	Material process	登陆
	15	Relational process	成为
(6)	16	Material process	转战

	17	Relational process	成为
(7)	18	Material process	发展
(8)	19	Relational process	拥有
(9)	20	Material process	设有
(10)	21	Relational process	有
(11)	22	Material process	揽
(12)	23	Material process	推动
(13)	24	Relational process	依托
	25	Relational process	实现
	26	Relational process	确保
(14)	27	Behavioral process	依托
	28	Material process	养护
	29	Material process	撷取
	30	Material process	奠定
(15)	31	Behavioral process	把关
	32	Material process	打造
	33	Behavioral process	保障
(16)	34	Material process	汇聚
	35	Material process	成立
	36	Material process	采用
	37	Material process	开发
(17)	38	Material process	开设
	39	Material process	提供
	40	Material process	护航
(18)	41	Relational process	认为
	42	Behavioral process	确保
	43	Behavioral process	独善其身
	44	Material process	开创
(19)	45	Mental process	专注
	46	Behavioral process	承担
	47	Behavioral process	有目共睹
	48	Material process	得到
(20)	49	Material process	开发
(21)	50	Relational process	成为
	51	Behavioral process	引领

	52	Behavioral process	步入
(22)	53	Behavioral process	致力
	54	Material process	提供
	55	Verbal process	有口皆碑
	56	Mental process	不忘
	57	Behavioral process	引领
	58	Behavioral process	同行

By analyzing types of process of the remaining text, the process distribution of all Chinese corporate profiles is shown in the table below:

Table 27 Distribution of Types of Process in Chinese corporate profiles

Text No.	Relational process	Material process	Mental process	Behavioral process	Verbal process	Existential process	Total
1	5	31	3	6	0	0	45
2	9	27	5	4	0	0	45
3	8	29	4	15	1	0	57
4	10	35	4	10	0	0	59
5	7	29	1	6	0	0	43
6	11	37	3	10	0	0	61
7	6	31	1	5	0	0	43
8	6	33	3	7	0	0	49
9	5	30	1	3	0	0	39
10	4	25	1	2	0	0	32
11	7	38	1	4	0	0	50
12	3	31	2	5	0	0	51
13	3	35	3	5	0	0	46
14	4	40	4	5	0	0	53
15	2	36	1	2	0	0	41
16	2	33	1	5	0	0	41
17	1	30	2	7	0	0	40
18	3	31	0	3	0	0	37
19	2	33	1	5	0	0	41
20	4	35	0	7	0	0	46
21	5	30	0	7	0	0	42
22	7	37	3	10	0	0	57

23	4	25	2	6	0	0	37
24	6	31	3	7	0	0	47
25	6	35	0	4	0	0	45
26	3	33	1	5	0	0	42
27	5	34	0	7	0	0	46
28	7	40	2	5	0	0	54
29	3	26	0	5	0	0	34
30	5	31	1	7	0	0	44
31	5	29	0	7	0	0	41
32	7	38	1	8	0	0	54
33	5	33	2	7	0	0	45
34	7	39	3	9	0	0	58
35	6	35	1	4	0	0	46
36	4	31	0	5	0	0	40
37	5	32	1	7	0	0	45
38	4	27	0	5	0	0	36
39	5	33	0	5	0	0	43
40	6	37	2	7	0	0	42

The ratio of different process types in the corpus is:

Table 28 Distribution Ratio of Process Type

	Relational process	Material process	Mental process	Behavioral process	Verbal process	Existential process	Sum
Sum	207	1305	63	243	1	0	1819
%	11.4	72	3.5	13	0	0	100

From the table, it is found that the type of material process is the most common and exceeds half, accounting for 72% of the total. In the Chinese enterprise profile, material processes are mainly used to describe the basic information of a company, its current status, and some honors it has received. For example:

为消费者**提供**安全、新鲜、营养、健康的乳制品是全体光明人的责任和追求。(Text 1)

坚持**发展**实体经济、发展先进制造业、**抢占**战略性新兴产业、积极发展商超零售业，在巩固饮料行业龙头地位的同时，逐步进军奶粉、机械、印刷、零售、奶牛养殖等新产业，实现多元化发展，向世界500强**进军**。(Text 8)

雅戈尔集团**创建**于1979年，经过32年的发展，逐步**确立**了以品牌服装为主业，涉足地产开

发、金融投资领域。(Text 18)

The relational process accounts for 11.5% of the total, which is similar to the 13% percentage of the behavioral process. The relational process mainly describes the company's current position in the same industry. For example:

作为中国最早的奶粉生产企业之一，飞鹤乳业打造了一条从奶源到终端，完全自主掌控的全产业链，成为我国唯一拥有全产业链的婴幼儿奶粉企业。(Text 3)
此外，还用来描述旗下品牌、分公司、员工、科技使用情况等，例如：
目前，伊利集团**拥有**液态奶、冷饮、奶粉、酸奶和原奶五大事业部，所属企业近百个，旗下有纯牛奶、乳饮料、雪糕、冰淇淋、奶粉、奶茶粉、酸奶、奶酪等1000多个产品品种。(Text 2)

Behavioral processes are often used for certain behaviors that lie between material and mental processes, such as:

集团控股子公司维维食品饮料股份有限公司于2000年在上交所成功上市，秉承"健康生活，欢乐维维"的理念，**致力**于打造"国际化、大型、综合性"食品企业。(Text 7)
公司**奉行**"与时俱进、勇于探索"的核心价值观，秉承"管理规范化、经营连锁化、品牌国际化、信息网络化"的"新四化"经营理念，形成包括夹克、T恤、衬衫、毛衫、牛仔、西服、休闲鞋、皮具及服饰配件等九大系列在内的完善的服饰产品系统，提供给消费者一条龙的服务体系。(Text 17)

As for the mental process, the existential process and the verbal process, they are rarely referred to in Chinese corporate profiles. The mental process involves providing consumers with product service quality assurance or development, business philosophy, etc. For example:

九牧王品牌自推出以来，公司管理层始终**视**高品质为企业的立命之本。（文本 14）
维维的发展，一直**恪守**着"追求卓越"的企业精神，把产品质量视作企业的生命。（文本 7）

2) Mood System

Text 5 is taken as an example to analyze the mood system.

关于雨润（http://www.yurun.com.hk/yurunfood/about.html）

（1）雨润集团是一家集食品、物流、商业、旅游、房地产、金融和建筑等七大产业于一体的中国500强企业，[2]创建于1993年。

（2）集团总部位于江苏省南京市，[4]下属子（分）公司两百多家，遍布全国三十个省、直辖市和自治区。

（3）[5]2011年，集团员工总数近11万人，实现销售总额907亿元，[6]生猪屠宰产能达4500万头，稳居世界首位，[7]"雨润牌"低温肉制品连续十四年销量位列国内第一。

（4）[8]目前，在中国企业500强中排名128位，中国制造业500强第56位，中国民营企业500强第5位，中国肉食品加工业第1位。

（5）[9]2005年10月3日，雨润集团的部分食品业务在香港联合交易所成功上市。

（6）[10]集团旗下已有雨润食品（1068.HK）、南京中商（600280.SH）两家上市公司。

Table 29 Analysis of Mood System in Text 5

Sentence No.	Clause No.	Subject	Infinite	Type of Mood
(1)	[1]	雨润集团	是	Indicative mood
	[2]	(雨润集团)	创建	Indicative mood
(2)	[3]	集团总部	位于	Indicative mood
	[4]	分公司	遍布	Indicative mood
(3)	[5]	(公司)	实现	Indicative mood
	[6]	生猪屠宰产能	稳居	Indicative mood
	[7]	销量	位列	Indicative mood
(4)	[8]	(公司)	排名	Indicative mood
(5)	[9]	部分食品业务	上市	Indicative mood
(6)	[10]	集团	有	Indicative mood

(Due to the linguistic characteristics of Chinese, verbs do not change due to changes in tense and voice, so tenses are omitted in the analysis of mood systems.)

By analyzing Chinese enterprise profile of Text 5, it can be seen that all 10 clauses adopt an indicative mood, with basic information about the company and the subject of the sentences being "company" or "group".

After conducting the above analysis on the remaining corpora, the mood of all 40 Chinese corporate profiles in the corpus is obtained:

Table 30 The Mood System of Chinese corporate profiles

Text No.	Number of Clauses	Type of Mood			Subject		
		Indicative mood	Imperative mood	Interrogative mood	First person	Second person	Third person
1	35	35	0	0	0	0	35
2	38	38	0	0	0	0	38
3	45	45	0	0	0	0	45
4	33	33	0	0	0	0	33
5	10	10	0	0	0	0	10
6	57	56	1	0	3	0	54
7	43	43	0	0	0	0	43
8	16	16	0	0	0	0	16
9	53	53	0	0	0	0	53
10	47	46	1	0	0	0	47
11	12	12	0	0	1	0	11
12	31	30	1	0	0	0	31
13	55	55	0	0	0	0	55
14	53	53	0	0	0	0	53
15	27	27	0	0	0	0	27
16	63	62	1	0	0	0	63
17	27	26	1	0	1	1	25
18	36	36	0	0	0	0	36
19	37	37	0	0	0	0	37
20	39	39	0	0	0	0	39
21	35	34	1	0	3	1	31
22	26	26	0	0	0	0	26
23	31	31	0	0	1	0	30
24	27	25	2	0	4	1	22
25	33	32	1	0	0	0	33
26	35	35	0	0	0	0	35
27	29	29	0	0	0	0	29
28	28	28	0	0	0	0	28
29	32	32	0	0	0	0	32
30	25	25	0	0	0	0	25

31	31	31	0	0	0	0	31
32	34	34	0	0	3	0	31
33	32	32	0	0	2	0	30
34	28	26	2	0	0	1	27
35	31	30	1	0	0	2	29
36	38	38	0	0	0	0	38
37	24	24	0	0	1	0	23
38	27	27	0	0	3	0	24
39	25	25	0	0	0	0	25
40	31	31	0	0	0	0	31

The distribution ratio of different types of mood in the corpus is:

Table 31 Distribution ratio of mood system

	Number of clauses	Type of Mood			Subject		
		Indicative mood	Imperative mood	Interrogative mood	First person	Second person	Third person
Sum	1359	1347	12	0	22	6	1331
%	100	99.1	0.9	0	1.6	0.4	98

In terms of mood types, it can be seen from the above table that the indicative mood is up to 99%, the imperative mood is nearly 1%, and there is no the interrogative mood. The indicative tone is mainly used to state facts, and the content involved in a company introduction is mainly to state the basic facts or situation of the enterprise or company. Imperative mood is often used to describe the vision of an enterprise or company, to express the company's enthusiasm towards and care for consumers, and attract consumers' attention. For example:

希望公司在更宽广的道路上前行！（Text 10）
在广大消费者的支持下，公司一定有更美好的未来！（Text 19）

In terms of subjects, the first person subject is 1.6%, the second person subject is less than 1%, and the third-person pronoun subject is as high as 98%. Using the third person as the subject expresses a more objective attitude to consumers. However, if you blindly introduce the company and brand from a condescending perspective, there is a lack of interaction and interpersonal significance.

3) Modality System

Through observation and statistics, the use of modal verbs in Chinese corporate profiles is as follows:

Table 32 Distribution of Modal Verbs in Chinese corporate profiles

Text No.	可能(May)	能够(Can)	希望、将会 (Hope,will)	（想）要 (Want)	应该 (Should)	必须 (Must)
1						
2						
3		√				
4						
5		√				
6		√				√
7						
8						
9		√				
10						
11						
12						
13						
14		√				
15						
16						
17			√			
18						
19						
20		√				
21						
22		√	√			√
23						
24						
25		√				
26						

27						
28						
29						
30						
31	√					
32		√				
33						
34						
35						
36		√				
37		√				
38						
39						
40						

The distribution frequency is:

Table 33 Distribution Frequency of Modal Verbs

	Low		Middle		High		Sum
	may	can	hope	want	should	must	
Total	1	11	2	0	0	2	16
%	6.25	68.75	12.5	0	0	12.5	100

It can be seen that modal verbs nost commonly used in Chinese corporate profiles, such as "can", "hop", "must" and "will", which to a certain extent expresses the confidence of enterprises and promises to consumers. The great number of modal verbs is meant to show good prospects of enterprises.

4) Theme System

Taking Text 12 as an example.

关于歌莉娅(http://www.goelia.com.cn/about)

(1) [1]歌莉娅女性时尚服饰品牌，诞生于1995年，[2]品牌的创办企业——广州市格风服饰有限公司，位于广州市白云区的现代化工业园1998年2月28日奠基成立。

(2) [3]公司一直以把最好与人分享的精神，以筑梦踏实的态度贯彻在企业和品牌的经营中。

(3) [4]公司集女装研发、生产、专卖销售为一体，是专业生产销售女性时尚服饰的大型综合性企业，拥有"歌莉娅""格风""Orange桔子"三个注册品牌。

(4) [5]主打品牌歌莉娅以环球之旅采撷灵感，品牌首创旅行文化、花舍文化等概念引领着行业时尚、清新的风潮。

(5) [6]于2009年6月30日诞生在广州市北京路225号、一栋传承岭南文化的老楼里的"歌莉娅225"，更是融汇歌莉娅的品牌和独树一帜的旅游+花文化于一体。

(6) [7]"歌莉娅225"的建立意味着歌莉娅由女性服饰品牌走向多元文化品牌，代表着新纪元的品牌远景。

(7) [8]歌莉娅不再只是装扮女孩的外表，更关注她的内心；

(8) [9]在品牌自我成长的过程中，带动消费者的集体成长，[10]并致力于成为美好生活的引领者和记录者，[11]从而更从容优雅地面对世界。

(9) [12]它不仅是推广和展现歌莉娅品牌文化及"环球之旅"的一个更立体和多元化的平台，[13]也是时尚和感性的里程碑。

(10) [14]经过十余年的发展，格风公司将占地近4万平方米的大型花园式工业园打造成一个多次获得国际及亚太地区设计奖项的时尚基地。

(11) [15]由2千多名员工组成的专业设计、营销和生产队伍，[16]并拥有先进的技术研发能力、现代化的物流和质检中心以及强大的电子商务平台，[17]同时也积淀了浓厚的企业文化："厚德、革新、健行"！

(12) [18]近年来，公司在品牌整体形象、企业与品牌的知名度、美誉度和企业综合实力上通过与国际级团队的合作实现迅速提升，[19]目前已在国内各大城市及挪威、科威特、新加坡、埃及等多个国家开设了歌莉娅旗舰店和形象店。

(13) [20]公司已经准备在2012年开始陆续推出新系列和新品牌，进一步扩大市场占有率。

The analysis of the theme system of this text is expressed as follows:

Table 34 Theme System Analysis of Text 12

Sentence Number	Clause Number	Them			Marked theme	Unmarked theme
		Discourse theme	Interpersonal theme	Experiential theme		
(1)	[1]			歌莉娅女性时尚服饰品牌		√
	[2]			品牌的创办企业		√
(2)	[3]			公司		√
(3)	[4]			公司		√
(4)	[5]			主打品牌歌莉娅		√
(5)	[6]			于2009年6月30	√	

				日		
(6)	[7]			"歌莉娅225"的建立		√
(7)	[8]			歌莉娅		√
(8)	[9]			在品牌自我成长的过程中	√	
	[10]	并		（歌莉娅）		√
	[11]	从而		（歌莉娅）		√
(9)	[12]			它		√
	[13]	也		（它）		√
(10)	[14]			经过十余年的发展	√	
(11)	[15]			2千多名员工		√
	[16]	并		（歌莉娅）		√
	[17]	同时		（歌莉娅）		√
(12)	[18]			近年来	√	
(13)	[19]			目前	√	
	[20]			公司		√

From this, it can be seen that there are a total of 20 thematic combinations in the profile of "About Goelia", of which 15 are single themes and 5 are marked themes, mainly including time adverbs and prepositional phrases, all of which are discourse themes. There is no interpersonal theme, and the experiential theme often uses "company" and rarely uses pronouns.

The thematic systems of the remaining texts are analyzed by using the same method, with the results shown in Table 35.

Table 35 Distribution of Theme Systems in Chinese Corporate Profiles

Text No.	Multiple theme	Single theme	Marked theme	Unmarked theme
1	2	20	5	17
2	3	16	2	17
3	3	17	4	16
4	1	19	3	17
5	3	21	2	22
6	3	23	4	22
7	1	28	3	26
8	1	17	3	15
9	4	25	3	26
10	2	23	3	22

11	1	19	2	18
12	5	15	5	15
13	2	23	4	21
14	3	25	4	24
15	4	21	2	23
16	5	21	4	22
17	3	24	2	25
18	3	21	1	23
19	4	22	3	23
20	3	21	1	23
21	4	23	1	26
22	4	25	3	26
23	2	21	5	18
24	3	20	2	21
25	1	19	3	17
26	3	17	2	18
27	2	21	5	18
28	4	23	2	25
29	4	25	1	28
30	2	24	3	23
31	2	21	2	21
32	3	19	4	18
33	3	23	1	25
34	1	17	3	15
35	1	22	3	20
36	1	19	2	18
37	3	17	4	16
38	2	21	1	22
39	4	22	1	25
40	1	24	1	24
Total	106	844	109	841
%	11.2	88.8	11.5	88.5

From the above table, it can be seen that the single theme accounts for nearly 89% of the total themes, while multiple themes only account for 11.2%. Among the multiple themes, 74 combinations are "discourse theme+experiential theme", and another 32 combinations are "interpersonal theme+experiential theme". The combination of multiple themes is also relatively simple, involving discourse themes such as "and", "also", "thus", and "but". The interpersonal theme mainly consists of time adverbs and prepositional phrases. From the perspective of the entire discourse, Chinese corporate profiles mainly use relatively short and small sentences, while English corporate profiles often use relatively long and complex sentences or subordinate clauses to express themselves.

Among the experiential themes, the marked theme accounts for 11.5%, emphasizing key factors related to the enterprise and company. The content mainly involves the company's geographical location and different achievements at different stages of development, such as:

于2009年6月30日诞生在广州市北京路225号、一栋传承岭南文化的老楼里的"歌莉娅225", 更是融汇歌莉娅的品牌和独树一帜的旅游+花文化于一体。(Text 12)

经过十余年的发展，格凤公司将占地近4万平方米的大型花园式工业园打造成一个多次获得国际及亚太地区设计奖项的时尚基地。(Text 12)

6.3.3 Linguistic Features of English Translation of Chinese Corporate Profiles

1) Transitivity System

The translation text corresponding to Chinese corporate profiles Text 3 from the English translation corpus is selected for analysis.

About Feihe (http://ady.feihe.com/about_us.html)

(1) Founded in 1962, Feihe is one of the leading producers and distributors of premium infant formula, milk powder, soybean, rice cereal and walnut products in China.

(2) We were incorporated in the State of Utah on December 31, 1985.

(3) Effective May 7, 2003, we acquired 100% of the issued and outstanding capital stock of American Flying Crane, or AFC, a Delaware corporation that operates a dairy business in China through various subsidiaries.

(4) In connection with that acquisition, we changed our name to American Dairy, Inc.

(5) With nearly five decades of expertise in milk product development, ADI FEIHE

produces a widely diversified menu of nutritious products in addition to standard fresh milk production.

(6) Today, we own various subsidiaries in the PRC that operate our business, including: Heilongjiang Feihe Dairy Co., Limited, or Feihe Dairy, which produces, packages and distributes milk powder and other dairy products;

(7) Gannan Flying Crane Dairy Products Co., Limited, or Gannan Feihe, which produces milk products;

(8) Shanxi Feihe santai Biotechnology Scientific and Commercial Co., Limited, or Shanxi Feihe, which produces walnut and soybean products;

(9) Langfang Flying Crane Dairy Products Co., Limited, or Langfang Feihe, which packages and distributes finished products;

(10) Heilongjiang Aiyingquan International Trading Co., Limited, or Aiyingquan, which markets and distributes water and cheese, specifically marketed for consumption by children;

(11) Heilongjiang Flying Crane Trading Co., Limited, or Feihe Trading, which sells milk and soybean related products;

(12) Qiqihaer Feihe Soybean Co., Limited, or Feihe Soybean, which manufactures and distributes soybean products;

(13) and Beijing Feihe Biotechnology Scientific and Commercial Co., Limited, or Beijing Feihe, which markets and distributes dairy products.

(14) We believe the market for dairy products in China;

(15) particularly the market for high quality infant milk formula and other dairy products is growing.

(16) Our growth strategy involves increasing market share during this growth phase.

(17) To implement this strategy, we plan to:

(18) Strengthen distribution logistics in strategic PRC markets.

(19) We plan to focus on improving sales at existing sales points, leveraging our extensive distribution network to generate revenues in a cost-effective manner.

(20) Our distribution network has grown in first-tier markets in the PRC, including Beijing, Shanghai, Guangzhou, Shenzhen and other major second and third-tier cities in the Pearl River Delta.

(21) Our extensive distribution network, which reaches many provincial capital and sub-provincial cities, has special channels into first-tier markets that we plan to expand.

(22) We believe that improving our distribution logistics in our network is an important driver of our gross margins.

(23)Strengthen our premium quality rand awareness.

(24)We believe that our products enjoy a reputation for high quality among those familiar with them, and our products routinely pass government and internal quality inspections.

(25)We have increased our advertising expenses and plan to continue advertising on influential provincial stations in China, in order to market our products as premium and super-premium products.

(26)We believe many consumers in China tend to regard higher prices as indicative of higher quality and higher nutritional value, and as a result consumers with higher disposable incomes are increasingly inclined to purchase higher priced products, particularly in the areas of infant formula and nutritional products.

(27) Maintaining quality through world-class production processes.

(28) We believe we can maintain our production of high quality dairy products by continuing to source high quality milk through exclusive contracts with the Dairy Farms and other dairy farmers, expanding our company-owned collection.

The above analysis is presented in a table as follows:

Table 36 Process Type Analysis of the English Translation of "Feihe Dairy"

Sentence No.	Process No.	Type of Process	Process
(1)	1	Material process	Founded
	2	Relational process	is
(2)	3	Material process	were incorporated
(3)	4	Material process	acquired
	5	Material process	operates
(4)	6	Material process	changed
(5)	7	Material process	produces
(6)	8	Relational process	own
	9	Material process	operate
	10	Material process	produces
	11	Material process	packages
	12	Material process	distributes
(7)	13	Material process	produces

(8)	14	Material process	produces
(9)	15	Material process	packages
	16	Material process	distributes
(10)	17	Material process	markets
	18	Material process	distributes
(11)	19	Material process	sells
(12)	20	Material process	manufactures
	21	Material process	distributes
(13)	22	Material process	markets
	23	Material process	distributes
(14)	24	Mental process	believe
(15)	25	Behavioral process	is growing
(16)	26	Mental process	involves
(17)	27	Mental process	plan
(18)	28	Material process	strengthen
(19)	29	Mental process	plan
	30	Material process	leveraging
(20)	31	Behavioral process	has grown
(21)	32	Behavioral process	reach
	33	Relational process	has
	34	Mental process	plan
(22)	35	Mental process	believe
	36	Relational process	is
(23)	37	Material process	strengthen
(24)	38	Mental process	believe
	39	Mental process	enjoy
	40	Material process	pass
(25)	41	Material process	have increased
	42	Mental process	plan
	43	Material process	market
(26)	44	Mental process	believe
	45	Mental process	tend
	46	Mental process	inclined

		Behavioral process	maintaining
(27)	47	Behavioral process	maintaining
(28)	48	Mental process	believe
	49	Behavioral process	maintain
	50	Material process	expanding

The process analysis of the remaining texts in the corpus is completed by using the same method, and the results are as follows:

Table 37　Distribution of Process Types in English Translation of Chinese corporate profiles

Text No.	Relational process	Material process	Mental process	Behavioral process	Verbal process	Existential process	Total number
1	5	21	3	3	0	0	32
2	7	25	1	2	0	0	35
3	5	28	12	5	0	0	50
4	5	27	1	3	0	0	36
5	10	30	1	3	0	1	45
6	6	32	3	5	0	0	46
7	10	35	2	6	0	0	53
8	8	33	4	5	0	0	50
9	3	35	2	4	0	0	44
10	3	30	1	7	0	0	41
11	4	27	2	5	0	0	38
12	3	24	2	3	0	0	32
13	5	29	2	5	0	0	41
14	7	31	1	3	0	0	42
15	5	26	2	3	0	0	36
16	3	34	2	4	0	0	43
17	4	29	2	1	0	0	36
18	3	35	3	3	0	0	44
19	3	29	1	4	0	0	37
20	5	38	3	7	0	0	53
21	5	37	2	6	0	1	51
22	8	35	2	9	0	2	56
23	5	25	2	6	0	1	39
24	6	35	3	5	0	0	49

25	6	23	0	7	0	0	36
26	3	28	1	6	0	0	38
27	3	33	0	5	0	1	42
28	5	30	2	7	0	1	45
29	7	36	0	5	0	0	48
30	4	23	1	3	0	1	32
31	6	30	0	5	0	1	42
32	5	28	1	7	0	0	41
33	8	35	2	6	0	0	51
34	4	30	3	5	0	0	42
35	8	35	1	7	0	0	51
36	6	33	0	6	0	1	46
37	5	29	1	3	0	1	39
38	4	30	0	4	0	0	38
39	5	25	0	5	0	0	35
40	7	37	2	4	0	0	50

According to statistics, the distribution ratios of different process types are:

Table 38 Distribution Ratio of Process Types in English Translation of Chinese corporate profiles

	Relational process	Material process	Mental process	Behavioral process	Verbal process	Existential process	Sum
Total	214	1215	73	192	0	11	1705
%	12.5%	71.3%	4.3%	11.3%	0	0.6	100%

From the research results of the corpus of English translation of Chinese corporate profiles, it can be seen that material processes are also the most widely used, with a percentage as high as 71.3%. After studying the translated texts, it is found that they correspond closely to the Chinese company profiles, so the distribution and percentage of process types are also very similar to the situation in the Chinese corpus. For example:

We were **incorporated** in the State of Utah on December 31, 1985. (Text 3)

In connection with that acquisition, we **changed** our name to American Dairy, Inc. (Text 3)

The relational process accounts for 12.5% of the total, while the behavioral process accounts for 11.3%. The percentage of both is almost the same. For example:

Relational process:

Feihe **is** one of the leading producers and distributors of premium infant formula, milk powder, soybean, rice cereal and walnut products in China. (Text 3)

Today, we **own** various subsidiaries in the PRC that operate our business, including: Heilongjiang Feihe Dairy Co., Limited, or Feihe Dairy, which produces, packages and distributes milk powder and other dairy products. (Text 3)

Behavioral process:

Our extensive distribution network **reaches** many provincial capital and sub-provincial cities. (Text 3)

Our distribution network **has grown** in first-tier markets in the PRC, including Beijing, Shanghai, Guangzhou, Shenzhen and other major second and third-tier cities in the Pearl River Delta. (Text 3)

The psychological process only accounts for 4.3%, mainly involving the company's commitments and guarantees. For example:

We **believe** that our products enjoy a reputation for high quality among those familiar with them, and our products routinely pass government and internal quality inspections. (Text 3)

The company **plans** to focus on improving sales at existing sales points.(Text 3)

2) Mood System

The English translation of text 5 and its corresponding Chinese profile are chosen for analyzsis of the mood system.

About Yurun(http://www.yurun.com.hk/en/yurunfood/about.html）

(1) [1]Yurun Group Co. Ltd, headquartered in Nanjing, Jiangsu Province, China, [2] is one of China's Top 500 enterprises with the business areas of food processing, real estate, tourism, trade & commerce and logistics.

(2) [3] It has nearly 100 subsidiaries and branch companies [4] located in more than 28 provinces, municipalities and autonomous regions, such as Jiangsu, Anhui, Beijing and Shanghai.

(3) [5] The total number of employees has reached 43000.

(4) [6] In 2006, Yurun was ranked the124th among China's Top 500 enterprises, the 56th in China's manufacturing industry, and the 7th amongChina's

Top 500 privately-owned companies.

(5) [7] On October 3, 2005, China Yurun Food Co., Ltd., one of the main food producers of Yurun Group, got successfully listed on Hong Kong StockExchange Market, [8]thus making an access to overseas capital.

(6) [9] Till the present, Yurun boasts 3 listed companies: Yurun Food (Stock symbol: 1068HK), china Power New Energy (0735.HK) and Nanjing Central Emporium.

The above analysis is presented in the table as follows:

Table 39 Analysis of Mood System in Text 5

Sentence No.	Clause No.	Subject	Infinite	Tense	Mood System
(1)	[1]	Yurun Group Co. Ltd	(is) headquartered	Present	Indicative mood
	[2]	Yurun Group Co. Ltd	is	Present	Indicative mood
(2)	[3]	It	has	Present	Indicative mood
	[4]	100 subsidiaries and branch companies	(is) located	Present	Indicative mood
(3)	[5]	The total number of employees	has reached	Present	Indicative mood
(4)	[6]	Yurun	was ranked	Past	Indicative mood
(5)	[7]	Yurun	got	Past	Indicative mood
	[8]	Yurun	(is) making	Present	Indicative mood
(6)	[9]	Yurun	boasts	Present	Indicative mood

From the English translation of Text 5, it can be seen that there are a total of 9 clauses, the main content of which is the basic information of the company, which corresponds to the introduction of the Chinese "Yurun Group". The only difference is that in terms of the use of verbs, Text 5 mainly uses the present tense, which appears 7 times in total, while the past tense tense only appears 2 times. This is because Text 5 mainly introduces the current situation of the company, and seldom talks about the development and entrepreneurial history of the company.

The mood analysis of the remaining texts is completed by using the same method, and the results are as follows:

Table 40 Distribution of Mood System in English Translation of corporate profiles

	Number of Clauses	Type of Mood			Subject			Tense		
		Indicative	Imperative	Interrogative	First person	Second person	Third person	Past	Present	Future
1	33	33	0	0	0	0	33	10	22	1
2	35	35	0	0	0	0	35	3	31	1
3	43	43	0	0	0	0	43	4	37	2
4	30	30	0	0	0	0	30	3	26	1
5	9	9	0	0	0	0	9	2	7	0
6	55	54	1	0	3	0	52	5	50	0
7	41	41	0	0	0	0	41	3	37	1
8	18	18	0	0	0	0	18	1	16	1
9	50	50	0	0	0	0	50	3	45	2
10	45	44	1	0	0	0	45	5	39	1
11	15	15	0	0	1	0	14	3	12	0
12	30	30	0	0	0	0	30	8	20	2
13	55	55	0	0	0	0	55	5	48	2
14	50	50	0	0	0	0	50	7	40	3
15	30	30	0	0	0	0	30	5	23	2
16	62	61	1	0	0	0	62	9	50	3
17	26	25	1	0	1	1	24	4	20	2
18	35	35	0	0	0	0	35	4	29	2
19	36	36	0	0	0	0	36	3	32	1
20	40	40	0	0	0	0	40	4	34	2
21	37	36	1	0	3	1	33	5	29	3
22	35	35	0	0	0	0	35	3	31	1

	Total	Indicative	Imperative	Interrogative	First person	Second person	Third person	Past	Present	Future
23	40	40	0	0	1	0	39	7	31	2
24	33	32	1	0	4	1	28	9	24	0
25	26	26	0	0	0	0	26	5	20	1
26	23	23	0	0	0	0	23	8	14	1
27	34	34	0	0	0	0	34	6	25	3
28	35	35	0	0	0	0	35	8	25	2
29	36	36	0	0	0	0	36	9	25	2
30	33	33	0	0	0	0	33	10	22	1
31	34	34	0	0	0	0	34	7	24	3
32	29	29	0	0	3	0	26	8	20	1
33	33	33	0	0	2	0	31	5	27	1
34	32	31	1	0	0	1	31	8	23	1
35	27	25	2	0	0	2	25	9	16	2
36	26	26	0	0	0	0	26	7	19	0
37	22	22	0	0	1	0	21	4	17	1
38	25	25	0	0	3	0	22	7	17	1
39	21	21	0	0	0	0	21	8	11	2
40	23	23	0	0	0	0	23	9	13	1

The distribution ratio of different types of mood is:

Table 41 Distribution Ratio of Mood System in English Translation

	Total number of clauses	Type of Mood			Subject			Tense		
		Indica-tive	Impera-tive	Interro-gative	First person	Second person	Third person	Past	Present	Future
Sum	1342	1333	9	0	22	6	1314	233	1051	58
%	100	99.3	0.7	0	1.6	0.4	98	17.4	78.3	4.3

From the above table, we find that:

Mood: There are 1342 clauses in the corpus of English translation, of which 1333 are indicative and 9 are imperative mood.

Subject: Only 22 clauses use the first person as the subject, while the number of third-person subjects is up to 1314, which means that a total of 1336 clauses use the company as the subject, while only 6 clauses use the second person, where the second-person refers to potential consumers.

Tense: The present tense is the most widely used, accounting for 78.3% of the total number of clauses, followed by the past tense tense, accounting for 17.4% of the total, and the future tense is rarely used, accounting for only 4.3%. For example:

The company **will** step into a brand new period.(Text 8)

3) Modality System

The use of modal verb in the English translation of the Chinese corporate profiles is observed as follows:

Table 42 Distribution of Modal Verbs

Text No.	should	might(may)	could(can)	must	need	will(would)
1						
2						
3						
4			√			
5						
6						√
7			√			
8						
9						
10						
11			√			√
12						
13						
14						
15			√			
16						
17						
18						
19						
20						√
21						
22			√			

23							
24							
25		√					
26				√			
27							
28				√			
29							
30				√			
31							
32							
33							
34							
35		√					
36							√
37				√			
38							
39				√			
40							

The frequency of the use of modal verb is:

Table 43 Frequency of Modal Verbs

	Low		Middle		High		Sum
	might(may)	could(can)	should	will(would)	must	need	
Total	2	10	0	4	0	0	16
%	12.5	62.5	0	25	0	0	100

From this, it can be seen that in the English translation of Chinese corporate profiles, the most commonly used ones are could (can), will (would), might (may), etc.

3) Theme System

The English translation text corresponding to Chinese company introduction Text 12 are selected and a thematic system analysis on it is conducted.

ABOUT GOELIA(http://www.goelia.com.cn/en/about)
(1) [1] GOELIA is founded in 1995, more than 16 years ago.
(2) [2] We are a ladies' fashion brand with headquarters in China.

(3) [3] To discover, to live and to share a fashionable and healthy lifestyle with our customers is our vision.

(4) [4] GOELIA has built-up and continuously expanded our customer base by offering trendy products with limitless styling possibilities, rest-assuring quality, reasonable pricing and easily accessible sales networks.

(5) [5] Now we have more than 500 shops all over China covering more than 200 cities.

(6) [6] We also have shops in Norway, Egypt, Kuwait, Syria, Singapore, and Indonesia.

(7) [7] Most of our customers are in their mid-twenties to early-thirties,
[8] who are starting their very important era in both their personal and professional life,
[9] during which values and lifestyle are cultivated.

(8) [10] GOELIA is aiming to be an important partner of our customers in the grooming of their personal styles, both in fashion and in everyday life.

(9) [11] We believe that [12]sharing our experiences in travel is a good way to communicate our values and insights.

(10) [13] We have started our "World Tour" more than 10 years ago and have just completed the 24th stop for 2011Winter (Edinburgh of Scotland).

(11) [14] Since 2002, our brand will choose a city as the "muse" of a particular season and fuse the inspirations from this "muse" city into the upcoming fashion trend.

(12) [15] During the journeys, we try to discover the beauty of the cities through the eye of GOELIA.

(13) [16] Products and promotions are then evolved.

(14) [17] GOELIA is offering a brand experience [18]that is not only trendy, but also with stories and perspectives. (15)[19] "Discover more, live more" is the best description of our brand philosophy.

Present in a table as follows:

Sentence No.	Clause No.	Subject			Marked Theme	Unmarked Theme
		Discourse theme	Interpersonal theme	Experiential theme		
(1)	[1]			GOELIA		√
(2)	[2]			We		√
(3)	[3]			To discover	√	

(4)	[4]			GOELIA		√
(5)	[5]			Now	√	
(6)	[6]			We		√
(7)	[7]			Most of our customers		√
	[8]			who		√
	[9]			during which		√
(8)	[10]			GOELIA		√
(9)	[11]			We		√
	[12]			sharing our experiences in travel		√
(10)	[13]			We		√
(11)	[14]			Since 2002	√	
(12)	[15]			During the journeys	√	
(13)	[16]			Products and promotions		√
(14)	[17]			GOELIA		√
	[18]			that		√
(15)	[19]			"Discover more, live more"		√

From the above table, it can be seen that there are a total of 19 thematic combinations, all of which are single themes. The four marked themes are all time adverbs.

The results of thematic analysis of all English translated texts are as follows:

Table 45 Distribution of Theme System in Texts of English Translation

Text No.	Multiple Themes	Single Theme	Marked Theme	Unmarked Theme
1	3	17	4	16
2	2	19	3	18
3	5	17	4	18
4	3	15	5	13
5	1	16	1	16
6	3	20	2	21
7	3	19	2	20
8	1	17	3	15
9	4	20	2	22
10	2	19	3	18
11	4	15	3	16

12	0	19	4	15
13	3	17	5	15
14	3	15	5	13
15	5	19	3	21
16	2	20	3	19
17	2	17	3	16
18	1	15	1	15
19	3	17	2	18
20	4	21	3	22
21	3	15	3	15
22	4	21	5	20
23	2	20	2	20
24	2	22	4	20
25	4	19	5	18
26	4	15	5	14
27	5	17	4	18
28	3	19	3	19
29	5	21	4	22
30	4	22	5	21
31	3	23	5	21
32	3	25	4	24
33	3	18	4	17
34	2	21	3	20
35	2	19	3	18
36	2	21	1	22
37	2	15	3	14
38	1	17	2	16
39	1	20	2	19
40	1	22	2	21
Sum	110	746	130	726
%	12.9	87.1	15.2	84.8

From the above table, it can be seen that the proportion of multiple themes is 12.9%, with the subject being the "discourse theme+experiential theme", 7 being the "interpersonal theme + experiential theme",and only 5 being the "discourse theme + interpersonal theme + experiential theme". The 103 discourse themes are mainly composed of words such as but, while, however, so, etc., while the 12 interpersonal themes are mainly composed of course, only, then, just, etc.

Among the experiential themes, the marked theme accounts for 15.2%. For example:

As a leading enterprise of agricultural industrialization in China, Bright Dairy & Food Co., Ltd has always committed to the corporate mission of "to innovate life and share health".(Text 1)

Established in 1987, Hangzhou Wahaha Group Co., Ltd has developed into China's largest and most profitable beverage company. (Text 8)

6.4 Corpus-based Contrastive Analysis of Corporate Profiles

The above analyzes the schematic structure and presentation style of all texts in the the corpora of English, Chinese, and English translation of Chinese corporate profiles from the perspective of genre analysis, and summarizes their respective characteristics. The following is a comparison of structures and linguistic features (vocabulary grammar) of these texts to identify similarities and differences, thus providing a basis for evaluating the quality of translated texts and how to improve the translation in the next section.

6.4.1 Comparison of Schematic Structure of Three Types of Texts (GSP Model)

1) Comparison between English and Chinese corporate profiles

Looking back at the structural features and GSP model of English and Chinese texts based on the English and Chinese enterprise profile corpora, it is known that the structural features of both are as follows:

Table 46 Distribution of Structural Elements in English corporate profiles

	I	BI	CA	EP	CLS	CF	CIC	CPI	LS	EH	FS	SA
Sum	40	39	34	9	9	21	16	19	2	19	21	0
%	100	97.5	85	22.5	22.5	52.5	40	47.5	5	47.5	52.5	0

Table 47 Distribution of Structural Elements in Chinese corporate profiles

	I	BI	CA	EP	CLS	CF	CIC	CPI	LS	EH	FS	SA
Sum	40	37	34	23	17	22	29	17	13	0	4	7
%	100	92.5	85	57.5	42.5	55	72.5	42.5	32.5	0	10	17.5

Scenarios of the GSP models are:

The GSP model for English enterprise profile is:

） I^ BI^ [CA. FS]. [(CIC). (CPI)] (EP) (CLS) (LS) (EH) ^ CF
※ ※ ※ ※

I^ EP. BI (LS) (FS) ^ CIC^ CA (CLS) (CPI) (SA) ^ CF
※ ※　　　　　　※ ※ ※

By comparison, it is found that the English translation of Chinese corporate profiles is almost identical to the Chinese version of their source text in terms of the frequency of GSP model and structural elements. In other words, the English translation completely follows the structure of the Chinese source texts, without considering the characteristics of this genre structure in the target language.

2) Comparison between English Translation of Chinese corporate profiles and English corporate profiles

As can be seen from the previous text, the structural characteristics of both are:

Table 50 Distribution Frequency of Structural Elements in English corporate profiles

	I	BI	CA	EP	CLS	CF	CIC	CPI	LS	EH	FS	SA
Sum	40	39	34	9	9	21	16	19	2	19	21	0
%	100	97.5	85	22.5	22.5	52.5	40	47.5	5	47.5	52.5	0

Table 51 Distribution of Structural Elements in English Translation of Chinese corporate profiles

	I	BI	CA	EP	CLS	CF	CIC	CPI	LS	EH	FS	SA
Sum	40	37	34	23	17	22	29	17	13	0	4	7
%	100	92.5	85	57.5	42.5	55	72.5	42.5	32.5	0	10	17.5

The GSP model of English corporate profiles is:

I^ BI^ [CA. FS]. [(CIC). (CPI)] (EP) (CLS) (LS) (EH) ^ CF
※ ※ ※ ※

The GSP model of the English translation of Chinese corporate profiles is:

I^ EP. BI (LS) (FS) ^ CIC^ CA (CLS) (CPI) (SA) ^ CF
※ ※　　　　　　　　　※ ※ ※

From this, it can be seen that the similarities and differences in the structure between the Chinese and English corporate profiles mentioned above are fully applicable to the translation of Chinese corporate profiles into English and the English corporate profiles.

6.4.2 Comparison of the Presentation Styles of Three Types of Texts(Vocabulary and Grammar Level)

1) Comparison between English and Chinese Corporate Profiles

(1) Transitivity System

Combining the process type analysis of the English corpus in the previous section with the process type analysis of the Chinese corpus, the results are as follows:

Table 52 Comparison of Process Types between English and Chinese corporate profiles

	English Corpus		Chinese Corpus	
Process Type	Total	Percentage	Total	Percentage
Relational process	212	18.7	208	11.5
Material process	594	52.3	1305	72
Mental process	106	9.3	63	3.5
Behavioral process	176	15.5	236	13
Verbal process	13	1.2	0	0
Existential process	34	3.0	0	0
Sum	1135	100	1812	100

From this, it is not difficult to find that material process is the most commonly used in Chinese and English corporate profiles, but the gap between the two is still significant: the proportion of material processes used in Chinese is as high as 72%, which is 20 percentage points higher than the proportion of 52.3% used in English; Secondly, the other process types that are most commonly used, according to their proportion to the entire process type, are relational process (18.7%), behavioral process (15.5%), mental process (9.3%), existential process (3.0%), and verbal process (1.2) in English, while in Chinese, behavioral process (13%), relational process (11.5%), psychological process (3.5), verbal process. Neither does existential process nor verbal process appear at all.

By analyzing the behavioral, mental, and verbal processes in English corporate profiles, it is found that their main function is to create an interactive communication with consumers by bringing them closer, of which the language form is more lively. However, the use of these process types in Chinese company profiles is missing or insufficient, and the language expression is too formal and lacks change, making it a little bit sluggish.

(2) Mood System

By integrating the mood analysis of English corporate profiles with that of Chinese corporate profiles, it can be concluded that:

			English Corpus		Chinese Corpus	
			Total	%	Total	%
Number of Clauses	Sum		1254	100	1359	100
Mood Type	Indicative mood		1217	97.0	1347	99.1
	Imperative mood		33	2.7	12	0.9
	Interrogative mood		4	0.3	0	0
Subject	First person		107	8.5	22	1.6
	Second person		32	2.6	6	0.4
	Third person		1115	88.9	1331	98
Tense	Past tense		596	47.5	×	×
	Present tense		637	50.8	×	×
	Future tense		21	1.7	×	×

The similarities and differences between the two are clearly presented in the above table.

The declarative mood is the most important choice in both Chinese and English, with a proportion of almost 100% among the three types of moods. The difference is that a certain amount of Imperative mood is used in English business profiles to strengthen communication with consumers, but in Chinese, imperative mood rarely appears, which results in lacking interactivity. In terms of personal pronoun, English corporate profiles often use the first person "we" and second person "you". The first person refers to the company's leaders and employees as a whole, demonstrating the cohesion and affinity of the company, while the use of the second person 'you' refers to the company's invitation to consumers represented by leaders and employees, which is intimate and friendly. On the contrary, the most commonly used personal pronoun is the third-person pronoun, which often take "this company", "the company", or the name of the company as the subject of the sentence, which lacks care and consideration for other employees inside the enterprise and the vast number of consumers outside.

(3) Modality System

After integrating the comparative analysis of modal verbs in the English and Chinese corporate profiles, Table 54 is obtained:

	Chinese Enterprise Profile						
	Low		Middle		High		Sum
	might(may)	could(can)	will(would)	should	must	need	
Total	1	11	2	0	0	2	16
%	6.25	68.75	12.5	0	0	12.5	100
	English Enterprise Profile						
	Low		Middle		High		Sum
	might(may)	could(can)	will(would)	should	must	need	
Total	0	18	9	1	0	0	28
%	0	64.3	32.1	3.6	0	0	100

Similarities: The most frequently used modal verb are "can/could", "will/would" in both Chinese and English company profiles, which to some extent expresses the confidence of enterprises and promises to consumers. More modal words are used to express oaths and good prospects.

Differences: Although modal verbs are rarely used in the two corpora, more are used in the Corpus of English corporate profiles.

(4) Theme System

By integrating the thematic analysis of the English and Chinese corporate profiles from previous sections, the following table is obtained:

Table 55 Comparison of Theme Systems between English and Chinese corporate profiles

	The English Corpus		The Chinese Corpus	
	Sum	%	Sum	%
Multiple Theme	140	20	106	11.2
Single Theme	552	80	844	88.8
Marked Theme	108	15.6	109	11.5
Unmarked Theme	584	84.4	841	88.5
Sum	692	100	950	100

From the comparison of the theme systems of English and Chinese corporate profiles, it is found that both profiles have a common feature in thematic selection: the frequency of using a single theme is higher than that of multiple themes, and the number of unmarked themes is more than that of marked themes. There are differences as well. In English corpora, the proportion of multiple themes and marked themes is higher than that in Chinese corporate profiles, which are 20% vs. 11.2% and 15.6% vs. 11.5, respectively.

2) Comparison of Chinese Corporate Profiles and Their English Translations

Transitivity System

By integrating the process type analysis of the Chinese corpus with that of the English translation corpus, Table 56 is obtained:

Table 56 Comparison of Process Types of Chinese corporate profiles with Their English Translations

	The Chinese Corpus		The Corpus of English Translations	
Process Type	Sum	%	Sum	%
Relational Process	208	11.5	214	12.5

Material Process	1305	72	1215	71.3
Mental Process	63	3.5	73	4.3
Behavioral Process	236	13	192	11.3
Verbal Process	0	0	0	0
Existential Process	0	0	11	0.6
Sum	1812	100	1705	100

From the above data, it can be seen that the English texts of the corporate profiles are literal translations of the corresponding Chinese profiles, so they are very close in numbers and percentages, with only slight differences.

Mood System

Similarly, by integrating the analysis of the mood system in Chinese corporate profiles with that of the English translations,

Table 57 is obtained:

			The Chinese Corpus		The English Corpus	
			Sum	%	Sum	%
Number of Clauses	Sum		1359	100	1342	100
Type of Mood	Indicative Mood		1347	99.1	1333	99.3
	Imperative Mood		12	0.9	9	0.7
	Interrogative Mood		0	0	0	0
Subject	First Person		22	1.6	22	1.6
	Second Person		6	0.4	6	0.4
	Third Person		1331	98	1314	98
Tense	Past Tense		×	×	233	17.4
	Present Tense		×	×	1051	78.3
	Future Tense		×	×	58	4.3

These two are almost the same, but due to its unique characteristics, it is not possible to reflect different tenses on verbs in Chinese, while verbs in the translated texts could naturally reflect different tenses.

(5) Modality System

By integrating the analysis of modality system in Chinese corporate profiles and their corresponding translated English versions, the results are as follows:

Table 58 Comparison of Modal Verbs in Chinese corporate profiles and Their English Translations

	Chinese corporate profiles						
	Low		Medium	High			Sum
	might(may)	could(can)	will (would)	should	must	need	
Sum	1	11	2	0	0	2	16
%	6.25	68.75	12.5	0	0	12.5	100
	English Translation of Chinese corporate profiles						
	Low		Medium	High			Sum
	might(may)	could(can)	will (would)	should	must	need	
Sum	2	10	4	0	0	0	16
%	12.5	62.5	25	0	0	0	100

Similarities: In terms of different levels of expression of modal verbs, the Chinese corporate profiles and their English translations are very similar at each level. For example, in the selection of the low-level modal verb "can/could", the Chinese enterprise profile is 68.75%, and their English translations is 62.5%; The medium-level modal verb "should" does not appear in both Chinese corporate profiles and their English translations; Neither does the high-level modal verb "must". It can be concluded from these data that there is a certain correspondence between the two in the selection of modal verbs.

Difference: The high-level modal verb "must" appear twice in Chinese corporate profiles, which is not the case in English translations, so the English translations are more gentle.

(6) Theme System

By integrating the thematic analysis of Chinese corporate profiles with that of the translated English versions,

Table 59 is obtained:

	The Chinese Corpus		The English Translation Corpus	
	Sum	%	Sum	%
Multiple Theme	106	11.2	110	12.9
Single Theme	844	88.8	746	87.1
Marked Theme	109	11.5	130	15.2
Unmarked Theme	841	88.5	726	84.8
Sum	950	100	1710	85.6

It can be seen that there is not much difference between the two.

3) English corporate profiles and English Translations of Chinese Corporate Profiles

Due to the fact that the English translations of Chinese corporate profiles are almost identical to the source Chinese profiles, as mentioned above, the similarities and differences between the English and Chinese corporate profiles are basically the same as the situation we described earlier for the English and Chinese corporate profiles. For example, in terms of transitivity systems:

	The English Corpus		The English Translation Corpus	
Process Type	Sum	%	Sum	%
Relational Process	212	18.7	214	12.5
Material Process	594	52.3	1215	71.3
Mental Process	106	9.3	73	4.3
Behavioral Process	176	15.5	192	11.3
Verbal Process	13	1.2	0	0
Existential Process	34	3.0	11	0.6
Sum	1135	100	1705	100

Comparing the proportion of various process types in the English translation corpus on the right side of the table with previous Chinese corpus, it is found that the proportion of each process type in the translation corpus are material process (71.3%), relational process (12.5%), behavioral process (11.3%), psychological process (4.3%), and existential process (0.6%), respectively; In the Chinese corpus, proportions, as mentioned earlier, are material process (72%), behavioral process (13%), relational process (11.5), psychological process (3.5), verbal process (0%), and existential process (0%). Considering the significant differences between Chinese and English languages and the possible errors in identifying process types, it is believed that although there have been some changes in the selection of process types in the translated texts compared to source texts, the changes are minimal, indicating that the former is a one-to-one mechanical translation of the latter.

(7) Mood System

Table 61 Comparison of Mood System between English corporate profiles and English Translations of Chinese corporate profiles

		English Enterprise Corpus		English Translation Corpus	
		Sum	%	Sum	%
Number of Clauses	Sum	1254	100	1342	100
Type of Mood	Indicative Mood	1217	97.0	1333	99.3
	Imperative Mood	33	2.7	9	0.7
	Interrogative Mood	4	0.3	0	0
Subject	First Person	107	8.5	22	1.6
	Second Person	32	2.6	6	0.4
	Third Person	1115	88.9	1314	98
Tense	Past Tense	596	47.5	233	17.4
	Present Tense	637	50.8	1051	78.3
	Future Tense	21	1.7	58	4.3

This is basically consistent with the situation in the Chinese and English corpora mentioned earlier.

(8) Transitivity System

By integrating the analysis of modal verbs in English corporate profiles with the analysis of modal verbs in Chinese corporate profiles, the result is as follows:

Table 62 Comparison of Modal Verbs in English corporate profiles and English Translations of Chinese corporate profiles

	English corporate profiles						
	Low		Medium		High		Sum
	might(may)	could(can)	will(would)	should	must	need	
Sum	0	18	9	1	0	0	28
%	6.20	64.3	32.1	3.6	0	0	100
	English Translations of Chinese corporate profiles						
	Low		Medium		High		Sum
	might(may)	could(can)	will(would)	should	must	need	
Sum	2	10	4	0	0	0	16
%	12.5	62.5	25	0	0	0	100

In terms of modal verbs, although modal verb are not commonly used in both corpora, they still appear more frequently in the corpus of English corporate profiles, making the overall style of writing seem more lively and communicative.

(9) Theme System

Similarly, by integrating the thematic system analysis of English corporate profiles with that of the English translation corpus, the comparative results are:

Table 63 Comparison of Theme System between English corporate profiles and English Translation of Chinese corporate profiles

	The English Corpus		The English Translation Corpus	
	Sum	%	Sum	%
Multiple Theme	140	20	110	12.9
Single Theme	552	80	746	87.1
Marked Theme	108	15.6	130	15.2
Unmarked Theme	584	84.4	726	84.8
Sum	672	100	836	100

It is found that, except for those integrated themes, whether it is a single theme, a marked theme, or an unmarked theme, the number of which in translated versions is higher than that of English corporate profiles. The reason is that many sentences in the translated profiles are composed of clauses, and compared to English corporate profiles, complex clauses are less used, reflecting the influence of Chinese clauses on the translator's English writing.

6.5 Evaluation and Improvement of Translation Quality for Corporate Profiles

Through the above comparison and analysis, it is found that English translations of Chinese corporate profiles are literal translations that are completely based on source Chinese texts and writing habits with which Chinese customers are familiar, without considering the language habits and aesthetic expectations of the target language readers. As a result, there are significant differences not only in wording but also in macro structure between the corporate profiles translated into English and the authentic English corporate profiles of English-speaking countries.

6.5.1 Judgment and Modification Suggestions on the Quality of the Translation from the Perspective of Structure

In order to maximize the compatibility between the translated text and the social, cultural as well as pragmatic habits of the target language, and to achieve the expected reception effect of this genre of translation in the target language society, we randomly select a corpus from the translation corpus and analyze its structure from the perspective of structure of the genre; Then, with the help of the English enterprise profile structure summarized in the previous section, it is adjusted to improve and enhance the quality of the translation.

The previous discussion indicates that generally speaking, a business introduction includes 12 steps or elements, among which I, BI, CA, CF, FS elements are necessary, and the others are optional. Moreover, there are rules to follow in the ranking of these elements, which cannot be done arbitrarily. Taking the translation of the profile of "Anta"as an example.

(I) **About ANTA** （http://en.anta.com/about.html）

（BI）In 1994, ANTA's first shoe workshop was established in Jinjiang, Fujian. Now ANTA Sports is the most famous and top sports goods brand in China. （**EH**）In 2007, ANTA Group made a successful IPO in Hong Kong (ANTASPORTS 02020.HK). Until 2010, the market capitalization of ANTA Group became the 4th largest sports goods' company in the world (over USD5.7 billion, Oct 2010), ANTA brand value was USD 800 million evaluated by Forbes Brand value ranking (2010). From 2006 to 2010, the annual growth of ANTA turnover is over 35%, which is the highest in sports goods industry.

(**EP**) ANTA Group has now become one of leading sport brand company among the competitors. (**CIC**) *"Integrating the sports spirit of'Beyond yoursel'into everyone's* *life*", in accordance with this concept, **(CA)** ANTA follows the channel strategy of brand store networks and boasts more than 7,500 franchise brand stores(/shops) in the world. **(CLS)** While in overseas market, ANTA has penetrated into 15 countries and regions including Italy, Turkey, Czech Republic and Serbia in Europe, Kazakhstan, Nepal, Saudi Arabia, Kuwait, Vietnam, Singapore and the Philippines in Asia.

(CIC)As the pioneer of sports technology in China, ANTA always regards technology innovation as core company competitiveness. In order to meet different consumer preferences and requirements, ANTA is paying attention to frontier sports technology, cooperating with high-tech companies such as Huntsman, DuPont, 3M, and adopting the most advanced anti-bacterial technology such as Teflon, New Sherry materials, from the detail, ANTA implant the high-tech into everybody's life.

(SA) For the brand publicity, ANTA Group signed many world leading athletes as brand spokesmen, which include NBA Star Kevin Garnett (Boston Celtics),Luis Scola(Houston Rocket),women tennis player Jelena Jankovic, and world men table tennis world champion Wang Hao. ANTA has been sponsoring 152 sports teams with a total 4,000 person/times annually, engaging over 300 different product lines and over 200,000 items. **(CF)** We are young but we are strong enough to go forward faster, join us and let's "*Keep Moving*"together.

Namely, the structural feature of the profile is:

$$I^\wedge BI^\wedge EH^\wedge EP^\wedge CIC^\wedge CA^\wedge CIS^\wedge CIC^\wedge SA^\wedge CF$$

Put into words, the formula means that the introduction of Anta mentioned above has the following structure: first, pointing out the name of this enterprise clearly at the beginning; Next, reporting the basic information of the enterprise (when and where it was established, and what is the current situation); Next, describing the development and achievements of the enterprise in recent years; Then stating the glorious history of enterprise development; On this basis, pointing out its position in the industry logically; Next, elaborating on the development concept of the enterprise and the achievements achieved in brand management and market development under this concept, as well as its layout in the international market; Afterwards, discussing the technology-based concept pursued by the enterprise and how to carry out technological cooperation and innovation with world-class companies under this concept; Next, from the perspective of promoting the brand, listing what social activities the enterprise has organized and implemented; Finally, proposing the bright future of the enterprise.

In fact, the structural arrangement of the above enterprise introduction, as shown in the previous analysis, fully follows its corresponding source profile step by step- the structure of Chinese enterprise introduction. The problem is that for applied genres with prominent vocative functions such as corporate profiles, the main purpose of producing texts is to exert the "power behind words" of them, driving readers to "put it into action" after reading the texts. Therefore, when translating Chinese corporate profiles into English, it is aimed at promoting products or services to consumers in English-speaking countries from the perspective of sales effectiveness. Translations naturally need to consider the reading habits and aesthetic expectations formed by consumers in the target language under their long-term cultural traditions, and strive to make the translated text "pleasing", in order to achieve the possibility of moving from "being touched" to "taking action". Therefore, we cannot but pay attention to the writing standards of this genre of texts in the target language. From the perspective of genre analysis, it is necessary to have a clear understanding of the structural and linguistic characteristics of English corporate profiles, so as to follow the examples when translating Chinese corporate profiles into English, and to improve the acceptance of these translated texts in English speaking countries - achieving good translation results. From the perspective of translation quality, only in this way can we enhance the smoothness and elegance of the translation in the eyes of readers in the target language, and achieve the "expressiveness and elegance" requirements of traditional Chinese Translators Journal studies for measuring translation quality.

Then, what are the characteristics of the English corporate profiles? Based on corpus analysis in previous sections, we have summarized its structural and linguistic features at a preliminary level. As mentioned earlier, in terms of commonalities, I (identification), BI (basic information), CA (company's achievements), and CF (future development) constitute indispensable basic elements in a company's profile regarding the structural characteristics and differences between English and Chinese of this genre. Secondly, in terms of order, I always comes first, CF always appears at the end or back of the company profile, and can be repeated with CA in a company's profile. Starting from this, when making structural adjustments to the translation, it is necessary to ensure that the above structural elements are both present and in order.

On the other hand, regarding the differences, which are the structural differences described earlier, namely:

First, CIC generally appears along with CPI (the company's commitment and guarantee), and is placed after it, indicating that such a commitment is based on what business philosophy the company adheres to, and there are reasons for making such a commitment, which is easier for consumers to accept. While in Chinese corporate profiles,

CIC is placed before CA (company achievements), indicating that due to the belief in the correct business philosophy, many honors and achievements have been achieved. Here, due to the lack of corresponding CPI elements in the source Chinese texts of the case, the translation can only be readjusted according to CLC ^ CA.

Second, although LS is not a necessary element, it appears much more frequently in Chinese than in English (32.5%>5%). However, on the other hand, this part of the content has been replaced by EH in this case.

Third, FS (Entrepreneurial Stories) appears frequently in English corporate profiles, reaching up to 52.5%, which fully reflects the significance attached to interpersonal meaning by English corporate profiles. It is already a necessary element. While FS only appears four times in Chinese profiles, accounting for only 10% of the total. The main function of FS is to help consumers understand more stories about the company and brand, hoping to impress consumers with all these stories. However, this element did not appear in this case.

Fourth, EP (evaluations and positions) is a necessary element in Chinese corporate profiles, with a frequency of 57.5%. However, in English corporate profiles, its proportion is only 22.5%. In terms of order, in English corporate profiles, the position of EP is relatively arbitrary, but in Chinese profiles, EP always appears after I and is located at the beginning of the topic sentence, in order to win the trust of consumers in the shortest possible time. Based on this, we can adjust EP to be after EH in the translation as an inevitable result of the glorious development history of the enterprise.

Fifth, EH (entrepreneurship history) accounts for 47.5% of English corporate profiles, while it has not appeared once in the corpus of Chinese profile. But this may be related to our judgment on the content of EH and CA, in fact, these two are sometimes difficult to distinguish. In this case, we believe that the content which describes the development of the enterprise at different time periods can be seen as the development history of the enterprise at the structural level, thus can be reflected in the translation.

Based on the above description of the structural characteristics and similarities and differences between Chinese and English corporate profiles, as well as on the explanation that the translated texts should align with the target in terms of structure, the original translation structure

I^BI^EH^EP^CIC^CA^CIS^CIC^SA^CF

can be adjusted to

I^BI^CIC^CA^CLS^EH^EP ^CIC^CA^SA^CF

which is

(I) **About ANTA** (http://en.anta.com/about.html)

(BI) In 1994, ANTA's first shoe workshop was established in Jinjiang, Fujian. Now ANTA Sports is the most famous and top sports goods brand in China. **(CIC)** "*Integrating the sports spirit of 'Beyond yourself' into everyone's life*", in accordance with this concept, **(CA)** ANTA follows the channel strategy of brand store networks and boasts more than 7,500 franchise brand stores(/shops) in the world. **(CLS)** While in overseas market, ANTA has penetrated into 15 countries and regions including Italy, Turkey, Czech Republic and Serbia in Europe, Kazakhstan, Nepal, Saudi Arabia, Kuwait, Vietnam, Singapore and the Philippines in Asia. **(EH)** In 2007, ANTA Group made a successful IPO in Hong Kong (ANTASPORTS 02020.HK). Until 2010, the market capitalization of ANTA Group became the 4th largest sports goods' company in the world (over USD5.7 billion, Oct 2010), ANTA brand value was USD 800 million evaluated by Forbes Brand value ranking (2010). From 2006 to 2010, the annual growth of ANTA turnover is over 35%, which is the highest in sports goods industry. **(EP)** ANTA Group has now become one of leading sport brand company among the competitors. **(CIC)** As the pioneer of sports technology in China, ANTA always regards technology innovation as core company competitiveness. **(CA)** In order to meet different consumer preferences and requirements, ANTA is paying attention to frontier sports technology, cooperating with high-tech companies such as Huntsman, DuPont, 3M, and adopting the most advanced anti-bacterial technology such as Teflon, New Sherry materials, from the detail, ANTA implant the high-tech into everybody's life **(SA)** For the brand publicity, ANTA Group signed many world leading athletes as brand spokesmen, which include NBA Star Kevin Garnett (Boston Celtics), Luis Scola (Houston Rocket), women tennis player Jelena Jankovic, and world men table tennis world champion Wang Hao. ANTA has been sponsoring 152 sports teams with a total 4,000 person/times annually, engaging over 300 different product lines and over 200,000 items. **(CF)** We are young but we are strong enough to go forward faster, join us and let's "*Keep Moving*" together.

That is to say, the structure of this company profile is adjusted according to the commonalities and differences between Chinese and English texts of this genre, and its logical structure is as follows:

The company name (I) is provided first, followed by the basic information (BI), then the company's ideas and concepts (CIC), the achievements in brand management and market development under this idea and concept (CA), and its location and supply scope in the international market (CLS); Following this approach is the report on the glorious development history (EH) of the enterprise and its logical position in the industry (EP); Next, another concept for enterprise development is introduced - the great important role played by technology (CLC), which explains how to engage in technological cooperation and innovation (CA) with world-class enterprises; Next, from the perspective of promoting the brand, describing what social activities (SA) the enterprise has organized and implemented; Finally, the bright future (CF) of the enterprise.

In this way, without adding or deleting the original content (of course, if conditions permit, if the translator is able to obtain relevant information about the enterprise, the translation should provide the FS and other structural sections required for the structure of the English enterprise introduction, and the language expression should also be aligned with the target language specification — detailed later, then the translation effect will naturally be better), the modified translation has made structural adjustments to align with the target language. Compared to the original translation, the modified version is more in line with the reading habits of readers of the target language, thus naturally appears more "faithful and elegant".

In other words, the original translation is completely constrained by the inherent structure of Chinese profile, without considering the aesthetic or normative rules of the English, which naturally results in not being smooth and elegant t in the eyes of the target language readers. In this way, judging from the second stage of the translation quality assessment model constructed earlier, which measures the translation quality from the perspective of "smoothness" and "elegance", the original translation is far from being satisfying.

6.5.2 Judgment and Modification Suggestions on the Quality of the Original Translation from the Perspective of Representation Style

To maximize the accordance of the translation with the norms and pragmatic habits of this genre in the target language, and to achieve the expected acceptance effect in the target language society, it is not only necessary to align with the corresponding genre in the target language at the structural level, but also to be in accord with it in terms of stylistic and linguistic characteristics. Here, we also take the translation of "Anta" profile as an example to analyze its linguistic characteristics; Then, based on the generic characteristics of the English corporate profiles summarized in the previous text, we intend to criticize, adjust and improve the quality of the translation.

The previous discussion indicates that in general, a business introduction generally includes 12 step elements, among which I, BI, CA, CF, FS are necessary and the others are optional. Moreover, there are rules to follow in the ranking of these elements, which cannot be done arbitrarily. Taking the profile translation of "Anta" as an example.

（1） **Analysis of Process Types from the Perspective of Transitivity**

About ANTA（http://en.anta.com/about.html）

(M) In 1994, ANTA's first shoe workshop was established in Jinjiang, Fujian. (R)Now ANTA Sports is the most famous and top sports goods brand in China. (M)In 2007, ANTA Group made a successful IPO in Hong Kong (ANTASPORTS 02020.HK). (R) Until 2010, the market capitalization of ANTA Group became the 4th largest sports goods'company in the world (over USD5.7 billion, Oct 2010), (R)ANTA brand value was USD 800 million evaluated by Forbes Brand value ranking (2010). (R) From 2006 to 2010, the annual growth of ANTA turnover is over 35%, (R) which is the highest in sports goods industry.

(R) ANTA Group has now become one of leading sport brand company among the competitors. (M) *"Integrating the sports spirit of 'Beyond yourself' into everyone's life"*, in accordance with this concept, ANTA follows the channel strategy of brand store networks and (V) boasts more than 7,500 franchise brand stores (/shops) in the world. (M) While in overseas market, ANTA has penetrated into 15 countries and regions including Italy, Turkey, Czech Republic and Serbia in Europe, Kazakhstan, Nepal, Saudi Arabia, Kuwait, Vietnam, Singapore and the Philippines in Asia.

(M2) As the pioneer of sports technology in China, ANTA always regards technology innovation as core company competitiveness. (M2) In order to meet different consumer preferences and requirements, ANTA is paying attention to frontier sports technology, (M) cooperating with high-tech companies such as Huntsman, DuPont, 3M, and (B) adopting the most advanced anti-bacterial technology such as Teflon, New Sherry materials,from the detail, (M)ANTA implant the high-tech into everybody's life.

(B) For the brand publicity, ANTA Group signed many world leading athletes as brand spokesmen, (R)which include NBA Star Kevin Garnett (Boston Celtics),Luis Scola(Houston Rocket),women tennis player Jelena Jankovic, and world men table tennis world champion Wang Hao. (M) ANTA has been sponsoring 152 sports teams with a total 4,000 person/times annually, (B)engaging over 300 different product lines and over 200,000 items. (R)We are young but we are strong enough to go forward faster,(B) join us and let's "*Keep Moving*" together.

Note: The letter M in parentheses in the text represents material processes, M2 represents mental process, R represents relational process, and B represents behavioral process. From this, it can be seen that the entire text consists of 21 clauses, of which 7 are material processes, 8 are relational processes, 4 are behavioral processes, 2 are mental processes, and 1 is verbal process.

(2) **Mood Analysis**

About ANTA (http://en.anta.com/about.html)

(D) In 1994, ANTA's first shoe workshop was established in Jinjiang, Fujian. (D) Now ANTA Sports is the most famous and top sports goods brand in China. (D) In 2007, ANTA Group made a successful IPO in Hong Kong (ANTASPORTS 02020.HK).

(D) Until 2010, the market capitalization of ANTA Group became the 4th largest sports goods' company in the world (over USD5.7 billion, Oct 2010), (D) ANTA brand value was USD 800 million evaluated by Forbes Brand value ranking (2010). (D) From 2006 to 2010, the annual growth of ANTA turnover is over 35%, (D) which is the highest in sports goods industry.

(D) ANTA Group has now become one of leading sport brand company among the competitors. (D) "*Integrating the sports spirit of 'Beyond yourself' into everyone's life*", in accordance with this concept, ANTA follows the channel strategy of brand store networks and boasts more than 7,500 franchise brand stores(/shops) in the world. (D) While in overseas market, ANTA has penetrated into 15 countries and regions including Italy, Turkey, Czech Republic and Serbia in Europe, Kazakhstan, Nepal, Saudi Arabia, Kuwait, Vietnam, Singapore and the Philippines in Asia.

(D)As the pioneer of sports technology in China, ANTA always regards technology innovation as core company competitiveness. (D) In order to meet different consumer preferences and requirements, ANTA is paying attention to frontier sports technology, cooperating with high-tech companies such as Huntsman, DuPont, 3M, and adopting the most advanced anti-bacterial technology such as Teflon, New Sherry materials, from the detail, (D) ANTA implant the high-tech into everybody's life.

(D) For the brand publicity, <u>ANTA Group</u> signed many world leading athletes as brand spokesmen, (D) <u>which</u> include NBA Star Kevin Garnett (Boston Celtics),Luis Scola (Houston Rocket),women tennis player Jelena Jankovic, and world men table tennis world champion Wang Hao. (D) <u>ANTA</u> has been sponsoring 152 sports teams with a total 4,000 person/times annually, engaging over 300 different product lines and over 200,000 items. (D) <u>We</u> are young but we are strong enough to go forward faster, (I) join us and let's *"Keep Moving"* together.

Note: The letter D in parentheses represents the indicative mood, I represents the imperative mood, and the underlined part is the subject. It can be seen that except for one place where imperative mood is used, the whole text is all in indicative mood; no modal word is used; Except for one where the subject is 'we' and one where the implicit subject is 'you', all other phrases are ANTA or ANTA Group or phrases containing ANTA Group, such as the market capitalization of ANTA Group, ANTA brand value, the annual growth of ANTA turnover, etc.

(3) **Thematic analysis**

About ANTA (http://en.anta.com/about.html)

In 1994, ANTA's first shoe workshop was established in Jinjiang, Fujian. **Now ANTA Sports** is the most famous and top sports goods brand in China. **In 2007,** ANTA Group made a successful IPO in Hong Kong (ANTASPORTS 02020.HK). **Until 2010,** the market capitalization of ANTA Group became the 4th largest sports goods' company in the world (over USD5.7 billion, Oct 2010), **ANTA brand value** was USD 800 million evaluated by Forbes Brand value ranking (2010). **From 2006 to 2010,** the annual growth of ANTA turnover is over 35%, **which** is the highest in sports goods industry.

ANTA Group has now become one of leading sport brand company among the competitors."<u>*Integrating the sports spirit of 'Beyond yourself' into everyone's life*</u>", in accordance with this concept, ANTA follows the channel strategy of brand store networks and boasts more than 7,500 franchise brand stores(/shops) in the world. **While in overseas market,** ANTA has penetrated into 15 countries and regions including Italy, Turkey, Czech Republic and Serbia in Europe, Kazakhstan, Nepal, Saudi Arabia, Kuwait, Vietnam, Singapore and the Philippines in Asia.

<u>**As the pioneer of sports technology in China**</u>, ANTA always regards technology innovation as core company competitiveness. **<u>In order to meet different consumer preferences and requirements,</u>** ANTA is paying attention to frontier sports technology,

cooperating with high-tech companies such as Huntsman, DuPont, 3M, and adopting the most advanced anti-bacterial technology such as Teflon, New Sherry materials, from the detail, ANTA implant the high-tech into everybody's life.

For the brand publicity, ANTA Group signed many world leading athletes as brand spokesmen, **which** include NBA Star Kevin Garnett (Boston Celtics), Luis Scola (Houston Rocket), women tennis player Jelena Jankovic, and world men table tennis world champion Wang Hao. **ANTA** has been sponsoring 152 sports teams with a total 4,000 person/times annually, engaging over 300 different product lines and over 200,000 items. **We** are young but we are strong enough to go forward faster, **join** us and let's "*Keep Moving*" together.

Note: The bold part here represents the theme, while the highlighted part in bold indicates the marked theme. The entire article consists of 17 themes, all of which are single themes, of which 9 are marked themes.

Through a three-dimensional analysis of the linguistic characteristics of the text (process type, mood, theme), combined with the previous analysis and summary of the representation styles in the self-built corpus of English corporate profiles and the corpus of English translation of Chinese corporate profiles, we know that material and relational processes are the most commonly used process types, while other process types, such as verbal process, mental process, behavioral process, and existential process, are less commonly used, Among them, relatively speaking, the proportion of these processes used in English is higher than that in Chinese profiles and translated English profiles that fully correspond to Chinese. However, in this case, except for the absence of existential processes, all other process types have appeared, and the proportions of various process types are relatively balanced, especially the proportions of relational and behavioral processes are relatively high.

In terms of mood, the analysis shows that in addition to the indicative mood, there is a small amount of imperative mood in English corporate profiles to invite more consumers to learn about the company, its products and services. But there is almost no imperative mood in the English translation of Chinese corporate profiles; In addition, personal pronoun such as "you" and "we" are seldom used as subjects in the translated texts, instead of which "Group" is used, or the company name is directly used. In terms of tense, the most commonly used tense in English corporate profiles is the past tense. The past tense is used to describe the entrepreneurial story of the company or brand founder, and introduces the history of the company.

As far as this case is concerned, we find that the original translation basically displays the overall characteristics of the above-mentioned English translation corpus with respect to the use of mood, such as the high proportion of indicative mood, the low proportion of modal words, the subject is mostly the third-person pronoun—company's name, and the tense is mostly the present tense or the present perfect tense. Therefore, from the perspective of smoothness and expressiveness, the translation quality is not high. Naturally, in addition to the problems in the structure - the source text of the translation - the Chinese enterprise profile lacks FS that is often found in the English profiles, since it is about the history of founders, it inevitably involves the use of the past tense - mainly because the translation completely and mechanically follows the source text step by step. Therefore, in order to improve the readability and acceptance of the translation in the target language society, translators must study the linguistic characteristics of such genres in the target language country, and strive to reflect in the translation, with the highest level being "faithful in original flavor", "as if it is a re creation in the source language".

As for the theme system, as mentioned earlier, the biggest difference between Chinese and English corporate profiles is that compared to English profiles, there are more themes in translated texts, with a higher proportion of single themes. This is mainly because translated texts use more short and simple sentences, while English profiles use more complex sentences. The root cause is that translated texts are mechanical conversion from Chinese to English. The biggest difference between Chinese and English is that Chinese often uses short run-on sentences, while English tends to use complex sentences. Recognizing this difference requires corresponding adjustments during translation. Based on the overall generic characteristics of Chinese and English corporate profiles described above and the differences between this case and English corporate profiles, we believe that, in addition to the structural adjustments and modifications made to the original translation, further improvements can be made in terms of mood and thematic system at the level of words and expressions.

In terms of mood, the indicative and interrogative mood can be moderately increased; In terms of subject, first and second person can be increased; If possible, modal words can also be added. In terms of themes, by expanding the use of complex sentences, the overall number of themes is reduced, and the proportion of multiple themes is increased, making the text more coherent.

Following the above approach, the original translation is modified (in bold and italicized) as follows:

About ANTA(http://en.anta.com/about.html)

In 1994, *we ANTA witnessed* our first shoe workshop in Jinjiang, Fujian, *and now we are already* the most famous and top sports goods brand in China. *Firmly believing in* "*Integrating the sports spirit of 'Beyond yourself' into everyone's life*", *we* follow the channel strategy of brand store networks and boast more than 7,500 franchise brand stores(/shops) in the world. *As for* the overseas market, *we have* penetrated into 15 countries and regions including Italy, Turkey, Czech Republic and Serbia in Europe, Kazakhstan, Nepal, Saudi Arabia, Kuwait, Vietnam, Singapore and the Philippines in Asia.In 2007, *we ANTA Group* made a successful IPO in Hong Kong (ANTASPORTS 02020.HK), and *3 years later, until 2010, our market capitalization* became the 4th largest sports goods' company in the world (over USD5.7 billion, Oct 2010), and *our brand value* was USD 800 million evaluated by Forbes Brand value ranking (2010). *Incredibly*, from 2006 to 2010, *our annual growth of turnover* is over 35%, 7D which is the highest in sports goods industry. *What a wonder!*

As a result, ANTA Group have now become one of leading sport brand company among the competitors. As the pioneer of sports technology in China, *ANTA* always regard technology innovation as core company competitiveness. In order to meet *your* different consumer preferences and requirements, *we ANTA* are paying attention to frontier sports technology, cooperating with high-tech companies such as Huntsman, DuPont, 3M, and adopting the most advanced anti-bacterial technology such as Teflon, New Sherry materials, from the detail, *we* implant the high-tech into everybody's life. For the brand publicity, *we* signed many world leading athletes as brand spokesmen, which include NBA Star Kevin Garnett (Boston Celtics),Luis Scola(Houston Rocket),women tennis player Jelena Jankovic, and world men table tennis world champion Wang Hao. *In addition, we ANTA* have been sponsoring 152 sports teams with a total 4,000 person/times annually, engaging over 300 different product lines and over 200,000 items. *Young as we may be*, but we are strong enough to go forward faster, join us and let's "Ke ep Moving" together.

The first and second sentences of the original translation are two simple sentences, the subject is the third-person pronoun, the name of the enterprise. The modified version combines them into a complex sentence, and converts the singular third-person pronoun subject into the plural first person, which shortens the distance with the reader. At the same time, by adding the modal adjunct'already'and contrasting it with the marked theme'In 1994'at the beginning of the sentence, it highlights the miracle of rapid development of the enterprise and naturally attracts readers'attention. The second sentence is a clause complex that includes mental process. The first half is the concept upheld by the enterprise, which marks the theme and the starting point of information, while the latter is the focus of readers'attention, which is the actions and achievements of the enterprise under this concept. Similarly, the following third sentence is a logical continuation of the second sentence and a further expression of the development of the enterprise according to the above concept. However, the original translation is completely a mechanical conversion of Chinese, the use of four sentences makes it structurally loose. The revised translation integrates them into a complex sentence, which is more compact and coherent. The fourth sentence is not included in the original translation, but the meaning is implied. Here, an exclamation sentence structure is used to enhance the interaction with the reader. As mentioned earlier, the fifth sentence is an EP element in structure, which is a judgment of the company's position in the industry. From the perspective of the sequential arrangement of elements in this text, its position is appropriate because the description of achievements gained by the enterprise in the fourth and third sentences strongly supports its current position. In other words, its position is a natural result of its previous achievements. Therefore, the phrase "As a result" is added here to make it easier for readers to see the connection between the sentences. From the perspective of schematic structure, the sixth sentence actually introduces another concept upheld by the enterprise and the actions taken by the enterprise under it (seventh and eighth sentences). In addition, the addition of second person possessive pronouns in the seventh sentence that were not present in the original translation is also aimed at bridging the gap with readers.

The ninth and tenth sentences both describe what activities the enterprise has carried out in brand promotion, but they describe different types of activities, so adding "In addition" at the beginning of the tenth sentence will more clearly connect and show the relationship between the two. Revising the plain and straightforward "we are young" to "Young as we may be" in the eleventh sentence to better contrast with the latter half of the sentence'but we are strong enough to go forward faster', which undoubtedly has stronger expressive power and more prominent vocative function.

In addition, the original translation blindly uses third-person pronouns ANTA or ANTA Group as the subject, which not only expands the distance from the reader but also repeats too much. For this reason, the first person "we" is added, but on the other hand, in order to avoid repetition, We Anta, We Anta Group, We Anta, Anta and other forms are also rotated.

References:
[1] Halliday, M. A. K. & Hasan, R. Language, Context and Text: Aspects of Language in a Social-Semiotic Perspective[M]. Victoria: Deakin University Press,1985.
[2] Nwogu, K. N. The medical research paper: Structure and function [J]. English for Specific Purposes. 1997,16(2), 119-138.

Chapter 7: Research on the Translation Quality of Sports News Discourses

This chapter introduces the content, steps, and methods of corpus construction for three types of sports news (BBC English sports news, Xinhua Chinese sports news, and translated English sports news on Xinhua Net). Based on this, firstly, from the perspective of structure, by analyzing all text components in the three corpora, the GSP model is summarized; Secondly, starting from the transitivity system, mood system, and thematic system, the lexical and grammatical characteristics (representing styles) of these generic texts in the three corpora are analyzed; Then, a comparison is made between the three types of sports news included in three corpora from the dimensions of structure and style that reflect the characteristics of these generic texts, and commonalities and differences are drawn; Finally, starting from the second stage of the translation quality assessment model constructed in Chapter 6, which judges and measures whether the translation is smooth and expressive, and using the generic characteristics of BBC English sports news as a benchmark, this chapter assesses and proposes improvement suggestions for the English translation quality of Xinhua Sports News, achieving empirical analysis of the translation quality assessment model constructed in Chapter 6.

7.1 Construction of the Corpus of Sports News Discourses

This study established three comparable corpora consisting of 40 native English sports news texts, 40 native Chinese sports news texts, and 40 translated English sports news texts in domestic China, each containing 11,013, 25,437, and 19,728 characters. The main research object of this section is the coverage of the 2012 London Olympics, with corpus from the London Olympics column at official BBC website, Xinhua Net and its English version. These websites are the main official media for news coverage, ensuring the authority and credibility of the corpus. In order to make the analysis more convincing, this study strives to ensure that the reporting themes of the three parallel texts from the three corpora are consistent when selecting the corpus. Firstly, we will select a news report about an athlete winning a gold medal from Xinhua Net, and then search for its corresponding reports in the 2012 Olympic Games column on Xinhua's English website and BBC's official website. For example, we select a news report on Xinhua Net titled "Zhou Lulu's'easy'Victory Ends China Power's Competition in London with 5 Gold Medals". This is a report about the Chinese women's weightlifting team member Zhou

Lulu who won the gold medal in women's ±75kg weightlifting competition and broke the world record. Then the corresponding reports found on the English website of Xinhua Net and the official website of the BBC are "Chinese lifter Zhou Lulu nails gold with world record in women's+75kg" and "Records tumble as Zhou takes gold". Following this method, three monolingual parallel corpora have been established in the following directory. The specific content of the corpora is shown in the attachment.

Table 1 List of Corpus for Three Types of Sports News Texts

Texts No.	BBC Sports News	Xinhua Sports News	Xinhua English Sports News
1	Olympics boxing: China's Zou Shiming retains light flyweight title	邹市明再获拳击冠军为中国夺第38块金牌	Zou Shiming repeats Beijing success
2	Wu defends Olympic crown	"了不起的战士"吴静钰	Wu Jingyu defends taekwondo title at London
3	Round-up: China bag maximum medal haul	少帅刘国梁再创佳绩 "亦师亦友"更是"真核心"	China wins table tennis men's team gold
4	Lin thrills to claim gold	林丹再胜李宗伟 男单卫冕第一人	"Super Dan" wins final battle against arch-rival Lee Chong Wei
5	Xu claims Laser Radial gold	徐莉佳为中国水上军团夺得伦敦奥运会首枚金牌	China wins Laser Radial class in Olympic sailing regatta
6	Records tumble as Zhou takes gold	周璐璐果然"轻松"夺冠中国力量伦敦五金收官	Chinese lifter Zhou Lulu nails gold with world record in women's +75kg
7	Wu takes gold with perfect 10	吴敏霞轻取女子3米板 迎来个人奥运首金	Chinese Wu wins Olympic women's 3m springboard gold
8	China triumph seals Badminton sweep	中国羽毛球男双"风云"组合圆梦伦敦	Chinese badminton players Cai and Fu win gold medals in men's doubles
9	Golden Sun lowers world record	游泳综合：孙杨再次改写历史 "菲鱼"完美谢幕	Sun Yang wins gold and breaks world record in 1,500 meters freestyle

10	China dominance continues	同室操戈 裁判"搅局"李晓霞赢得女单冠军	Li Xiaoxia wins table tennis gold medal
11	Yi Siling wins first gold medal of Games	美女枪手易思玲夺冠后落泪：压力终于释放了	Yi shot for the gold and hit the mental mark
12	Impressive Li claims gold	中国男举"未开张" 李雪英捍卫女举荣誉	Chinese lifter Li sets Olympic records and wins women's 58kg gold
13	Guo gets 10m Air Pistol gold	郭文珺一枪定乾坤惊天逆转实现卫冕	Guo Wenjun picks up pistol gold
14	Lin lifts his way to title	举重：男举绝地反击林清峰发狠夺冠	China's Lin Qingfeng wins men's 69kg weightlifting gold at Olympic
15	Qin and Luo add to favourites' haul	秦凯/罗玉通男双3米板轻松取胜	Chinese Luo/Qin win men's synchronised 3m springboard Olympic gold
16	China claim another Diving gold	陈若琳/汪皓女双10米台夺金	China amasses third diving gold at London Olympic
17	Zhang gold earns Grand Slam	张继科奥运单打摘金 成就男单"最快大满贯"	China's Zhang Jike crowned Olympic champion
18	Gold for Chinese pair	中国男双跳台冠军性格南辕北辙的缘全组合	China continues gold streak in Olympic diving
19	Brilliant Bolt completes sprint double	田径：博尔特"溜达"着创历史田径场终破世界纪录	Imperious Bolt blazes to sprint double-double
20	Round-up: Phelps signs off in typical style	7月31日综合：中美继续角力菲鱼成为传奇	Phelps out on a golden high
21	China continue table Tennis dominance	中国女乒再度加冕奥运团体桂冠	Chinese women win table tennis team gold in Olympic Games

22	Deng edges out Sui to claim gold	冯喆、邓琳琳两冠"解气"中国队有力回击4金收官	China's Deng Linlin wins women's beam gymnastic Olympic gold
23	Hurdles hope Liu injured in heats	刘翔跟腱撕裂单脚跳向终点赢得全场掌声	Liu Xiang crashes out of men's 110m hurdles at Olympic Games
24	Britain's gold medallists celebrated with new Royal Mail stamps	英各界盛赞东道主"首金日"	Britain wins 1st gold in women's rowing pair
25	Ye dominates medley heats	叶诗文再演逆转大戏 200米混合泳又夺一金	Ye nets second gold, Phelps sets medal record
26	China surprise Czech Republic	分胜捷克队中国女篮伦敦首战迎来开门红	China oust Czech 66-57 in women's basketball opener
27	Chen defends Platform crown	陈若琳女子10米台轻松卫冕 胡亚丹仅获第9	Chen Ruolin wins women's 10m platform gold at London Olympic Games
28	Chen Race Walks home to gold	陈定"生日"夺金创历史 中国男子竞走现集团优势	History-making walker Chen Ding may become idol of college students
29	China win women's Doubles	田卿/赵芸蕾摘得羽毛球女双金牌	Chinese badminton players Tian Qing and Zhao Yunlei snatch gold in women's doubles
30	China fights to women's Team epee gold	中国玫瑰剑道绽放 女子重剑创造历史	China beats South Korean to win women's epee team event gold medal at Olympics
31	Li claims gold in all-Chinese final	"黑马"李雪芮勇夺奥运女单金牌	Li Xuerui wins Olympic women's badminton singles, Wang Xin withdraws over injury
32	Gold for on-song Dong	董栋笑言错过4年的金牌有点沉	China's Dong beats Russia's Ushakov to win men's trampoline
33	Lu lifts into record books	吕小军陆浩杰包揽男举77公斤级金银牌	Lu Xiaojun of China breaks world record to win men's 77kg weightlifting gold in Olympic Games

34	Fantastic Feng secures gold	冯喆：裁判比我紧张 我终于放心了	Feng wins third gymnastic gold for China at London Olympic
35	Gymnast Zou claims Floor gold	邹凯成中国奥运金牌最多的选手	Chinese Zou retains his Olympic floor title in London
36	Kiprotich claims Marathon gold	乌干达选手夺奥运会马拉松金牌	Kiprotich delighted with gold medal as everyone a winner in marathon
37	Kulhavy edges out rivals to claim gold	山地自行车男子越野赛结束捷克选手夺得冠军	Jaroslav Kulhavy of Czech Republic wins men's cycling mountain gold
38	Boudia edges out rivals to claim gold	男10米台：美国鲍迪亚夺冠 邱波、戴利获二、三	American Boudia wins Olympic men's platform diving gold
39	Round-up: Weightlifting sees records tumble	伦敦奥运男子举重105公斤以上级伊朗包揽冠亚军	Iran's lifter wins Olympic men's over-105kg gold
40	Olympics swimming: Liuyang Jiao wins 200m butterfly gold for China	焦刘洋破奥运纪录赢中国游泳第四金	Jiao surges to China's 4th swim gold

Next, we will conduct generic analysis on the 120 texts in the aforementioned corpus, with the specific steps as follows:

(1) By analyzing and discriminating the various components of the texts in the three corpora, determining which parts are necessary and optional as well as their order and recursion are determined, the GSP model is summarized;

(2) Starting from the transitivity system, mood system, and thematic system that reflect the style of generic expression, the grammatical and lexical characteristics of this genre in the three corpora are analyzed;

(3) By comparing GSP models, vocabulary and grammar among the three corpora, commonalities and differences are identified;

(4) Finally, starting from parameters of smoothness and expressiveness that measure the quality of translation in the translation quality assessment model, improvement suggestions for the quality of English translation of Chinese texts based on the textual structure and linguistic feature dimensions that reflect the characteristics of English sports

news are proposed, and empirical analysis of the aforementioned constructed translation quality assessment model is achieved.

7.2 Corpus-based Generic Structure of Sports News Discourses
7.2.1 Components of Generic Structure of Sports News

Firstly, one piece of sports news is randomly selected from each aforementioned corpus and a schematic structure analysis is conducted to illustrate the methods for generic structural studies. By using the same method, the analysis and statistics of all remaining news in the three corpora are completed.

After completing the structural analysis of all texts in the three corpora, approximately 13 structural elements (moves) of the genre of sports news have been summarized based on their different communicative purposes. They are: H:Heading, L:Lead, RS:Results and Significance, P:Performance, D:Details, AB:Athlete Background, IC:Interview Champion, CET: Champion Express Thanks/Celebrate, CC: Coach's Comment, IO:Interview Other Athletes, OCC:Opponent Coach's Comment, SG:Scores of Great Britain, S:Supplementary Information. Of course, in terms of collective meaning, specifically for a specific piece of sports news, it rarely includes all the aforementioned structural elements. Most discourses only include certain parts of these elements. In addition, BBC English sports news, Xinhua sports news, and translated English sports news on Xinhua Net also exhibit different characteristics in the selection of these elements.

The names and functions of these 13 structural elements are:

1. Heading (H):Heading is a highly concise news report.

2. Lead (L):Lead is usually the first paragraph of the body of the news report with no more than 35 words. It uses extremely concise and precise language to convey the most noteworthy content of the news event, helping readers quickly obtain information, and providing four major elements of news, namely "people", "event", "time", and "locality". (Melven Mencher 2003)[1]

3. Results and Significance: Comments on the results of the competition, especially their significance to the country.

4. Performance:Elaboration on the performance of athletes in the competition, especially their scoring performance.

---

[1] Melven Mencher.News Reporting and Writing, Ninth Edition[M].Beijing: McGraw-Hill Education (Asia) Co. and Qsinghua University Press,2003:34.

5. Details:Description of the details of the competition.

6. Athlete Background:Introduction to the background of the athletes, such as which awards they have won and how they have performed in other competitions.

7. Interview Champion:Interview with champions and the award speeches delivered by champions.

8. Champion Express Thanks/Celebrate:Acknowledgement and celebrations of champions.

9. Coach's Comment: Comment of coaches of the award-winning athletes on their competition and performance.

10. Interview Other Athletes: Interview with other athletes.

11. Opponent Coach's Comment:Opinions or comments of opponents' coaches.

12. Scores of Great Britain: The performance of British athletes, such as scores, ranks, etc.

13. Supplementary Information: Other relevant information about the competition.

7.2.2 The GSP Model of BBC English Sports News

We randomly select one sample (Text 8) from the corpus of BBC English sports news which contains 40 articles and conduct a structural analysis on it. Its structure is as follows:

1. (H) Headline:*China triumph seals Badmin ton sweep*

2. (L) Cai Yun and Fu Haifeng completed a Chinese clean sweep of the Badminton gold medals at London 2012 with victory in the men's Doubles final.

3. RS) The top seeds edged out Denmark's Mathias Boe and Carsten Mogensen 21-16 21-15 at Wembley Arena to ensure China ended the tournament with an emphatic statement.

4. (**P**) The Danes were fired up for the occasion and Boe was even warned to keep his aggression in check.But the third seeds could not trouble the Chinese world number twos enough as they were edged out in both games.

5. (**IO**) Boe complained that the umpire had not spotted that one of his shots hit a Chinese player on its way out at a crucial juncture of the second game.

6. (**S**) But the Danes looked second-best throughout, duly taking silver while Cai and Yun fully deserved their victory.In the bronze match, Republic of Korea pair Chung Jae Sun and Lee Yong Dae beat Malaysian duo Koo Kien Keat and Tan Boon Heong.

From the above analysis, it can be seen that this piece of news includes six moves, and its structure can be summarized as follows:

H^L^RS^P^IO^S

That is, the heading of this news article is "China Triumph Seals Badminton Sweep", then the reporter summarizes the main content of this news with a lead, which is "Cai Yun and Fu Haifeng Has Won the Men's Doubles Final in the 2012 Olympic Games". Subsequently, the results and significance of this game are described:China eliminates Danish players, adding a touch of glory to Chinese badminton. Then there is a description of the players'performance in the game, interviews with the opponents, and some supplementary information about the game.

Following the same method, the structural analysis of all sports news articles in three corpora was completed, and the results are shown in Tables 2 and 3.

Table 2 Structure of BBC English Sports News Articles

Text No.	Structural Components and Their Order
1	H^L^D
2	H^L^AB^P
3	H^L^AB^RS^S^P^S
4	H^L^RS^P^D^S^IC^IO
5	H^L^D^P
6	H^L^D^P^IC
7	H^L^P^AB^P^S^IC
8	H^L^RS^P^IO^S
9	H^L^RS^AB^P^S
10	H^L^RS^P^S^P^D^S
11	H^L^AB^P^IC
12	H^L^P^SG
13	H^L^AB^P^S^IC^IO
14	H^L^RS^S^P
15	H^L^RS^P^IC
16	H^L^P^SG^IC
17	H^L^AB^P^RS
18	H^L^P^SG
19	H^L^AB^P^IC
20	H^L^AB^P^S^IC^S
21	H^L^RS^S^RS^P

22	H^L^P^D	
23	H^L^AB^P^IC^S^OCC	
24	H^L^SG^RS^S	
25	H^L^AB^P^IO^S	
26	H^L^D^OCC^P	
27	H^L^RS^P^AB^IC	
28	H^L^AB^P	
29	H^L^P^D^S	
30	H^L^P^D	
31	H^L^P^AB^P^S^P^RS	
32	H^L^P^RS^IC	
33	H^L^P^D^S	
34	H^L^P^RS^IC	
35	H^L^P^RS	
36	H^L^AB^P^D	
37	H^L^P^D	
38	H^L^P	
39	H^L^AB^P^S^RS^S^P^D^S	
40	H^L^P	

The distribution of each structural elements is as follows:

Table 3 Distribution of Structural Elements in BBC English Sports News Texts

Text No.	H	L	RS	AB	P	D	IC	IO	OCC	SG	S
1	√	√				√					
2	√	√			√	√					
3	√	√	√	√	√						√
4	√	√	√		√	√	√	√			√
5	√	√			√	√					
6	√	√			√	√	√				
7	√	√		√	√		√				√
8	√	√	√		√			√			
9	√	√	√	√	√						√

	1	2	3	4	5	6	7	8	9	10	11
10	√	√	√			√			√		√
11	√	√		√	√		√				
12	√	√		√						√	
13	√	√		√	√		√	√			√
14	√	√	√		√						√
15	√	√	√		√		√		√		
16	√	√			√		√			√	
17	√	√	√	√	√						
18	√	√			√					√	
19	√	√		√	√		√				
20	√	√		√	√		√				√
21	√	√	√		√						√
22	√	√			√	√					
23	√	√		√	√		√		√		√
24	√	√	√							√	√
25	√	√		√	√			√			√
26	√	√			√	√			√		
27	√	√	√	√	√		√				
28	√	√			√	√					
29	√	√			√	√					√
30	√	√			√	√					
31	√	√	√	√	√						√
32	√	√	√				√				
33	√	√			√	√					√
34	√	√	√		√		√				
35	√	√	√		√						
36	√	√		√	√	√					
37	√	√			√	√					
38	√	√			√						
39	√	√	√	√	√	√					√
40	√	√			√						

This table is a description of the structural components of texts in the corpus, namely the description of moves. The symbol "√" indicates that the move appears in the text.

The frequency of each move in the corpus is shown in Table 4 after statistical analysis.

Table 4 The Occurrence Rate of Moves in BBC English Sports News

	H	L	RS	P	D	AB	IC	IO	OCC	SG	S
Sum	40	40	16	38	13	16	13	4	2	4	15
%	100	100	40	95	32.5	40	32.5	10	5	10	37.5

From the above statistics, it can be seen that BBC sports news include the following moves: heading, lead, results and significance, performance, details, athlete background, interview champion, coach's comment, interview other athletes, opponent coach's comment, scores of Great Britain and supplementary information. The occurrence rate of moves like "heading","lead" and "performance" all exceeds 50%, making them essential moves in English sports news. The occurrence rate of other factors is less than 50%, which means that they are selective elements.

In terms of the sequence and recursion of structural elements, it can be found from the table that "heading" and "lead" appear at the beginning of each news article, and their positions cannot be interchanged, they form a whole."Results and significance" is not an essential element and its position is flexible. In general, "athlete background" appears together with"performance", and "athlete background" appears before "performance" (because"athlete background" is an unnecessary element,"performance" may not necessarily appear when it appears). "Details" generally appear after "performance" and can be repeated. The position of "supplementary information" is relatively flexible.

Therefore, the GSP model of BBC sports news articles is:

[H^L]^[(AB)^P]^(D)(RS)(IC)(IO)(OCC)(SG). (S)

7.2.3 The GSP Model of Xinhua Sports News

In order to correspond with BBC English sports news, sample 8 of Chinese sports news is analyzed as below.

（H）中国羽毛球男双"风云"组合圆梦伦敦

（L）新华网伦敦8月5日奥运专电（记者姬烨白旭）北京奥运会羽毛球男双亚军蔡赟/傅海峰终于在伦敦完成了自己的奥运梦想！

（RS）在5日的伦敦奥运会羽毛球男双决赛中，"风云"以21:16和21:15战胜世界第三的丹麦组合鲍伊/摩根森，在他们的第三次奥运之旅中终获金牌。而一向被视为软肋的国羽男双也终于摘得了奥运首金。这样，中国羽毛球队在本届奥运会中史无前例地包揽5金，并且还获得2银1铜。

（CET）获得胜利后，蔡赟也像之前摘得男单冠军的林丹一样，奔向场边，尽情地享受观众的欢呼，而傅海峰则在场地中央掩面哭泣。

（AB）为了这枚奥运金牌，两人足足等了8年。2004年雅典奥运会，他们止步八强；2008年北京奥运会，他们在决赛惜败。

（IC）"这是具有历史意义的时刻，奥运会拿了五金，对于（中国）羽毛球队来说，简直不敢想象，"蔡赟说。（D）在男双决赛中，面对半决赛淘汰了韩国名将郑在成/李龙大的鲍伊/摩根森，经验丰富的蔡赟/傅海峰没有给对手太多机会。首局比赛，他们在12平后打出一波6:1的高潮，奠定了领先优势。第二局，丹麦组合放手一搏，"风云"依然稳扎稳打，并以20:14拿到了6个冠军点。

（IC）"我们跟他们彼此相互很了解，而且他们打得非常优秀，如果我们稍微有一个环节处理不好，他们就会连赢很快，所以我们今天要把比分咬住。"傅海峰说。

（CC）看到"风云"夺得男双金牌，昔日国羽的男双队员、如今队内的总教练李永波也与他们相拥而泣。"我希望通过这个冠军能够改变大家的印象，那就是中国男双已经不是我们的软肋。我希望奥运冠军是我们男双的一个新起点"。

（S）在上午进行的铜牌争夺战中，郑在成/李龙大以23:21和21:10击败马来西亚组合古健杰/陈文宏，获得季军。

The structure of this news article can be summarized as follows:

H^L^RS^CET^AB^IC^D^IC^CC^S

This sports news article not only includes heading, lead, results and significance, supplementary information, but also athletes' celebration after winning the award, athlete background, details, and comment of athletes and coaches.

The structure of the remaining sports news articles is analyzed by using the same method,Their structural elements and distribution are as follows:

Table 5 Structure of Xinhua Sports News Articles

Text No.	Structural Elements and Their Sequence
1	H^L^CET^RS^D^P^S^IC
2	H^L^RS^P^D^CC^AB^IC^S^IO^S^IC^IO
3	H^L^S^CET^S
4	H^L^CET^P^IC^IO^D^S^IC^S^CC
5	H^L^RS^S^AB^P^D^S
6	H^L^RS^AB^D^IC^D^CET^IC^CC^P^IO^P^S
7	H^L^RS^S^D^P^IC^AB^IC^S^IO
8	H^L^RS^CET^AB^IC^D^IC^CC^S
9	H^L^P^CET^IC^S^P^S
10	H^L^S^D^IO^D^P^AB
11	H^L^D^P^IC
12	H^L^RS^P^IC^P^IO^S^P^IO^P^S^IO
13	H^L^AB^D^IC^P^CC^AB^IC^D^IC^P^S
14	H^L^RS^D^P^AB^CET^IC^CC^IC^S
15	H^L^RS^P^AB^IC^D^IC
16	H^L^RS^P^D^IC^AB^P^S
17	H^L^RS^D^P^D^P^D^P^AB^S
18	H^L^RS^AB^D^IC^S^IC^AB^IC^AB^IC
19	H^L^P^D^IC^RS^D^S^CET
20	H^L^RS^P^S^RS^P^S^P^S
21	H^L^CET^RS^P^D^S
22	H^L^RS^P^CET^IC^P^CET^IC^P^S
23	H^L^OCC^S^D^OCC
24	H^L^RS^P^S^IC^S
25	H^L^D^P^IC^S^D^IC
26	H^L^P^RS^S
27	H^L^P^RS^CET^IC^AB^IC^P^S^IO^S
28	H^L^RS^P^IC^D^IC^P^IC^IO^S^AB^D
29	H^L^D^P^CET^IC^IO
30	H^L^RS^P^CC^S

	31	H^L^RS^CET^AB^CET^IC^P^IC^IO^P
	32	H^L^S^IC^AB^P^S
	33	H^L^D^IC^D^P^IC^IO^S
	34	H^L^IC
	35	H^L^S^RS^IC^P^IC^CET^IC
	36	H^L^P^CET^IC^AB^IC^S
	37	H^L
	38	H^L^D^CET^P^S^IO^AB^IO^S^
	39	H^L^S
	40	H^L^P^IC^AB^IC^D^IO^IC^CC^CET

The structure of all 40 news articles in this corpus is as follows:

Table 6 Distribution of Structural Elements in Xinhua Sports News Articles

Text No.	H	L	RS	AB	P	D	CET	IC	CC	IO	OCC	S
1	√	√	√		√	√	√	√				√
2	√	√	√	√	√	√		√	√	√		√
3	√	√					√					√
4	√	√			√	√	√	√	√	√		√
5	√	√	√	√	√	√						√
6	√	√	√	√	√	√	√	√	√	√		√
7	√	√	√	√	√	√		√		√		√
8	√	√	√	√		√	√	√	√			√
9	√	√			√		√			√		√
10	√	√		√	√	√				√		√
11	√	√			√	√		√				
12	√	√	√		√		√			√		
13	√	√		√	√	√		√				√
14	√	√	√	√	√	√	√	√	√			√
15	√	√	√	√	√	√		√				
16	√	√	√	√	√	√		√				√
17	√	√	√	√	√	√						√
18	√	√	√	√		√		√				
19	√	√	√		√	√	√	√				√

	H	L	RS	P	D	AB	IC	CC	IO	OCC	CET	S
20	√	√	√		√							√
21	√	√	√		√	√						√
22	√	√	√		√		√	√				√
23	√	√				√					√	√
24	√	√	√		√			√				√
25	√	√			√	√		√				√
26	√	√	√		√							√
27	√	√	√	√	√		√	√		√		√
28	√	√	√	√	√	√		√		√		√
29	√	√		√	√	√	√	√		√		
30	√	√	√		√				√	√		√
31	√	√	√	√	√		√	√		√		
32	√	√	√	√	√			√		√		√
33	√	√			√	√		√		√		√
34	√	√						√				
35	√	√	√		√		√	√		√		√
36	√	√			√	√	√	√				√
37	√	√										
38	√	√		√	√	√	√			√		√
39	√	√										√
40	√	√		√	√	√	√	√	√	√		

Based on this, the frequency of each move appearing in the 40 articles in the corpus is:

Table 7: Frequency of Moves in Xinhua Sports News Articles

	H	L	RS	P	D	AB	IC	CC	IO	OCC	CET	S
Sum	40	40	23	30	21	19	28	8	10	1	17	30
%	100	100	57.5	75	52.5	47.5	70	17.5	25	2.5	42.5	70

From the above three tables, it can be seen that moves included in Xinhua sports news are: heading, lead, results and significance, performance, details, athletes background, interview champion, champion express thanks/celebrate, interview with award-winning coach, interview champion's coach, and supplementary information.

From the analysis, it can be seen that the occurrence rate of moves like heading, lead, results and significance, performance, details, interview champion, and supplementary information has all exceeded 50%. In Chinese sports news articles, these moves are necessary elements. If the occurrence rate is less than 50%, then the elements are optional.

The structural elements of Chinese sports news display the following characteristics: heading and lead appear in pairs, both are located at the beginning of the article and cannot be exchanged with each other; Results and significance follow closely after heading and lead; Performance and details are generally presented in pairs, and their positions can be exchanged or repeated; The position of interview champion is relatively flexible and can appear repeatedly; Interviewing champion's coach usually occurs after interview champion (but interview champion's coach is an optional element); The location of supplementary information is relatively flexible and can be repeated.

Therefore, the GSP model for Chinese sports news articles is:

$$[H{\wedge}L]{\wedge}RS{\wedge}(AB).[P.D].[IC{\wedge}(CC)](CET)(IO)(OCC).S$$

7.2.4 Structure of Translated English Sports News on Xinhua Net

Next, one sample (Text 8) from the corpus of translated English sports news on Xinhua Net is also selected to make structural analysis.

(H) Chinese badminton players Cai and Fu win gold medals in men's doubles

(L) LONDON, Aug. 5 (Xinhua)—Chinese badminton players Cai Yun and Fu Haifeng beat their rivals 2-0 Sunday afternoon and clinched gold medals in men's doubles in the Wembley Arena.

(RS) These are the first gold medal won by Chinese in that event. This means Chinese raked in all the five badminton gold medals produced at the London Olympics.

(P) Mathias Boe and Carsten Mogensen from Denmark won the silver, while the bronze fell into the pockets of Jung Jae Sung and Lee Yong Dae of South Korea.

(C) Cai and Fu geared up quickly in the first game to rule the court, where the Danish only started to become aggressive after being outscored 1-4. They impressed the audience by catching up to the Chinese pair, who enjoyed 11-6 advantage before the interval, and leveling the scores at 12-12. But some mistakes from Boe and Mogensen sent their rivals to a 21-16 victory.In the second game the Danish made desperate attempts. Li Yongbo, China's badminton head coach, shouted from the stand every now and then to remind Cai and Fu to"run quickly". With Cai Yun's last shot missed by the rivals, China won, 21-15.Cai Yun rushed out of the court for celebration, while his partner Fu shed tears in excitement.

(IC) "This is the exact result we aimed for," said Cai, 32. "We have been playing together for over 10 years, and have entered the Olympic three times. Last time in Beijing we only achieved silver, and we were regretful."

(AB) The combination of Fu Haifeng's power with his regular partner Cai Yun's speed enabled the pair to become the world's leading men's doubles team since 2004. After the Beijing Olympic, however, they seemed to be in a downturn.

(IC) "After failure, we were more mature," said Cai. "For match we were not afraid of failure, we tried to enjoy it. We were not scared at all, not nervous. Part of the reason we won was we were full of confidence." Fu, 28, said the title was like "a dream coming true". "This will probably be the greatest recognition of our badminton career," he said. "Next time, our performance might be even better because we don't have any pressure now that we have achieved this goal. Next time we will play in a different state of mind."

(CC) Li Yongbo was delighted because their victory not only signalled a clean sweep of badminton golds at the London Olympic, but also suggested a breakthrough of the men's doubles, as the gold in men's doubles seemed always elusive in the past.

"I hope that these medals could change people's perception on the event," he said. "Many people considered men's doubles the Achilles'heel for China's national badminton team. In fact, Cai and Fu have harvested 14 world titles. This victory is a new starting point for us."

(IO) The disappointed Boe said, "right now it doesn't feel that good. We hoped for more but of course after half an hour or a little bit later today we willprobably be satisfid with reaching final and getting silver."

While his partner said they have tried to believe they would win the whole time. "We tried to fight even though it was 14-18, we still tried and told each other to focus."

(OCC) Finn Traerup-Hansen, coach from the Danish team, said he was "extremely happy" with the result. Earlier Joachim Fischer and Christinna Pedersen have pocketed bronze medals in mixed doubles. "That's extraordinary for a country of 5.5 million people," he said. "So of course we are very happy."

From this, it can be seen that the structure of this article can be summarized as follows:

H^L^RS^P^D^IC^AB^IC^CC^IO^OCC

This sports news article includes heading, lead, results and significance, performance, details, interview champion, athlete background, interviews champion's coach, interview opponent athlete, and interview opponent's coach. By using the same method, the structural elements and their order of 40 translated English sports news articles are as follows:

Table 8 Structural Elements of Translated English Sports News on Xinhua Net

文本编号	结构要素及其顺序
1	H^L^RS^P^D^S
2	H^L^RS^P
3	H^L^RS^P^D^CC^IC^OCC^IO
4	H^L^RS^D^P^IC^IO^S
5	H^L^RS^P^S^D^IC^AB^IC
6	H^L^RS^P^D^IC^P^IO
7	H^L^P
8	H^L^RS^P^D^IC^AB^IC^CC^IO^OCC
9	H^L^P^D^S
10	H^L^D^P
11	H^L^P^S^P^IC^RS^AB^IC^D^IC^CC^IC^CC^S
12	H^L^P^D^IC^P^IO^P
13	H^L
14	H^L^P
15	H^L^P^D^IC^P^IO^P^IO^RS
16	H^L^P^D^IC^P^OCC^P^IO^S
17	H^L^RS^P
18	H^L^P^D^S
19	H^L^P^AB^S
20	H^L^P^IC^D^IC
21	H^L^RS^P^S
22	H^L^P
23	H^L^S
24	H^L^P^RS^D^AB^D^S
25	H^L^D^S^D^IC^P^IC^P^IC^P^S^P^IC^S^IC^P^IC^P^S

26	H^L^RS^IC^P^D^OCC^CC^S
27	H^L^RS^P^S
28	H^L^RS^AB^S^IC^AB^P^IC
29	H^L^RS^D^IC^S^IC^IO
30	H^L^RS
31	H^L^RS^P^D^S^IC^S^RS^P^IC^S^IO
32	H^L^P^D^IC^P^IO^P^IO
33	H^L^P^RS^P
34	H^L^RS^AB^P^IC^S^IC^IO^S
35	H^L^RS^P^IC^AB^IC^IO
36	H^L^D^IC^IO^S^IO^S
37	H^L^RS^IC^P^S
38	H^L^P
39	H^L^P
40	H^L^RS^IC^P^S^IC^P^IC^P^IC

The distribution of structural elements in articles in the corpus of translated English sports news is as follows.

Table 9 Distribution of Structural Elements in Translated English Sports News

Text No.	H	L	RS	P	D	IC	AB	CC	IO	OCC	S
1	√	√	√	√	√						√
2	√	√	√	√							
3	√	√	√	√	√	√		√	√	√	
4	√	√	√	√	√	√			√		√
5	√	√	√	√	√	√	√				√
6	√	√	√	√	√	√			√		
7	√	√		√							
8	√	√	√	√	√	√	√	√	√	√	
9	√	√	√	√							
10	√	√		√	√						
11	√	√	√	√	√	√	√	√			√
12	√	√		√	√	√			√		
13	√	√									

	1	2	3	4	5	6	7	8	9	10
14	√	√		√						
15	√	√	√	√	√	√			√	
16	√	√		√	√	√			√	√	√
17	√	√	√	√						
18	√	√		√	√					√
19	√	√		√			√			√
20	√	√		√	√	√				
21	√	√	√	√						√
22	√	√		√						
23	√	√								√
24	√	√	√	√	√		√			√
25	√	√		√	√	√				√
26	√	√	√	√	√	√		√	√	√
27	√	√	√	√						√
28	√	√	√	√		√	√			√
29	√	√	√		√	√	√	√		√
30	√	√	√							
31	√	√	√	√	√	√			√	√
32	√	√		√	√	√			√	
33	√	√	√	√						
34	√	√	√	√		√	√		√	√
35	√	√	√	√		√	√		√	
36	√	√			√	√			√	√
37	√	√	√	√		√				√
38	√	√		√						
39	√	√		√						
40	√	√	√	√		√				√

After the description of the structural characteristics of translated English sports news articles on Xinhua Net, the occurrence rate of each move appearing in these articles was calculated and the results are shown in Table 10.

Table 10: Occurrence Rate in Translated English Sports News Articles

	H	L	RS	P	D	AB	IC	CC	IO	OCC	S
Sum	40	40	23	35	21	6	21	4	14	4	20
%	100	100	56	87.5	52.5	15	52.5	10	35	10	50

As mentioned earlier, only when the occurrence rate of a move exceeds 50% can it be called a necessary one; On the contrary, it is an optional move. According to this standard, it can be seen that in the translated English sports news on Xinhua Net, heading, lead, results and significance, performance, details, interviews champion, and supplementary information are necessary moves. The occurrence rate of other elements appearing is less than 50%, which belongs to optional elements.

Although the necessary and optional elements as well as the occurrence sequence that each translated English news article contains are complex, there are still some rules to follow: heading (H) and lead (L) must appear in each piece of news, and heading appears before lead. The sequence and position of the two in the article cannot be exchanged; Results and significance (RS) generally appear in the first step of the game review; Performance (P) and details (D) are relatively flexible in terms of positions; Interview champion (IC) usually appears in pairs with athletes background (AB), and their positions can be shifted (AB is an optional element, so AB can not appear when IC appears); The position of supplementary information (S) is relatively flexible and can appear repeatedly. Based on the above summary, it can be concluded that the GSP model for translated English sports news on Xinhua Net is as follows:

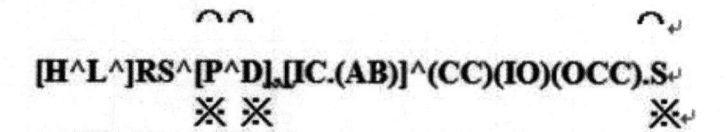

[H^L^]RS^[P^D].[IC.(AB)]^(CC)(IO)(OCC).S

7.3 Corpus-based Linguistic Analysis of Sports News Discourses

As mentioned earlier, we use language to achieve three "meta functions" or "pure rational functions" :ideational function, interpersonal function, and textual function. Ideational function is mainly achieved through the transitivity system and the vocabulary-grammar system, interpersonal function is reflected through the mood system and modality system, and textual function is mainly achieved through the theme system.

The transitivity system, mood system, and theme system, which reflect the ideational function, interpersonal function, and textual function of language, will be used as analytical tools to conduct a lexical and grammatical analysis of the linguistic features -

representation styles - of English, Chinese, and translated English texts in sports news corpora.

7.3.1 Linguistic Characteristics of BBC English Sports News Discourses

The transitivity system has three components: the process itself, the participants in the process, and the additional situations associated with the process. For example, in the sentence'Lion lazily chases tourists in the jungle.''Lion'is the participant,'chase'is the process,'tourist'is the participant,'lazily'and 'in the jungle'are additional situations. In the process of transitivity, "the process itself " is generally achieved through verbs or verb phrases, "participants" are generally achieved through nouns or noun phrases, and additional situations are generally achieved through adverbs, adverb phrases, or prepositional phrases. Usually, the transitivity system consists of six major processes: material, mental, relational, behavioral, verbal, and existential. These processes have been discussed in detail in the previous chapters, and will not be further elaborated here.

1) Transitivity system

The BBC English sports news entitled "China Triumph Seals Badminton Sweep" (Text 8) is selected as an example to conduct the analysis of transitivity process types.

China triumph seals Badminton sweep

(1) Cai Yun and Fu Haifeng completed a Chinese clean sweep of the Badminton gold medals at London 2012 with victory in the men's Doubles final.

(2) The top seeds edged out Denmark's Mathias Boe and Carsten Mogensen 21-16 21-15 at Wembley Arena to ensure China ended the tournament with an emphatic statement.

(3) The Danes were fired up for the occasion and Boe was even warned to keep his aggression in check.

(4) But the third seeds could not trouble the Chinese world number twos enough as they were edged out in both games.

(5) Boe complained that the umpire had not spotted that one of his shots hit a Chinese player on its way out at a crucial juncture of the second game.

(6) But the Danes looked second-best throughout, duly taking silver

(7) while Cai and Yun fully deserved their victory.

(8)In the bronze match, Republic of Korea pair Chung Jae Sun and Lee Yong Dae beat Malaysian duo Koo Kien Keat and Tan Boon Heong.

The process type analysis of this text is as follows:

Table 11 Process Type Analysis of Text 8

Clause No.	Process No.	Type of Process	Verbs Involved
1	1	Material	completed
2	2	Material	edged out
3	3	Material	were fired up
4	5	Material	trouble
5	7	Verbal	complained
6	10	Behavioral	looked
7	12	Material	beat

The process type analysis of all 40 BBC English sports news articles is completed by using the same method, and the statistics are as follows.

Table 12 Distribution Process Type of BBC English Sports News Texts

Text No.	Material	Mental	Relational	Behavioral	Verbal	Existential	Sum
1	4	0	0	0	0	0	4
2	5	0	0	1	0	1	7
3	8	1	2	0	1	1	13
4	11	0	2	0	2	0	15
5	8	0	2	0	0	1	11
6	5	0	1	0	1	0	7
7	6	0	0	0	4	0	10
8	8	1	0	1	2	0	12
9	4	0	1	0	0	0	5
10	19	0	3	0	0	1	23
11	4	0	0	0	1	0	5

12	3	0	0	0	0	0	3
13	4	1	1	0	2	0	8
14	4	0	0	0	0	0	4
15	1	0	3	0	3	0	7
16	3	0	0	0	3	0	6
17	6	0	1	0	0	0	7
18	5	0	0	0	0	1	6
19	6	1	1	0	1	0	9
20	20	2	4	0	2	1	29
21	5	0	4	0	0	0	9
22	3	0	1	0	0	0	4
23	3	0	0	1	2	2	8
24	6	0	3	0	0	0	9
25	3	1	4	0	2	0	10
26	5	1	1	0	1	0	8
27	4	0	4	0	4	0	12
28	7	0	0	1	0	0	8
29	13	0	0	0	0	0	13
30	8	0	1	0	0	1	10
31	11	0	1	0	0	0	12
32	4	0	0	0	3	0	7
33	5	0	0	2	0	0	7
34	3	0	1	0	1	0	5
35	4	0	0	0	0	0	4
36	11	1	1	0	0	0	13
37	6	0	0	1	0	1	8
38	3	0	1	0	0	0	4
39	9	0	3	0	1	0	13
40	4	0	0	0	0	0	4

The distribution ratios of different process types are:

Table 13 Distribution Ratio of BBC English Sports News Process Types

	Material	Mental	Relational	Behavioral	Verbal	Existential	Sum
Sum	249	9	46	6	35	10	355
%	70.2	2.5	13.0	1.7	9.9	2.8	100

From the above analysis, it can be seen that the proportion of material process is 70.2%, which is the most commonly used in BBC English sports news. The content expressed by material process is "doing", which involves results and significance, performance, details and so on. For example:

The world number one had **stormed through** the opening rounds, and **stopped** her semi-final early with a convincing 19-7 victory over Lucija Zaninovic of Croatia. (Text 2)

The Chinese swimmer **had broken** Grant Hackett's long-standing world mark at last year's World Championships in Shanghai. (Text 9)

China triumph **seals** Badminton sweep。（Text 8）

In addition to material process, relational and verbal processes are also very common, with a proportion of 13% and 9.9% respectively. The relational process is mainly used to describe characteristics and attributes, and is more common when introducing results and significance, background of athletes and the game, such as:

That **was** Japan's first Olympic medal in the sport.（Text 3）

Xu **was** still ahead around the third and fourth marks, although Bouwmeester pulled herself up from eighth to third in the penultimate downwind leg.（Text 5）

Because athletes'words are often cited in sports news reports, the proportion of verbal process is relatively high, such as:

Boe **complained** that the umpire had not spotted that one of his shots hit a Chinese player on its way out at a crucial juncture of the second game. (Text 8)

Phelps **told** Bowman: "I have looked up to Michael Jordan all my life. He became the best Basketball player there ever was. I've been able to become the best swimmer of all time, we got here together. Thank you." (Text 20)

As for the three processes of mental behavioral, and existential, their frequency is relatively low in BBC English sports news.

2) Mood System

Sports news not only conveys specific information, but also conveys certain emotional meaning. The function of emotional meaning lies in "interacting with others, establishing and maintaining relationships, influencing others' behavior, expressing one's own views and perspectives on everything in the world, or changing others' views about the world"[1]. The above functions of sports news are mainly realized by the interpersonal meaning of sports news discourses, while meaning at lexical and grammatical levels is realized by the mood system.

One article from the 40 BBC English sports news is randomly selected for mood analysis. Next, text 1 is selected from the corpus of BBC English Sports News.

Olympics boxing: China's Zou Shiming retains light flyweight title

(1) [1]Zou Shiming of China successfully defends his Olympic light flyweight title by edging a controversial contest with Thailand's Kaeo Pongprayoon.

(2) [2]Leading 6-4 after two rounds, Zou came under a sustained assault in the third and was penalised for pushing - adding two points to his opponent's score.

(3) [3]But Pongprayoon was handed the same penalty moments later, allowing top seed Zou a 13-10 triumph.

The mood analysis of the above news article is detailed in the table below.

Table 14 Analysis of Mood System of Text 1

Sentence No.	Clause No.	Subject	Determiner	Tense	Mood Type
1	[1]	Zou shiming	defends	Present Tense	Indicative
2	[2]	Zou	came	Past Tense	Indicative
3	[3]	Pongprayoon	was	Past Tense	Indicative

According to the above method, the analysis of the mood system in 40 BBC English

---

[1] Thompson, G. Introducing Functional Grammar [M]. London: Edward Arnold, 1996:28.

sports news texts is completed, and the statistics are as follows.

Table 15 Distribution of Mood Types in BBC English Sports News Texts

No.		Mood Type			Subject						Tense		
					第一人称		第二人称		第三人称				
Text No.	Number of Clauses	Indica-tive	Impera-tive	Interro-gative	athlete /coach	other	athlete /coach	other	athlete /coach	other	past	present	future
1	3	3	0	0	0	0	0	0	3	2	2	1	0
2	6	6	0	0	0	0	0	0	5	1	6	0	0
3	15	15	0	0	1	0	0	0	3	11	8	7	0
4	13	13	0	0	0	0	0	0	8	5	13	0	0
5	8	8	0	0	0	0	0	0	7	1	8	0	0
6	8	8	0	0	0	0	0	0	5	3	5	3	0
7	13	13	0	0	2	0	0	0	7	4	11	2	0
8	7	7	0	0	0	0	0	0	7	0	7	0	0
9	5	5	0	0	0	0	0	0	5	0	5	0	0
10	19	19	0	0	0	0	0	0	16	3	16	2	1
11	9	9	0	0	1	0	0	0	5	3	6	3	0
12	3	3	0	0	0	0	0	0	3	0	3	0	0
13	8	8	0	0	0	0	0	0	6	2	7	1	0
14	4	4	0	0	0	0	0	0	1	3	4	0	0
15	10	10	0	0	4	0	0	0	4	2	7	3	0
16	9	9	0	0	3	0	0	0	6	0	9	0	0
17	7	7	0	0	0	0	0	0	6	1	5	2	0
18	5	5	0	0	0	0	0	0	5	0	5	0	0
19	12	12	0	0	5	0	0	0	5	2	12	0	0
20	26	26	0	0	1	0	0	0	17	8	25	1	0
21	9	9	0	0	0	0	0	0	2	7	5	3	1
22	4	4	0	0	0	0	0	0	3	1	4	0	0
23	17	17	0	0	2	0	1	0	9	5	13	4	0
24	7	7	0	0	0	0	0	0	0	7	1	4	2
25	9	9	0	0	1	0	0	0	7	1	9	0	0
26	6	6	0	0	0	0	0	0	3	3	6	0	0

27	9	9	0	0	2	0	0	0	6	1	7	2	0
28	6	6	0	0	0	0	0	0	5	1	6	0	0
29	9	9	0	0	0	0	0	0	9	0	9	0	0
30	8	8	0	0	0	0	0	0	7	1	8	0	0
31	8	8	0	0	0	0	0	0	6	2	8	0	0
32	9	9	0	0	1	0	0	0	6	2	9	0	0
33	5	5	0	0	0	0	0	0	4	1	5	0	0
34	7	7	0	0	1	0	0	0	4	2	6	1	0
35	4	4	0	0	0	0	0	0	3	1	4	0	0
36	10	10	0	0	0	0	0	0	9	1	10	0	0
37	8	8	0	0	0	0	0	0	8	0	8	0	0
38	4	4	0	0	0	0	0	0	3	1	4	0	0
39	13	13	0	0	0	0	0	0	4	9	12	1	0
40	3	3	0	0	0	0	0	0	2	1	1	2	0

The distribution ratio of the three types of mood and their related personal and tense parameters in the corpus was as follows:

Table 16 Analysis and Statistics of Mood System

	Number of Clauses	Mood Type			Subject			Tense		
		Indicative	Imperative	Interrogative	First person	Second person	Third person	Past	Present	Future
Sum	345	345	0	0	24	1	320	299	42	4
%	100	100	0	0	7	0.2	92.8	87	12	1

From this, it is found that:

Mood type: There are a total of 345 small sentences in 40 BBC English sports news articles, all of which use an indicative tone, accounting for 100%. For example:

The most notable statistic is that China has now won 24 of the 28 Table Tennis gold medals on offer after delivering a second successive clean sweep in London. (Text 3)

Xu was still ahead around the third and fourth marks, although Bouwmeester pulled herself up from eighth to third in the penultimate downwind leg. (Text 5)

Subject selection: the first person subjects account for 6.5%, the second person subjects are less than 1%, and the third-person subjects account for an overwhelming majority which is about 93%. The proportion of athletes as subjects is as high as 72%, for example:

We actually have a better feeling now than we did after Beijing because more new people have seen our sport. (Text 3)

You see him running well in certain competitions, but not many people know how he achieves this level. (Text 23)

The Irish sailor, though, dropped down to ninth during the second leg as Xu moved into the lead, despite being forced to do a penalty turn. (Text 5)

Sun Yang continued to steer the 1500m Freestyle into uncharted territory as he lowered his own world record to clinch his second gold at the London 2012 Olympic Games. (Text 9)

Tense: The past tense is the most frequently used, accounting for 87% of the total; the present tense is 12%, and the proportion of future tense is the smallest, accounting for about 1%. From the content described by these tenses, the past tense is mainly used to report games and details that have occurred, and achievements that have been gained by athletes in the past; the present tense mainly appears in direct speech and background introduction when athletes or coaches comment, and the future tense is used to forecast upcoming events. For example:

New gold medal stamps **have gone** (present perfect tense) on sale today to celebrate the successes of Great Britain's first gold medallists of the London 2012 Olympic Games: rowers Helen Glover and Heather Stanning, and cyclist Bradley Wiggins.(Text 24)

Ye Shiwen **returned** (past tense) to the Olympic pool after her super-fast 400m Individual Medley swim to easily head the field in the heats of the shorter medley event.(Text 25)

In the last eight, they **will be joined** (future tense) by Austria, Hong Kong and Portugal, who eased to 3-0 successes against Egypt, Brazil and host nation Great Britain respectively. (Text 10)

3) Modality System

Modality is about being "positive" or "negative". Here, "yes" and "no" are not in simple binary opposition to each other but at a transitional level, which is a tendency related to being "positive" or "negative". Halliday (1985)[1] used the following table to summarize a list of modal operators according to different degrees:

Table 17 List of English Modal Operators

Model operators	low	median	high
Positive	can, may, could, might	will, would, should, is/was to	must, ought to, need, has/had to
Negative	needn't, doesn't, didn't need to/ have to	won't, wouldn't, shouldn't, isn't/wasn't to	mustn't, oughtn't to, can't, couldn't, mayn't, hasn't

According to Table 17, modal operators contained in all 40 BBC sports news articles have been summarized and their distribution is as follows:

Table 18 Distribution of Modal Operators in BBC English Sports News

Text No.	might(may)	could(can)	will(would)	should	must	need
1						
2						
3	√		√			
4	√					
5		√				
6			√			
7		√				
8		√				
9						
10			√			
11						
12						

---

[1] Halliday, M. A. K. *An Introduction to Functional Grammar* [M]. London: Edward Arnold, 1985:76.

13						
14						
15	√					
16			√			
17		√	√			
18						
19	√	√	√			
20		√	√		√	
21		√				
22			√			
23		√	√			
24			√			
25			√			
26						
27						
28						
29			√			
30						√
31		√	√			
32			√			
33						
34		√				
35						
36						
37						
38						
39	√					
40						

The occurrence rate of these modal operators is:

Table 19 Occurrence Rate of Modal Operators

	Low		Media		High		Sum
	might(may)	could(can)	will(would)	should	must	need	
Total No.	5	14	22	0	1	1	43
%	11.7	32.6	51.1	0	2.3	2.3	100

It can be seen from the above table that low degree modal operators (might, may, could) and the medium degree modal operators "will (would)" are much more frequently used than high degree modal operators. "Can" usually appears in the direct speech of athletes and coaches, while "could" is often used to describe the state of athletes or coaches;'will (would)'is mainly used to describe or forecast future events. For example:

I **can** handle more pressure than before.(Text 7)

Afterwards, Deng **could** hardly hide his delight.(Text 34)

In the last eight, they **will** be joined by Austria, Hong Kong and Portugal, who eased to 3-0 successes against Egypt, Brazil and host nation Great Britain respectively. (Text 10)

4) Theme System

Next, text 1 from the corpus of BBC English sports news entitled "Olympics boxing: China's Zou Shiming Retains Light Flyweight Title" is selected as an example for theme analysis.

Olympics boxing: China's Zou Shiming retains light flyweight title

(1) [1] Zou Shiming of China successfully defends his Olympic light flyweight title by edging a controversial contest with Thailand's Kaeo Pongprayoon.

(2) [2] Leading 6-4 after two rounds, Zou came under a sustained assault in the third and was penalised for pushing - adding two points to his opponent's score.

(3) [3] But Pongprayoon was handed the same penalty moments later, allowing top seed Zou a 13-10 triumph.

The above analysis is presented in a table as follows:

Table 20 Theme Analysis of Text 1

Clause No.	Theme No.	Theme Type			Marked	Unmarked
		Textual	Interpersonal	Experiential		
1	1			Zou shiming		√
2	2			Zou		√
3	3	But		Pongprayoon	√	

From this, it can be seen that there is a compound theme composed of textual and experiential themes as well as a marked theme in these clauses. Using the same method, all texts from the BBC sports news corpus are analyzed and the results are as follows:

Table 21 Distribution of Theme Systems in BBC English Sports News Texts

Text No.	Number of Compound Themes	Number of Single Themes	Number of Marked Themes	Number of Unmarked Themes
1	1	2	1	2
2	0	7	1	6
3	3	12	2	13
4	3	13	1	15
5	1	8	1	8
6	3	7	0	10
7	3	12	1	14
8	4	5	1	8
9	2	5	1	6
10	6	19	4	21
11	0	5	0	5
12	0	3	0	3
13	1	7	0	8
14	4	2	0	6
15	2	9	1	10
16	2	9	0	11
17	2	5	0	7
18	3	5	1	7

19	6	11	2	15
20	8	24	6	26
21	1	11	2	10
22	1	6	0	7
23	3	16	3	16
24	1	8	0	9
25	0	10	1	9
26	2	6	1	7
27	1	10	0	11
28	0	6	0	6
29	1	9	1	9
30	1	8	1	8
31	1	8	0	9
32	2	9	2	9
33	0	5	0	5
34	1	5	2	4
35	1	4	0	5
36	4	10	1	13
37	0	8	0	8
38	2	3	0	5
39	3	12	2	13
40	0	3	0	3
Sum	79	327	39	367
%	20	80	9	91

From the above table, it can be seen that unmarked themes account for 91%, and compound themes account for 20%.

7.3.2 Linguistic Features of Chinese Sports News Texts on Xinhua Net

1) Transitivity System

Chinese sports news text 8 "Chinese Badminton Men's Doubles 'Fengyun'

Combination Realizes Dreams in London" from Xinhua Net is selected as an example.

中国羽毛球男双"风云"组合圆梦伦敦

（1）北京奥运会羽毛球男双亚军蔡赟／傅海峰终于在伦敦**完成**了自己的奥运梦想！
（2）在5日的伦敦奥运会羽毛球男双决赛中，"风云"以21:16和21:15**战胜**世界第三的丹麦组合鲍伊／摩根森，在他们的第三次奥运之旅中**终获**金牌。（3）而一向被视为软肋的国羽男双也终于**摘得**了奥运首金。
（4）这样，中国羽毛球队在本届奥运会中史无前例地**包揽**5金，（5）并且还**获得**2银1铜。
（6）**获得**胜利后，蔡赟也像之前摘得男单冠军的林丹一样，**奔向**场边，尽情地**享受**观众的欢呼，（7）而傅海峰则在场地中央**掩面哭泣**。（8）为了这枚奥运金牌，两人足足**等**了8年。（9）2004年雅典奥运会，他们**止步**八强；2008年北京奥运会，他们在决赛**惜败**。
（10）"这**是**具有历史意义的时刻，奥运会**拿**了五金，对于（中国）羽毛球队来说，简直不敢**想象**，"蔡赟**说**。
（11）在男双决赛中，面对半决赛淘汰了韩国名将郑在成／李龙大的鲍伊／摩根森，经验丰富的蔡赟／傅海峰没有**给**对手太多机会。
（12）首局比赛，他们在12平后**打出**一波6:1的高潮，**奠定**了领先优势。（13）第二局，丹麦组合**放手一搏**，"风云"依然稳扎稳打，并以20:14**拿到**了6个冠军点。
（14）"我们跟他们彼此相互很了解，而且他们**打得**非常优秀，如果我们稍微有一个环节**处理**不好，他们就会连**赢**很快，所以我们今天要把比分**咬住**，"傅海峰**说**。
（15）**看到**"风云"夺得男双金牌，昔日国羽的男双队员、如今队内的总教练李永波也与他们**相拥而泣**。（16）"我**希望**通过这个冠军能够**改变**大家的印象，那就是中国男双已经不**是**我们的软肋。（17）我**希望**奥运冠军**是**我们男双的一个新起点"。
（18）在上午进行的铜牌争夺战中，郑在成／李龙大以23:21和21:10**击败**马来西亚组合古健杰／陈文宏，获得季军。

Process types of the above text are summarized into the following table:

Table 22 Process Type Analysis of Text 8

Clause No.	Process No.	Type of Process	Process Verbs
1	1	Material	完成
2	2	Material	战胜
	3	Material	终获
3	4	Material	摘得
4	5	Material	包揽
5	6	Material	获得

6	7 8	Material Mental	奔向 享受
7	9	Behavioral	掩面哭泣
8	10	Material	等
9	11 12	Material Material	止步 惜败
10	13 14 15 16	Verbal Relational Behavioral Mental	说 是 拿 想象
11	17	Material	给
12	18	Material	打出
13	19 20 21	Material Material Behavioral	放手一搏 稳扎稳打 拿到
14	22 23 24 25 26	Material Material Material Behavioral Verbal	打 处理 赢 咬住 说
15	27 28	Mental Behavioral	看到 相拥而泣
16	29 30	Mental Relational	希望 改变 是
17	31	Mental	希望
18	32	Material	击败

(Note: For the sake of simplification, the process types in subordinate clauses such as attributive clauses and adverbial clause are not counted.)

According to the above method, statistics on the process types of 40 Chinese sports news articles on Xinhua Net are conducted and results are shown in the table below.

Table 23 Process Type Distribution of Chinese Sports News Texts on Xinhua Net

Text No.	Material	Mental	Relational	Behavioral	Verbal	Existential	Sum
1	20	1	3	3	1	1	29
2	17	2	5	2	3	1	30
3	20	1	4	3	0	2	30
4	24	2	2	3	6	0	37
5	39	1	4	1	0	1	46
6	33	1	3	2	4	2	45
7	18	1	7	0	4	0	30
8	18	5	2	5	2	0	32
9	29	2	4	1	1	0	37
10	25	0	3	1	2	0	31
11	5	0	0	0	3	0	8
12	27	2	0	0	4	1	34
13	27	3	2	0	2	1	35
14	37	2	3	4	5	0	51
15	14	0	3	0	3	0	20
16	18	1	1	0	3	0	23
17	34	2	5	2	1	0	44
18	15	2	6	1	6	1	31
19	31	1	7	0	1	0	40
20	47	1	12	2	1	1	64
21	24	1	4	0	0	0	29
22	25	0	3	1	3	2	34
23	10	4	4	8	2	0	28
24	10	4	2	0	5	0	21

25	17	1	3	0	2	0	23
26	85	0	4	0	0	1	90
27	20	1	7	0	2	1	31
28	19	1	8	2	4	0	34
29	9	0	3	1	2	0	15
30	22	1	2	0	3	0	28
31	33	0	3	1	4	0	41
32	9	1	1	1	4	0	16
33	41	4	5	2	2	1	55
34	8	2	3	0	2	0	15
35	15	0	2	0	4	1	22
36	21	2	1	0	2	0	26
37	1	0	0	0	0	0	1
38	35	0	10	0	2	1	48
39	2	0	0	0	0	0	2
40	24	1	4	2	2	0	33

The ratio of different process types in the corpus is:

Table 24 Distribution Ratio of Process Types of Chinese Sports News on Xinhua Net

	Material	Mental	Relational	Behavioral	Verbal	Existential	Sum
Sum	928	53	145	48	97	18	1289
%	72	4.1	11.3	3.7	7.5	1.4	100

According to statistics, it is not difficult to see that material types also account for a high proportion in Chinese sports news on Xinhua Net, and this proportion is far higher than other process types, accounting for 73%. In Chinese sports news, material processes are mainly used to describe performance, details and results. For example:

来自中国贵州的 31 岁拳击手邹市明，伦敦当地时间 11 日晚在伦敦奥运会拳击馆，以一套独创的"海盗式打法"，**击败**老对手泰国"黑马"卡奥·庞普里亚杨，**蝉联**奥运会男子拳击最小级别的冠军……（Text 1）

从8日上午起,她先后以10:2、14:0、19:7的大比分连续**淘汰**三名对手进入决赛。(Text 2)

In addition, the relational process is also relatively common, accounting for 11%, which is mainly used to introduce details, performance and so on. For example:

决赛的对手**是**本届奥运会49公斤级最大的黑马卡奥·庞普里亚杨。(Text 1)

事实上,在本届奥运会之前,吴静钰**是**所有对手最熟悉、最下功夫研究和最想打败的对象。(Text 2)

Similar to BBC English sports news, the proportion of verbal processes in Chinese sports news is also high. This type of process is mainly used to report on comment of athletes and coaches, such as:

邹市明**说**:"奥运会任何事情都可能发生,这也是奥运会的魅力所在。一年前,我就承诺要把奥运会金牌当做礼物献给刚出生不久的孩子,今天我做到了,我兑现了一个父亲的承诺。"(Text 1)

李宗伟尽管心情低落,但也不由得**感叹**:"林丹太伟大了,世界只有一个林丹,感觉很难击败他。"(Text 4)

In contrast, the occurrence rate of behavioral, mental, and existential processes in Chinese sports news is relatively low.

2) Mood System

Similarly, text 1 of the Chinese sports news corpus entitled "Zou Shiming won the 38th gold medal for China after winning the boxing championship again" is selected to analyze the mood system.

邹市明再获拳击冠军 为中国夺第38块金牌

(1) [1]来自中国贵州的31岁拳击手邹市明,伦敦当地时间11日晚在伦敦奥运会拳击馆,以一套独创的"海盗式打法",击败老对手泰国"黑马"卡奥·庞普里亚杨,蝉联奥运会男子拳击最小级别的冠军,同时也为中国体育代表团献上第38块金牌。

(2)[2]现场裁判宣布最终结果后,邹市明快步跑到拳击台边,接过教练递过来的一面鲜艳的五星红旗,披在身上,绕着拳击台,和看台上的观众、媒体记者们欢庆胜利。(3)[3]国际拳联主席吴经国兑现了赛前的承诺,来到拳击台上,为邹市明颁奖。(4)[4]四年前的北京奥运会上,同样是吴经国为首夺奥运会拳击冠军的邹市明颁奖,邹市明当时的那块金牌,是中国选手在奥运会拳击场上零的突破。

(5)[5]作为伦敦奥运会49公斤级头号种子,邹市明最大的对手只有他自己。(6)[6]技术的优势能否弥补体能和心理的障碍,考验着这位奥运会冠军和世界冠军。

(7)[7]决赛的对手是本届奥运会49公斤级最大的黑马卡奥·庞普里亚杨。(8)[8]这位泰国老将,酷似邹市明的打法,在此前的四场比赛中全部获胜,尤其是在半决赛中以13:12,淘汰实力强劲的俄罗斯选手大卫·阿拉佩特扬,显示出极佳的竞技状态和很强的实力。

(9)[9]邹市明在决赛中,时而如一阵急速的山野之风,在与对手即将遭遇的刹那擦身而过;又像一头敏捷的猎豹,瞅准时机,出拳快如狂风暴雨。

(10)[10]卡奥·庞普里亚杨,三个回合都力图逼迫邹市明近身赤搏,几度险些得手。(11)[11]不过,邹市明腾挪闪躲间,出拳迅猛,用三个回合2:1、4:3和7:6的比分,令泰国选手终场铃声响起的瞬间,跪地痛哭失声。

(12)[12]邹市明的夺冠之战并不轻松,分组抽签将几名夺冠呼声很高的选手悉数抽到了他所在的半区。此次伦敦奥运之行,四战皆为硬仗。

(13)[13]首役以巧制胜,14:11力擒夺冠呼声很高的古巴22岁新秀索托;次战又以13:10的比分惊险战胜哈萨克斯坦选手扎基波夫。

(14)[14]半决赛的对手爱尔兰名将巴恩斯,得到全场上万拳迷山呼海啸般的呐喊助威声,状态有如神助,几乎令邹市明折戟,不过最后仅凭借着点数的小分,邹市明幸运地淘汰了这位北京奥运会半决赛曾经零封过的老对手,晋级决赛。

(15)[15]颁奖仪式后,邹市明抱着前来现场观赛的一岁多的儿子,在妻子的陪伴下,一家三口喜不自禁。(16)[16]邹市明说:"奥运会任何事情都可能发生,这也是奥运会的魅力所在。一年前,我就承诺要把奥运会金牌当做礼物献给刚出生不久的孩子,今天我做到了,我兑现了一个父亲的承诺。"

Table 25 Mood Analysis of Text 1

Sentence No.	Clause No.	Subject	Determiner	Mood Type
1	[1]	邹市明	击败	Indicative

2	[2]	邹市明	欢庆	Indicative
3	[3]	吴经国	颁奖	Indicative
4	[4]	那块金牌	是	Indicative
5	[5]	邹市明	只有	Indicative
6	[6]	技术的优势	考验	Indicative
7	[7]	决赛的对手	是	Indicative
8	[8]	这位泰国老将	淘汰	Indicative
9	[9]	邹市明	出拳	Indicative
10	[10]	卡奥·庞普里亚杨	得手	Indicative
11	[11]	邹市明	出拳	Indicative
12	[12]	邹市明	并不轻松	Indicative
13	[13]	首役	力擒	Indicative
14	[14]	爱尔兰名将巴恩斯	得到	Indicative
15	[15]	邹市明	抱着	Indicative
16	[16]	邹市明	说	Indicative

After completing the mood analysis of all texts in the corpus, the statistics are as follows:

No.		Mood			Subject					
Text No.	Number of Clauses	Indica-tive	Impera-tive	Interro-gative	First person		Second person		Third person	
					athlete /coach	other	athlete /coach	other	athlete /coach	other
1	16	16	0	0	0	0	0	0	12	4
2	24	24	0	0	3	0	0	0	21	0
3	15	15	0	0	0	0	0	0	11	4
4	16	16	0	0	0	0	0	0	15	1
5	23	23	0	0	0	0	0	0	13	10
6	21	21	0	0	1	0	0	0	16	4
7	12	12	0	0	0	0	0	0	10	2
8	14	14	0	0	0	0	0	0	12	2
9	16	16	0	0	1	0	0	0	15	0

10	14	14	0	0	1	0	0	0	7	6
11	9	9	0	0	3	0	0	0	6	0
12	16	16	0	0	1	0	0	0	11	4
13	20	20	0	0	1	0	0	0	16	3
14	20	20	0	0	0	0	0	0	15	5
15	7	7	0	0	1	0	0	0	6	0
16	13	13	0	0	0	0	0	0	10	3
17	14	14	0	0	0	0	0	0	9	5
18	21	21	0	0	3	0	0	0	13	5
19	21	21	0	0	0	0	0	0	20	1
20	38	38	0	0	0	0	0	0	32	6
21	12	12	0	0	0	0	0	0	8	4
22	18	18	0	0	0	0	0	0	15	3
23	18	18	0	0	0	0	0	0	13	5
24	14	14	0	0	0	0	0	0	11	3
25	9	9	0	0	0	0	0	0	9	0
26	48	48	0	0	0	0	0	0	47	1
27	16	16	0	0	0	0	0	0	12	4
28	21	21	0	0	0	0	0	0	13	8
29	9	9	0	0	0	0	0	0	7	2
30	20	20	0	0	0	0	0	0	17	3
31	23	23	0	0	0	0	0	0	22	1
32	11	11	0	0	0	0	0	0	11	0
33	22	22	0	0	0	0	0	0	17	5
34	8	8	0	0	0	0	0	0	7	1
35	11	11	0	0	0	0	0	0	10	1
36	11	11	0	0	0	0	0	0	10	1
37	1	1	0	0	0	0	0	0	1	0
38	16	16	0	0	0	0	0	0	8	8
39	2	2	0	0	0	0	0	0	2	0
40	15	15	0	0	0	0	0	0	15	0

The distribution ratio of the mood system in the corpus is as follows:

Table 27 Distribution Ratio of Mood System

	Total number of clauses	Indicative mood	Interrogative mood	First person	Second person	Third person
Total	655	655	0	15	0	640
%	100	100	0	2	0	98

It is not difficult to see that:

Mood type: There are a total of 655 clauses in Chinese sports news, which is much more numerous than BBC English news. The proportion of indicative mood remains at 100%. For example:

现场裁判宣布最终结果后,邹市明快步跑到拳击台边,接过教练递过来的一面鲜艳的五星红旗,披在身上,绕着拳击台,和看台上的观众、媒体记者们欢庆胜利。(Text 1)

面向温布利体育馆的数千名观众,身披五星红旗的林丹再度献上标志性军礼,而又一次落败的李宗伟则倒在地上。(Text 4)

Subject selection: Only 2% of Chinese sports news articles use the first person as the subject, and none of the 40 articles , use the second person as the subject,while 98% of the articles use the third-person pronoun as the subject. Similar to BBC English sports news, 80% of Chinese sports news articles use athletes or coaches as subjects, such as:

"**我**在决赛时一直猜不透她下一招想干什么,是要踢我脸,还是别的部位,这让我很困惑"。(Text 2)

李宗伟尽管心情低落,但也不由得感叹:"林丹太伟大了,世界只有一个林丹,感觉很难击败他。"(Text 4)

3) Modality System

Modal verbs in the Chinese sports news on Xinhua Net have been analyzed, and the statistical results are as follows.

Table 28 Distribution of Modal Verbs

Text No.	might(may)	could(can)	will(would)	should	must	need
1	√			√		
2				√		
3		√				

4		√				√
5		√				
6		√	√	√		
7		√		√		
8		√	√	√		
9						
10				√		
11						
12		√				
13				√		
14				√		
15		√				
16				√		
17		√			√	
18				√		
19		√				
20	√			√		
21						
22		√				
23		√			√	
24			√			
25						
26						
27	√				√	
28		√				
29						
30						
31		√		√	√	
32	√	√	√			
33		√				
34		√		√		
35		√		√		

36		√				√
37						
38		√				
39						
40	√			√		

The occurrence rate of modal verbs in the corpus is as follows:

Table 29 Occurrence Rate of Modal Verbs

	Low		Medium		High		Sum
	might(may)	could(can)	will(would)	should	must	need	
Total No.	5	23	5	17	4	3	57
%	8.9	41	7.2	30.3	7.2	5.4	100

In terms of the degree of these modal verbs, the proportion of low degree modal verbs ("might", "can", "could") and medium degree modal verbs ("will", "should") is high. From the perspective of distribution, more than 50% of the discourses use these two degrees of modal verbs. Among them, the verbs with the highest rate of occurrence are "could(can)" and "should", which are 41% and 30.3% respectively. They are mostly used to reflect comments of athletes or coaches on their own performance, or their expectations for the game by expressing their own will with a subjective color. For example:

斯里卡亚赛后高兴地说："今天是我妈妈的生日，我很开心**能**把这块奖牌送给她作为生日礼物。"（Text 12）

"我**希望**通过这个冠军能够改变大家的印象，那就是中国男双已经不是我们的软肋。我**希望**奥运冠军是我们男双的一个新起点。"（Text 8）

斯蒂芬·基普洛奇说："今天比赛的速度很快，我知道我不会过早地摆脱肯尼亚选手的封锁，因为他们实力很强，我只能跟着他们。最后关键时刻，我全力以赴，我**必须**为金牌做最后的努力。"（Text 36）

4) Theme System

Similarly, text 1 of the Chinese sports news on Xinhua Net, "Zou Shiming won the 38th gold medal for China after winning the boxing championship again", is selected for theme analysis.

邹市明再获拳击冠军 为中国夺第 38 块金牌

(1) [1]<u>来自中国贵州的 31 岁拳击手邹市明</u>，伦敦当地时间 11 日晚在伦敦奥运会拳击馆，以一套独创的"海盗式打法"，击败老对手泰国"黑马"卡奥·庞普里亚杨，蝉联奥运会男子拳击最小级别的冠军，同时也为中国体育代表团献上第 38 块金牌。

(2) [2]<u>现场裁判宣布最终结果后</u>，邹市明快步跑到拳击台边，接过教练递过来的一面鲜艳的五星红旗，披在身上，绕着拳击台，和看台上的观众、媒体记者们欢庆胜利。

(3) [3]<u>国际拳联主席吴经国</u>兑现了赛前的承诺，来到拳击台上，为邹市明颁奖。

(4) [4]<u>四年前的北京奥运会上</u>，同样是吴经国为首夺奥运会拳击冠军的邹市明颁奖，邹市明当时的那块金牌，是中国选手在奥运会拳击场上零的突破。

(5) [5]<u>作为伦敦奥运会 49 公斤级头号种子</u>，邹市明最大的对手只有他自己。

(6) [6]<u>技术的优势能否弥补体能和心理的障碍</u>，考验着这位奥运会冠军和世界冠军。

(7) [7]<u>决赛的对手是本届奥运会 49 公斤级最大的黑马卡奥·庞普里亚杨</u>。

(8) [8]<u>这位泰国老将</u>，酷似邹市明的打法，在此前的四场比赛中全部获胜，尤其是在半决赛中以 13:12，淘汰实力强劲的俄罗斯选手大卫·阿拉佩特扬，显示出极佳的竞技状态和很强的实力。

(9) [9]<u>邹市明</u>在决赛中，时而如一阵急速的山野之风，在与对手即将遭遇的刹那擦身而过；又像一头敏捷的猎豹，瞅准时机，出拳快如狂风暴雨。

(10) [10]<u>卡奥·庞普里亚杨</u>，三个回合都力图逼迫邹市明近身赤搏，几度险些得手。(11) [11]<u>不过</u>，邹市明腾挪闪躲间，出拳迅猛，用三个回合 2:1、4:3 和 7:6 的比分，令泰国选手终场铃声响起的瞬间，跪地痛哭失声。

(12) [12]<u>邹市明的夺冠之战</u>并不轻松，分组抽签将几名夺冠呼声很高的选手悉数抽到了他所在的半区。

(13) [13]<u>此次伦敦奥运之行</u>，四战皆为硬仗。

(14) [14]<u>首役</u>以巧制胜，14:11 力擒夺冠呼声很高的古巴 22 岁新秀索托；

(15) [15]<u>次战</u>又以 13:10 的比分惊险战胜哈萨克斯坦选手扎基波夫。

(16) [16]<u>半决赛的对手爱尔兰名将</u>巴恩斯，得到全场上万拳迷山呼海啸般的呐喊助威声，状态有如神助，几乎令邹市明折戟，不过最后仅凭借着点数的小分，邹市明幸运地淘汰了这位北京奥运会半决赛曾经零封过的老对手，晋级决赛。

(17) [17]<u>颁奖仪式后</u>，邹市明抱着前来现场观赛的一岁多的儿子，在妻子的陪伴下，一家三口喜不自禁。

(18) [18]<u>邹市明说</u>："奥运会任何事情都可能发生，这也是奥运会的魅力所在。一年前，我就承诺要把奥运会金牌当做礼物献给刚出生不久的孩子，今天我做到了，我兑现了一个父亲的承诺。"

The thematic analysis of this news is shown in Table 30.

Table 30 Theme Analysis of Text 1

Clause No.	Theme No.	Thematic Type			Marked	Unmarked
		Textual	Interpersonal	Experiential		
1	1			邹市明		√
2	2			现场裁判宣布最终结果后	√	
3	3			国际拳联主席吴经国		√
4	4			四年前的北京奥运会上	√	
5	5			作为伦敦奥运会49公斤级头号种子	√	
6	6			技术的优势		√
7	7			决赛的对手		√
8	8			这位泰国老将		√
9	9			邹市明		√
10	10			卡奥·庞普里亚杨		√
11	11	不过		邹市明		√
12	12			邹市明的夺冠之战		√
13	13			此次伦敦奥运之行	√	
14	14			首役		√
	15			次战		√
15	16			半决赛的对手爱尔兰名将巴恩斯		√
16	17			颁奖仪式后	√	
17	18			邹市明		√

Through analysis, there is a compound theme composed of one textual and experiential theme, as well as five marked themes. The thematic analysis of the remaining texts in the corpus completed by using the same method, and the results are shown in the table below.

Table 31 Theme System Distribution of Chinese Sports News Texts on Xinhua Net

Text No.	Number of Compound Themes	Number of Single Themes	Number of Marked Themes	Number of Unmarked Themes
1	1	17	5	13
2	1	26	7	20
3	3	14	9	8
4	2	21	11	12
5	7	23	7	23
6	2	20	5	17
7	2	13	3	12
8	3	16	9	10
9	2	18	3	17
10	7	11	7	11
11	2	9	3	8
12	2	16	5	13
13	7	18	4	21
14	0	23	4	19
15	1	7	1	7
16	1	12	1	12
17	3	14	4	13
18	1	26	6	21
19	4	21	10	15
20	3	36	7	32
21	7	11	8	10
22	4	17	6	15

23	2	17	5	14
24	0	13	3	10
25	0	10	2	8
26	2	43	3	42
27	0	21	4	17
28	0	21	3	18
29	2	7	5	4
30	0	19	5	14
31	7	18	5	20
32	0	10	1	9
33	7	23	3	27
34	0	10	0	10
35	1	10	1	10
36	0	11	3	8
37	0	1	0	1
38	2	19	3	18
39	0	2	0	2
40	3	17	3	17
Sum	91	661	174	578
%	12	88	23	77

From this, it can be seen that compound themes account for 12%. Those that are composed of discourse themes and experiential themes are still the main form of compound themes. Marked themes account for 23%.

7.3.3 Linguistic Features of Translated English Sports News Texts
1) Transitivity System

Correspondingly, news sample 8 "Chinese badminton players Cai and Fu win gold medals in men's doubles" is selected as the research object for the transitivity analysis of translated English sports news on Xinhua Net.

Chinese badminton players Cai and Fu win gold medals in men's doubles

LONDON, Aug. 5 (Xinhua) — (1) Chinese badminton players Cai Yun and Fu Haifeng **beat** their rivals 2-0 Sunday afternoon, and **clinched** gold medals in men's doubles in the Wembley Arena.

(2) These **are** the first gold medal won by Chinese in that event.

(3) This **means** Chinese **raked** in all the five badminton gold medals produced at theLondon Olympic.

(4) Mathias Boe and Carsten Mogensen from Denmark **won** the silver, while the bronze **fell into** pockets of Jung Jae Sung and Lee Yong Dae from South Korea.

(5) Cai and Fu **geared up** quickly in the first game to rule the court, where the Danish only **started** to become aggressive after being outscored 1-4.

(6) They **impressed** the audience by catching up the Chinese pair, who **enjoyed** 11-6 advantage before the interval, and levelling the scores 12-12.

(7) But some mistakes from Boe and Mogensen **sent** their rival to a 21-16 victory.

(8) In the second game the Danish **made** desperate attempts.

(9) Li Yongbo, China's badminton head coach, **shouted** from the stand every now and then to remind Cai and Fu to "run quickly".

(10) With Cai Yun's last shot missed by the rivals, China **won**, 21-15.

(11) Cai Yun **rushed out** of the court for celebration, while his partner Fu **shed tears** in excitement.

(12) "This **is** the exact result we aimed for," **said** Cai, 32.

(13) "We **have been playing** together for over 10 years, and **have entered** the Olympic three times. Last time in Beijing we only **achieved** silver, and we **were** regretful."

(14) The combination of Fu Haifeng's power with his regular partner Cai Yun's speed **enabled** the pair to become world's leading men's doubles team since 2004.

(15) After the Beijing Olympic, however, they **seemed** to be in a downturn.

(16) "After failure, we **were** more mature," **said** Cai.

(17) "For match we **were** not afraid of failure, we **tried** to enjoy it. We **were not scared** at all, not nervous. Part of the reason we won **was** we were full of confidence."

(18) Fu, 28, **said** the title was like "a dream coming true".

(19) "This will probably **be** the greatest recognition of our badminton career," he **said**.

(20) Next time, our performance might **be** even better because we don't **have** any pressure now that we **have achieved** this goal. Next time we will **play** in a different state of mind.

(21) Li Yongbo **was** delighted because their victory not only **signalled** a clean sweep of badminton golds at the London Olympic, but also **suggested** a breakthrough of the men's doubles, as the gold of men's doubles **seemed** always elusive in the past.

(22) "I **hope** that these medals could **change** people's perception on the event," he **said**.

(23) "Many people **considered** men's doubles the Achilles'heel for China's national badminton team.

(24) In fact, Cai and Fu have **harvested** 14 world titles.

(25) This victory **is** a new starting point for us."

(26) The disappointed Boe **said**, "right now it doesn't **feel** that good.

(27) We **hoped** for more but of course after half an hour or a little bit later today we will probably **be** satisfied with reaching final and getting silver."

(28) While his partner **said** they **have tried** to believe they would **win** the whole time, "We **tried** to fight even though it was 14-18, we still **tried** and told each other to focus."

(29) Finn Traerup-Hansen, coach from the Danish team, **said** he **was** "extremely happy" with the result. Earlier Joachim Fischer and Christinna Pedersen **have pocketed** bronze medals in mixed doubles, "That's extraordinary for a country of 5.5 million people," he **said**. "So of course we **are** very happy."

Process types are analyzed sentence by sentence, and the results are shown in the table below:

Table 32 Process Type Analysis of Sample 8

Clause No.	Process No.	Process Type	Process Verb
1	1	Material	beat

	2	Material	clinched
	3	Material	raked
2	4	Relational	are
3	5	Relational	means
4	6	Material	won
	7	Material	fell into
5	8	Material	geared up
	9	Material	started
6	10	Mental	impressed
	11	Mental	enjoyed
7	12	Material	sent
8	13	Material	made
9	14	Verbal	shouted
10	15	Material	won
11	16	Behavioral	rushed
	17	Behavioral	shed tears
12	18	Verbal	said
	19	Relational	is
13	20	Material	have been playing
	21	Material	have entered
	22	Material	achieved
	23	Relational	were
14	24	Mental	enabled
15	25	Relational	seemed
16	26	Verbal	said
	27	Relational	were

17	28	Relational	were not afraid
	29	Relational	were not scared
	30	Relational	was
18	31	Verbal	said
	32	Relational	was
19	33	Verbal	said
	34	Relational	will be
20	35	Relational	might be
	36	Material	don't have
	37	Material	have achieved
	38	Material	will play
21	39	Mental	was delighted
	40	Relational	signalled
	41	Relational	suggested
	42	Relational	seemed
22	43	Mental	hope
	44	Material	change
	45	Verbal	said
23	46	Mental	considered
24	47	Material	have harvested
25	48	Relational	is
26	49	Verbal	said
	50	Mental	feel
27	51	Mental	hoped
	52	Relational	be

28	53	Verbal	said
	54	Material	have tried
	55	Material	win
	56	Material	tried
	57	Material	tried
29	58	Verbal	said

Process types of all texts in the corpus of translated English sports news on Xinhua Net are analyzed, and the statistics are as follows:

Table 33 Distribution of Process Types for Xinhua English Translated English Sports News Texts

Text No.	Material	Mental	Relational	Behavioral	Verbal	Existential	Sum
1	10	0	1	1	0	0	12
2	3	0	1	0	0	1	5
3	13	0	3	1	6	0	23
4	12	2	12	4	8	1	39
5	14	1	7	1	4	1	28
6	10	0	5	0	3	0	18
7	2	0	1	0	0	0	3
8	23	8	20	2	10	0	63
9	9	0	3	0	1	0	13
10	2	0	2	0	0	0	4
11	19	1	4	1	12	0	37
12	13	1	5	0	5	0	24
13	1	0	0	0	0	0	1
14	2	0	0	0	0	0	2
15	13	0	2	0	11	1	27
16	5	1	7	0	5	0	18
17	4	0	3	0	0	0	7
18	5	0	4	0	0	0	9

19	11	0	3	0	0	0	0	14
20	9	1	2	0	7	0		19
21	9	0	2	0	0	0		11
22	3	0	0	0	0	0		3
23	2	0	1	0	0	0		3
24	10	0	5	0	0	0		15
25	22	0	6	0	9	0		37
26	10	1	1	0	4	0		16
27	4	0	2	0	0	0		6
28	5	1	4	1	5	0		16
29	14	0	1	3	7	0		25
30	1	0	1	0	0	0		2
31	10	0	6	0	5	0		21
32	5	0	5	0	5	0		15
33	4	0	1	0	0	0		5
34	6	1	5	0	5	0		17
35	7	0	3	0	5	0		15
36	2	1	8	0	3	0		14
37	4	0	1	0	1	0		6
38	3	0	0	0	0	0		3
39	3	0	0	0	0	0		3
40	27	1	6	3	9	1		47

The distribution ratio of different process types in the corpus is:

Table 34 Distribution ratio of Process Types for Xinhua Translated English texts

	Material	Mental	Relational	Behavioral	Verbal	Existential	Sum
Sum	331	20	143	17	130	5	646
%	51.3	3.1	22.1	2.6	20.1	0.8	100

From it, it can be seen that in translated English sports news texts, the number of material process types has decreased compared to Xinhua Chinese sports news, but the proportion is still the highest. It is mainly used to describe details, performance, results and supplementary information, such as:

Lee, the No. 1 seed, **changed** his direction abruptly, posing threats to the Beijing Olympic champion with diagonal smashes. (Text 4)
Chinese Wu Minxia **scored** 414 points to win the Olympic women's 3m springboard diving gold medal on Sunday. (Text 7)

The proportion of relational and verbal processes has increased. The proportion of relational processes has increased to 22.1%, which is mainly used to describe details, athletes background and other information, such as:

These **are** the first gold medal won by Chinese in that event. (Text 8)
It **was** China's fifth gold medal at these Olympics in the swimming pool and the seventh world record to be smashed in London. (Text 9)

In addition, the proportion of verbal processes is also 20.1%, which is relatively high compared to BBC English sports news and Xinhua Chinese sports news. Verbal processes are mainly used to report on what athletes and coaches say during interviews, such as:

The disappointed Boe **said**, "right now it doesn't feel that good. We hoped for more but of course after half an hour or a little bit later today we will probably be satisfied with reaching final and getting silver." (Text 8)
"Without the rise of youngsters, we can't keep our roster strong and energetic in the long term," the coach **said**. (Text 11)

In general, material, relational and verbal processes are the three types with a higher proportion of appearance in texts of three corpora, among which the material process is most frequently used to describe details, performance and results.

2) Mood System

The following is the analysis of the mood system of text 1 "Zou Shiming repeats Beijing success" selected from the corpus of Xinhua translated English sports news:

Zou Shiming repeats Beijing success

(1) Zou Shiming won his second successive Olympic gold medal on Saturday, beating Thailand's Kaeo Pongprayoon in a battle of two of the oldest fighters at the London Games to cap his total dominance of the light-flyweight division.

(2) [2] Zou, who won China's first Olympic boxing medal, a bronze, eight years ago and its first gold in front of home fans at the Beijing Games, added a second Olympic win to a career haul that also includes three world amateur championships.

(3) [3] The canny 31-year-old, who survived a couple of scares to reach the final, grinned all the way to the ring and was probably still smiling inside when he was slightly fortunate to be narrowly ahead after the first round.

(4) [4] Pongprayoon, at 32 the oldest among the men's 20 finalists, was cheered on by the majority of the crowd, including a noisy section of Thai fans, but their encouragement turned to boos after the second round when he was again unlucky to lose by a single point.

(5) [5] Pongprayoon continued to be a nuisance against his taller opponent in the final round, catching Zou with a big left but the now double Olympic champion, who was warned for holding, hung on to win 13-10.

(6) [6] Pongprayoon, who also received a warning in the final seconds of the bout, fell to the ground in tears and beat the canvass in frustration as a flag-waving Zou was booed.

(7) [7] Pongprayoon's cornerman even raised his fighter's hand in defiance to the delight of the crowd.

(8) [8] Losing semi-finalists Ireland's Paddy Barnes and David Ayrapetyan of Russia took bronze.

The mood analysis results of this text are shown in the table below.

Table 35 Analysis of Mood System of Text 1

Clause No.	Clause No.	Subject	Infinite	Tense	Mood Type
1	[1]	Zou Shiming	won	Past tense	Indicative mood
2	[2]	Zou	added	Past tense	Indicative mood
3	[3]	The canny 31-year-old	grinned	Past tense	Indicative mood
4	[4]	Pongprayoon	was	Past tense	Indicative mood

5	[5]	Pongprayoon	continued	Past tense	Indicative mood
6	[6]	Pongprayoon	fell	Past tense	Indicative mood
7	[7]	Pongprayoon's	raised	Past tense	Indicative mood
8	[8]	Ireland's Paddy Barnes	took	Past tense	Indicative mood

Using the same method, the analysis of mood types for all texts in the corpus is analyzed, and the results are shown in the table below:

Table 36 Statistics of Mood Types in Translated English Sports News on Xinhua Net

No.		Mood			Subject						Tense		
Text No.	Number of Clauses	Indicative	Imperative	Interrogative	First person		Second person		Third person		past	present	future
					athlete /coach	other	athlete /coach	other	athlete /coach	other			
1	8	8	0	0	0	0	0	0	8	0	8	0	0
2	5	5	0	0	0	0	0	0	4	1	5	0	0
3	19	19	0	0	0	0	0	0	13	6	17	1	1
4	41	41	0	0	0	0	0	0	28	13	37	4	0
5	20	20	0	0	0	0	0	0	18	2	19	1	0
6	17	17	0	0	2	0	0	0	13	2	14	3	0
7	2	2	0	0	0	0	0	0	2	0	2	0	0
8	35	35	0	0	4	0	0	0	24	7	26	7	2
9	9	9	0	0	0	0	0	0	6	3	9	0	0
10	4	4	0	0	0	0	0	0	3	1	4	0	0
11	38	38	0	0	3	0	0	0	21	14	31	7	0
12	18	18	0	0	0	0	0	0	16	2	18	0	0
13	1	1	0	0	0	0	0	0	1	0	1	0	0
14	2	2	0	0	0	0	0	0	2	0	2	0	0
15	27	27	0	0	0	0	0	0	22	5	25	2	0
16	17	17	0	0	0	0	0	0	14	3	17	0	0
17	7	7	0	0	0	0	0	0	6	1	7	0	0
18	9	9	0	0	0	0	0	0	6	3	8	1	0

19	11	11	0	0	0	0	0	0	10	1	9	2	0
20	17	17	0	0	1	0	0	0	12	4	15	1	1
21	9	9	0	0	0	0	0	0	5	4	9	0	0
22	2	2	0	0	0	0	0	0	2	0	2	0	0
23	2	2	0	0	0	0	0	0	1	1	2	0	0
24	11	11	0	0	0	0	0	0	5	6	8	3	0
25	32	32	0	0	0	0	0	0	22	10	30	2	0
26	17	17	0	0	1	0	0	0	9	7	14	3	0
27	4	4	0	0	0	0	0	0	3	1	4	0	0
28	19	19	0	0	4	0	0	0	12	3	15	4	0
29	26	26	0	0	2	0	0	0	19	5	20	6	0
30	2	2	0	0	0	0	0	0	2	0	2	0	0
31	20	20	0	0	1	0	0	0	15	4	18	2	0
32	21	21	0	0	4	0	1	0	12	4	15	6	0
33	4	4	0	0	0	0	0	0	3	1	4	0	0
34	17	17	0	0	1	0	0	0	11	5	14	2	1
35	17	17	0	0	1	0	0	0	13	3	14	3	0
36	12	12	0	0	0	0	0	0	8	4	10	2	0
37	6	6	0	0	0	0	0	0	4	2	5	1	0
38	2	2	0	0	0	0	0	0	2	0	2	0	0
39	2	2	0	0	0	0	0	0	2	0	2	0	0
40	40	40	0	0	1	0	0	0	32	7	34	6	0

Statistics of the distribution of mood types, subjects and tenses in the corpus are as follows:

Table 37 Statistics of Mood System Analysis

	Number of Clauses	Mood type			Subject			Tense		
		Indica-tive	Impera-tive	Interro-gative	First person	Second person	Third person	Past tense	Present tense	Future tense
Sum	572	572	0	0	25	1	546	498	69	5
%	100	100	0	0	4.3	0.2	95.5	87	12	1

Mood type: Analysis shows that compared to Chinese sports news on Xinhua Net, the number of clauses in translated English sports news has decreased to a total of 572, but compared to BBC English sports news, the number is still higher. The most frequently used mood type in translated English sports news is indicative, the proportion of which is up to 100%. For example:

Lin didn't seem to be in form in the first game, lashing the shuttlecock out of the court for at least nine times and delivering at least five returns into the net. (Text 4)
Kashirina won silver with a total of 332kg. (Text 6)

Subject selection:95.5% of the English sports news texts translated by Xinhuanet use the Third-person pronoun as the subject, and 76.8% of the English sports news texts use athletes or coaches as the subject. For example:

But **I** told me I need to try my best. (Text 35)
Zhang Jike, the London Olympic singles gold medalist, got a slow start in the following match against South Korea's Joo Sae-Hyuk. (Text 3)
Tense: Similar to BBC English sports news, English translated sports news on Xinhua Net also use the past tense, reporting on events that have occurred and past performances of athletes. But present and future tenses are also used, such as:

I **hope** (present tense) we can be friends forever. (Text 4)
The medal **will** (future tense) for sure boost the confidence of his team and help promote the sport in Germany. (Text 3)

3)Modality System

According to statistics, the distribution of modal verbs in the corpus is as follows:

Table 38 Distribution of Modal Verbs

Text No.	might(may)	could(can)	will(would)	should	must	need
1						
2						
3		√	√			
4		√	√			

5			√			
6			√			
7						
8	√	√	√			
9		√				
10						
11		√				
12		√	√			
13		√				
14						
15		√	√			√
16						
17						
18						
19			√			
20		√	√			
21						
22						
23						
24		√				
25		√	√			√
26		√				
27						
28	√	√	√		√	√
29						
30		√	√	√		
31						
32		√	√			√
33						
34			√			√
35			√			√
36		√	√			

37							
38							
39							
40		√	√				√

The occurrence rate of modal verbs is:

Table 39 Occurrence Rate of Modal Verbs

	Low		Medium		High		Sum
	might(may)	could(can)	will(would)	should	must	need	
Total	3	39	31	2	1	8	84
%	3.4	46.3	36.8	2.2	1.8	9.5	100

It can be seen from the above that the occurrence rate of low degree modal verb ("might","may","could", "can") and medium degree modal verbs (will, would) is comparatively high.

Among these modal verbs, "could (can)" has a high proportion of 46.3%; The occurrence rate of 'will (would)' is 36.8%. For example:

"I hope that these medals **could** change people's perception on the event," he said. (Text 8)

The 25-year-old is the first man to win two 200 Olympic golds and, as he did in 2008, he **will** look to complete the treble in the 4x100 relay. (Text 19)

"The players were very exhausted. It **would** have been impossible for us to win even the bronze medal. But they fought hard and played well. I am so proud of them," Yoo said. (Text 3)

4) Theme System

Next, Text 1 of translated English sports news is selected as an example to analyze its thematic system:

Zou Shiming repeats Beijing success

(1) [1] Zou Shiming won his second successive Olympic gold medal on Saturday, beating Thailand's Kaeo Pongprayoon in a battle of two of the oldest

fighters at the London Games to cap his total dominance of the light-flyweight division.

(2) [2] Zou, who won China's first Olympic boxing medal, a bronze, eight years ago and its first gold in front of home fans at the Beijing Games, added a second Olympic win to a career haul that also includes three world amateur championships.

(3) [3] The canny 31-year-old, who survived a couple of scares to reach the final, grinned all the way to the ring and was probably still smiling inside when he was slightly fortunate to be narrowly ahead after the first round.

(4) [4] Pongprayoon, at 32 the oldest among the men's 20 finalists, was cheered on by the majority of the crowd, including a noisy section of Thai fans, [5] but their encouragement turned to boos after the second round when he was again unlucky to lose by a single point.

(5) [6] Pongprayoon continued to be a nuisance against his taller opponent in the final round, catching Zou with a big left but the now double Olympic champion, who was warned for holding, hung on to win 13-10.

(6) [7] Pongprayoon, who also received a warning in the final seconds of the bout, fell to the ground in tears and beat the canvass in frustration as a flag-waving Zou was booed.

(7) [8] Pongprayoon's cornerman even raised his fighter's hand in defiance to the delight of the crowd.

(8) [9] Losing semi-finalists Ireland's Paddy Barnes and David Ayrapetyan of Russia took bronze.

The thematic analysis of the above text is shown in the table below:

Table 40 Thematic Analysis of Text 1

Clause No.	Theme No.	Type of theme			Marked	Unmarked
		Textual	Interpersonal	Experiential		
1	1			Zou Shiming		✓
2	2			Zou		✓
3	3			The canny 31-year-old		✓
4	4			Pongprayoon		✓

	5	but		their encouragement		√
5	6			Pongprayoon		√
6	7			Pongprayoon		√
7	8			Pongpray's cornerman		√
8	9			Losing semi-finalists	√	

As shown in the above table, the text has a total of 9 theme systems, of which one is a compound system composed of experiential and textual themes, and one is a marked theme.

Thematic analysis on all translated English sports news texts is conducted by using the same method, and the results are as follows:

Table 41 Distribution of Theme Systems in Translated English Sports News Texts on Xinhua Net

Text No.	Theme System	The Number of Compound Themes	The Number of Single Themes	The Number of Marked Themes	The Number of Unmarked Themes
1	9	1	8	1	8
2	5	0	5	0	5
3	23	1	22	2	21
4	45	2	43	7	38
5	23	1	22	4	19
6	18	0	18	4	14
7	2	0	2	0	2
8	36	3	33	5	31
9	11	1	10	3	8
10	4	0	4	2	2
11	38	3	35	3	35
12	20	3	17	4	16
13	1	0	1	0	1
14	2	0	2	0	2
15	33	1	32	0	33

16	21	1	20	2	19
17	7	0	7	2	5
18	9	1	8	2	7
19	12	1	11	3	9
20	23	5	18	5	18
21	9	0	9	1	8
22	2	0	2	0	2
23	3	0	3	1	2
24	13	3	10	3	10
25	38	6	32	7	31
26	22	0	22	2	20
27	4	0	4	0	4
28	21	5	16	5	16
29	29	1	28	5	24
30	2	0	2	0	2
31	24	3	21	2	22
32	26	5	21	7	19
33	4	0	4	0	4
34	17	1	16	1	16
35	26	7	19	2	24
36	19	4	15	2	17
37	12	1	11	0	12
38	2	0	2	0	2
39	2	0	2	0	2
40	62	13	59	6	56
Sum	679	73	616	93	586
%		11	89	14	86

From the above table, it can be seen that compound themes account for 11% of the total, of which the combination of textual theme and experiential theme is still the main form. 22 news articles contain the compound themes composed of "textual theme+experiential theme". In addition, marked themes in translated English sports news on Xinhua Net account for 14%.

7.4 Corpus-based Comparative Analysis of Sports News Discourses

Previously, we have analyzed the structure and presentation styles of all texts in corpora of English, Chinese, and translated English translated sports news from a generic perspective, and have summarized their respective characteristics. The following is a comparison of these three kinds of texts to identify similarities and differences, providing a basis for evaluating the quality of translated texts and how to improve them in the next section.

7.4.1 Structural Comparison of Three Types of Texts (GSP Model)

Based on the structural analysis of 120 sports news texts from the self-built corpora, we have summarized and sorted out the generic characteristics of sports news structure in three corpora, and drawn their corresponding GSP models. Next, we will compare and analyze similarities and differences in terms of generic structure of sports news texts in different corpora.

1) Comparison between Xinhua Chinese Sports News and BBC English Sports News

By integrating the structural features of Chinese sports news and English sports news texts, the occurrence rate is:

Table 42 Occurrence Rate of Moves in Xinhua Chinese Sports News Texts

	H	L	RS	P	D	AB	IC	CC	IO	OCC	CET	S
Total	40	40	23	30	21	19	28	7	10	1	17	30
%	10	100	57.5	75	52.5	47.5	70	17.5	25	2.5	42.5	70

Table 43 Occurrence Rate of Moves in BBC English Sports News Texts

	H	L	RS	P	D	AB	IC	IO	OCC	SG	S
Total	40	40	16	38	13	16	13	4	2	4	15
%	100	100	40	95	32.5	40	32.5	10	5	10	37.5

And the GSP model is:
The GSP model of Xinhua Chinese sports news texts is:

[H^L]^RS^(AB).[P.D].[IC^(CC)](CET)(IO)(OCC).S

The GSP model of BBC English sports news texts is:

[H^L]^[(AB)^P]^(D)(RS)(IC)(IO)(OCC)(SG). (S)

After comparison, it is found that the structural differences between the two are as follows:

Similarities: For both Xinhua Chinese sports news and BBC English sports news, heading, lead and performance are necessary elements, the occurrence rate of them are all 100%. In addition, the occurrence rate of performance is also high, indicating that sports news focus on the game itself and related details.

Differences: In Xinhua Chinese sports news, heading, lead, results and significance, performance, interview champion and supplementary information are all necessary moves. On the contrary, in BBC English sports news, the necessary elements are reduced to heading, lead and performance, indicating that BBC English sports news is more concise than Chinese sports news which focus on the game itself, and "results and significance" is no longer a necessary element. In addition, both Xinhua Chinese sports news and BBC English sports news have their own unique moves: in Xinhua Chinese sports news, "champion express thank" appears as a unique move, accounting for a considerably high proportion (42.5%), which is consistent with our domestic reporting style; In BBC English Sports News, 'scores of Great Britain' constitutes its unique move. Being the host country of this Olympics, even without winning a medal, BBC English sports news focus more on reporting on their country's ranking and achievements.

2) **Comparison between Xinhua Chinese Sports News and Xinhua Translated English Sports News**

Based on the description of the structural characteristics of Xinhua Chinese sports news and Xinhua translated English sports news (step frequency and GSP mode) in the previous text, it is not difficult to summarize the structural similarities and differences between the two as follows:

Table 44 Occurrence Rate of Moves in Xinhua Sports News Texts

	H	L	RS	P	D	AB	IC	CC	IO	OCC	CET	S
Sum	40	40	23	30	21	19	28	7	10	1	17	30
%	100	100	57.5	75	52.5	47.5	70	17.5	25	2.5	42.5	70

Table 45: Occurrence Rate of Movement in Translated English Sports News Texts

	H	L	RS	P	D	AB	IC	CC	IO	OCC	S
Sum	40	40	23	35	21	6	21	4	14	4	20
%	100	100	56	87.5	52.5	15	52.5	10	35	10	50

Their respective GSP models are:

The GSP model of Xinhua Chinese sports news is:

[H^L]^RS^(AB).[P.D].[IC^(CC)](CET)(IO)(OCC).S

The GSP model of translated English sports news on Xinhua Net is:

[H^L^]RS^[P^D].[IC.(AB)]^(CC)(IO)(OCC).S

Similarities: Both Xinhua translated English sports news and Chinese sports news are composed of elements such as heading, lead, results and significance, performance, details, interview champions and supplementary information. Their necessary elements are almost identical. In terms of order, Xinhua translated English sports news basically follow the suit of their source Chinese texts, and retains high consistency in occurrence rate of elements.

Differences: It is worth noting that the two types of texts also exhibit certain differences in structure. Firstly, compared to translated English news texts, Chinese texts include the element 'Champion express thank/celebrate'; Secondly, although the order of moves in the two types of texts is consistent, the frequency of their occurrence is not the same: in Chinese news, the occurrence rate of "interview champion" and "supplementary information" are both 70%, while in translated English news, the occurrence rate of these two moves has decreased to 52.5% and 50%. From this, it can be seen that the content of Chinese news reports is more comprehensive and detailed, with a greater emphasis on the delicate expression of the subjective feelings of the award-winning contestants. Once again, the occurrence frequency o "athlete background" and "champion express thank/celebrate" in Chinese reports is also high, both approaching 50%, while the frequency of these elements in domestic translated English news is relatively low. This difference indicates that Chinese news reports are centered around contestants and contain more information than translated English news. Finally, in terms of order arrangement, moves in Chinese news are more casual, and their positions are more likely to vary than translated English news. This may be due to the fact that Chinese news focus on parataxis, while English news focus on hypotaxis, so in terms of discourse structure, the position of moves in Chinese news are more various.

3) **Comparison between Xinhua Translated English Sports News and BBC English Sports News**

From the previous analysis, it can be seen that the structural characteristics of both are as follows:

Table 46: Frequency of Moves in Translated English Sports News on Xinhua Net

	H	L	RS	P	D	AB	IC	CC	IO	OCC	S
Sum	40	40	23	35	21	6	21	4	14	4	20
%	100	100	56	87.5	52.5	15	52.5	10	35	10	50

Table 47 Frequency of Moves in BBC English Sports News Texts

	H	L	RS	P	D	AB	IC	IO	OCC	SG	S
Sum	40	40	16	38	13	16	13	4	2	4	15
%	100	100	40	95	32.5	40	32.5	10	5	10	37.5

Their respective GSP models are:

The GSP model of translated English sports news on Xinhua Net is:

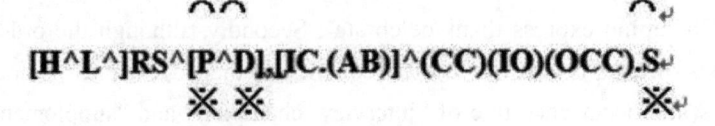

$$[H^\wedge L^\wedge]RS^\wedge[P^\wedge D],[IC.(AB)]^\wedge(CC)(IO)(OCC).S$$

The GSP model of BBC sports news is:

[H^L]^[(AB)^P]^(D)(RS)(IC)(IO)(OCC)(SG). (S)

※※　※※　　　　　　　　　※

From above, it can be seen that:

Similarities: As mentioned earlier, the common moves are "heading", "lead", and "performance", aiming to convey the latest information in the simplest form to attract readers.

Differences: As shown in the previous analysis, there are only three necessary elements in BBC English sports news (title, introduction, and player performance), the structure of them is more concise and clear. However, the structure of domestic English news is more complex with more detailed content. Specifically, (1) Chinese news are more detailed, performance (P) and details (D) are both necessary moves that appear in almost every report; (2) Chinese people are accustomed to emphasizing the significance of gold medals for their country. The move (RS) is necessary in Xinhua sports news, while in BBC sports news, it is a selective step - Western news reporters pay more attention to the game itself, results and significance of the game is the focus of news reporting; (3) Sports news on Xinhua Net focus more on interview champions, especially their experiences before, during and after the game. In BBC sports news, however, interviews champion (IC) is an optional move, which further confirms that English news reports place more emphasis on game itself; (4) In addition, as the host country of this Olympic Games, if British athletes achieve good results, BBC news will definitely mention it, and this move is missing in the Xinhua translated English news.

In short, BBC English news reports are more concise, while domestic news reports usually contain more detailed information about games to cater to readers'interests. Therefore, compared to BBC English sports news, domestic news reports have added information like"interview champion", and they put more emphasis on other optional moves.

7.4.2 Comparison of Vocabulary and Grammar among Three Types of Texts

Based on our previous analysis of the transitivity, mood (modality) and theme of BBC English sports news, Xinhua Chinese sports news, and translated Xinhua English sports news, we will next compare them in pairs and elaborate on their similarities and differences.

1）Comparison between BBC English Sports News and Xinhua Chinese Sports News Type of Process

Based on the description of characteristics of process types of these two types of sports news in Tables 13 and 24, the following table is obtained:

Table 48 Comparison of Process Types of BBC English Sports News and Xinhua Sports News

Type of Process	BBC English Sports News		Chinese Sports News on Xinhua Net	
	Total	%	Total	%
Material	249	70.2	928	72
Mental	9	2.5	53	4.1
Relational	46	13	145	11.3
Behavioral	6	1.7	48	3.7
Verbal	35	9.9	97	7.5
Existential	10	2.8	18	1.4
Sum	355	100	1289	100

Similarities: Material processes are the most commonly used in Chinese and English sports news, both exceeding 70%. In sports news reporting, material processes are usually used to describe the progress of sports events, consistent with the purpose of sports news reporting. Secondly, the verbal process usually occurs during interviews with athletes, reproducing their award-winning speeches. One of the most important purposes of sports news reporting is to attract readers'attention, and directly citing interviews that record the true emotions of champions is crucial for attracting readers' attention. Thirdly, the relational process is also frequently used in sports news reporting, as it typically describes the nature, attributes and environment of things. In sports news reports, the subject is usually the athlete or the game itself, and the relational process can accurately describe the athlete's condition, environment and results of games. Fourthly, there is also a certain proportion of mental processes. News reporters usually use mental processes to describe opinions or comments of athletes, coaches and authorities on results of games, which is also essential for sports news reporting. Fifthly, behavioral processes are also used in sports news reports, such as in news reports about China's men's doubles badminton championship, which are reflected as follows: Li Yongbo, China's badminton head coach, shouted from the stand every now and then to remind Cai and Fu to" run quickly "In this sentence, the news reporter uses "shout" to express the anxiety of coach Li Yongbo and his strong desire to win. Another example is "Yi Siling smiled after she saw the screen which shows her results". The reporter uses "smile"to express her joy after winning the game. Sixthly, the existential process is least used in sports news reporting. The existential process is usually used to describe a static state, but sports events are usually dynamic. Therefore, the existential process conflicts with the essence of sports news reporting and is thus not suitable.

Differences: In English sports news, the specific proportions are: relational process (13%), verbal process (9.9%), mental process (2.5%), existential process (2.8%), and behavioral processes (1.7%); In Chinese, the proportions are: relational process (11.3%), verbal process (7.5%), mental process (4.1%), behavioral process (3.7%), and existential process (1.4%). Through statistical analysis of various process types, it is found that the number of processes in Chinese sports news far exceeds that in English. In other words, BBC English sports news is more concise, while Chinese sports news is more detailed.

Mood System

Based on the mood system analysis of these two types of sports news texts in Tables 16 and 27, the following table is obtained:

			BBC English Sports News		Chinese Sports News on Xinhua Net	
			Total	%	Total	%
Number of Clauses	Sum		345	100	655	100
Type of Mood	Indicative		345	100	655	97.0
	Imperative		0	0	0	2.7
	Interrogative		0	0	0	0.3
Subject	First person		24	7	15	2
	Second person		1	0.2	0	0
	Third person		320	92.8	640	98
Tense	Past tense		299	87	×	×
	Present tense		42	12	×	×
	Future tense		4	1	×	×

Similarities: In terms of the type of mood, indicative mood is the most important choice in this genre. The third-person pronoun subject has a absolute advantage, accounting for more than 90%. Since sports news reports matches that have already taken place, the past tense is used most frequently.

Differences: Mainly reflected in the length, i.e. the number of clauses. BBC English sports news is more concise than domestic translated English sports news (345<572), but compared to Chinese sports news, translated English sports news on Xinhua net has made a significant reduction in the number of clauses (572<655).

Modality System

According to Table 19 and Table 39 in previous sections, the differences are as follows:

	BBC English Sports News						
	Low		Medium		High		Sum
	might(may)	could(can)	will(would)	should	must	need	
Number of Texts	5	10	14	0	1	1	22
Total	5	14	22	0	1	1	43
%	11.7	32.6	51.1	0	2.3	2.3	100
	Translated English Sports News on Xinhua Net						
	Low		Medium		High		Sum
	might(may)	could(can)	will(would)	should	must	need	
Number of Texts	2	17	14	1	1	7	22
Total	3	39	31	2	1	8	84
%	3.4	46.3	36.8	2.2	1.8	9.5	100

Similarities: From the perspective of length, Xinhua translated English sports news and BBC English sports news are very similar in the use of modal verbs, the number of texts from both corpora is 22. From the perspective of the type of modal verb used, both Xinhua translated English sports news and BBC English sports news tend to use low level modal verb, such as "might (may)", "could (can)" and medium level modal verb "will (would)".

Differences: In terms of quantity, 84 modal verbs are used in Xinhua translated English sports news, while modal verbs used in BBC English sports news are less than half (43). In terms of the degree of modal verbs, both Xinhua English sports news and BBC English sports news tend to use a lower degree modal verbs. However, in terms of high degree modal verbs, "need" is used more frequently in Xinhua translated English sports news(9.5%>2.3%). This modal verb corresponds to "需要" and "要" in Chinese, and shows a certain consistency with the high frequency use of "需要(要)" in Chinese sports news.

Theme System

Similarly, by integrating the thematic analysis (Table 21) of Xinhua translated English sports news (Table 41) and BBC English sports news from the previous section, it can be concluded that:

	BBC English Sports News		Xinhua Translated English Sports News	
	Sum	%	Sum	%
Compound Theme	79	20	73	11
Single Theme	327	80	616	89
Marked Theme	39	9	93	14
Unmarked Theme	367	91	586	86
Sum	406	100	679	100

Similarities: Both single themes and unmarked themes are the main forms. Although there are differences in the proportion of compound themes used in the two types of news, textual themes and experiential themes are the main forms of compound themes commonly used in marked themes.

Differences: The length of Xinhua translated English news is 1/3 higher than that of BBC sports News (679>406). In addition, the ratio of marked themes in Xinhua translated English sports news is quite close to that of BBC English sports news (14%>9%), which has significantly decreased compared to the ratio of Chinese sports news towards BBC sports news (23%>9%). This indicates that domestic news translators have significantly compressed their coverage of relevant background information by taking into consideration of differences in reading habits between Chinese and English. However, from the perspective of acceptability and improvement of translation quality, it is still necessary to further compress the introduction of background information and other aspects but focus on the event itself, refine the report content and wording and make the translation more in line with the aesthetic expectations of English readers.

Finally, to summarize: in the three corpora, marked themes account for 14%, 9%, and 23% of the total thematic systems respectively; Unmarked themes account for 86%, 91% and 77% respectively. For marked themes, most of them are used to emphasize the time and place of events and are achieved through adverbs or adverb phrases of time and place. Further research on the position of marked themes in texts of three corpora reveals that marked themes typically appear in moves about background knowledge. For example,

In 2002, Xu was old enough to change from Optimist class to Europe.

After China's National Games in 2009, Xu took a long break from sailing and enrolled in Shanghai Communications University. (Xinhua translated English text 5)

After winning 17 Olympic gold medals in his total of 21, Michael Phelps wasn't going to let a fact that he was about to swim the last race of his competitive career disturb his concentration or ambition when there was another medal on offer. (Xinhua translated English text 20)

That is to say, when introducing background information, time and place are usually the most concerned information, so the marked theme is most commonly seen in this move of the generic structure. This further explains why the use of marked themes in English and English translated sports news is lower than that of Chinese texts, as the former weakens the description of background information.

7.5 Assessment and Improvement of Translation Quality of Sports News

In recent years, with the continuous expansion of the influence of foreign media and culture, Chinese journalistic translation has noticed the differences between reporting methods of Chinese news and English with respect to generic structure and presentation style, and has made some adjustments in the English editing and translation of sports news. However, compared with the BBC English sports news, there is still a lot of room for improvement in the structure and presentation style of English translation of Chinese sports news. In order to examine whether there have been any adjustments made to the English translation of sports news in China compared to Chinese sports news, and how it needs to be improved compared to English sports news, we have established three corpora: BBC English sports news, Chinese sports news, and English translation of domestic sports news, and conducted parallel comparisons of the texts in the three corpora in terms of generic structure and presentation style. Through the detailed analysis and comparison of the above two sections, it has been found that there are significant differences in the GSP model between Xinhua Chinese sports news and BBC English sports news in terms of process type, mood, modality and theme. The English translation of Xinhua news takes into account these differences and makes targeted improvements to meet the reading habits of English readers. The translation is not simply a one-to-one correspondence of Xinhua Chinese sports news. However, the analysis also indicates that in order to fully utilize the functions of domestic sports news English translation, further improvement is needed to improve its quality, especially in terms of smoothness and elegance, in order to better meet the aesthetic expectations of English readers.

7.5.1 Quality Judgment and Modification Suggestions for the Original Translation from the Perspective of Generic Structure

As a common sub genre of news, sports news has its unique structure and presentation style. In translating such texts, we should not only pay attention to the specific content of the source text, but also pay attention to the manifestation of its content, that is, the macro structure of the text and the specific lexical-grammatical features. The translation of sports news should achieve effects similar to those of the source text. The translator should not only focus on conveying the content of the source text, but also adjust the structure and presentation style of translated texts from the perspective of the recipients. This adjustment often leads to conflicts between content and form, and translators need to make trade-offs in terms of content or form.

In the translation of sports news, the traditional concept of "meaning equivalence" is no longer the only or most important criterion for measuring the quality of translation. In order to achieve the creative purpose or purpose of this genre of texts, it is often necessary to adjust the structure and wording from the perspective of the genre during translation. In this way, in a sense, translators of sports news and other genres are no longer just translators, but also editors and writers. When translating, they should use the structure and presentation style of generic texts in the source language as a guide, and make changes in content, structure, wording and other aspects in translated texts relative to source texts.

Based on the previous analysis of the schematic structure of sports news texts in the corpus, we have summarized and compared the structural characteristics of English and Chinese sports news. Next, we try to discuss how to adjust the structure of similar Chinese sports news when translated into English based on the generic structure of the BBC English news, so as to achieve the effect of the source texts in translated texts.

In order to assess and improve the quality of translated , we start with the comparison of GSP model between Xinhua translated sports news and BBC English sports news texts. We randomly select Text 34 from the corpus of Xinhua translated sports news and conduct structural analysis on it. Then, by using the structure of similar BBC news as a benchmark, we elaborate on how to improve the quality of translation.

（H）Feng wins third gymnastic gold for China at London Olympic

(L) LONDON, Aug. 7 (Xinhua) —Chinese gymnast Feng Zhe held his nerve to win the Olympic men's parallel bars gold medal here on Tuesday.

(R&S) It was the third title claimed by the Chinese gymnastic team at the London Games. The Asian powerhouse also won gold medals in men's team and women's beam events.

(S) As the third one to compete, Feng was under much pressure after teammate Zhang Chenglong fell off the apparatus.

(AB) But the 2010 world champion in the discipline managed to earn a highest score of 15.955 points.

(P) Marcel Nguyen of Germany was 0.166 points behind and took the silver. The bronze went to French Hamilton Sgaot who scored 15.566 points.

(IC) "We finally vented out our frustration," said Feng. "Our skills are outstanding, but it is hard to say whether our performances are to the taste of the judges. This is the problem for all the events whose results are determined by judges."

(T) Feng referred to the scoring controversy in Monday's rings final, where teammate Chen Yibing had looked assured of victory after a superb opening routine only to final Arthur Nabarrete Zanetti of Brazil pull off a shock by earning the highest score.

(IC) "I felt sorry for Chen, but he did his best," said Feng, who has many fans in China for his baby-faced looks and sense of humor. "It tells how cruel sport competition is. I just need to do my best here," he added.

(IO) Nguyen said he was fairly satisfied with his silver medal, though he had a slight glitch with the grip and didn"t dismount properly. "This is the best thing I have ever had in life," he said. "I will never forget them."

(S) Japanese Tanaka Kazuhito and Tanaka Yasuke brothers, whose parents are both gymnasts as well, finished fourth and eighth respectively in men's parallel bars final.

The above is the structural analysis of this translated English sports news text on Xinhua Net. The schematic structure is expressed as follows:

H^L^RS^S^AB^P^IC^S^IC^IO^S

The meaning expressed by this formula is that in terms of structure, the news report is unfolded as follows: the heading points out the key content of the news; The lead introduces the elements of news(time, location, people, events); Next, the description of results and significance (for the country or for individuals); Next is a brief introduction to the champion, and a detailed description of the contestants' performance on the field; After that, the champion's speech and supplementary information about Chen Yibing, interview the champion and opponents, and finally the description of the performance of the other two athletes.

From the previous analysis, it can be seen that there are omissions in English translation of this Xinhua sports news text in moves like "athlete background" and "supplementary detailed information", and complete omission of "champion celebration" in Chinese sports news. However, in terms of structure, traces of Chinese generic characteristics are still retained, and the translator has not completely broken free from the constraints of the structure of Chinese news articles. The structure is still very similar to Chinese news text.

Based on corpus analysis, we have summarized the structural and linguistic features of English sports news represented by the BBC. As mentioned earlier, there are structural characteristics and differences between English and Chinese. Firstly, in terms of commonalities, H (heading), L (lead), and P (performance) constitute indispensable basic elements in a sports news article. Secondly, in terms of sequence, H always comes first, L always appears after H, and the position of P is relatively flexible. However, if AB (athlete background) appears, P must appear after AB, and other elements such as D (game details), IC (interview champion), IO (interview opponent), OCC (interview opponent coach), and S (supplementary information) are optional and flexible. Starting from this, when making structural adjustments to the translation, it is necessary to consider the above structural elements and occurrence order.

On the other hand, regarding the differences, which are the structural differences described earlier, namely:

Firstly, RS is not an essential element in BBC English sports news and its position is relatively flexible; In the translated English and Chinese news on Xinhua Net, RS generally appears after L and is a necessary element. In this sports news, RS can be omitted and part of its content can be transferred to S (supplementary information).

Secondly, D is an optional element in Chinese sports news, and P usually appears in pairs with D, but in BBC English sports news, P usually appears in pairs with AB, which means that when introducing an athlete's performance, a brief introduction of the player's background is usually given.

Thirdly, IC (interview champion) appears at a frequency of 52.5% in translated English Xinhua sports news, which is a necessary element. However, in BBC English sports news, its proportion is only 35%. In terms of order, in BBC English sports news, the position of IC is relatively flexible, but in Xinhua Chinese and translated English news, IC generally appear together with AB, that is, when interviewing champions, the background information of athletes is also explained. Based on this, we can simplify IC during the translation process.

Fourthly, finally, the proportion of S (supplementary information) in BBC English sports news is 37.5%, while it is 50% in Xinhua translated English sports news. It can be repeated and positioned flexibly, so it can be simplified and merged according to the specific content of the news report, such as deleting what is not very related to the competition, and integrating the part that can be included in the introduction of "athlete background".

Based on the above requirements for the similarities and differences in the structure and feature descriptions of similar genres in both Chinese and English, as well as the translated text being aligned structurally with the target language version, we can adjust the original translation structure from

H^L^RS^S^AB^P^IC^S^IC^IO^S

to

H^L^S^AB^P^IC^IO^S

That is to say, based on the structure of English sports news of the similar genre summarized in the previous section, we believe that the following adjustments can be made to the structure of the above translation:

(1) From the analysis of the structural characteristics of English sports news in the previous section, it can be seen that the main body of sports news reporting presents readers with specific content during the process of the game, such as player performance, opponent performance, competition details and relevant background. In other words, what English readers are most concerned about is the game itself, results, significance and other aspects are not the most concerned parts. Therefore, when translating from Chinese to English, corresponding adjustments should be made in order.

(2) Given that BBC sports news of the similar genre is more concise, Xinhua sports news can simplify the results and meaning of the competition when translating, focusing on the results rather than the meaning. In addition, athlete background is not a necessary element in BBC English sports news. For the sake of brevity in the text, it can be omitted in the supplementary information move to shorten the length. Namely:

(H)**Feng wins third gymnastic gold for China at London Olympic**

(L) LONDON, Aug. 7 (Xinhua)—Chinese gymnast Feng Zhe held his nerve to win the Olympic men's parallel bars gold medal here on Tuesday.

(S) As the third one to compete, Feng was under much pressure after teammate Zhang Chenglong fell off the apparatus.

(P) But the 2010 world champion in the discipline managed to earn a highest score of 15.955 points.

Marcel Nguyen of Germany was 0.166 points behind and took the silver. The bronze went to French Hamilton Sabot who scored 15.566 points.

(IC) "We finally vented out our frustration," said Feng. "Our skills are outstanding, but it is hard to say whether our performances are to the taste of the judges. This is the problem for all the events whose results are determined by judges."

(IO) Nguyen said he was fairly satisfied with his silver medal, though he had a slight glitch with the grip and didn"t dismount properly. "This is the best thing I have ever had in life," he said. "I will never forget them."

(S) It was the third title claimed by the Chinese gymnastic team at the London Games. The Asian powerhouse also won gold medals in men's team and women's beam events. Japanese Tanaka Kazuhito and Tanaka Yasuke brothers, whose parents are both gymnasts as well, finished fourth and eighth respectively in men's parallel bars final.

That is to say, according to the commonalities and differences between Chinese and English texts of this genre, the logical structure of the translated text is adjusted as follows:

First is heading (H), followed by lead (L) (covering the four elements of the news: time, location, people, and events), and then provide information about the athlete (S), including athlete background (AB), performance (P) (champion performance, opponent performance, etc.). Then, in order to enrich the news content, are interview champion (IC) and interview opponent (IO), and finally is supplementary information (S), such as results and significance, ranking achieved by other athletes. In this way, while maintaining the main content of the original text, the revised version has made structural adjustments to the target language, which is more in line with the reading habits of readers in the target language country, and the translation appears more "smooth".

In other words, although the original translation takes into account the habits of the target language, it still follows the framework of Chinese sports news in terms of structure, and does not pay enough attention to the structure or standard of English sports news texts.

From the perspective of "smoothness" and "elegance", which are two major parameters for measuring translation quality, the original translation quality is not good enough and there is much room for improvement.

7.5.2 Judgment and Improvement Suggestions on the Quality of the Original Translation from the Perspective of Representation Style

The translation must conform to the norms and habits of the target language to the greatest extent possible, and achieve the expected reception in the target language society. Similarly, it must also be reflected at the stylistic level - linguistic characteristics that are similar to it. Here we still take Text 34 on Xinhua Net as an example, from the perspective of systemic functional linguistics, to analyze the linguistic characteristics of the text in terms of transitivity system, mood system (including modality system) and theme system.

（1） Analysis of Process Types from the Perspective of Transitivity

Feng wins third gymnastic gold for China at London Olympic

LONDON, Aug. 7 (Xinhua)— (**M**) Chinese gymnast Feng Zhe held his nerve to win the Olympic men's parallel bars gold medal here on Tuesday.

(**R**) It was the third title claimed by the Chinese gymnastic team at the London Games. (**R**) The Asian powerhouse also won gold medals in men's team and women's beam events.

(**R**) As the third one to compete, Feng was under much pressure (**M**) after teammate Zhang Chenglong fell off the apparatus. (**M**) But the 2010 world champion in the discipline managed to earn a highest score of 15.955 points.

(**R**) Marcel Nguyen of Germany was 0.166 points behind and (**M**) took the silver. (**M**) The bronze went to French Hamilton SGAot (**M**) who scored 15.566 points.

(**M**) "We finally vented out our frustration," (**V**) said Feng. (R) "Our skills are outstanding, but it is hard to say whether our performances are to the taste of the judges. (**R**) This is the problem for all the events （**B**） whose results are determined by judges."

（**V**） Feng referred to the scoring controversy in Monday's rings final, （**M2**） where teammate Chen Yibing had looked assured of victory after a superb opening routine only to (M)final Arthur Nabarrete Zanetti of Brazil pull off a shock by earning the highest score.

（**M2**） "I felt sorry for Chen, （**M**） but he did his best," (**V**) said Feng, (**R**) who has many fans in China for his baby-faced looks and sense of humor.

(**V**) "It tells(R)how cruel sport competition is. （**M2**）I just need to do my best here," （**V**） he added.

(V) Nguyen said (R) he was fairly satisfied with his silver medal, (M)though he had a slight glitch with the grip and (B) didn't dismount properly.

(R) "This is the best thing (R) I have ever had in life," (V) he said. (M2) "I will never forget them."

(R) Japanese Tanaka Kazuhito and Tanaka Yasuke brothers, whose parents are both gymnasts as well, finished fourth and eighth respectively in men's parallel bars final.

(In the text, the letter M in parentheses represents material processes, M2 represents mental processes, R represents relational processes, and V represents verbal processes. It can be seen that there are a total of 10 material processes, 10 relational processes, 7 verbal processes, 4 mental processes, and 2 behavioral processes in the entire text.)

In the above case, it is evident that compared to English sports news of the similar genre, relational and verbal processes account for a large proportion in Xinhua translated English News, far exceeding the material process. The reporting focus is not placed on the field and athlete performance—which is the focus of similar English news reports. Therefore, the relational and verbal process can be appropriately reduced to highlight the game itself when translating.

(2) Analysis from the perspective of mood and modality system

Feng wins third gymnastic gold for China at London Olympic

LONDON, Aug. 7 (Xinhua) — (D) Chinese gymnast Feng Zhe (3)held his nerve to win the Olympic men's parallel bars gold medal here on Tuesday.

(D)It (3) was the third title claimed by the Chinese gymnastic team at the London Games. (D)The Asian powerhouse (3) also won gold medals in men's team and women's beam events.

(D)As the third one to compete, Feng (3) was under much pressure after teammate Zhang Chenglong fell off the apparatus. (D)But the 2010 world champion (3) in the discipline managed to earn a highest score of 15.955 points.

(D)Marcel Nguyen (3) of Germany was 0.166 points behind and took the silver.(D)The bronze (3) went to French Hamilton SGAot who scored 15.566 points.

(D) "We finally vented out our frustration," said Feng (3) . (D) "Our skills (3) are outstanding, but it is hard to say whether our performances are to the taste of the judges. (D) This (3) is the problem for all the events whose results are determined by judges."

(D) Feng (3) referred to the scoring controversy in Monday's rings final, where teammate Chen Yibing had looked assured of victory after a superb opening routine only to final Arthur Nabarrete Zanetti of Brazil pull off a shock by earning the highest score.

(D) "I felt sorry for Chen, but he did his best," said Feng (3), who has many fans in China for his baby-faced looks and sense of humor.

(D) "It tells how cruel sport competition is. I just need to do my best here," he (3) added.

(D) Nguyen (3) said he was fairly satisfied with his silver medal, though he had a slight glitch with the grip and didn''t dismount properly.

(D) "This is the best thing I have ever had in life," he (3) said. (D) "I (1) **will** never forget them."

(D) Japanese Tanaka Kazuhito and Tanaka Yasuke brothers (3), whose parents are both gymnasts as well, finished fourth and eighth respectively in men's parallel bars final.

(The letter D in parentheses indicates the indicative mood, the underlined part is the subject, the number 3 in parentheses after the subject indicates the third-person pronoun, and the number 1 indicates the first person.)

From this, it can be seen that the entire article is in indicative mood; Except one subject is I, the rest are all third-person pronouns. Modal words are seldomly used, and the only one that has been used is "will".

Based on the data analyzed above, whether it is domestic English translated sports news or BBC English sports news, it is recommended to avoid or minimize the use of subjective modal words to ensure the objectivity of the news content and try to avoid mixing personal attitudes and viewpoints. However, in terms of subject type, the third-person pronoun is blindly used in the translated English news text, which increases the distance from the reader and can be improved in this regard.

（3） Theme analysis

Feng wins third gymnastic gold for China at London Olympic

LONDON, Aug. 7 (Xinhua) —Chinese gymnast Feng Zhe held his nerve to win the Olympic men's parallel bars gold medal here on Tuesday.

It was the third title claimed by the Chinese gymnastic team at the London Games. The Asian powerhouse also won gold medals in men's team and women's beam events.

As the third one to compete, Feng **(M)**was under much pressure after teammate Zhang Chenglong fell off the apparatus. But the 2010 world champion **(C)**in the discipline managed to earn a highest score of 15.955 points.

Marcel Nguyen of Germany was 0.166 points behind and took the silver. The bronze went to French Hamilton SGAot who scored 15.566 points.

"We finally vented out our frustration," said Feng. "Our skills are outstanding, but it is hard to say whether our performances are to the taste of the judges. This is the problem for all the events whose results are determined by judges."

Feng referred to the scoring controversy in Monday's rings final, where teammate Chen Yibing had looked assured of victory after a superb opening routine only to final Arthur Nabarrete Zanetti of Brazil pull off a shock by earning the highest score.

"I felt sorry for Chen, but he did his best," said Feng, who has many fans in China for his baby-faced looks and sense of humor.

"It tells how cruel sport competition is. I just need to do my best here," he added.

Nguyen said he was fairly satisfied with his silver medal, though he had a slight glitch with the grip and didn't dismount properly.

"This is the best thing I have ever had in life," he said. "I will never forget them."

Japanese Tanaka Kazuhito and Tanaka Yasuke brothers, whose parents are both gymnasts as well, finished fourth and eighth respectively in men's parallel bars final.

(The underlined part in the text represents the theme, while the letter M in parentheses represents the marked theme and C represents the compound theme. It is not difficult to see from the above annotation that the entire text is almost in single themes except for 1 marked theme and 1 compound theme, which appears dull.)

Based on the above analysis, we propose the following improvement suggestions for Xinhua translated English sports news based on the differences in linguistic features between Xinhua Chinese sports news and its English translation, and BBC English sports news, taking the latter as a reference:

1. In terms of experiential significance, more material processes should be used to reduce other types of processes and to focus on the game itself.

The previous analysis shows that although material processes are the most frequently used type in all three corpora, their frequency is not the same:their proportions in the Chinese, English, and translated English corpora are 72%, 70.2%, and 51.3%, respectively.

2. The frequency of verbal processes being used should be further reduced.

From the previous analysis, it can be seen that the proportion of verbal processes ranks second in all three corpora, but the frequency is completely different in the three corpora. In BBC English sports news, the frequency of verbal processes is 9.9%, while in domestic translated English news, the frequency of verbal processes is 20.1%. Due to differences in habits of news writing between the East and the West, very few English news quotes interviews with athletes. In response to this, no corresponding adjustments have been made to translated English news.

Here we can delete all the content about interviews with Feng Zhe and other athletes. Because most of the content in the interview with Feng Zhe is about the regret and injustice expressed by him for another Chinese gymnast, Chen Yibing, who missed the gold medal due to the unfair scoring of the referee in the ring game. We can fully understand such content in the Chinese report, because the audiences of the news are from Chinese, and Chinese readers have the same psychological feelings about the results of Chen Yibing's game. Therefore, the interview and report of Feng Zhe on Chen Yibing can arouse the resonance of readers. However, in foreign reports, audiences have become foreign readers, who do not have the same feelings as Chinese readers about the results of Chen Yibing's competition. In this case, it would be superfluous for the readers of the translated text to translate the interview with Feng Zhe into English without adjustment. Therefore, when translating, corresponding adjustments should be made according to the audience's reading expectations and the writing habits of English news, such as reducing the verbal processes while increasing the number of material processes, and focusing on the performance of athletes on the field. This can better achieve the communicative purpose of this genre of text.

In terms of theme, the translated text has more themes than English sports news, and the proportion of single themes is higher than that of English. This is mainly because the translated text uses more short and simple clauses, while BBC English sports news uses more complex clauses. The root behind it is that the translated text is a mechanical translation of Chinese sports, and the biggest difference between Chinese and English is that the former often uses short and concise flowing clauses, while the latter tends to use complex sentences. Recognizing this difference requires translation to respond accordingly. From the perspective of textual meaning, which is the organization of the text, BBC English sports news texts rarely contain relevant background information. On the contrary, in Chinese news texts, background information accounts for a large amount of space. This indicates that due to the influence of different cultures on news writing, Chinese people are more accustomed to making reports as detailed as possible and presenting all information related to athletes and games to readers. However, for BBC English news, it places more emphasis on the game itself and does not pay much attention to relevant background information. Similar to Chinese sports news on Xinhua Net, translated English news focuses on describing background information, so the marked theme is slightly higher than that of BBC English sports news. Therefore, in the translation process, compound sentences can be added, the overall number of themes can be reduced, and the proportion of multiple themes can be expanded, thus the text can be more coherent.

In summary, the revised translation is as follows:

Feng wins third gymnastic gold for China at London Olympic

LONDON, Aug. 7 (Xinhua) — (1) (M) <u>Chinese gymnast Feng Zhe</u> **held** his nerve to win the Olympic men's parallel bars gold medal here on Tuesday.

(2) (M) <u>As the third one to compete, the 2010 world champion in the discipline</u> **managed** to earn a highest score of 15.955 points, not influenced by his teammate Zhang Chenglong's falling off the apparatus.

(3) <u>And, Marcel Nguyen of Germany,</u> <4> (M) <u>who</u> **had** a slight glitch with the grip and didn't (B) **dismount** properly,(R) **got** the silver with only 0.166 points behind <5> (R) <u>but he</u> **felt** fairly satisfied with the result,<6> (M) <u>and the bronze</u> **went to** French Hamilton (M) who **scored** 15.566 points.

(4) (R) <u>Born in a gymnastic family, Japanese Tanaka Kazuhito and Tanaka Yasuke brothers,</u> **finished** fourth and eighth respectively in men's parallel bars final.

(5) (R) <u>It</u> was the third title claimed by the Chinese gymnastic team at the London Games, <7> (R) <u>besides, the Asian powerhouse</u> also **won** gold medals in men's team and women's beam events.

The original translation of this news is influenced by the Chinese structure of the source text. Through interviews with champions, there are a lot of words about Chen Yibing's rings incident and the results of the game being vulnerable to unfair adjudication. However, this kind of content is not directly related to the game itself. Therefore, according to the consideration of English sports news' focus on the event itself, it is deleted here. However, all the content that readers pay attention to, such as athlete performance (self, opponent), competition details (such as:highest score of 15.955 points, with only 0.166 points behind, he had a slim glitch with the grip and didn't dismount properly, not influenced by his teammate Zhang Chenglong's falling off the apparatus), is retained. In addition, in terms of expression, by combining some small clauses, the writing structure is compact and tightly connected. In this way, the revised version is closer to generic characteristics of English sports news in terms of the GSP model, as well as linguistic features such as process type, mood and theme selection. From the perspective of the target language reader, it appears more smooth. (There are a total of 5 sentences in the revised translation, represented by (), 7 small sentences, and marked with ◇, including

5 material processes, 5 relational processes, and 1 behavioral relational process; 9 theme combinations (indicated by underscores), with 6 marked themes; In terms of tense use, except for the title, they are all in the past tense, and no modal words are used. The mood is all indicative, which basically conforms to the linguistic characteristics of this type of English genre)

References:

[1]Melven Mencher.News Reporting and Writing, Ninth Edition[M].Beijing: McGraw-Hill Education (Asia) Co. and Qsinghua University Press,2003.

[2]Halliday, M. A. K. An Introduction to Functional Grammar [M]. London: Edward Arnold,1985.

[3]Thompson, G. Introducing Functional Grammar [M]. London: Edward Arnold,1996.

Chapter 8 Translation Quality Studies of Museum Introduction Discourses

This chapter elaborates on the content, steps, and methods of constructing corpora of three types of museum introductions (English introductions of foreign museums, Chinese introductions of domestic museums, and English translations of domestic museum introductions). Based on this, first of all, the GSP model is summarized by analyzing textual components in the three corpora from the perspective of schematic structure; Secondly, starting from the transitivity system, mood system and theme system, lexical and grammatical characteristics (reflecting styles) of this genre of texts in three corpora are analyzed; Thirdly, similarities and differences are found by comparing three types of museum introductions included in the corpora from dimensions of structure and style that reflect the characteristics of discourses; Finally, starting from the second stage of the translation quality assessment model constructed in Chapter 6, which judges and measures whether the translation is smooth and unobstructed, this paper evaluates and proposes improvement suggestions for the quality of English translation of domestic museum introductions by using the characteristics of foreign museum introductions as a benchmark , and achieves empirical analysis of the translation quality evaluation model constructed in Chapter 6.

8.1 Construction of Corpus of Museum Introduction Discourses

This project has selected 40 different types of museum introductions from official foreign tourism website Aviewoncities, China Culture and the English version of China Culture respectively, the total number of which is 120. Three analogical corpora have thus been accordingly established, namely the English introduction corpus of foreign museums, the Chinese introduction corpus of domestic museums, and the English translation corpus of domestic museum introductions. For example, Text 5 of the English introduction corpus of foreign museums is a space museum, specifically "National Air&Space Museum", and the corresponding Chinese and its translated English introductions of domestic museums are "Hong Kong Space Museum".

Therefore, the directory of the established corpus of museum introduction is as follows. (Specific corpus can be found in the appendix)

No.	English Introductions of Foreign Museums	Chinese Introductions of Domestic Museums	English Translations of Domestic Museums Introductions
1	British Museum	故宫博物院	Palace museum
2	Vatican Museums	首都博物馆	The Capital Museum
3	Orsay Museum	中国地质博物馆	Geological Museum of China
4	National Museum of Natural History	上海自然博物馆	Shanghai Museum of Natural Science
5	National Air & Space Museum	香港太空馆	Hong Kong Space Museum
6	Victoria and Albert Museum	秦始皇兵马俑博物馆	Qin Terra Cotta Army museum
7	Metropolitan Museum of Art	中国佛教图书文物馆	Relic Hall of Chinese Buddhism Books
8	Field Museum	铜绿山古铜矿遗址博物馆	Museum of the Former Site of Ancient Tonglvshan Copper Mine
9	Museum of Science and Industry	中国台湾自然科学博物馆	Taiwan National Museum of Natural Science
10	Louvre	澳门博物馆	Macau museum
11	Capitoline Museums	天津戏剧博物馆	Tianjin Museum of Theatre
12	Museums Quartier	天津博物馆	Tianjin museum
13	Museum of Fine Art in Vienna	广州美术馆	GuangZhou art gallery
14	Naval History Museum	西安半坡博物馆	Banpo Museum
15	Van Gogh Museum	南阳汉画馆	Nanyang Museum of Han Dynasty Stone Carving
16	Maritime Museum	香港海洋公园（海洋博物馆）	Hong Kong Ocean Park
17	Rijksmuseum	中国丝绸博物馆	China National Silk Museum

18	Middelheim Sculpture Museum	平遥双林寺彩塑艺术馆	Shuanglin Temple Art Gallery of Painted Sculptures at Pingyao
19	Royal Museum	皇家博物院	Puppet Manchurian Imperial Palace Museum
20	Plantin-Moretus Museum	北京大钟寺古钟博物馆	Ancient Bells Museum at the Great Bell Temple
21	National Archaeological Museum	周口店遗址博物馆	Zhoukoudian relics museum
22	Benaki Museum	中国台北故宫博物院	Tai Bei Palace Museum
23	Acropolis Museum	中国茶叶博物馆	Chinese tea museum
24	Pergamon Museum	辽宁省博物馆	Liaoning Provincial Museum
25	Museum Island	中国科技博物馆	Museum of Chinese Science and Technology
26	Museum of Fine Arts in Boston	中国美术馆	China National Museum of Fine Arts
27	Hungarian National Museum	青海省博物馆	QingHai Province Museum
28	Military History Museum	中国人民革命军事博物馆	The Military Museum of the Chinese People's Revolution
29	Senckenberg Museum	中国台北昆虫科学博物馆	Taipei Insect Science Museum
30	History Museum in Frankfurt	中国台湾历史博物馆	National History Museum of Taiwan
31	National Coach Museum	中国邮票博物馆	China's Museums of Stamps
32	National Azulejo Museum	景德镇陶瓷历史博物馆	Jingdezhen Ceramics Museum
33	Gulbenkian Museum	广东民间工艺馆	Guangdong Folk Arts and Crafts Museum
34	Prado Museum	澳门艺术博物馆	Macao Museum of Art

35	Deutsches Museum	北京自然博物馆	Beijing Natural History Museum
36	National World War II Museum	南京太平天国历史博物馆	The History Museum of Taiping Heavenly Kingdom
37	Rodin Museum	上海博物馆	Shanghai Museum
38	Russian Museum	中国国家博物馆	The National Museum of China
39	Vasa Museum	洛阳石刻艺术馆	Luoyang Museum of Stone Carving Art
40	Museum of Anthropology	厦门大学人类学博物馆	Museum of Anthropology of Xiamen University

Next, an analysis of the 120 discourses in the aforementioned three corpora as has been done in Section 1 of Chapter 6 and Chapter 7 will be conducted. Description and comparison will be made of the GSP model and lexical and grammatical features of the three corpora to identify similarities and differences. Starting from parameters like "smooth and unobstructed" used in the translation quality assessment model to measure the quality of the translated texts, this project aims to summarize structural and linguistic features represented by introductions of English museums to provide improvement suggestions for the quality of English translations of Chinese museum introductions, and further conduct empirical research on the translation quality evaluation model constructed in Chapter 6.

8.2 Corpus-based Generic Structure of Museum Introductions
8.2.1 Structural Elements of Museum Introductions

In order to summarize the GSP model for museum introductions in English, Chinese, and English translations, structural analyses of them are conducted to understand the structural composition of these genres of discourses. Next, one museum introduction will be selected randomly from each of the three corpora mentioned above to conduct a structural analysis of its outline, identify and statistically analyze the structural elements of this genre, and to demonstrate the method of generic structural analysis. Then, following the same method, the analysis, identification and statistics of all remaining discourses in the three corpora will thus be completed.

After analyzing all the structural elements of discourses in three corpora, based on their different communicative purposes embedded in these discourses, it can be found that the genre of museum introduction generally has 11 structural elements, namely: designation, location, completed time, historical events, building introduction, collections and exhibits introduction, social activities, academic contributions, evaluation and position, and visiting guide.

The names (including the initial letters of English names) and functions of these 11 structural elements are as follows:

Designation: Namely, the title of the museum.

Location: The geographical location of the museum.

Completed Time: When the museum was established and completed.

Historical Events: Its mainly about the historical allusions related to the construction process of the museum.

Building Introduction: Mainly the description and introduction of the museum building itself, such as the building area, layout of the exhibition hall, etc.

Collections and Exhibits Introduction: Introduction to the items collected in the museum.

Social Activities: Including exhibitions held or economic, educational and other social activities participated in by museums.

Academic Contributions: It refers to published publications or related works.

Evaluation and Position: The evaluation of the museum and an introduction to its importance.

Visiting Guide: Including opening hours, ticket prices, and other information.

8.2.2 The GSP Model of English Introductions to Foreign Museums

Next, text 8 from the English introduction corpus of foreign museums has been randomly selected for structural analysis.

(D) Field Museum

(http://www.aviewoncities.com/chicago/fieldmuseum.htm)

(EP) Chicago's Field Museum is considered one of the finest natural history museums in the U.S. It even gained national acclaim when Steven Spielberg made it the home base for the esteemed archaeologist in his Indiana Jones movies.

(HE) Movie appearances aside, however, the Field Museum was originally founded to house the biological and anthropological collections assembled for the World's Columbian Exposition of 1893. That collection still remains the core of the Field's permanent collection. However, in more than a century, the museum has grown into a home for more than 20 million specimens and a 25,000 volume natural history library.

（CEI） The Field Museum boasts a number of both permanent and temporary exhibits that will appeal to museum goers of all ages.

Nature Exhibits

Nature exhibits include areas dedicated to the animals of Africa, North American birds, plants of the world, sea mammals and an underground adventure.

One of the African exhibits tells the story of the Lions of Tsavo, two lions that once terrorized East Africa. Other exhibits include Evolving Planet, a journey through 4 billion years of life on earth and Moving Earth, where you can discover why the plates on the earth move. Also in the nature section are several galleries with profile rocks and fossils. Other galleries focus on Jade, diamonds and other gems.

Culture Exhibits

Permanent culture-related exhibits include a look inside Ancient Egypt, a chance to view a full scale Pawnee earth lodge, the hall of the Ancient Americas and the lacquer ware art of Japan. There's also a Maori Meeting House and an exhibit on life in Tibet as well as exhibits on Eskimos and Northwest Coast Indians.

Temporary Exhibits

Temporary exhibits change several times a year and the Field Museum has been a stop for some of the finest major traveling exhibits of the last several decades, including an excellent exhibit about Jackie Kennedy, the wonderful King Tut exhibition, and the Auschwitz Album, a photographical tour of the infamous Nazi death camp.

Sue

Kids will certainly want to visit the T-Rex named Sue, described as the largest, most complete, and best-preserved Tyrannosaurus Rex ever unearthed, standing 12 feet high and 42 feet long (3.6 x 12.8 meter).

（VG） Visiting the Museum

The Field Museum also has four gift shops on site where visitors can purchase a number of wonderful items, from inexpensive souvenirs to beautiful jewelry and hand-crafted artwork. There's also a better-than-average café at which to grab a bite to eat.

Visitors can explore the three floors of the museum on their own or take a guided "highlights" tour which departs twice each day and gives you the inside story on some of the museum's most popular artifacts.

As mentioned above, the schematic structure of Text 8 is:

  D ^EP^HE^CEI^VG

This museum introduction begins by highlighting its name - the Field Museum and its status as one of the most outstanding natural history museums in the United States, and is renowned nationwide as the main filming location for the *Indiana Jones* series. Subsequently, a brief explanation is given about changes in the museum's collection from the early days to the present from three aspects: natural exhibits, cultural exhibits, and temporary exhibits. This includes the most well preserved Rex Tyrannosaurus fossil, which is one of the main interests of children. Finally, the introduction provides guide information for tourists to visit: there are 4 souvenir and gift shops within the museum, as well as coffee shops for rest, and visitors are advised to visit on their own or browse under the guidance of introduction or the staff.

After analyzing the remaining museum English introductions in the corpus by using the above method, their structural elements and order are shown in the table below:

Table 2 schematic structure of English Introductions of Foreign Museums

Text No.	Structural Elements and Order
1	D^EP ^EP^L^CEI^BI
2	D^L^CT^ EP^HE^CEI
3	D^EP^VG^HE^BI^CEI
4	D^EP^ CEI^HE^BI^L
5	D^ EP^CT^CEI
6	D^CT^EP^BI^CEI
7	D^L^EP^HE^BI^CEI
8	D^EP^HE^CEI^VG
9	D^EP^L^HE^BI^CEI
10	D^EP^HE^BI^CEI^VG
11	D^CT^L^BI^HE^CEI
12	D^L^BI^CEI
13	D^EP^L^HE^CT^HE^BI^CEI
14	D^L^EP^HE^CEI
15	D^EP^CEI^BI
16	D^EP^CEI
17	D^EP^EP^CEI^BI
18	D^HE^L^CT^BI^CEI^VG
19	D^CT^EP^L^HE^BI^CEI

20	D^EP^HE^CEI^EP
21	D^EP^CT^BI^CEI
22	D^HE^CEI
23	D^L^HE^CT^BI^CEI
24	D^EP^L^CT^HE^CEI
25	D^EP^HE^CEI
26	D^L^EP^HE^BI^CEI
27	D^EP^BI^CT^CEI
28	D^L^HE^CEI
29	D^EP^EP^HE^CEI
30	D^L^HE^BI^CEI
31	D^EP^CT^L^HE^BI^CEI
32	D^L^HE^CEI^BI^CEI
33	D^EP^HE^CT^CEI
34	D^HE^EP^HE^CEI^VG
35	D^EP^L^EP^CEI^HE^VG
36	D^EP^CT^HE^CEI
37	D^L^HE^CEI
38	D^CT^HE^BI^CEI
39	D^CT^EP^HE^CEI
40	D^EP^BI^CEI

The distribution of various structural elements is as follows:

Table 3 Distribution of Structural Elements in English Introductions of Foreign Museums

文本编号	D	L	CT	HE	BI	CEI	SA	AC	EP	VG
1	√	√			√	√			√	
2	√	√	√	√		√			√	
3	√			√	√	√			√	√
4	√	√		√	√	√			√	
5	√		√			√			√	
6	√		√		√	√			√	
7	√			√	√	√			√	
8	√			√		√			√	√

9	√	√		√	√	√			√	
10	√			√	√	√			√	√
11	√	√	√	√	√	√				
12	√	√			√	√				
13	√	√	√	√	√	√			√	
14	√	√		√		√			√	
15	√				√	√			√	
16	√					√			√	
17	√				√	√			√	
18	√	√	√	√	√	√				√
19	√	√	√	√	√	√			√	
20	√			√		√			√	
21	√		√		√	√			√	
22	√			√		√				
23	√	√	√	√	√	√				
24	√	√	√	√		√			√	
25	√			√		√			√	
26	√	√		√	√	√			√	
27	√		√		√	√			√	
28	√	√		√		√				
29	√			√		√			√	
30	√	√		√	√	√				
31	√	√	√	√	√	√			√	
32	√	√		√	√	√				
33	√		√	√		√			√	
34	√			√		√			√	√
35	√	√		√		√			√	√
36	√		√	√		√			√	
37	√	√		√		√				
38	√		√	√	√	√				
39	√		√	√		√			√	
40	√				√	√			√	

The frequency of occurrence of each structural element is:

Table 4 Frequency of Structural Elements in English Introductions of Foreign Museums

	D	L	CT	HE	BI	CEI	SA	AC	EP	VG
Sum	40	19	16	30	23	40	0	0	30	6
%	100	47.5	40	75	57.5	100	0	0	75	15

Through the analysis of Tables 2, 3, and 4, it can be found that the frequency of elements like designation, historical events, building introduction, collection and exhibit introduction and evaluation and position exceed 50%, making them essential structural elements of museum introductions. Most English introductions of foreign museum include these elements. In contrast, the frequency of occurrence of other elements is less than 50%, making them optional.

In terms of the sequence of these structural elements, although the order of appearance of essential and optional elements in the introduction of museums is relatively complex, it still follows certain rules. For example, the museum name (D) must always appear first, and evaluation and position (EP) always appear at the beginning of the introduction, directly informing tourists of the museum's significance, which is in line with the habit of western discourses by providing the summary first and details later; Building introduction (BI) often appears before the collection and exhibition introduction (CEI), and these two elements mainly inform visitors about the layout of the museum and the main collection exhibiting in a specific area; The position of historical events (HE) is not fixed, but it must appear before CEI; Positions of optional elements such as museum address (L) and complete time (CT) are relatively flexible, and visiting guide (VG) always appears at the end of the introduction to provide more detailed information for tourists. Thus, it is concluded that the GSP model for English museum introductions is as follows:

$$D \wedge EP \wedge (L) (CT) \overset{\frown}{HE} \wedge \overset{\frown}{BI} \, CEI \, (\wedge VG)$$
※ ※ ※

Elements of D, EP, HE, BI and CEI are necessary, while the rest are optional. Elements of D and EP always appear at the beginning of the introduction. The positions of L, CT, and HE are relatively flexible, HE can appear repeatedly and always appear before CEI. When BI appears, it often appears before CEI; CEI can be duplicated; VG always appears at the end of the introduction.

8.2.3 The GSP Model of Chinese Introductions of Domestic Museums

Similarly, Text 4 has been selected randomly from the corpus as an example to analyze the structure of the Chinese introductions of domestic museums.

（D）上海自然博物馆
(http://www.chinaculture.org/gb/cn_bwyg/2004-06/28/content_47697.htm)

（EP）上海自然博物馆是中国最大的自然博物馆之一。（L）位于上海市中心。（BI）该馆大楼带有英国古典建筑风格，建筑面积为12880平方米。

（CT）上海自然博物馆于1956年11月筹建。1960年建成动物学分馆对外开放。1984年建成植物学分馆，该分馆包括标本大楼和陈列厅两个部分，是中国唯一的植物学馆。标本大楼面积为3053平方米，除珍藏各类植物标本外，还设有研究室和实验室；陈列厅设在上海植物园内。总面积为4726平方米。其中约二分之一已对外展出。

（CEI）上海自然博物馆有丰富的馆藏标本和图书资料。除了接收原英国人办的亚洲文会上海博物馆标本，法国人办的震旦博物院的部分自然标本外，主要通过采集、收购、赠送、交换等途径获得各类自然标本。到1985年，馆藏各类标本有20余万件，其中动物标本6.2万多件，植物标本13.5万多件，古生物标本1700多件，新旧石器标本700多件，矿物与岩石标本1700多件。在这些标本中，有一定数量的模式标本和国内第一次发现的新记录标本。有中国特有的和世界著名的珍稀生物标本，有6亿年前的化石。该馆还藏有供科学研究和科学教育用的中、外文各类专业图书资料6万余册。

（BI）该馆基本陈列面积共5700平方米。陈列内容包括古动物史、人类发展史、动物和植物的进化四大部分。

（CEI）在古动物史陈列，展示了动物的发生和发展，从水生到陆生，从简单到复杂，从低等到高等进化的漫长过程。展厅中央陈列了一条体长22米、肩高3.5米的原大恐龙模型——合川马门溪龙。它的右侧是一头黄河古象模型，体长8米，体高4米，一对门牙有3米长。

人类发展史陈列，用大量实物、模型、出土文物以及二、三百万年前的前期猿人生活情况的景象，揭示了人类的起源、人类社会的形成和发展。

在动物陈列分设无脊椎动物、鱼类、两栖动物，爬行动物，鸟类和哺乳动物6个陈列厅。除了展出中国一级保护动物长臂猿、金丝猴、大熊猫、云豹、金钱豹、雪豹、虎、亚洲象、儒艮、野驴、梅花鹿、野牦牛、羚牛、野骆驼、褐马鸡、扬子鳄、白鲟等外，还有中国二级保护动物及野生已绝灭的麋鹿（即"四不像"）等许多珍禽异兽。此外，也展出许多外国著名动物，如非洲的狮子、长颈鹿、狒狒和黑猩猩，澳大利亚的鸭嘴兽、袋鼠和鸸鹋，美洲的狮子，日本的高脚蟹等等。

古尸陈列室共陈列5具古尸，其中新疆楼兰地区发掘的楼兰女尸，据碳14测定，认为距今3880±95年，是中国已知古尸中年代最早的一具。植物陈列，分序厅、植物进化厅和植物的改造与利用厅。内容包括原始的藻类，没有叶绿素的真菌，菌藻共生的地衣，陆生维管植物的先驱——蕨类、陆生植物的一个旁枝——苔藓，直到高等的秋子植物。沿着陈列线，一个个生态景象的衔接，展示植物演化的进程。陈列厅的中央是一个巨大的石炭纪蕨类立体景箱，它再现了2亿多年前地球上最早的沼泽森林，也是植物从水生到陆生后出现的第一批大森林。已经在地球上绝灭的鳞木、封印木等蕨类矗立于森林上层，无数草木蕨类覆盖在沼泽湿地上。

（SA）该馆还办有"中国历代古尸""一九八〇年云南日全食观测""珍稀动物""宝石""优生优育""生物工程""南极考察和知识""中国特产动物——麋鹿"等展览。

（AC）该馆除了编写一批动物、植物、人类、古生物、天文等专业学科的书籍和图集外，还编辑《考察与研究》学术专辑和综合性科普双月刊《自然与人》。

The schematic structure of Text 4 is:

D^EP^L^BI^CT^CEI^BI^CEI^SA^AC

The structure of this introduction is: first, the name is given and its status as one of the largest natural science museums in China is indicated. Subsequently, information on the establishment and opening of the museum is introduced. The collections of the museum are elaborated, which are mainly animal and plant specimens or ore specimens. It goes on to explain that the museum consists of four exhibition halls, and collections displayed in each hall are introduced separately. Finally, it is introduced that in addition to the permanent display of aforementioned collections, the museum also holds other exhibition activities and stores multiple books, making significant academic contributions to natural science research. The remaining texts in the corpus have been analyzed by using the same method, the structural elements and the order in which each element appears are:

Table 5 schematic structure of Chinese Introductions of Domestic Museums

Text No.	Elements and Their Order
1	D^EP^L^CT^HE
2	D^EP^L^CT^BI^CEI^SA
3	D^EP^L^HE^CT^CEI^SA^AC
4	D^EP^L^BI^CT^CEI^BI^CEI^SA^AC
5	D^EP^L^CT^BI^CEI
6	D^L^HE^CT^BI^CEI
7	D^L^CT^EP^CEI^SA^AC
8	D^EP^L^CT^HE^BI^CEI
9	D^L^CEI

10	D^CT^L^BI^CEI^VG
11	D^EP^L^CT^BI^CEI^SA
12	D^CT^L^EP^BI^CEI^EP
13	D^CT^L^BI^CEI^AC
14	D^L^HE^CT^CEI
15	D^EP^L^CT^CEI^SA
16	D^L^CT^CEI
17	D^L^CT^BI^CEI
18	D^L^EP^CT^BI^CEI
19	D^L^CT^BI^EP
20	D^EP^L^CT^CEI^AC
21	D^L^CT^BI^HE^CEI
22	D^L^BI^HE^CEI^AC
23	D^L^CT^EP^BI^CEI
24	D^EP^CT^SA^EP
25	D^L^CT^CEI^SA^AC
26	D^L^CT^EP^BI^CEI^SA
27	D^EP^L^BI^CEI^SA^AC
28	D^EP^BI^SA^EP
29	D^EP^L^BI^CT^CEI^SA
30	D^CT^L^BI^CEI^SA
31	D^L^CT^CEI^SA
32	D^L^CT^BI^CEI^AC
33	D^CT^L^BI^EP^CEI^SA
34	D^L^CT^BI^EP^CEI^EP
35	D^EP^L^CT^CEI^AC
36	D^L^BI^CEI^AC
37	D^EP^L^CT^CEI^SA^AC
38	D^CT^EP^CEI
39	D^L^CT^CEI^SA
40	D^L^CT^CEI^AC

The distribution of each structural element is as follows:

Table 6 Distribution of Structural Elements in Chinese Introductions of Domestic Museums

文本编号	D	L	CT	HE	BI	CEI	SA	AC	EP	VG
1	√	√	√	√					√	
2	√	√	√		√	√	√		√	
3	√	√	√	√		√	√	√	√	
4	√	√	√		√	√	√	√	√	
5	√	√	√		√	√			√	
6	√	√	√	√	√	√				
7	√	√	√			√	√	√	√	
8	√	√	√	√	√	√			√	
9	√	√				√				
10	√	√	√		√	√				√
11	√	√	√		√	√	√		√	
12	√	√	√		√	√			√	
13	√	√	√		√	√		√		
14	√	√	√	√		√				
15	√	√	√			√	√		√	
16	√	√	√			√				
17	√	√	√		√	√				
18	√	√	√		√	√			√	
19	√	√	√		√				√	
20	√	√	√			√		√	√	
21	√	√	√	√	√	√				
22	√	√		√	√	√		√		
23	√	√	√		√	√			√	
24	√	√	√				√		√	
25	√	√	√			√	√	√		
26	√	√	√		√	√	√			
27	√	√			√	√	√	√	√	
28	√				√		√		√	
29	√	√	√		√	√	√		√	
30	√	√	√		√	√	√			

	D	L	CT	HE	BI	CEI	SA	AC	EP	VG
31	√	√	√			√	√			
32	√	√	√		√	√		√		
33	√	√	√		√	√	√		√	
34	√	√	√		√	√			√	
35	√	√	√			√		√	√	
36	√	√			√	√		√		
37	√	√	√			√	√	√	√	
38	√		√			√			√	
39	√	√	√			√	√			
40	√	√	√			√		√		

The frequency of occurrence of each structural element is:

Table 7 Frequency of Structural Elements in Chinese Introductions of Domestic Museums

	D	L	CT	HE	BI	CEI	SA	AC	EP	VG
Sum	40	38	36	7	24	36	17	13	23	1
%	100	95	90	17.5	60	90	42.5	32.5	57.5	2.5

From this, it can be seen that the occurrence frequency of elements like museum name (D), building information (BI), collection and exhibition introduction (CEI) and evaluation and status (EP) is all over 50%, which indicates that they are necessary elements. But compared to the English introduction of foreign museums, elements of museum location (L) and completed time (CT) have become new necessary elements, while historical events (HE) has become optional. Social activities (SA), academic contributions (AC), and visiting guides (VG) remain optional.

In terms of sequence, D is always at the beginning, but the position of EP has changed: in some cases it still appears at the beginning, while in other cases it appears at the end of the introduction; L and CT often appear in pairs and their positions can be interchanged, but in most cases, L precedes CT; BI always appears before CEI and both of them are still the focus of the introduction, which aim at informing visitors about the layout of the museum and main collections and exhibits in different regions. CEI does not necessarily appear in the introduction whatsoever. In addition, SA and AC have started to appear in the Chinese introductions, but their frequency is not high and they are still optional elements. Their order with respect to VG is relatively fixed and always appear at the end of the introduction. In the Chinese introductions, HE has become an optional element, the position of which is relatively flexible but usually appears before CEI.

In this way, the GSP model of introductions of domestic museums can be abstracted as:

D^ EP [L.CT] (HE) BI ^CEI (^SA) (^AC) (^ VG).

That is to say, for the Chinese introductions of domestic museums, D, EP, L, CT, BI and CEI are necessary elements, while the rest are optional. L and CT often appear together, but their positions can be interchanged; The positions of EP and HE are relatively flexible; So it is with SA and AC; VG always appears at the end of the introduction.

8.2.4 The GSP Model of English Translation of Domestic Museum Introductions

In order to be consistent with the source text, Text 4 is selected as an example to analyze its structural features.

(**D**) Shanghai Museum of Natural Sciences
(http://www.chinaculture.org/gb/en museum/2003-09/24/content 30409.htm)
(**EP**) The Shanghai Museum of Natural Sciences is one of the largest museums of natural sciences in China. (**L**)Located at downtown Shanghai, (**BI**)the museum features some British traditional style and covers an area of 12,880 square meters.

(**CT**) Prepared in November 1956, the Shanghai Museum of Natural Sciences opened the Division Museum of Animals to the public in 1960, and the Division Museum of Plants in 1984. The building for exhibition of samples covers a floor space of 3,053 square meters. The exhibition halls of the museum are situated in the Shanghai Botanic Garden and cover a total space of 4,726 square meters.

(**CEI**) The museum has a collection of 240,000 samples, including over 62,000 pieces of animal specimens, 135,000 plant specimens, 700 specimens of the Stone Age, and 1,700 specimens of minerals, which are of high value to research on natural evolvement.

The largest exhibit is a dinosaur skeleton of over four storeys high. There are also some rare species, which cannot be found elsewhere outside China, on display, such as a Yellow River mammoth, a giant salamander, a giant panda, and an alligator from the Yangtze River. Besides, the museum boasts more than 60,000 volumes of documents and books on scientific research.

(BI) The museum features four exhibition halls: the Hall of the History of the Ancient Animals, the Hall of History of Ancient Anthropology, the Hall of Animals and the Hall of Plants.

(CEI) The Hall of the History Ancient Animals houses fossil remains from the Paleozoic, Mesozoic and Cenozoic eras, forming a wordless chronicle of prehistoric life and displaying the evolvement of animals from aquicolous animals to terraneous animals, and from simple formation to complex one. Among the exhibits is a restored model of a Mamenxi dinosaur with the length of 22 meters, which is 140 million years old.

In the Hall of Ancient Anthropology is a huge collection of specimens, restored models and unearthed relics, which details the genesis and evolvement of human beings.

The Hall of Animals displays invertebrates, fishes, amphibious animals, reptiles, birds and mammals, many of which are on the national list of first-class and second-class protected animals. The Hall for Plants displays primitive alga, epiphyte, lichen and so on.

The famous Chinese mummies are exhibited in the Hall of the Mummies, such as a female mummy unearthed in Loulan of Xinjiang Uygur Autonomous Region.

(SA) In addition to permanent exhibitions, the museum often organizes other displays, such as Ancient Mummies of China, Rare Animals, Biologic Engineering, Chinese Special Animal - Elk and so on.

(AC) The museum has compiled a good many of books on animals, plants, human and astronomy such as *Research and Study* and *Nature and Human*.

As mentioned above, the schematic structure of Text 4 can be expressed as:

D^EP^L^BI^CT^CEI^BI^CEI^SA^AC

The remaining texts in the corpus of English translation of domestic museum introductions have been analyzed by using the same method, their structural elements and sequence of occurrence are:

Table 8 Schematic Structure of Texts in English Translation of Domestic Museum Introductions

Text No.	Structural Elements and Occurrence Order
1	D^EP^L^CT^HE^EP^BI^CEI^BI^CEI^EP
2	D^L^CT^HE^BI^CEI^SA
3	D^L^ CT^EP^BI ^CEI^SA^AC
4	D^EP^L^BI^CT^CEI^BI^CEI^SA^AC
5	D^L^EP^CT^BI ^CEI^SA

6	D^EP^L^HE^CT^CEI^EP
7	D^L^CT^CEI^SA
8	D^L^CT^HE^BI^CEI
9	D^L^EP^CEI
10	D^CT^L^BI^CEI
11	D^L^CT^EP^BI^HE^CEI
12	D^L^BI^CEI^VG
13	D^L^CT^BI^CEI
14	D^L^CT^EP^BI^EP^CEI
15	D^EP^CT^CEI^SA
16	D^L^CT^BI^CEI
17	D^CT^L^BI^CEI
18	D^L^CT^EP^BI^CEI
19	D^CT^L^BI^CEI^SA^AC
20	D^L^CT^CEI^EP^AC
21	D^L^CT^BI^HE^EP^CEI
22	D^L^BI^HE^CEI^AC
23	D^L^CT^BI^CEI^VG
24	D^L^EP^CT^EP^CEI^EP
25	D^L^CT^BI^CEI^EP
26	D^L^EP^CT^BI^CEI^SA^AC
27	D^CT^CEI^SA^AC
28	D^EP^CT^CEI^EP
29	D^L^EP^BI^CT^CEI^AC
30	D^L^BI^CT^CEI^AC^SA
31	D^L^CT^CEI^SA
32	D^L^CT^BI^CEI^SA
33	D^CT^L^BI^CEI^SA
34	D^L^CT^EP^BI^CEI^EP
35	D^EP^L^CT^BI^CEI^SA
36	D^L^CT^HE^CEI^SA
37	D^EP^CT^L^CEI^SA

38	D^BI^CT^EP^BI ^CEI
39	D^L^CT^CEI
40	D^L^CT^CEI^SA

The distribution of each structural element is as follows:

Table 9 Distribution of Structural Elements in the English Translation of Domestic Museum Introductions

Text No.	D	L	CT	HE	BI	CEI	SA	AC	EP	VG
1	√	√	√	√	√	√			√	
2	√	√	√	√	√	√	√			
3	√	√	√		√	√	√	√	√	
4	√	√	√		√	√	√	√	√	
5	√	√	√		√	√	√		√	
6	√	√	√	√		√			√	
7	√	√	√			√	√			
8	√	√	√	√	√	√				
9	√	√				√			√	
10	√	√	√		√	√				
11	√	√	√	√	√	√			√	
12	√	√			√	√				√
13	√	√	√		√	√				
14	√	√	√		√	√			√	
15	√		√			√	√		√	
16	√	√	√		√	√				
17	√	√	√		√	√				
18	√	√	√		√	√			√	
19	√	√	√		√	√	√	√		
20	√	√	√			√		√	√	
21	√	√	√	√	√	√			√	
22	√	√		√	√	√		√		
23	√	√	√		√	√				√
24	√	√	√			√			√	
25	√	√	√		√	√			√	

#	D	L	CT	HE	BI	CEI	SA	AC	EP	VG
26	√	√	√		√	√	√	√	√	
27	√		√			√	√	√		
28	√		√			√			√	
29	√	√	√		√	√		√	√	
30	√	√	√		√	√	√	√		
31	√	√	√			√	√			
32	√	√	√		√	√	√			
33	√	√	√		√	√	√			
34	√	√	√		√	√			√	
35	√	√	√		√	√	√			
36	√	√	√	√		√	√			
37	√	√	√			√	√		√	
38	√		√		√	√			√	
39	√	√	√			√				
40	√	√	√			√	√			

The frequency of occurrence of each structural element is:

Table 10 Frequency of Structural Elements in English Translation of Domestic Museum Introductions

	D	L	CT	HE	BI	CEI	SA	AC	EP	VG
Sum	40	36	37	8	27	40	17	9	20	2
%	100	90	92.5	20	67.5	100	42.5	22.5	50	5

Based on analysis of the above table, it can be found that in the English translation of domestic museum introductions, the proportion of elements such as name (D), location (L), completed time (CT), building information (BI), collection and exhibition introduction (CEI), and evaluation and position (EP) exceeds 50%, indicating that they are necessary elements. The remaining elements are still optional, the case of which is consistent with the Chinese museum introductions.

In terms of the sequence, D is always at the beginning; Similar to introductions of Chinese museums, the position of EP is flexible and repeatable; L and CT generally appear simultaneously with interchangeable positions, both of which are behind D. The order of other elements is no different from the Chinese introductions of the domestic museums.

The GSP model of it is:

D^ [L.CT] ^ EP (HE) BI ^CEI (^SA) (^AC) (^ VG)

8.3 Corpus-based Analysis of Characteristics of Museum Introductions

In this section, transitivity system, mood system (including modality), and thematic system that represent ideational, interpersonal and textual function have been used as tools to make the lexical and grammatical studies of the linguistic features of the English, Chinese, and translated English texts in three museum introduction corpora, including their expression patterns.

8.3.1 Linguistic Features of English Introductions of Foreign Museums
1. Transitivity System

The transitivity system includes three elements: participant, process, and environment. Among them, process is the core element of the transitivity system. The following transitivity analysis focuses on process types, which is called process type analysis. Text 8 in the corpus is taken as an example.

Field Museum

(http://www.aviewoncities.com/chicago/fieldmuseum.htm)

(1) Chicago's Field Museum is considered one of the finest natural history museums in the U.S.

(2) It even gained national acclaim when Steven Spielberg made it the home base for the esteemed archaeologist in his Indiana Jones movies.

(3) Movie appearances aside, however, the Field Museum was originally founded to house the biological and anthropological collections assembled for the World's Columbian Exposition of 1893.

(4) That collection still remains the core of the Field's permanent collection.

(5) However, in more than a century, the museum has grown into a home for more than 20 million specimens and a 25,000 volume natural history library.

(6) The Field Museum boasts a number of both permanent and temporary exhibits that will appeal to museum goers of all ages.

Nature Exhibits

(7) Nature exhibits include areas dedicated to the animals of Africa, North American birds, plants of the world, sea mammals and an underground adventure.

(8) One of the African exhibits tells the story of the Lions of Tsavo, two lions that once terrorized East Africa.

(9) Other exhibits include Evolving Planet, a journey through 4 billion years of life on earth and Moving Earth, where you can discover why the plates on the earth move.

(10) Also in the nature section are several galleries with profile rocks and fossils.

(11) Other galleries focus on Jade, diamonds and other gems.

Culture Exhibits

(12) Permanent culture-related exhibits include a look inside Ancient Egypt, a chance to view a full scale Pawnee earth lodge, the hall of the Ancient Americas and the lacquer ware art of Japan.

(13) There's also a Maori Meeting House and an exhibit on life in Tibet as well as exhibits on Eskimos and Northwest Coast Indians.

Temporary Exhibits

(14) Temporary exhibits change several times a year and the Field Museum has been a stop for some of the finest major traveling exhibits of the last several decades, including an excellent exhibit about Jackie Kennedy, the wonderful King Tut exhibition, and the Auschwitz Album, a photographical tour of the infamous Nazi death camp.

Sue

(15) Kids will certainly want to visit the T-Rex named Sue, described as the largest, most complete, and best-preserved Tyrannosaurus Rex ever unearthed, standing 12 feet high and 42 feet long (3.6 x 12.8 meter).

Visiting the Museum

(16) The Field Museum also has four gift shops on site where visitors can purchase a number of wonderful items, from inexpensive souvenirs to beautiful jewelry and hand-crafted artwork.

(17) There's also a better-than-average café at which to grab a bite to eat.

(18) Visitors can explore the three floors of the museum on their own or take a guided "highlights" tour which departs twice each day and gives you the inside story on

some of the museum's most popular artifacts.

The process type of the text is presented in a table as follows:

Table 11 Process Type Analysis of Text 8

Sentence No.	Process No.	Process Type	Process Verb
(1)	1	Mental Process	is considered
(2)	2	Material Process	gained
	3	Relational Process	made
(3)	4	Material Process	was founded
(4)	5	Relational Process	remains
(5)	6	Relational Process	has grown
(6)	7	Relational Process	boasts
	8	Material Process	appeal
(7)	9	Relational Process	include
(8)	10	Verbal Process	tells
	11	Material Process	terrorized
(9)	12	Relational Process	include
	13	Material Process	discover
	14	Material Process	move
(10)	15	Existential Process	are
(11)	16	Material Process	focus
(12)	17	Relational Process	include
(13)	18	Existential Process	is
(14)	19	Material Process	change
	20	Relational Process	has been
(15)	21	Mental Process	want
(16)	22	Relational Process	has
	23	Material Process	purchase
(17)	24	Existential Process	is

(18)	25	Material Process	explore
	26	Material Process	take
	27	Material Process	departs
	28	Material Process	gives

Similar analysis has been made to the remaining texts, the distribution of the six process types in all museum introductions in the corpus is as follows:

Table 12 Distribution of Process Types in English Introductions of Foreign Museums

Text No.	Relational Process	Material Process	Mental Process	Behavioral Process	Verbal Process	Existential Process	Total
1	32	29	3	1	0	5	70
2	15	16	6	0	2	0	39
3	14	12	5	1	1	2	35
4	11	9	0	1	0	0	21
5	31	28	3	0	1	1	64
6	20	31	5	2	0	0	58
7	29	36	3	0	1	5	74
8	10	14	2	0	1	3	30
9	15	27	1	0	0	1	44
10	27	25	3	1	1	2	59
11	14	16	2	0	0	1	33
12	11	18	0	1	0	2	32
13	15	16	0	0	0	3	34
14	10	23	6	0	0	2	41
15	8	13	2	0	1	0	24
16	9	9	0	0	0	4	22
17	17	11	3	0	0	0	31
18	10	15	2	0	0	1	28
19	8	13	0	0	0	0	21
20	10	13	2	0	0	0	25
21	28	19	0	1	0	2	50
22	4	15	3	0	0	3	25
23	17	29	5	1	1	5	58

24	15	15	1	1	0	1	33
25	14	28	2	0	1	2	47
26	21	12	1	0	0	0	34
27	19	14	5	0	0	0	38
28	7	18	0	0	0	1	26
29	8	10	0	0	0	4	22
30	13	13	3	0	1	0	30
31	18	26	2	1	2	1	50
32	19	27	2	0	0	0	48
33	14	32	1	0	0	1	48
34	14	14	3	0	0	0	31
35	16	13	8	0	2	1	40
36	13	14	1	0	4	2	34
37	3	12	2	0	0	1	18
38	17	23	4	0	0	1	45
39	26	51	2	1	0	5	85
40	24	27	4	0	2	1	58

The proportion of different types of processes is:

Table 13 Distribution Ratio of Process Types in English Introductions of Foreign Museums

	Relational Process	Material Process	Mental Process	Behavioral Process	Verbal Process	Existential Process	Sum
Total	626	786	97	12	21	63	1605
%	39.0	49.0	6.0	0.8	1.3	3.9	100

According to the data in the above table, it can be seen that material process is the most commonly used type of English introductions in foreign museums, accounting for 49.0%. The content expressed in material processes is mostly "doing", which refers to how museums are constructed, their historical development and changes. For example:

The history of the National Air and Space Museum **started** in 1946, when Congress **created** the National Air Museum as a part of the Smithsonian Institution. (Text 5)

Palazzo Nuovo **was built** in the 17th century after a design by Michelangelo **to complement** the Palazzo dei Conservatori. (Text 11)

The Exhibition Wing **was designed** by Japanese architect Kisho Kurokawa and **was opened** in 1999. (Text 15)

The second most commonly used process is relational process, which accounts for 39.0% of the total process. The relationship process is mainly used to describe the characteristics and attributes of museums, such as the relationship between museums and internal structures, the characteristics of museum collections and so on. For example:

Nature exhibits **include** areas dedicated to the animals of Africa, North American birds, plants of the world, sea mammals and an underground adventure. (Text 8)
The Museum of Fine Arts in Boston **is** one of the country's largest museums, with impressive collections of American, Asian and European art. (文本 26)
The museum **has** an impressive collection, with thousands of pieces of weaponry. (Text 28)

Mental process also accounts for a certain percentage, which is about 6.0%. Mental process mainly is used to describe people's cognition, desires and emotions. For example:

The railway station **was planned** by the Compagnie d'Orléans, who **wanted** to bring electrified trains right into the heart of Paris. （Text 3）
Most architecture buffs **love** the staircase in the central hall, where sunshine enters through an atrium and floods into the museum galleries. （Text 15）
In addition to Dutch artistic masterpieces, visitors will also **enjoy** a look at Dutch history through the display of a variety of artifacts that represent the Dutch state and nation from the Middle Ages through the 20th century. （Text 17）

2）Mood System

Text 8 is taken as an example:

Field Museum
（http://www.aviewoncities.com/chicago/fieldmuseum.htm）

(1) [1] Chicago's Field Museum is considered one of the finest natural history museums in the U.S. (2) [2] It even gained national acclaim [3] when Steven Spielberg made it the home base for the esteemed archaeologist in his Indiana Jones movies.

(2) [4] Movie appearances aside, however, [5] the Field Museum was originally founded to house the biological and anthropological collections assembled for the World's

Columbian Exposition of 1893. (4) [6] That collection still remains the core of the Field's permanent collection. (5) [7] However, in more than a century, the museum has grown into a home for more than 20 million specimens and a 25,000 volume natural history library.

(5) [8] The Field Museum boasts a number of both permanent and temporary exhibits [9] that will appeal to museum goers of all ages.

Nature Exhibits

(7) [10] Nature exhibits include areas dedicated to the animals of Africa, North American birds, plants of the world, sea mammals and an underground adventure.

(8) [11] One of the African exhibits tells the story of the Lions of Tsavo, two lions [12] that once terrorized East Africa. (9) [13] Other exhibits include Evolving Planet, a journey through 4 billion years of life on earth and Moving Earth, [14]where you can discover why the plates on the earth move. (10) [15] Also in the nature section are several galleries with profile rocks and fossils. (11) [16] Other galleries focus on Jade, diamonds and other gems.

Culture Exhibits

(12) [17] Permanent culture-related exhibits include a look inside Ancient Egypt, a chance to view a full scale Pawnee earth lodge, the hall of the Ancient Americas and the lacquer ware art of Japan. (13) [18] There's also a Maori Meeting House and an exhibit on life in Tibet as well as exhibits on Eskimos and Northwest Coast Indians.

Temporary Exhibits

(13) [19] Temporary exhibits change several times a year and [20] the Field Museum has been a stop for some of the finest major traveling exhibits of the last several decades, [21] including an excellent exhibit about Jackie Kennedy, the wonderful King Tut exhibition, and the Auschwitz Album, a photographical tour of the infamous Nazi death camp.

Sue

(15) [22] Kids will certainly want to visit the T-Rex named Sue, [23]described as the largest, most complete, and best-preserved Tyrannosaurus Rex ever unearthed, [24] standing 12 feet high and 42 feet long (3.6 x 12.8 meter).

Visiting the Museum

(16) [25] The Field Museum also has four gift shops on site [26] where visitors can purchase a number of wonderful items, from inexpensive souvenirs to beautiful jewelry and hand-crafted artwork. (17) [27] There's also a better-than-average café [28] at which to grab a bite to eat.

(18) [29] Visitors can explore the three floors of the museum on their own [30] or take a guided "highlights" tour [31] which departs twice each day [32] and gives you the inside story on some of the museum's most popular artifacts.

If represented by a table, it is as follows:

Table 14 Analysis of Mood System in Text 8

Sentence No.	Clause No.	Subject	Infinite	Tense	Mood Type
(1)	[1]	Chicago's Field	is	Present Tense	Indicative Mood
(2)	[2]	It	gained	Past Tense	Indicative Mood
(3)	[4]	movie	appearances	Present Tense	Indicative Mood
	[5]	the Field	was	Past Tense	Indicative Mood
(4)	[6]	That collection	remains	Present Tense	Indicative Mood
(5)	[7]	the museum	has	Present Tense	Indicative Mood
(6)	[8]	The Field Museum	boasts	Present Tense	Indicative Mood
	[9]		will appeal	Future Tense	Indicative Mood
(7)	[10]	Nature exhibits	include	Present Tense	Indicative Mood
(8)	[11]	One of the African exhibits	tells	Present Tense	Indicative Mood
	[12]		terrorized	Past Tense	Indicative Mood
(9)	[13]	Other exhibits	include	Present Tense	Indicative Mood
	[14]	you	discover	Present Tense	Indicative Mood
(10)	[15]	in the nature	are	Present Tense	Indicative Mood
(11)	[16]	Other galleries	focus	Present Tense	Indicative Mood
(12)	[17]	Permanent	include	Present Tense	Indicative Mood
(13)	[18]	There	is	Present Tense	Indicative Mood
(14)	[19]	Temporary exhibits the Field Museum	change	Present Tense	Indicative Mood
	[20]		has	Present Tense	Indicative Mood
	[21]		(include)	Present Tense	Indicative Mood

(15)	[22]	Kids	will want	Future Tense	Indicative Mood
	[23]	Sue	(is)	Present Tense	Indicative Mood
	[24]	Sue	(stands)	Present Tense	Indicative Mood
(16)	[25]	The Field Museum	has	Present Tense	Indicative Mood
	[26]		purchase	Present Tense	Indicative Mood
(17)	[27]	There	is	Present Tense	Indicative Mood
	[28]	(visitors)	grab	Present Tense	Indicative Mood
(18)	[29]	Visitors	explore	Present Tense	Indicative Mood
	[30]	Visitors	take	Present Tense	Indicative Mood
	[31]	which	departs	Present Tense	Indicative Mood
	[32]	which	gives	Present Tense	Indicative Mood

According to the above analysis, the whole text is in the indicative tone. The main purpose of indicative mood is to provide basic information about the museum. From the perspective of tense, the past tense is mainly used to describe the history and development of the museum, while the present tense is mainly used to introduce the current structure, layout, exhibits, and other information about the museum. The main subject is mostly the museum or related matters.

Based on the above analysis of the remaining texts in the corpus, the following statistics are obtained:

Table 15 Analysis of the Mood System of All Texts in English Introduction of Foreign Museums

Text No.	The Number of Clauses	Type of Mood			Subject			Tense		
		Indicative Mood	Imperative Mood	Interrogative Mood	Destination	Tourists	Other Subjects	Past Tense	Present Tense	Future Tense
1	84	84	0	0	42	6	36	30	54	0
2	40	40	0	0	13	0	27	30	10	0
3	36	35	1	0	16	2	18	13	23	0
4	23	22	1	0	11	2	10	10	13	0
5	72	72	0	0	28	7	37	24	46	2

6	60	60	0	0	25	4	31	35	25	0
7	81	80	1	0	32	6	43	33	48	0
8	32	32	0	0	15	5	12	4	28	1
9	49	48	1	0	22	1	26	26	23	0
10	66	65	1	0	34	11	21	18	45	3
11	40	40	0	0	21	2	17	11	29	0
12	36	35	1	0	19	4	13	8	28	0
13	36	36	0	0	17	1	18	16	20	0
14	52	51	1	0	13	7	32	13	35	4
15	31	31	0	0	13	3	15	11	20	0
16	32	32	0	0	11	2	19	8	23	1
17	35	35	0	0	15	6	14	6	25	4
18	28	28	0	0	15	1	12	10	18	0
19	24	24	0	0	12	0	12	18	6	0
20	25	25	0	0	12	0	13	14	11	0
21	57	55	2	0	16	3	38	15	42	0
22	31	31	0	0	12	2	17	9	20	2
23	57	57	0	0	18	2	37	22	35	0
24	38	37	1	0	17	4	17	16	20	2
25	48	48	0	0	32	2	14	31	14	3
26	37	37	0	0	19	0	18	15	22	0
27	46	45	1	0	16	6	26	11	35	0
28	33	33	0	0	6	0	27	18	15	0
29	27	27	0	0	12	2	13	6	19	2
30	32	32	0	0	12	0	20	13	18	1
31	52	52	0	0	16	1	35	25	27	0
32	51	51	0	0	11	2	38	20	30	1
33	45	45	0	0	12	0	33	27	18	0
34	35	35	0	0	17	1	17	26	9	0
35	39	39	0	0	21	7	11	10	26	3
36	37	37	0	0	13	2	22	11	24	2
37	21	20	1	0	5	3	13	11	10	0
38	42	42	0	0	14	0	28	24	18	0

| 39 | 84 | 84 | 0 | 0 | 8 | 1 | 75 | 58 | 26 | 0 |
| 40 | 57 | 57 | 0 | 0 | 19 | 6 | 32 | 18 | 38 | 1 |

The distribution ratio of mood types and the subject, tense, etc. in the corpus is as follows:

Table 16 Analysis and Statistics of Mood System

	The Number of Clauses	Mood Type			Subject			Tense		
		Indicative Mood	Imperative Mood	Interrogative Mood	Destin-ation	Tourists	Other subjects	Past Tense	Present Tense	Future Tense
Total	1752	1740	12	0	682	114	956	724	996	32
%	100	99.3	0.7	0	38.9	6.5	54.6	41.3	56.8	1.9

From the above table, it can be found that:

Mood type: The indicative mood is the most commonly used which is up to 99.3%. This mood is mainly used to state basic information about museum structures and exhibits. The imperative mood accounts for 0.7%, which mainly aims to recommend some unique exhibits to tourists, attract them to visit, or invite them to browse the website to learn more about the museum, such as:

Don't miss the small statue of a harpist. (Text 21)

For an overview of everything the Museums Quartier has to offer, **have a look at** their website. (Text 12)

Subject selection: There are three types of subjects: destination, tourists, and other subjects. Destination as the subject refers to buildings related to museums, such as museum names or exhibition halls, which accounts for 38.9% of subjects in English introductions of foreign museums; Tourists as the subject is mostly reflected in the form of "you", "visitor", etc. in the text, accounting for 6.5% of the total; And other subjects refer to specific references such as exhibits, designers and years as subjects, accounting for 54.6%. For example:

The Boston Museum of Fine Arts was founded in 1870 and is one of the oldest museums in America. (Text 26)

You can not only enjoy the rare historical collections (Text 12)

He placed them in a structure atop Capitoline Hill. (Text 11)

Tense: The present tense is the most commonly used, accounting for 56.8% of the total number of clauses. The past tense is slightly less used, accounting for 41.3%, while the future tense is the least used, accounting for about 1.9%. From the content described by these tenses, the present tense is mainly used to describe the current situation of museums or basic information such as exhibits and services, while the past tense is mainly used to introduce the history and development of museums, and the future tense is mostly used to describe the experiences that tourists can get when visiting. For example:

This highly-acclaimed art museum **is** one of the most-visited attractions in Madrid. (Text 34)

The history of Lisbon's National Coach Museum goes back to the year 1900, when a collection of Portuguese royal coaches **was** put on display at the Universal Exhibition in Paris. (Text 31)

You'**ll be** thrilled by the artifacts, photos, models, and other displays that grace the museum's five stories, especially if you're a navy buff. (Text 14)

3) Modality System

The modality system is mainly implemented by two subsystems, one is modalization and the other is modulation. When people communicate, it is not an absolute affirmation or negation.

When the modal system is used to discuss possibility or frequency, it is the modalization system. When discussing intention, it is the modulation system.

Modal words come in various forms, such as modal verbs, modal adverbs, and modal clauses. Here we only examine the use of modal verbs.

Tables 17 to 18 provide an analysis and statistics on the use of modal verbs in the corpus of English introductions of foreign museums.

Table 17 Distribution of Modal Verbs in English Introductions of Foreign Museums

Text No.	should	might(may)	could(can)	must	need	will(would)
1			√			√
2						√
3			√			
4			√			

5							√
6				√			√
7	√			√			
8				√			√
9							
10				√			√
11							
12				√			√
13							√
14							√
15							√
16							√
17				√			√
18				√			
19							
20							√
21	√						
22				√			√
23							
24				√			√
25							√
26							
27							
28							
29							√
30							
31				√			
32			√	√			
33							
34	√			√			√
35				√			√
36				√			√

37						
38			√			√
39			√	√		√
40			√			√

The frequency of use of modal verbs is:

Table 18 Distribution of Modal Verbs

	Low		Medium		High		Sum
	may (might)	can(could)	should	will (would)	must	need	
Total	1	20	3	23	1	0	48
%	2.1	41.7	6.2	47.9	2.1	0	100

It can be seen from the above tables, the most commonly used modal verbs in English introductions are could (can) and will (would).

4）Theme System

Text 8 is taken as an example:

Field Museum

(http://www.aviewoncities.com/chicago/fieldmuseum.htm)

(1) [1] Chicago's Field Museum is considered one of the finest natural history museums in the U.S.

(2) [2] It even gained national acclaim [3] when Steven Spielberg made it the home base for the esteemed archaeologist in his Indiana Jones movies.

(3) [4] Movie appearances aside, however, the Field Museum was originally founded to house the biological and anthropological collections assembled for the World's Columbian Exposition of 1893.

(4) [5] That collection still remains the core of the Field's permanent collection.

(5) [6] However, in more than a century, the museum has grown into a home for more than 20 million specimens and a 25,000 volume natural history library.

(6) [7] The Field Museum boasts a number of both permanent and temporary exhibits [8] that will appeal to museum goers of all ages.

Nature Exhibits

(7) [9] Nature exhibits include areas dedicated to the animals of Africa, North American birds, plants of the world, sea mammals and an underground adventure.

(8) [10] One of the African exhibits tells the story of the Lions of Tsavo, two lions [11] that once terrorized East Africa.

(9) [12] Other exhibits include Evolving Planet, a journey through 4 billion years of life on earth and Moving Earth,[13] where you can discover [14] why the plates on the earth move.

(10) [15] Also in the nature section are several galleries with profile rocks and fossils.

(11) [16] Other galleries focus on Jade, diamonds and other gems.

Culture Exhibits

(12) [17] Permanent culture-related exhibits include a look inside Ancient Egypt, a chance to view a full scale Pawnee earth lodge, the hall of the Ancient Americas and the lacquer ware art of Japan.

(13) [18] There's also a Maori Meeting House and an exhibit on life in Tibet as well as exhibits on Eskimos and Northwest Coast Indians.

Temporary Exhibits

(14) [19] Temporary exhibits change several times a year [20] and the Field Museum has been a stop for some of the finest major traveling exhibits of the last several decades, including an excellent exhibit about Jackie Kennedy, the wonderful King Tut exhibition, and the Auschwitz Album, a photographical tour of the infamous Nazi death camp.

Sue

(15) [21] Kids will certainly want to visit the T-Rex named Sue, described as the largest, most complete, and best-preserved Tyrannosaurus Rex ever unearthed, standing 12 feet high and 42 feet long (3.6 x 12.8 meter).

Visiting the Museum

(16) [22] The Field Museum also has four gift shops on site [23] where visitors can purchase a number of wonderful items, from inexpensive souvenirs to beautiful jewelry and hand-crafted artwork.

(17) [24] There's also a better-than-average café at which to grab a bite to eat.

(18) [25] Visitors can explore the three floors of the museum on their own [26] or take a guided "highlights" tour [27] which departs twice each day [28] and gives you the inside story on some of the museum's most popular artifacts.

The thematic analysis of the above text is as follows:

Table 19 Thematic Analysis of Text 8

Sentence No.	Clause No.	Theme System			Marked	Unmarked
		Textual Theme	Interpersonal Theme	Experiential Theme		
(1)	[1]			Chicago's Field Museum		√
(2)	[2]			It		√
	[3]			when	√	
(3)	[4]			Movie appearances aside	√	
(4)	[5]			That collection		√
(5)	[6]	However		in more than a century	√	
(6)	[7]			The Field Museum		√
	[8]			that		√
(7)	[9]			Nature exhibits		√
(8)	[10]			One of the African exhibits		√
	[11]			that		√
(9)	[12]			Other exhibits		√
	[13]			where	√	
	[14]			why	√	
(10)	[15]	Also		in the nature section	√	
(11)	[16]			Other galleries		√
(12)	[17]			Permanent		√

				culture-related exhibits		
(13)	[18]			There		√
(14)	[19]			Temporary exhibits		√
	[20]	and		the Field Museum		√
(15)	[21]			Kids		√
(16)	[22]			The Field Museum		√
	[23]			where	√	
(17)	[24]			There		√
(18)	[25]			Visitors		√
	[26]	or				√
	[27]			which		√
	[28]	and				√

From the table, it can be seen that there are a total of 28 thematic combinations in this introduction, of which 25 are single themes and 3 are multiple themes. The seven marked themes are easy to recognize, which are mainly adverbs of place and time.

Through thematic analysis of all texts in the corpus, the thematic distribution is shown in the table below.

Table 20 Thematic Distribution of All Texts in English Introductions of Foreign Museums

Text No.	Multiple Theme	Single Theme	Marked Theme	Unmarked Theme
1	3	57	17	43
2	5	29	10	24
3	3	25	2	26
4	1	18	6	13
5	9	43	9	43
6	12	36	8	40
7	2	57	12	47
8	3	25	7	21
9	5	35	10	30
10	9	41	11	39

11	1	29	6	24
12	1	26	3	24
13	4	28	5	27
14	2	31	10	23
15	0	22	5	17
16	0	18	5	13
17	6	21	8	19
18	1	21	7	15
19	2	16	3	15
20	3	19	8	14
21	3	42	1	44
22	1	23	3	21
23	3	43	9	37
24	6	22	4	24
25	7	34	15	26
26	2	30	2	30
27	5	27	4	28
28	3	22	8	17
29	2	19	4	17
30	6	21	2	25
31	10	37	4	43
32	9	36	7	38
33	8	33	13	28
34	7	22	6	23
35	4	27	8	23
36	2	27	6	23
37	2	14	7	9
38	10	28	5	33
39	17	55	20	52
40	5	37	12	30
Total	184	1196	292	1088
%	13.3	86.7	21.2	78.8

As can be seen from the above, there are a total of 1380 themes, with the single theme accounting for nearly 86.7% of the total. Multiple themes account for 13.3%, with different combinations including "textual theme+experiential theme", "interpersonal theme+experiential theme", and "textual theme+interpersonal theme+experiential theme".

There are 292 marked themes, accounting for 21.2% of the total. These marked themes mainly involve the location of museums, the establishment and development status of museums at different time periods. For example:

Today, the Met, as it is often called, measures about a quarter-mile long (400 meters) and occupies approximately two million square feet (almost 200,000 square meters). (Text 7)

In 1956, one year after his death, the Gulbenkian Foundation was created which according to his will, supports the arts, science, education and social welfare.（Text 33）

8.3.2 Linguistic Features of Chinese Introductions of Domestic Museums
1）Transitivity System

Text 4 is taken as an example.

上海自然博物馆

(1)上海自然博物馆是中国最大的自然博物馆之一。(2)位于上海市中心。(3)该馆大楼带有英国古典建筑风格，建筑面积为12880平方米。

(4)上海自然博物馆于1956年11月筹建。(5)1960年建成动物学分馆对外开放。(6)1984年建成植物学分馆，该分馆包括标本大楼和陈列厅两个部分，是中国唯一的植物学馆。(7)标本大楼面积为3053平方米，除珍藏各类植物标本外，还设有研究室和实验室；陈列厅设在上海植物园内。(8)总面积为4726平方米。(9)其中约二分之一已对外展出。

(10)上海自然博物馆有丰富的馆藏标本和图书资料。(11)除了接收原英国人办的亚洲文会上海博物馆标本，法国人办的震旦博物院的部分自然标本外，主要通过采集、收购、赠送、交换等途径获得各类自然标本。(12)到1985年，馆藏各类标本有20余万件，其中动物标本（有）6.2万多件，植物标本（有）13.5万多件，古生物标本（有）1700多件，新旧石器标本（有）700多件、矿物与岩石标本（有）1700多件。(13)在这些标本中，有一定数量的模式标本和国内第一次发现的新记录标本。(14)有中国特有的和世界著名的珍稀生物标本，有6亿年前的化石。(15)该馆还藏有供科学研究和科学教育用的中、外文各类专业图书资料6万余册。

(16)该馆基本陈列面积共5700平方米。(17)陈列内容包括古动物史、人类发展史、动物和植物的进化四大部分。

(18)在古动物史陈列,展示了动物的发生和发展,从水生到陆生,从简单到复杂,从低等到高等进化的漫长过程。(19)展厅中央陈列了一条体长22米、肩高 3.5 米的原大恐龙模型——合川马门溪龙。(20)它的右侧是一头黄河古象模型,体长8米,体高4米,一对门牙有3米长。

(21)人类发展史陈列,用大量实物、模型、出土文物以及二、三百万年前的前期猿人生活情况的景象,揭示了人类的起源、人类社会的形成和发展。

(22)在动物陈列分设无脊椎动物、鱼类、两栖动物,爬行动物,鸟类和哺乳动物 6 个陈列厅。(23)除了展出中国一级保护动物长臂猿、金丝猴、大熊猫、云豹、金钱豹、雪豹、虎、亚洲象、儒艮、野驴、梅花鹿、野牦牛、羚牛、野骆驼、褐马鸡、扬子鳄、白鲟等外,还有中国二级保护动物及野生已绝灭的麋鹿(即"四不像")等许多珍禽异兽。(24)此外,也展出许多外国著名动物,如非洲的狮子、长颈鹿、 狒狒和黑猩猩,澳大利亚的鸭嘴兽、袋鼠和鸸鹋,美洲的狮子,日本的高脚蟹等。

(25)古尸陈列室共陈列5具古尸,其中新疆楼兰地区发掘的楼兰女尸,据碳14测定,认为距今3880±95 年,是中国已知古尸中年代最早的一具。(26)植物陈列,分序厅、植物进化厅和植物的改造与利用厅。(27)内容包括原始的藻类,没有叶绿素的真菌,菌藻共生的地衣,陆生维管植物的先驱——蕨类,陆生植物的一个旁枝——苔藓,直到高等的秋子植物。(28)沿着陈列线,一个个生态景箱的衔接,展示植物演化的进程。(29)陈列厅的中央是一个巨大的石炭纪蕨类立体景象,它再现了2亿多年前地球上最早的沼泽森林,也是植物从水生到陆生后出现的第一批大森林。(30)已经在地球上绝灭的鳞木、封印木等蕨类矗立于森林上层,无数草木蕨类覆盖在沼泽湿地上。

(31)该馆还办有"中国历代古尸""一九八〇年云南日全食观测""珍稀动物""宝石""优生优育""生物工程""南极考察和知识""中国特产动物——麋鹿"等展览。

(32)该馆除了编写一批动物、植物、人类、古生物、天文等专业学科的书籍和图集外,还编辑《考察与研究》学术专辑和综合性科普双月刊《自然与人》。

It is represented in the table as follows:

Sentence No.	Process No.	Process Type	Process Verb
(1)	1	Relational process	是
(2)	2	Relational process	位于
(3)	3	Relational process	带有
	4	Relational process	为
(4)	5	Material process	筹建
(5)	6	Material process	建成
	7	Material process	开放

(6)	8	Material process	建成
	9	Relational process	包括
	10	Relational process	是
(7)	11	Relational process	为
	12	Material process	珍藏
	13	Relational process	设有
	14	Relational process	设在
(8)	15	Relational process	为
(9)	16	Material process	展出
(10)	17	Relational process	有
(11)	18	Material process	接收
	19	Material process	获得
(12)	20	Existential process	有
	21	Relational process	（有）
	22	Relational process	（有）
	23	Relational process	（有）
	24	Relational process	（有）
	25	Relational process	（有）
(13)	26	Existential process	有
(14)	27	Existential process	有
	28	Existential process	有
(15)	29	Existential process	藏有
(16)	30	Relational process	共
(17)	31	Relational process	包括
(18)	32	Material process	展示
(19)	33	Material process	陈列
(20)	34	Relational process	是
	35	Relational process	长
	36	Relational process	高
	37	Relational process	有

(21)	38	Relational process	揭示
(22)	39	Material process	分设
(23)	40	Material process	展出
	41	Existential process	有
(24)	42	Material process	展出
(25)	43	Material process	陈列
	44	Material process	测定
	45	Mental process	认为
	46	Relational process	是
(26)	47	Material process	分
(27)	48	Relational process	包括
(28)	49	Material process	展示
(29)	50	Relational process	是
	51	Material process	再现
	52	Relational process	是
(30)	53	Relational process	矗立
	54	Material process	覆盖
(31)	55	Material process	办有
(32)	56	Material process	编写
	57	Material process	编辑

Process types of all texts in the corpus have been analyzed, the results are as follows:

Table 22 Distribution of Process Types for All Texts of Chinese Introductions of Domestic Museums

Text No.	Relational Process	Material Process	Mental Process	Behavioral Process	Verbal Process	Existential Process	Sum
1	18	50	1	0	7	0	76
2	13	9	0	0	0	3	25
3	17	23	0	0	1	5	46
4	28	22	1	0	0	6	57
5	11	17	3	0	0	1	32
6	27	29	0	0	0	2	58

7	15	16	0	0	1	1	33
8	8	18	1	0	0	0	27
9	2	4	0	0	0	0	6
10	15	23	0	0	0	1	39
11	9	13	0	3	2	1	28
12	15	13	1	0	0	0	29
13	4	6	0	0	0	1	11
14	10	7	0	0	0	1	18
15	23	7	0	3	0	0	33
16	24	19	0	1	0	3	47
17	9	7	0	0	0	0	16
18	9	4	0	0	0	0	13
19	15	11	0	0	1	0	27
20	17	12	0	0	0	2	31
21	7	11	1	0	0	0	19
22	8	22	0	0	2	3	35
23	7	10	1	1	0	0	19
24	11	12	3	1	2	0	29
25	11	21	2	1	0	1	36
26	18	8	0	0	0	0	26
27	10	9	0	0	0	4	23
28	3	13	2	0	0	5	23
29	7	12	0	0	0	3	22
30	13	14	0	0	0	1	28
31	5	4	0	0	0	1	10
32	8	6	0	0	0	3	17
33	11	8	2	0	0	0	21
34	14	11	1	0	0	0	26
35	22	7	0	0	0	1	30
36	12	14	0	0	0	2	28
37	14	8	0	0	0	6	28
38	12	36	4	0	0	0	52

| 39 | 11 | 12 | 0 | 0 | 0 | 0 | 23 |
| 40 | 6 | 8 | 0 | 0 | 0 | 0 | 14 |

The ratio of different types of processes appearing in the corpus is:

Table 23　Distribution Ratio of Process Types

	Relational Process	Material Process	Mental Process	Behavioral Process	Verbal Process	Existential Process	Sum
Total	499	556	23	10	16	57	1161
%	42.9	47.9	2.0	0.9	1.4	4.9	100

It can be seen that material processes rank the , accounting for 47.9% of the total. The material process is mainly used to describe the development of museums, the status of collections and so on. For example:

中国地质博物馆还通过为国民经济各个领域和社会各个行业**提供**地质标本、资料，**开展**地质科学技术咨询活动，直接**承接**国家和地方的生产、科学研究、教育任务，此外，还**举办**地学夏令营、摄影、放映电影、电视录像等科普活动。(Text 3)

Relational processes account for 42.9% of the total, second only to material processes. Relational processes are mainly used to describe the construction and characteristics of museums. For example:

中国佛教图书文物馆**是**宗教文物博物馆。(Text 7)

中国丝绸博物馆**位于**浙江省杭州市玉皇山北莲花峰下。(Text 17)

Existential processes account for 4.9% of the total, which are mainly used to introduce the treasures in museums and the specific location of the collections. For example:

藏品中约**有**石器 3000 件，陶器 1.4 万件，其他质地器物 3700 多件，人骨标本 200 多具，古生物化石和古人类化石标本约 200 多件。(文本 14)

由国外交换来的珍贵藏品**有**：新西兰的大恐鸟化石、澳大利亚的懒树獭、针鼹、琴鸟以及非洲的拉蒂曼鱼。(文本 35)

As for mental processes, behavioral processes and verbal processes, they are rarely used in Chinese introductions of domestic museums.

2）Mood System

Similarly, Text 4 has been taken to analyze the mood system.

上海自然博物馆

(1)[1]上海自然博物馆是中国最大的自然博物馆之一。(2)[2]位于上海市中心。(3)[3]该馆大楼带有英国古典建筑风格，[4]建筑面积为12880平方米。

(4)[5]上海自然博物馆于1956年11月筹建。(5)[6]1960年建成动物学分馆对外开放。(6)[7]1984年建成植物学分馆，[8]该分馆包括标本大楼和陈列厅两个部分，[9]是中国唯一的植物学馆。(7)[10]标本大楼面积为3053平方米，[11]除珍藏各类植物标本外，[12]还设有研究室和实验室；[13]陈列厅设在上海植物园内。(8)[14]总面积为4726平方米。(9)[15]其中约二分之一已对外展出。

(10)[16]上海自然博物馆有丰富的馆藏标本和图书资料。(11)[17]除了接收原英国人办的亚洲文会上海博物馆标本，法国人办的震旦博物院的部分自然标本外，[18]主要通过采集、收购、赠送、交换等途径获得各类自然标本。(12)[19]到1985年，馆藏各类标本有20余万件，其中动物标本6.2万件，植物标本13.5万件，古生物标本1700多件，新旧石器标本700多件、矿物与岩石标本1700多件。(13)[20]在这些标本中，有一定数量的模式标本和国内第一次发现的新记录标本。(14)[21]有中国特有的和世界著名的珍稀生物标本，[22]有6亿年前的化石。(15)[23]该馆还藏有供科学研究和科学教育用的中、外文各类专业图书资料6万余册。

(16)[24]该馆基本陈列面积共5700平方米。(17)[25]陈列内容包括古动物史、人类发展史、动物和植物的进化四大部分。

(18)[26]在古动物史陈列，展示了动物的发生和发展，从水生到陆生，从简单到复杂，从低等到高等进化的漫长过程。(19)[27]展厅中央陈列了一条体长22米、肩高3.5米的原大恐龙模型——合川马门溪龙。(20)[28]它的右侧是一头黄河古象模型，体长8米，体高4米，一对门牙有3米长。

(21)[29]人类发展史陈列大量实物、模型、出土文物以及二、三百万年前的前期猿人生活情况的景象，[30]揭示了人类的起源、人类社会的形成和发展。

(22)[31]在动物陈列分设无脊椎动物、鱼类、两栖动物，爬行动物，鸟类和哺乳动物6个陈列厅。(23)[32]除了展出中国一级保护动物长臂猿、金丝猴、大熊猫、云豹、金钱豹、雪豹、虎、亚洲象、儒艮、野驴、梅花鹿、野牦牛、羚牛、野骆驼、褐马鸡、扬子鳄、白鲟等外，[33]还有中国二级保护动物及野生已绝灭的麋鹿(即"四不像")等许多珍禽异兽。(24)[34]此外，也展出许多外国著名动物，如非洲的狮子、长颈鹿、狒狒和黑猩猩，澳大利亚的鸭嘴兽、袋鼠和鸸鹋，美洲的狮子，日本的高脚蟹等等。

(25)[35]古尸陈列室共陈列5具古尸,其中新疆楼兰地区发掘的楼兰女尸,据碳14测定,[36]认为距今3880±95年,[37]是中国已知古尸中年代最早的一具。(26)[38]植物陈列,分序厅、植物进化厅和植物的改造与利用厅。(27)[39]内容包括原始的藻类,没有叶绿素的真菌,菌藻共生的地衣,陆生维管植物的先驱——蕨类,陆生植物的一个旁枝——苔藓,直到高等的秋子植物。(28)[40]沿着陈列线,一个个生态景箱的衔接,展示植物演化的进程。(29)[41]陈列厅的中央是一个巨大的石炭纪蕨类立体景箱,[42]它再现了2亿多年前地球上最早的沼泽森林,[43]也是植物从水生到陆生后出现的第一批大森林。(30)[44]已经在地球上绝灭的鳞木、封印木等蕨类矗立于森林上层,[45]无数草木蕨类覆盖在沼泽湿地上。

(31)[46]该馆还办有"中国历代古尸""一九八〇年云南日全食观测""珍稀动物""宝石""优生优育""生物工程""南极考察和知识""中国特产动物——麋鹿"等展览。

(32)[47]该馆除了编写一批动物、植物、人类、古生物、天文等专业学科的书籍和图集外,[48]还编辑《考察与研究》学术专辑和综合性科普双月刊《自然与人》。

The above analysis can be represented in the following table:

Sentence No.	Clause No.	Subject	Infinite	Mood Type
(1)	[1]	上海自然博物馆	是	Indicative mood
(2)	[2]	（上海自然博物馆）	位于	Indicative mood
(3)	[3]	该馆大楼	带有	Indicative mood
	[4]	建筑面积	为	Indicative mood
(4)	[5]	上海自然博物馆	筹建	Indicative mood
(5)	[6]	动物分馆	建成	Indicative mood
(6)	[7]	植物分馆	建成	Indicative mood
	[8]	该分馆	包括	Indicative mood
	[9]	（植物分馆）	是	Indicative mood
(7)	[10]	标本大楼面积	为	Indicative mood
	[11]	（标本大楼）	珍藏	Indicative mood
	[12]	（标本大楼）	设有	Indicative mood
	[13]	陈列厅	设在	Indicative mood
(8)	[14]	总面积	为	Indicative mood
(9)	[15]	其中约二分之一	展出	Indicative mood
(10)	[16]	上海自然博物馆	有	Indicative mood
(11)	[17]	（上海自然博物馆）	接收	Indicative mood
	[18]	（上海自然博物馆）	获得	Indicative mood

(12)	[19]	馆藏各类标本	有	Indicative mood
(13)	[20]	这些标本	有	Indicative mood
(14)	[21]	（这些标本）	有	Indicative mood
	[22]	（这些标本）	有	Indicative mood
(15)	[23]	该馆	藏有	Indicative mood
(16)	[24]	该馆基本陈列面积	共	Indicative mood
(17)	[25]	陈列内容	包括	Indicative mood
(18)	[26]	古动物史陈列	展示	Indicative mood
(19)	[27]	展厅中央	陈列	Indicative mood
(20)	[28]	它的右侧	是	Indicative mood
(21)	[29]	人类发展史	陈列	Indicative mood
	[30]	（人类发展史）	揭示	Indicative mood
(22)	[31]	动物陈列	分设	Indicative mood
(23)	[32]	（动物陈列）	展出	Indicative mood
	[33]	（动物陈列）	还有	Indicative mood
(24)	[34]	（动物陈列）	展出	Indicative mood
(25)	[35]	古尸陈列室	陈列	Indicative mood
	[36]	碳14测定	认为	Indicative mood
	[37]	（楼兰女尸）	是	Indicative mood
(26)	[38]	植物陈列	分	Indicative mood
(27)	[39]	内容	包括	Indicative mood
(28)	[40]	一个个生态景象的衔	展示	Indicative mood
(29)	[41]	陈列厅的中央	是	Indicative mood
	[42]	它	再现	Indicative mood
	[43]	沼泽森林	也是	Indicative mood
(30)	[44]	鳞木、封印木等蕨类	矗立	Indicative mood
	[45]	草木蕨类	覆盖	Indicative mood
(31)	[46]	该馆	办有	Indicative mood

	(32)	[47]	该馆	编写	Indicative mood
		[48]	（该馆）	编辑	Indicative mood

(Due to the characteristics of Chinese language, verbs do not change due to changes in tense and voice, so tense parameters are omitted when analyzing mood systems)

From Table 24, it can be seen that all the clauses in the text adopt the indicative mood, and the content is basic information about the museum. The subjects of the sentences are mostly "Shanghai Museum of Natural Sciences" , "The Museum", etc.

After analyzing all texts in the corpus by using the same method, the mood system of all texts is:

Table 25 Distribution of Mood System in All Texts of Chinese Introduction of Domestic Museums

Text No.	The Number of Clauses	Mood Type			Subject		
		Indicative Mood	Imperative Mood	Interrogative Mood	Destination	Tourists	Other Subjects
1	70	70	0	0	22	0	48
2	24	24	0	0	15	0	9
3	47	47	0	0	32	0	15
4	47	47	0	0	33	0	14
5	27	27	0	0	20	1	6
6	52	52	0	0	26	0	26
7	28	28	0	0	20	0	8
8	27	27	0	0	11	0	16
9	6	6	0	0	6	0	0
10	44	39	5	0	22	3	19
11	28	28	0	0	10	1	17
12	31	31	0	0	17	0	14
13	12	12	0	0	10	0	2
14	18	18	0	0	12	0	6
15	27	27	0	0	7	0	20
16	42	42	0	0	31	2	9
17	20	20	0	0	11	0	9
18	12	12	0	0	7	0	5

19	24	24	0	0	23	0	1
20	26	26	0	0	11	0	15
21	18	18	0	0	13	0	5
22	36	36	0	0	20	0	16
23	18	18	0	0	14	1	3
24	30	30	0	0	20	1	9
25	35	35	0	0	18	2	15
26	27	27	0	0	27	0	0
27	24	24	0	0	15	0	9
28	26	26	0	0	3	8	15
29	21	21	0	0	17	0	4
30	27	27	0	0	16	0	11
31	21	21	0	0	6	0	15
32	18	18	0	0	13	0	5
33	22	22	0	0	15	0	7
34	24	24	0	0	23	0	1
35	29	29	0	0	13	0	16
36	28	28	0	0	16	0	12
37	29	29	0	0	14	0	15
38	42	42	0	0	19	1	22
39	21	21	0	0	9	0	12
40	14	14	0	0	10	0	4

The distribution ratio of different mood and subject types is as follows:

Table 26 Distribution Ratio of Mood System

	The Number of Clauses	Mood Type			Subject		
		Indicative Mood	Imperative Mood	Interrogative Mood	Destination	Tourists	Other Subjects
Sum	1122	1117	5	0	647	20	455
%	100	99.6	0.4	0	57.7	1.8	40.5

From it, it can be seen that:

Mood type: Almost all clauses are indicative, with very little proporion of imperative mood and no interrogative mood at all. The indicative mood, as the name suggests, is to state basic facts or situations about a museum. The imperative mood guides tourists on how to receive corresponding services, such as:

请向大堂入口处柜面作资料查询。（文本 10）

教师、学校及其他教育机构请致电博物馆(853)-3941215。（文本 10）

Subject selection: Only nearly 2% of the clauses use tourists as the subject, while 57.7% use museums as the subject, and 40.5% use other things (exhibits, designers, years, etc.) as the subject. Using museums and other things related to museums as subjects mainly aims to objectively provide information to readers; The main purpose of using tourists as the subject is to bring them closer and attract them to visit. In this regard, Chinese introductions of domestic museums is slightly lacking.

3）Modality System

According to statistics, main modal verbs that are used in this corpus is as follows:

Table 27 Distribution of Modal Verbs

Text No.	should	might(may)	could(can)	must	need	will(would)	should
1							
2							
3							
4							
5	√						
6					√		
7							
8							
9							
10							
11	√						
12	√						
13							
14							
15							

16	√							
17								
18								
19								
20	√							
21								
22								
23								
24								
25								
26								
27								
28								
29								
30								
31								
32								
33								
34								
35								
36								
37								
38	√							
39								
40								

The frequency of its occurrence is:

Table 28 Distribution Frequency of Modal Verbs

	Low		Medium		High		Sum
	may (might)	can(could)	should	will(would)	must	need	
Total	6	0	0	0	0	1	7
%	85..7	0	0	0	0	14. 3	100

From this, it can be seen that these modal words rarely appear in Chinese museum introductions. In all 40 introductions, only "(may) might" appears 6 times, "must" appears 1 time, and the rest do not appear.

4）Theme System

Text 4 has been taken as an example:

上海自然博物馆

（1）[1]上海自然博物馆是中国最大的自然博物馆之一。（2）[2]位于上海市中心。（3）[3]该馆大楼带有英国古典建筑风格，[4]建筑面积为12880平方米。

（4）[5]上海自然博物馆于1956年11月筹建。（5）[6]1960年建成动物学分馆对外开放。（6）[7]1984年建成植物学分馆，[8]该分馆包括标本大楼和陈列厅两个部分，是中国唯一的植物学馆。（7）[9]标本大楼面积为3053平方米，[10]除珍藏各类植物标本外，还设有研究室和实验室；[11]陈列厅设在上海植物园内。（8）[12]总面积为4726平方米。（9）[13]其中约二分之一已对外展出。

（10）[14]上海自然博物馆有丰富的馆藏标本和图书资料。（11）[15]除了接收原英国人办的亚洲文会上海博物馆标本，法国人办的震旦博物院的部分自然标本外，主要通过采集、收购、赠送、交换等途径获得各类自然标本。（12）[16]到1985年，馆藏各类标本有20余万件，[17]其中动物标本6.2万多件，植物标本13.5万多件，古生物标本1700多件，新旧石器标本700多件、矿物与岩石标本1700多件。（13）[18]在这些标本中，有一定数量的模式标本和国内第一次发现的新记录标本。（14）[19]有中国特有的和世界著名的珍稀生物标本，[20]有6亿年前的化石。（15）[21]该馆还藏有供科学研究和科学教育用的中、外文各类专业图书资料6万余册。

（16）[22]该馆基本陈列面积共5700平方米。（17）[23]陈列内容包括古动物史、人类发展史、动物和植物的进化四大部分。

（18）[24]在古动物史陈列，展示了动物的发生和发展，从水生到陆生，从简单到复杂，从低等到高等进化的漫长过程。（19）[25]展厅中央陈列了一条体长22米、肩高3.5米的原大恐龙模型——合川马门溪龙。（20）[26]它的右侧是一头黄河古象模型，[27]体长8米，[28]体高4米，[29]一对门牙有3米长。

（21）[30]人类发展史陈列，用大量实物、模型、出土文物以及二、三百万年前的前期猿人生活情况的景象箱，揭示了人类的起源、人类社会的形成和发展。

（22）[31]在动物陈列分设无脊椎动物、鱼类、两栖动物、爬行动物、鸟类和哺乳动物6个陈列厅。（23）[32]除了展出中国一级保护动物长臂猿、金丝猴、大熊猫、云豹、金钱豹、雪豹、虎、亚洲象、儒艮、野驴、梅花鹿、野牦牛、羚牛、野骆驼、褐马鸡、扬子鳄、白鲟等外，还有中国二级保护动物及野生已绝灭的麋鹿（即"四不像"）等许多珍禽异兽。（24）[33]此外，也展出许多外国著名动物,如非洲的狮子、长颈鹿、 狒狒和黑猩猩,澳大利亚的鸭嘴兽、袋鼠和鸸鹋,美洲的狮子,日本的高脚蟹等等。

(25)[34]古尸陈列室共陈列 5 具古尸,[35]其中新疆楼兰地区发掘的楼兰女尸,据碳 14 测定,认为距今 3880±95 年,是中国已知古尸中年代最早的一具。(26)[36]植物陈列,分序厅、植物进化厅和植物的改造与利用厅。(27)[37]内容包括原始的藻类,没有叶绿素的真菌,菌藻共生的地衣,陆生维管植物的先驱——蕨类,陆生植物的一个旁枝——苔藓,直到高等的秋子植物。(28)[38]沿着陈列线,一个个生态景象的衔接,展示植物演化的进程。(29)[39]陈列厅的中央是一个巨大的石炭纪蕨类立体景箱,[40]它再现了 2 亿多年前地球上最早的沼泽森林,[41]也是植物从水生到陆生后出现的第一批大森林。(30)[42]已经在地球上绝灭的鳞木、封印木等蕨类矗立于森林上层,[43]无数草木蕨类覆盖在沼泽湿地上。

(31)[44]该馆还办有"中国历代古尸""一九八〇年云南日全食观测""珍稀动物""宝石""优生优育""生物工程""南极考察和知识""中国特产动物——麋鹿"等展览。

(32)[45]该馆除了编写一批动物、植物、人类、古生物、天文等专业学科的书籍和图集外,[46]还编辑《考察与研究》学术专辑和综合性科普双月刊《自然与人》。

If represented in a table, it is as follows:

Table 29 Thematic Analysis of Text 4

Sentence No.	Theme No.	Theme			Marked Theme	Unmarked Theme
		Textual Theme	Interpersonal Theme	Existential Theme		
(1)	[1]			上海自然博物馆		√
(2)	[2]			位于	√	
(3)	[3]			该馆大楼建筑		√
	[4]			建筑面积		√
(4)	[5]			上海自然博物馆		√
(5)	[6]			1960 年	√	
(6)	[7]			1984 年	√	
	[8]			该分馆		√
(7)	[9]			标本大楼面积		√
	[10]			除珍藏	√	
	[11]			陈列厅		√
(8)	[12]			总面积		√
(9)	[13]	其中		约二分之一		√
(10)	[14]			上海自然博物馆		√
(11)	[15]			除了接收	√	

(12)	[16]			到1985年	√	
	[17]	其中		动物标本		√
(13)	[18]			在这些标本中	√	
(14)	[19]			有	√	
	[20]			有	√	
(15)	[21]			该馆		√
(16)	[22]			该馆基本陈列面积		√
(17)	[23]			陈列内容		√
(18)	[24]			在古动物史陈列	√	
(19)	[25]			展厅中央		√
(20)	[26]			它的右侧		√
	[27]			体长		√
	[28]			体高		√
	[29]			一对门牙		√
(21)	[30]			人类发展史陈列		√
(22)	[31]			在动物陈列	√	
(23)	[32]			除了展出	√	
(24)	[33]	此外		也展出	√	
(25)	[34]			古尸陈列室		√
	[35]	其中		新疆楼兰地区发掘的楼兰女尸		√
(26)	[36]			植物陈列		√
(27)	[37]			内容		√
(28)	[38]			沿着陈列线	√	
(29)	[39]			陈列厅的中央		√
	[40]			它		√
	[41]			也是		√
(30)	[42]			已经在地球上绝灭的鳞木、封印木等蕨类		√
	[43]			无数草木蕨类		√
(31)	[44]			该馆		√
(32)	[45]			该馆		√
	[46]	还				√

From the above table, it can be seen that there are a total of 46 thematic combinations in the introduction of Shanghai Museum of Natural Sciences, including 42 single themes and 14 marked themes (mainly including time, place adverbs, and prepositional phrases).

There is no interpersonal theme, while the experiential theme often uses words such as "the museum", "area", "display", and rarely uses pronouns.

The thematic analysis has been made fo the remaining texts by using the same method and the following table is obtained:

Table 30 Distribution of Theme System in Chinese Introductions of Domestic Museums

Text No.	Multiple Theme	Single Theme	Marked Theme	Unmarked Theme
1	8	58	27	39
2	1	17	5	13
3	5	39	11	33
4	4	42	14	32
5	1	28	5	24
6	2	56	12	46
7	3	28	5	26
8	1	19	6	14
9	1	4	0	5
10	5	39	2	42
11	0	30	8	22
12	5	22	2	25
13	1	9	3	7
14	1	19	4	16
15	1	32	9	24
16	1	41	12	30
17	0	13	3	10
18	2	11	3	10
19	4	15	7	12
20	2	30	4	28
21	0	18	4	14
22	0	27	15	12
23	0	13	2	11
24	0	34	5	29
25	3	28	6	25
26	0	27	3	24

27	2	16	5	13
28	0	24	5	19
29	3	12	4	11
30	2	19	3	18
31	1	9	3	7
32	1	14	3	12
33	0	27	6	21
34	1	19	3	17
35	0	27	3	24
36	0	26	8	18
37	0	27	12	15
38	3	33	14	22
39	4	17	3	18
40	0	12	3	9
Total	68	981	252	797
%	6.5	93.5	24.0	76.0

From the above table, it can be seen that the proportion of single themes used is as high as 93.5%, and the proportion of multiple themes is 6.5%. The combination of multiple themes is relatively simple, and the main textual themes involved are "and", "also", and "besides". Interpersonal themes mainly include adverbs of time and place, as well as prepositional phrases. Among the experiential themes, the marked theme accounts for 24.0%, mainly involving the geographical location of the museum, the establishment time of the museum, and the development status of each stage, such as:

1987年7月该园由赛马会的附属机构变为由港督委任董事局成员的独立法定机构。(文本16)

8.3.3 Linguistic Features of the English Translation of Domestic Museum Introductions
1) Transitivity System

Text 4 is taken as an example.

The Shanghai Museum of Natural Sciences

(1) The Shanghai Museum of Natural Sciences is one of the largest museums of natural sciences in China.(2) Located at downtown Shanghai, the museum features some

British traditional style and covers an area of 12,880 square meters.

(3) Prepared in November 1956, the Shanghai Museum of Natural Sciences opened the Division Museum of Animals to the public in 1960, and the Division Museum of Plants in 1984. (4) The building for exhibition of samples covers a floor space of 3,053 square meters. (5) The exhibition halls of the museum are situated in the Shanghai Botanic Garden and cover a total space of 4,726 square meters.

(6) The museum has a collection of 240,000 samples, including over 62,000 pieces of animal specimens, 135,000 plant specimens, 700 specimens of the Stone Age, and 1,700 specimens of minerals, which are of high value to research on natural evolvement.

(7) The largest exhibit is a dinosaur skeleton of over four storeys high. (8) There are also some rare species, which cannot be found elsewhere outside China, on display, such as a Yellow River mammoth, a giant salamander, a giant panda, and an alligator from the Yangtze River. (9) Besides, the museum boasts more than 60,000 volumes of documents and books on scientific research.

(10) The museum features four exhibition halls: the Hall of the History of the Ancient Animals, the Hall of History of Ancient Anthropology, the Hall of Animals and the Hall of Plants.

(11) The Hall of the History Ancient Animals houses fossil remains from the Paleozoic, Mesozoic and Cenozoic eras, forming a wordless chronicle of prehistoric life and displaying the evolvement of animals from aquicolous animals to terraneous animals, and from simple formation to complex one. (12) Among the exhibits is a restored model of a Mamenxi dinosaur with the length of 22 meters, which is 140 million years old.

(13) In the Hall of Ancient Anthropology is a huge collection of specimens, restored models and unearthed relics, which details the genesis and evolvement of human beings.

(14) The Hall of Animals displays invertebrates, fishes, amphibious animals, reptiles, birds and mammals, many of which are on the national list of first-class and second-class protected animals. (15) The Hall for Plants displays primitive alga, epiphyte, lichen and so on.

(16) The famous Chinese mummies are exhibited in the Hall of the Mummies, such as a female mummy unearthed in Loulan of Xinjiang Uygur Autonomous Region.

(17) In addition to permanent exhibitions, the museum often organizes other displays, such as Ancient Mummies of China, Rare Animals, Biologic Engineering, Chinese Special Animal - Elk and so on.

(18) The museum has compiled a good many of books on animals, plants, human and astronomy such as Research and Study and Nature and Human.

It can be represented in the following table:

Table 31 Analysis of Process Types in Text 4

Sentence No.	Process No.	Process Type	Verbs Involved
(1)	1	Relational process	is
(2)	2	Relational process	features
	3	Relational process	covers
(3)	4	Material process	opened
(4)	5	Relational process	covers
(5)	6	Relational process	are situated
	7	Relational process	cover
(6)	8	Relational process	has
	9	Relational process	are
(7)	10	Relational process	is
(8)	11	Existential process	are
	12	Material process	be found
(9)	13	Relational process	boasts
(10)	14	Relational process	features
(11)	15	Relational process	houses
(12)	16	Existential process	is
	17	Relational process	is
(13)	18	Existential process	is
	19	Material process	details
(14)	20	Material process	displays
	21	Relational process	are
(15)	22	Material process	displays
(16)	23	Material process	are exhibited
(17)	24	Material process	organizes
(18)	25	Material process	has compiled

After completing the process analysis of the remaining texts in the corpus, the results are as follows:

Table 32 Distribution of Process Types in English Translations of Introductions of Domestic Museums

Text No.	Relational Process	Material Process	Mental Process	Behavioral Process	Verbal Process	Existential Process	Sum
1	42	61	2	3	0	6	114
2	8	14	0	0	0	0	22
3	10	14	1	0	1	1	27
4	14	9	0	0	0	3	26
5	11	8	2	0	0	1	22
6	22	14	1	3	1	0	41
7	8	12	0	0	0	5	25
8	8	18	2	0	0	0	28
9	2	3	0	0	0	0	5
10	6	10	0	0	0	0	16
11	5	12	0	1	0	0	18
12	7	18	2	2	0	3	32
13	2	2	0	0	0	0	4
14	11	4	2	0	0	1	18
15	8	5	1	0	0	0	14
16	15	6	0	0	0	2	23
17	11	9	0	0	0	1	21
18	5	1	0	0	0	3	9
19	6	6	1	0	0	0	13
20	17	8	3	0	0	0	28
21	4	11	0	0	0	1	16
22	5	12	1	0	0	0	18
23	8	7	0	1	0	0	16
24	3	4	0	0	0	0	7
25	8	13	3	0	0	2	26

26	7	8	0	0	0	0	15
27	5	7	0	0	0	3	15
28	3	5	0	0	0	0	8
29	2	8	1	0	0	1	12
30	4	5	0	0	0	0	9
31	3	5	0	0	0	0	8
32	7	7	1	0	0	3	18
33	7	8	1	0	0	0	16
34	7	4	0	0	0	0	11
35	11	7	0	0	0	1	19
36	5	9	0	0	0	0	14
37	18	6	0	0	1	0	25
38	21	14	1	0	1	0	37
39	8	4	0	0	0	1	13
40	4	5	0	0	0	0	9

According to statistics, the distribution ratios of different process types are as follows:

Table 33 Distribution Ratio of Process Types in English Translations of Domestic Museum Introductions

	Relational Process	Material Process	Mental Process	Behavioral Process	Verbal Process	Existential Process	Total
Total	358	383	25	10	4	38	818
%	43.8	46.8	3.1	1.2	0.5	4.6	100

From this, it can be seen that material processes are also most widely used, with a percentage as high as 46.8%. Overall, the translated texts are basically translated in a one-to-one correspondence with their source texts—Chinese introductions of domestic museums, that's why most verbs are translated literally. Therefore, the percentage of material processes, relational processes, mental processes, behavioral processes, verbal processes and existential processes is basically the same as with their source texts, and the contents involved are also similar. For example:

The Hall **has collected** 2,100 items of relics, including 34 pieces of Class One Relics.

(Text 7)

The display **is divided into** three parts: the "Hall of Land Revolutionary War", "Hall of Anti-Japanese War," and "Hall of National Liberation War" (Text 28)

Relational processes account for 43.8% of the total number, second only to material processes. For example:

The museum **takes up** an area of about 50,000 square meters and **consists of** eight exhibition halls, namely the Prelude Hall, Relics Hall, Folk Custom Hall, Silkworm Hall, Silk Manufacturing Hall, Weaving Hall, Dying Hall and Achievements Hall. (文本 17)

The Museum **houses** an abundant collection of paintings, seals, western paintings, pottery and bronze. (文本 34)

Existential processes only account for 4.6%. For example:

There **are** some Buddhist sanctuaries to the east of the six eastern palaces and to the west of the six western palaces. (文本 1)

There **are** various kinds of man-made seacoasts suitable for living of different sea creatures. (文本 16)

2) Mood System

Text 4 from the corpus of translated introductions is taken as an example.

Shanghai Museum of Natural Sciences

(1) [1] The Shanghai Museum of Natural Sciences is one of the largest museums of natural sciences in China. (2) Located at downtown Shanghai, [2] the museum features some British traditional style and [3]covers an area of 12,880 square meters.

(3) [4] Prepared in November 1956, [5] the Shanghai Museum of Natural Sciences opened the Division Museum of Animals to the public in 1960, [6] and the Division Museum of Plants in 1984. (4) [7]The building for exhibition of samples covers a floor space of 3,053 square meters. (5) [8] The exhibition halls of the museum are situated in the Shanghai Botanic Garden [9]and cover a total space of 4,726 square meters.

(6) [10] The museum has a collection of 240,000 samples, including over 62,000 pieces of animal specimens, 135,000 plant specimens, 700 specimens of the Stone Age,

and 1,700 specimens of minerals, [11] which are of high value to research on natural evolvement.

(7) [12] The largest exhibit is a dinosaur skeleton of over four stories high. (8) [13] There are also some rare species, [14] which cannot be found elsewhere outside China, on display, such as a Yellow River mammoth, a giant salamander, a giant panda, and an alligator from the Yangtze River. (9) [15] Besides, the museum boasts more than 60,000 volumes of documents and books on scientific research.

(10) [16] The museum features four exhibition halls: the Hall of the History of the Ancient Animals, the Hall of History of Ancient Anthropology, the Hall of Animals and the Hall of Plants.

(11) [17] The Hall of the History Ancient Animals houses fossil remains from the Paleozoic, Mesozoic and Cenozoic eras, forming a wordless chronicle of prehistoric life and displaying the evolvement of animals from aquicolous animals to terraneous animals, and from simple formation to complex one. (12) [18] Among the exhibits is a restored model of a Mamenxi dinosaur with the length of 22 meters, [19] which is 140 million years old.

(13) [20] In the Hall of Ancient Anthropology is a huge collection of specimens, restored models and unearthed relics, [21] which details the genesis and evolvement of human beings.

(14) [22] The Hall of Animals displays invertebrates, fishes, amphibious animals, reptiles, birds and mammals, [23] many of which are on the national list of first-class and second-class protected animals. (15) [24] The Hall for Plants displays primitive alga, epiphyte, lichen and so on.

(16) [25] The famous Chinese mummies are exhibited in the Hall of the Mummies, [26] such as a female mummy unearthed in Loulan of Xinjiang Uygur Autonomous Region.

(17) [27] In addition to permanent exhibitions, the museum often organizes other displays, such as Ancient Mummies of China, Rare Animals, Biologic Engineering, Chinese Special Animal - Elk and so on.

(18) [28] The museum has compiled a good many of books on animals, plants, human and astronomy such as *Research and Study* and *Nature and Human*.

The mood analysis is as follows:

Table 34 Analysis of Mood System in Text 4

Sentence No.	Clause No.	Subject	Infinite	Tense	Mood Type
(1)	[1]	The Shanghai Museum of Natural Sciences	is	Present tense	Indicative mood
(2)	[2]	the museum	features	Present	Indicative
	[3]	the museum	covers	Present	Indicative
(3)	[4]	(the Shanghai Museum of Natural Sciences)	prepared	Present	Indicative
	[5]	the Shanghai Museum of Natural Sciences	opened	Present	Indicative
	[6]	(the Shanghai Museum of Natural Sciences)	(opened)	Present	Indicative
(4)	[7]	The building for exhibition of samples	covers	Present	Indicative
(5)	[8]	The exhibition halls of the museum	are	Present	Indicative
	[9]	(The exhibition halls of the museum)	cover	Present	Indicative
(6)	[10]	The museum	has	Present	Indicative
	[11]	which	are	Present	Indicative
(7)	[12]	The largest exhibit	is	Present	Indicative
(8)	[13]	There	are	Present	Indicative
	[14]	which	be found	Present	Indicative

(9)	[15]	the museum	boasts	Present	Indicative
(10)	[16]	the museum	features	Present	Indicative
(11)	[17]	The Hall of the History Ancient Animals	houses	Present	Indicative
(12)	[18]	Among the exhibits	is	Present	Indicative
	[19]	which	is	Present	Indicative
(13)	[20]	In the Hall of Ancient Anthropology	is	Present	Indicative
	[21]	which	details	Present	Indicative
(14)	[22]	The Hall of Animals	displays	Present	Indicative
	[23]	many of which	are	Present	Indicative
(15)	[24]	The Hall for Plants	displays	Present	Indicative
(16)	[25]	The famous Chinese mummies	are	Present	Indicative
	[26]	a female mummy	unearthed	Present	Indicative
(17)	[27]	the museum	organizes	Present	Indicative
(18)	[28]	The museum	has	Present	Indicative

The translated Text 4 consists of 28 clauses, which mainly involve basic information about the museum and correspond to the Chinese version of "Shanghai Museum of Natural Sciences". From the perspective of English verb tenses, the present tense appears 24 times, while the past tense only appears 4 times. This is because Text 4 mainly introduces the current situation of the museum and rarely reviews the history of development.

After analyzing all 40 translated English texts, whether their mood system can reflect certain personalities or commonalities are observed:

Table 35 Distribution of Mood Systems in All Translated Texts

Text No.	The Number of Clauses	Mood Type			Subject			Tense		
		Indica-tive	Impera-tive	Interro-gative	Desti-nation	Tourists	Other Subjects	Past Tense	Present Tense	Future Tense
1	116	116	0	0	48	1	67	66	50	0
2	25	25	0	0	13	1	11	8	17	0
3	34	34	0	0	25	0	9	6	28	0
4	28	28	0	0	22	0	6	5	23	0
5	22	22	0	0	14	1	7	2	20	0
6	40	40	0	0	25	1	14	19	20	1
7	33	33	0	0	12	0	21	14	19	0
8	35	35	0	0	13	0	22	11	22	2
9	6	6	0	0	6	0	0	0	6	0
10	20	20	0	0	10	1	9	8	12	0
11	21	21	0	0	15	0	6	9	12	0
12	36	36	0	0	15	7	14	3	30	3
13	8	8	0	0	6	0	2	2	6	0
14	20	20	0	0	11	0	9	5	15	0
15	14	14	0	0	8	0	6	1	13	0
16	26	26	0	0	22	1	3	3	23	0
17	19	19	0	0	11	0	8	3	16	0
18	17	17	0	0	8	0	9	6	11	0
19	18	18	0	0	13	0	5	10	8	0
20	26	26	0	0	8	0	18	5	21	0
21	20	20	0	0	6	0	14	11	9	0
22	19	19	0	0	12	0	7	9	10	0
23	17	17	0	0	12	2	3	3	14	0
24	12	12	0	0	10	0	2	8	4	0
25	25	25	0	0	16	0	9	3	22	0
26	18	18	0	0	16	0	2	2	16	0
27	20	20	0	0	7	0	13	8	12	0
28	10	10	0	0	10	0	0	3	7	0

29	22	22	0	0	9	0	13	0	22	0
30	12	12	0	0	9	0	3	3	9	0
31	24	24	0	0	8	0	16	14	10	0
32	25	25	0	0	14	0	11	6	19	0
33	18	18	0	0	13	0	5	9	9	0
34	11	11	0	0	9	0	2	1	10	0
35	24	24	0	0	12	0	12	8	16	0
36	16	16	0	0	10	0	6	6	10	0
37	31	31	0	0	12	0	19	5	26	0
38	39	39	0	0	23	0	16	11	28	0
39	20	20	0	0	8	0	12	6	14	0
40	11	11	0	0	11	0	0	2	9	0

The distribution ratio of different types of mood is:

Table 36 Distribution Ratio of Mood System in Translated English Texts

	The Number of Clauses	Mood Type			Subject			Tense		
		Indica-tive	Impera-tive	Interro-gative	Desti-nation	Tourists	Other Subjects	Past Tense	Present Tense	Future Tense
%	100	100	0	0	55.5	1.6	42.9	31.7	67.7	0.6

From this, it can be found that:

Mood type: All are in indicative mood. For example:

The Zhoukoudian Relics Museum of palaeoanthropology is located in Fangshan District in Beijing. (Text 21)

The temple consists of temple palaces and halls in three compounds. (Text 18)

Subject selection: The percentage of tourists as the subject is only 1.6%, while the percentage of destinations as the subject is as high as 55.5%. The proportion of other things (exhibits, designers, years, etc.) as the subject is 42.9%. For example:

The Palace Museum, historically and artistically one of the most comprehensive museum in China, was established on the basis of the Forbidden City. (Tex 1)

You can not only enjoy the rare historical collection but also enjoy the sunshine coming from the feather-shaped skylight in the dome. (Text 12)

In 1936, **anthropologist Jia Lanpo** discovered another three fossilized skulls of the Upper Cave Man. (Text 21)

Tense: The present tense is most widely used, accounting for 67.7%, followed by the past tense, accounting for 31.7%, and the future tense is rarely used, accounting for only 0.6%. For example:

The Museum, expected to be completed in October this year, is to be built into a large modern spot for the collection, protection and research of historic relics as well as a place for education, leisure and tour. Tianjin Art Museum and Historical Museum, **will** contain all the 150,000 pieces of valuable historical and cultural relics of the two museums, and aperiodic exhibitions will be held by turns. (Text 12)

3) Modality System

After observation, the use of modal verbs in the English translations of the museum introductions is as follows:

Table 37 Distribution of Modal Verbs

Text No.	should	might(may)	could(can)	must	need	will(would)
1						√
2			√			
3			√			
4						
5			√			
6			√			
7			√			
8			√			
9						
10			√			
11			√			
12			√			√
13						
14						
15						

16				√				
17								
18								
19								
20				√				
21								
22								
23				√				
24								
25								
26								
27								
28								
29								
30								
31								
32				√				
33								
34				√				
35				√				
36								
37								
38								
39				√				
40								

The frequency of use of modal verbs is:

Table 38 Frequency of Use of Modal Verbs

	Medium		Low		High		Sum
	might(may)	could(can)	should	will(would)	must	need	
Total	0	16	0	2	0	0	18
%	0	88.9	0	11.1	0	0	100

It can be seen that in the English translation of museum introductions, modal verbs are not often used, with the most commonly used being "can", "will", etc.

4) Theme System

Text 4 is also taken as the example.

Shanghai Museum of Natural Sciences

(1) [1] The Shanghai Museum of Natural Sciences is one of the largest museums of natural sciences in China. (2) [2] Located at downtown Shanghai, the museum features some British traditional style [3] and covers an area of 12,880 square meters.

(3) [4] Prepared in November 1956, the Shanghai Museum of Natural Sciences opened the Division Museum of Animals to the public in 1960, and the Division Museum of Plants in 1984. (4) [5] The building for exhibition of samples covers a floor space of 3,053 square meters. (5) [6] The exhibition halls of the museum are situated in the Shanghai Botanic Garden [7] and cover a total space of 4,726 square meters.

(6) [8] The museum has a collection of 240,000 samples, including over 62,000 pieces of animal specimens, 135,000 plant specimens, 700 specimens of the Stone Age, and 1,700 specimens of minerals, [9] which are of high value to research on natural evolvement.

(7) [10] The largest exhibit is a dinosaur skeleton of over four storeys high. (8) [11] There are also some rare species, [12] which cannot be found elsewhere outside China, on display, such as a Yellow River mammoth, a giant salamander, a giant panda, and an alligator from the Yangtze River. (9) [13] Besides, the museum boasts more than 60,000 volumes of documents and books on scientific research.

(10) [14] The museum features four exhibition halls: the Hall of the History of the Ancient Animals, the Hall of History of Ancient Anthropology, the Hall of Animals and the Hall of Plants.

(11) [15] The Hall of the History Ancient Animals houses fossil remains from the Paleozoic, Mesozoic and Cenozoic eras, forming a wordless chronicle of prehistoric life and displaying the evolvement of animals from aquicolous animals to terraneous animals, and from simple formation to complex one. (12) [16] Among the exhibits is a restored model of a Mamenxi dinosaur with the length of 22 meters, [17] which is 140 million years old.

(13) [18] In the Hall of Ancient Anthropology is a huge collection of specimens, restored models and unearthed relics, [19] which details the genesis and evolvement of human beings.

(14) [20] The Hall of Animals displays invertebrates, fishes, amphibious animals, reptiles, birds and mammals, [21] many of which are on the national list of first-class and second-class protected animals. (15) [22] The Hall for Plants displays primitive alga, epiphyte, lichen and so on.

(16) [23] The famous Chinese mummies are exhibited in the Hall of the Mummies, such as a female mummy unearthed in Loulan of Xinjiang Uygur Autonomous Region.

(17) [24] In addition to permanent exhibitions, the museum often organizes other displays, such as Ancient Mummies of China, Rare Animals, Biologic Engineering, Chinese Special Animal - Elk and so on.

(18) [25] The museum has compiled a good many of books on animals, plants, human and astronomy such as *Research and Study* and *Nature and Human*.

The analysis results are as follows:

Table 39 Theme System Analysis of Translated English Text 4

Sentence No.	Clause No.	Theme			Marked Theme	Unmarked Theme
		Textual Theme	Interpersonal Theme	Experiential Theme		
(1)	[1]			The Shanghai Museum of Natural Sciences		√
(2)	[2]			Located at downtown	√	
(3)	[3]	and				√
	[4]			Prepared in November 1956	√	
(4)	[5]			The building for exhibition of samples		√

(5)	[6]			The exhibition halls of the museum		√
	[7]	and				√
(6)	[8]			The museum		√
	[9]			which		√
(7)	[10]			The largest exhibit		√
(8)	[11]			There		√
	[12]			which		√
(9)	[13]	Besides		the museum		√
(10)	[14]			The museum		√
(11)	[15]			The Hall of the History Ancient Animals		√
(12)	[16]			Among the	√	
	[17]			which		√
(13)	[18]			In the Hall of Ancient Anthropology	√	
	[19]			which		√
(14)	[20]			The Hall of		√
	[21]			many of which		√
(15)	[22]			The Hall for Plants		√
(16)	[23]			The famous Chinese mummies		√
(17)	[24]			In addition to permanent exhibitions	√	
(18)	[25]			The museum		√

From the above table, it can be seen that there are a total of 25 thematic combinations, of which only 1 is a multiple theme and 5 are marked themes.

Thematic analysis is conducted on all English translated texts by using the same method, and the results are as follows:

Table 40 Theme System Distribution of All Texts in the Corpus of Translated Introductions

Text No.	Multiple Theme	Single Theme	Marked Theme	Unmarked Theme
1	12	82	41	53
2	4	17	3	18
3	1	26	7	20
4	1	24	5	20
5	0	17	5	12
6	5	29	10	24
7	4	19	8	15
8	3	21	6	18
9	0	5	2	3
10	1	13	6	8
11	1	12	5	8
12	5	23	8	20
13	0	4	2	2
14	2	15	3	14
15	1	11	2	10
16	6	12	3	15
17	2	14	1	15
18	1	8	3	6
19	0	11	4	7
20	5	21	3	23
21	0	16	4	12
22	1	13	6	8
23	2	12	4	10
24	1	6	0	7
25	1	17	3	15
26	0	10	2	8
27	1	11	3	9
28	0	7	2	5
29	1	9	2	8
30	2	6	1	7

31	0	7	0	7
32	1	15	4	12
33	1	13	4	10
34	0	8	2	6
35	1	16	3	14
36	0	11	5	6
37	0	22	8	14
38	4	28	3	29
39	0	10	1	9
40	0	7	2	5
Total	70	628	186	512
%	10.0	90.0	26.6	73.4

From the above table, it can be seen that the proportion of single themes is the highest, which is up to 90%, while multiple themes only account for 10%. Most of them are combinations of "textual theme+experiential theme". In the experiential theme, marked themes account for 26.6%. For example:

Located at the Taizhong Market of Taiwan Province, the Taiwan National Museum of Natural Science is the first of three science museums in Taiwan. (Text 9)

Founded in 1955, the Museum mainly collects cultural relics from the Central Plains besides some local cultural relics. (Text 30)

8.4 Corpus-based Comparative Analysis of Museum Introductions

We have analyzed the schematic structure and presentation style of all texts in corpara of English, Chinese, and translated English museum introductions from a generic analysis perspective, and summarized their respective characteristics. The following is a comparison of structures and linguistic features (vocabulary grammar) of these three kinds of texts to identify similarities and differences, providing a basis for evaluating the quality of the English translation of museum introductions and how to improve the translation in the next section.

8.4.1 Comparison of Schematic Structure of Three Types of Texts (GSP Model)

1) **Comparison between English Introductions of Foreign Museums and Chinese Introductions of Domestic Museums**

Firstly, we have reviewed the structural features of texts from corpora of Chinese introductions of domestic museums and English introductions of foreign museums, which are:

Table 41 Distribution Frequency of Structural Elements in English Introduction of Foreign Museums

	D	L	CT	HE	BI	CEI	SA	AC	EP	VG
Total	40	19	16	30	23	40	0	0	30	6
%	100	47.5	40	75	57.5	100	0	0	75	15

Table 42 Distribution Frequency of Structural Elements in Chinese Introductions of Domestic Museums

	D	L	CT	HE	BI	CEI	SA	AC	EP	VG
Total	40	38	36	7	24	36	17	13	23	1
%	100	95	90	17.5	60	90	42.5	32.5	57.5	2.5

The GSP model for English introductions of foreign museums is:

$$D^\wedge\ EP^\wedge\ (L)\ (CT)\ HE\ ^\wedge\ \overset{\frown}{BI}\ CEI\ \overset{\frown}{(^\wedge\ VG)}$$
※ ※ ※

The GSP model of Chinese introductions of domestic museums is:

$$D^\wedge\ EP\ [L.CT]\ \overset{\frown}{(HE)}\ BI\ ^\wedge CEI\ (^\wedge SA)\ (^\wedge AC)\ (^\wedge\ VG)$$
※ ※

From the above, it can be found that there are similarities and differences in terms of textual structure between the two types of museum introductions.

Similarities: D (Designation), BI (Building Information), CEI (Collections and Exhibits Introduction), and EP (Evaluation and Position) all account for over 50% of the elements, which are necessary and indispensable structural frameworks for genres such as museum introductions.

VG (Visiting Guide) always appears at the end of introductions, providing more detailed information for tourists.

HE (Historical Events) always appears before CEI (Collections and Exhibits Introduction).

BI (Architectural Overview) always appears before CEI (Collections and Exhibits Introduction).

Differences:

HE (Historical Events): Each museum has its own unique history, but due to differences in Chinese and Western cultures, there are differences in English introductions of foreign museums and Chinese introductions of domestic museums in this move. HE is to introduce historical allusions related to the construction process of the museum to visitors, which can increase their emotional understanding and impress them. In English introductions of foreign museums, HE is a necessary element with a proportion of approximately 75%, while in Chinese introductions of domestic museums, its proportion is only 17.5%, which is an optional element.

L (Location) and CT (Completed Time): The function of L and CT is to provide visitors with a general understanding of museums. In English introductions of foreign museums, L and CT are optional elements, and their positions in the GSP modes are also relatively flexible, accounting for 47.5% and 40% respectively; In Chinese introductions of museums, L and CT are necessary elements, these two often appear in pairs and their positions are interchangeable . However, in most cases, L appears before CT, accounting for 95% and 90% respectively.

SA (Social Activities)and AC (Academic Contributions): In English introductions of foreign museums, SA and AC do not appear, while in Chinese introductions of domestic museums, SA and AC appear as optional elements in a relatively fixed order with VG and generally appear before VG, accounting for 42.5% and 32.5%, respectively.

D (Designation) and EP (Evaluation and Position): In English introductions of foreign museums, D and EP often appear together in an uncertain order, but always appear at the beginning of the introduction, accounting for 100% and 57.5% respectively; In Chinese introductions of domestic museums, the position of EP has changed, with some still appearing at the beginning and some appearing at the end of introductions.

2） Comparison between China Museum introductions and Their English Translations

According to the previous analysis, the structural characteristics of the Chinese and English translations of domestic museum introductions are as follows:

Table 43: Distribution Frequency of Structural Elements in Chinese Introductions of Domestic Museums

	D	L	CT	HE	BI	CEI	SA	AC	EP	VG
Total	40	38	36	7	24	36	17	13	23	1
%	100	95	90	17.5	60	90	42.5	32.5	57.5	2.5

Table 44: Distribution Frequency of Structural Elements in English Translations of Domestic Museum Introductions

	D	L	CT	HE	BI	CEI	SA	AC	EP	VG
Total	40	36	37	8	27	40	17	9	20	2
%	100	90	92.5	20	67.5	100	42.5	22.5	50	5

The GSP model of domestic museum introductions is:

D^ EP [L.CT] (HE) BI ^CEI (^SA) (^AC) (^ VG).
※   ※

The GSP model of English translations of domestic museums is:

D^ [L.CT] ^ EP (HE) BI ^CEI (^SA) (^AC) (^ VG).
※

Compared to Chinese introductions of domestic museums, in translated English texts of domestic museums, except for the positions of L and CT ahead of EP, the other elements are completely consistent with Chinese introductions of museums. In other words, translated English texts completely follow the structure of the Chinese texts, hardly considering the structural characteristics of this genre in the target language.

3) **Comparison between English Translations of Domestic Museum Introductions and Foreign Museum Introductions**

According to the previous analysis, the structural characteristics of the English translations of domestic museums and foreign museum introductions are as follows:

Table 45 Distribution Frequency of Structural Elements in English Introductions of Foreign Museums

	D	L	CT	HE	BI	CEI	SA	AC	EP	VG
Total	40	19	16	30	23	40	0	0	30	6
%	100	47.5	40	75	57.5	100	0	0	75	15

Table 46 Distribution Frequency of Structural Elements in English Translations of Domestic Museum Introductions

	D	L	CT	HE	BI	CEI	SA	AC	EP	VG
Total	40	36	37	8	27	40	17	9	20	2
%	100	90	92.5	20	67.5	100	42.5	22.5	50	5

The GSP model of foreign museum introductions is:

D^ EP^ (L) (CT) HE ^ BI. CEI (^ VG)

The GSP model of translated English introductions of domestic museums is:

D^ [L.CT] ^ EP (HE) BI ^CEI (^SA) (^AC) (^ VG)

Due to the fact that the English version of domestic museum introductions is a mechanically literal translation of their source texts - introductions in Chinese, the description of similarities and differences in the structure between introductions of foreign museums in English and introductions of domestic museums in Chinese in the previous section is fully applicable to English translations of domestic museums and introductions of foreign museums in English.

8.4.2 Comparison of the Presentation Style of Three Types of Texts (at the lexical and grammatical level)

1) **Comparison of English Introduction to Foreign Museums and Chinese Introduction to Domestic Museums**

(1) **Transitivity System**

By integrating the transitivity analysis of introductions of foreign museums in

English and introductions of domestic museums in Chinese in the previous section, the results are obtained as follows:

Table 47 Comparison of Process Types between English Introductions of Foreign Museums and Chinese Introductions of Domestic Museums

Process Type	Introductions of Foreign Museums in English		Introductions of Domestic Museums in Chinese	
	Total	%	Total	%
Relational Process	626	39.0	499	42.9
Material Process	786	49.0	556	47.9
Mental Process	97	6.0	23	2.0
Behavioral Process	12	0.8	10	0.9
Verbal Process	21	1.3	16	1.4
Existential Process	63	3.9	57	4.9
Sum	1605	100	1161	100

Therefore, it is not difficult to find that material processes are most commonly used in both English and Chinese museum introductions, both of which are approaching 50%; The proportions of other process types are as follows: in English introductions, relational process (39.0%), mental process (6.0%), existential process (3.9%), verbal process (1.3%), and behavioral process (0.8%); Proportions of Chinese introductions are: relational process (42.9%), existential process (4.9%), mental process (2.0%), verbal process (1.4%) and behavioral process (0.9%).

From this, it can be found that introductions of foreign museums in English place more emphasis on describing mental processes to express emotions, cognition, and vision towards museums, facilitating spiritual communication with visitors or readers and easy resonance. In contrast, introductions of domestic museums in Chinese focus more on relational and existential processes, describing the internal structure, exhibition location, attributes and other aspects of museums with an emphasis on providing information.

(2) Mood System

By integrating Table 16 and Table 26, it can be concluded that:

		Introductions of Foreign Museums in English		Introductions of Domestic Museums in Chinese	
		Total	%	Total	%
The Number of Clauses	Sum	1752	100	1122	100
Mood Type	Indicative	1740	99.3	1117	99.6
	Imperative	12	0.7	5	0.4
	Interrogative	0	0	0	0
Subject	Destination	682	38.9	647	57.7
	Tourists	114	6.5	20	1.8
	Other subjects	956	54.6	455	40.5
Tense	Past tense	724	41.3	×	×
	Present tense	996	56.8	×	×
	Future tense	32	1.9	×	×

The similarities and differences between the two are clearly presented in the above table:

Similarities: The indicative mood is the most important mood choice in introductions of domestic and foreign museums, the proportion of which is almost 100% among three types of mood.

Differences: In terms of subject selection, although not many Chinese and English museum introductions choose tourists as the subject, the proportion of use in English is nearly four times that in Chinese. Using museums and other things related to museums as subjects demonstrates a relatively objective attitude towards readers, focusing on providing information; The main purpose of using tourists as the subject is to bring them closer and attract them to visit. In this regard, introductions of domestic museums in Chinese is still slightly lacking.

In terms of modal verbs, by integrating Tables 18 and 28 the results are as follows:

Table 49 Comparison of Modal Verbs between English Introductions of Foreign Museums and Chinese Introductions of Domestic Museums

	Introductions of Domestic Museums in Chinese						Sum
	Low		Medium		High		
	might(may)	could(can)	will(would)	should	must	need	
Total	6	0	0	0	0	1	7
%	87.5	0	0	0	0	14.3	100
	Introductions of Foreign Museums in English						Sum
	Low		Medium		High		
	might(may)	could(can)	will(would)	should	must	need	
Total	1	20	23	3	1	0	48
%	2.1	41.7	47.9	6.2	2.1	0	100

Although being rarely used in both corpora, the proportion of modal verbs used in English introductions of foreign museums is still higher than that of the Chinese corpus, and the overall style of English texts appears more lively and communicative.

(3) Theme System

Based on the previous Tables 20 and 30, it can be concluded that:

Table 50 Comparison of Thematic Analysis between English Introductions of Foreign Museums and Chinese Introductions of Domestic Museums

	Introductions of Foreign Museums in English		Introductions of Domestic Museums in Chinese	
	Total	%	Total	%
Multiple theme	184	13.3	68	6.5
Single theme	1196	86.7	981	93.5
Marked theme	292	21.2	252	24.0
Unmarked theme	1088	78.8	797	76.0
Sum	1380	100	1049	100

From it, it can be seen that in theme selection, the similarity is that single themes are used more frequently than multiple themes, and unmarked themes are used more frequently than marked themes; The difference is that in the corpus of English introductions of foreign museums, the proportion of multiple themes and unmarked themes used is higher than that in the case of domestic introductions in Chinese, which are

13.3% vs. 6.5% and 78.8% vs. 76.0% respectively.

2) Comparison of Chinese and English Translations of Domestic Museum Introductions

(1) Transitivity System

By integrating the process description of introductions of domestic museums and their English translations, the results are obtained as follows:

Table 51 Comparison of Translation Process Types between Chinese and English Introductions of Domestic Museums

Process Type	Introductions of Domestic Museums in Chinese		English Translations of Chinese Museum Introductions	
	Total	%	Total	%
Relational Process	499	42.9	358	43.8
Material Process	556	47.9	383	46.8
Mental Process	23	2.0	25	3.1
Behavioral Process	10	0.9	10	1.2
Verbal Process	16	1.4	4	0.5
Existential Process	57	4.9	38	4.6
Sum	1161	100	818	100

From the above data, it can be seen that apart from the reduced length of the translated English introductions compared to their source texts (818<1161), the proportion of various process types is very close, and the translated English texts basically correspond to their source texts.

(2) Mood System

By integrating Table 26 and Table 36, it can be obtained as follows:

Table 52 Comparison of Mood System between Chinese and English Translations of Domestic Museum Introductions

		Introductions of Domestic Museums in Chinese		English Translations of Domestic Museums	
		Total	%	Total	%
The Number of Clauses	Sum	1122	100	958	100
Mood Type	Indicative	1117	99.6	958	100

	Imperative	5	0.4	0	0
	Interrogative	0	0	0	0
Subject	Destination	647	57.7	532	55.5
	Tourists	20	1.8	15	1.6
	Other	455	40.5	411	42.9
Tense	Past tense	×	×	304	31.7
	Present	×	×	648	67.7
	Future tense	×	×	6	0.6

The two are almost the same, but due to the unique characteristics of Chinese, it is not possible to reflect tense differences in verbs.

In terms of the use of modal verbs, the comparison is as follows:

Table 53 Comparison of Modal Verbs Used in Chinese and English Translations of Domestic Museum Introductions

	Introductions of Domestic Museums in Chinese						
	Low		Medium		High		Sum
	might(may)	could(can)	will(would)	should	must	need	
Total	6	0	0	0	0	1	7
%	85.7	0	0	0	0	14.3	100
	English Translations of Domestic Museum Introductions						
	Low		Medium		High		Sum
	might(may)	could(can)	will(would)	should	must	need	
Total	0	16	2	0	0	0	18
%	0	88.9	11.1	0	0	0	100

From this, it can be seen that the use of modal verbs in both Chinese and English translations of museum introductions is not high. In Chinese texts, the most commonly used verbs are "能(够)" and "必须", while in English translations, they are "could (can)" and "will (would)".

(3) Theme System

By combining the previous thematic analysis of these two types of texts, it can be concluded that:

Table 54 Comparison of Theme System between Chinese and English Translations of Domestic Museum Introductions

	Introductions of Domestic Museums in Chinese		English Translations of Domestic Museum Introduction	
	Total	%	Total	%
Multiple Theme	68	6.5	70	10.0
Single Theme	981	93.5	628	90.0
Marked Theme	252	24.0	186	26.6
Unmarked Theme	797	76.0	512	73.4
Sum	1049	100	698	100

3) **Comparison of English Introductions of Foreign Museums and English Translations of Domestic Museums**

(1) **Transitivity System**

Table 55 Comparison of Process Types between Foreign Museum English Introductions and Translated Domestic Museum Introductions

	The Corpus of Translations of Foreign Museums		The Corpus of English Translations of Domestic Museums	
Process Type	总数	%	总数	%
Relational Process	626	39.0	358	43.8
Material Process	786	49.0	383	46.8
Mental Process	97	6.0	25	3.1
Behavioral Process	12	0.8	10	1.2
Verbal Process	21	1.3	4	0.5
Existential Process	63	3.9	38	4.6
Sum	1605	100	818	100

The differences are manifested in the following ways: firstly, in terms of total amount, the number of processes in English is twice that of the English translation of domestic museum introductions, which means that the length of foreign museum English introductions is much longer than that of English translations. Secondly, the proportion of various process types used in English, from high to low, is material (49), relational (39), mental (6), existential (3.9), verbal (1.3), and behavioral (0.8). Compared to foreign museum introductions, the case in the English translation of domestic museum introductions is material (46.8), relational (43.8), existential (4.6), mental (3.1), behavioral (1.2) and verbal (0.5), It can be seen that the proportion of relational processes used in the English translation of domestic museum introductions is much higher than that of foreign museum introductions.

（2）Mood System

Table 56 Comparison of Mood System between English Introduction of Foreign Museums and English Translations of Domestic Museum Introductions

		Introductions of Foreign Museums in English		Translated Introductions of Domestic Museums	
		Total	%	Total	%
The Number of Clauses	Sum	1752	100	958	100
Mood Type	Indicative	1740	99.3	958	100
	Imperative	12	0.7	0	0
	Interrogative	0	0	0	0
Subject	Destination	682	38.9	532	55.5
	Tourists	114	6.5	15	1.6
	Other Subjects	956	54.6	411	42.9
Tense	Past Tense	724	41.3	304	31.7
	Present Tense	996	56.8	648	67.7
	Future Tense	32	1.9	6	0.6

This is basically consistent with the situation of the aforementioned museum English introductions of foreign museums and Chinese introductions of domestic museums, that is, although the number of clauses in English translations of domestic museums is nearly half that of foreign museum English introductions, the proportion of mood types is similar. However, in terms of subject selection, the proportion of choosing tourists as the subject in English introductions of foreign museums is more than four times that of English translations of domestic museums.

(3) Modality System

The comparison between the two is as follows:

Table 57 Comparison of Modal Verbs in English Translations of Foreign Museums and English Translations of Domestic Museum Introductions

	English Introductions of Foreign Museums						
	Low	Medium		High			Sum
	might(may)	could(can)	will(would)	should	must	need	
Total	1	20	23	3	1	0	48
%	2.1	41.7	47.9	6.2	2.1	0	100

	English Translations of Domestic Museums						
	Low	Medium		High			Sum
	might(may)	could(can)	will(would)	should	must	need	
Total	0	16	2	0	0	0	18
%	0	88.9	11.1	0	0	0	100

In terms of modal verbs, although modal verbs are not commonly used in both corpora, compared to the English translation of domestic museum introductions, there are more types and a higher proportion of modal verbs used in foreign museum introductions. However, translated English texts have a particular preference for the use of "can (could)" and a higher proportion of them are used.

(4) Theme System

Through comparative analysis of two types of introductions, it can be concluded that:

Table 58 Comparison of Theme System between English Introduction of Foreign Museums and English Translation of Domestic Museum Introductions

	English Introductions of Foreign Museums		English Translations of Domestic Museums	
	Total	%	Total	%
Multiple Theme	184	13.3	70	10.0
Singe Theme	1196	86.7	628	90.0

Marked Theme	292	21.2	186	26.6
Unmarked Theme	1088	78.8	512	73.4
Sum	1380	100	698	100

It is found that regardless of the type of theme, the number of theme in translated texts is far less than that in English introductions of foreign museums, but the proportion is not much different. The root cause is that the length of foreign museum English introductions is nearly twice that of English translations of domestic museum introductions.

8.5 Assessment and Improvement of Translation Quality of Museum Introduction Discourses

Through the detailed comparison and analysis of the above two sections, it can be found that the English translation of museum introductions is basically the literal translation of their source texts—introductions of domestic museums in Chinese. Therefore, compared with English introductions foreign museums, there are significant differences in both structure and linguistic features. From the perspective of the smoothness, there are many problems.

8.5.1 Judgment and Improvement Suggestions on the Quality of the Original Translation from the Perspective of Schematic Structure

Next, Text 4 of English translations of Chinese museum introductions is taken as an example, and the schematic structure of foreign museum English introductions summarized in the previous section is used as a reference frame to conduct structural analysis, evaluation, and adjustment of the translated version, with the aim of improving the quality of such genre translations and their acceptance in the target language society.

The previous discussion indicates that generally speaking, a museum introduction consists of 10 elements, among which D (designation), HE (historical events), BI (building informaton), CEI (collections and exhibits introduction), EP (evaluation and position) are necessary elements, and the others are optional elements. Moreover, the order of these elements cannot be arbitrarily arranged.

For the convenience of discussion, the previous structural analysis of Text 4 is reviewed, namely:

(D) Shanghai Museum of Natural Sciences

(EP) The Shanghai Museum of Natural Sciences is one of the largest museums of natural sciences in China. (L)Located at downtown Shanghai, (BI)the museum features some British traditional style and covers an area of 12,880 square meters.

(CT) Prepared in November 1956, the Shanghai Museum of Natural Sciences opened the Division Museum of Animals to the public in 1960, and the Division Museum of Plants in 1984. The building for exhibition of samples covers a floor space of 3,053 square meters. The exhibition halls of the museum are situated in the Shanghai Botanic Garden and cover a total space of 4,726 square meters.

(CEI) The museum has a collection of 240,000 samples, including over 62,000 pieces of animal specimens, 135,000 plant specimens, 700 specimens of the Stone Age, and 1,700 specimens of minerals, which are of high value to research on natural evolvement.

The largest exhibit is a dinosaur skeleton of over four storeys high. There are also some rare species, which cannot be found elsewhere outside China, on display, such as a Yellow River mammoth, a giant salamander, a giant panda, and an alligator from the Yangtze River. Besides, the museum boasts more than 60,000 volumes of documents and books on scientific research.

(BI) The museum features four exhibition halls: the Hall of the History of the Ancient Animals, the Hall of History of Ancient Anthropology, the Hall of Animals and the Hall of Plants.

(CEI) The Hall of the History Ancient Animals houses fossil remains from the Paleozoic, Mesozoic and Cenozoic eras, forming a wordless chronicle of prehistoric life and displaying the evolvement of animals from aquicolous animals to terraneous animals, and from simple formation to complex one. Among the exhibits is a restored model of a Mamenxi dinosaur with the length of 22 meters, which is 140 million years old.

In the Hall of Ancient Anthropology is a huge collection of specimens, restored models and unearthed relics, which details the genesis and evolvement of human beings.

The Hall of Animals displays invertebrates, fishes, amphibious animals, reptiles, birds and mammals, many of which are on the national list of first-class and second-class protected animals. The Hall for Plants displays primitive alga, epiphyte, lichen and so on.

The famous Chinese mummies are exhibited in the Hall of the Mummies, such as a female mummy unearthed in Loulan of Xinjiang Uygur Autonomous Region.

(SA) In addition to permanent exhibitions, the museum often organizes other displays, such as Ancient Mummies of China, Rare Animals, Biologic Engineering, Chinese Special Animal - Elk and so on.

(AC) The museum has compiled a good many of books on animals, plants, human and astronomy such as *Research and Study* and *Nature and Human*.

The schematic structure of this text is:
D^EP^L^BI^CT^CEI^BI^CEI^SA^AC

That is to say, the structural features of the above-mentioned museum introduction text are as follows: pointing out the name and status of the museum clearly, then introducing the museum's location, building information, completed time, and overall introduce the museum's collections, mainly including animal and plant monographs and ore specimens, with a focus on introducing the main contents of each of the four exhibition halls. Finally, the ending section introduces the exhibition activities held and the books compiled, explaining that the museum has made significant academic contributions to natural sciences.

As shown in the previous analysis, the arrangement of the textual structure for museum introduction fully follows its corresponding source text - the structure of Chinese museum introduction, and follows suit step by step. For applied genres with strong vocative functions such as museum introductions, the main purpose of text production is to motivate and influence readers' inner feelings or external actions, exert the "power of words", and drive readers to "put into action" after reading the text. Therefore, when translating Chinese museum introductions into English, the aim is to attract readers from English speaking countries to come and visit. From the perspective of sales effectiveness, translation naturally takes into account the reading habits and aesthetic expectations of readers in the target language. Therefore, we must pay attention to the writing standards of this genre of text in the target language country, which means that we must have a clear understanding of the schematic structure and wording characteristics of the English museum introduction text. Therefore, when translating the Chinese museum introduction into English, we must strive to stand up to it and improve the smoothness and beauty of the translation in the eyes of readers in the target language country to realize the requirements of "expressiveness and elegance" according to traditional Chinese Translators Journal studies for measuring the essence of translation quality.

Based on corpus analysis in the previous article, we have summarized the schematic structure and linguistic features of English museum introductions. As mentioned earlier, structural characteristics of this genre and the differences between English and Chinese have been concluded. In terms of commonalities, firstly, D (designation), BI (building information), CEI (collections and exhibits introduction), and EP (evaluation and position) constitute essential basic elements in a museum introduction. Secondly, in terms of sequence, D always comes first, VG (visiting guide) always appears last, and HE can appear anywhere in the museum introduction. Therefore, when reconstructing the translated text, it is necessary to fully consider the above features.

On the other hand, as for differences, namely the structural differences between the two described earlier, they are:

Firstly, due to cultural differences between China and the West, the proportion of HE (historical events) in English museum introductions and Chinese museum introductions varies. The function of HE is to inform visitors of historical events during the establishment process of the museum, to increase their emotional understanding and leave a deep impression on them. In the introduction of English museums, HE is a necessary element, accounting for 75%; In Chinese, it becomes an optional element, accounting for 17.5%. There are significant differences between the two.

Secondly, L (location) and CT (completed time) are optional elements in the introduction of English museums, and their positions are relatively flexible, accounting for 47.5% and 40% respectively. In Chinese introductions, L and CT are necessary elements and must appear in pair. Although the positions can be interchanged, in most cases, L is located before CT, accounting for 95% and 90% respectively.

Thirdly, the main function of SA (social activities) and AC (academic contributions) is to inform visitors of which exhibits the museum has held, which social activities related to the economy, education and other fields it has participated in, and what publications or works it has published. However, there is no SA and AC in the introduction of foreign English museums, while in the introduction of domestic Chinese museums, SA and AC are optional structural elements, and their order is relatively fixed with VG. These three always appear in the last part of the text of this genre, accounting for 42.5% and 32.5% respectively.

Fourthly, the position of EP (evaluation and status) in English museum introductions is fixed, which always appears after D and before BI; As for the case in Chinese, EP can appear in any position and can be repeated.

Based on the above description of the structural features and similarities and differences of the Chinese and English museum introductions, as well as the requirement to strive to make the translated text be consistent with the target language in terms of structure, we can transform the structure of the original translation from:

D^EP^L^BI^CT^CEI^BI^CEI^SA^AC

to

D^L^EP^CT^CEI^BI^CEI^SA^AC

namely:

(D) Shanghai Museum of Natural Sciences

(L) Located at downtown Shanghai, (EP) the Shanghai Museum of Natural Sciences is one of the largest museums of natural sciences in China. (CT) Prepared in November 1956, the Shanghai Museum of Natural Sciences opened the Division Museum of Animals to the public in 1960, and the Division Museum of Plants in 1984. The building for exhibition of samples covers a floor space of 3,053 square meters. The exhibition halls of the museum are situated in the Shanghai Botanic Garden and cover a total space of 4,726 square meters.

(CEI) The museum has a collection of 240,000 samples, including over 62,000 pieces of animal specimens, 135,000 plant specimens, 700 specimens of the Stone Age, and 1,700 specimens of minerals, which are of high value to research on natural evolvement.

The largest exhibit is a dinosaur skeleton of over four storeys high. There are also some rare species, which cannot be found elsewhere outside China, on display, such as a Yellow River mammoth, a giant salamander, a giant panda, and an alligator from the Yangtze River. Besides, the museum boasts more than 60,000 volumes of documents and books on scientific research.

(BI) The museum features some British traditional style and covers an area of 12,880 square meters. The museum features four exhibition halls: the Hall of the History of the Ancient Animals, the Hall of History of Ancient Anthropology, the Hall of Animals and the Hall of Plants.

(CEI) The Hall of the History Ancient Animals houses fossil remains from the Paleozoic, Mesozoic and Cenozoic eras, forming a wordless chronicle of prehistoric life and displaying the evolvement of animals from aquicolous animals to terraneous animals, and from simple formation to complex one. Among the exhibits is a restored model of a Mamenxi dinosaur with the length of 22 meters, which is 140 million years old.

In the Hall of Ancient Anthropology is a huge collection of specimens, restored models and unearthed relics, which details the genesis and evolvement of human beings.

The Hall of Animals displays invertebrates, fishes, amphibious animals, reptiles, birds and mammals, many of which are on the national list of first-class and second-class protected animals. The Hall for Plants displays primitive alga, epiphyte, lichen and so on.

The famous Chinese mummies are exhibited in the Hall of the Mummies, such as a female mummy unearthed in Loulan of Xinjiang Uygur Autonomous Region.

（SA） In addition to permanent exhibitions, the museum often organizes other displays, such as Ancient Mummies of China, Rare Animals, Biologic Engineering, Chinese Special Animal - Elk and so on.

（AC） The museum has compiled a good many of books on animals, plants, human and astronomy such as *Research and Study* and *Nature and Human*.

That is to say, the museum's introduction structure is adjusted according to the commonalities and differences between Chinese and English texts of this genre, and its logical structure is as follows:

Firstly, give the designation (D) of the museum, followed by its location (L) and evaluation and position (EP). Then, point out the completed time (CT) of the museum, and provide an overall introduction to the museum's exhibits (CEI) and building information (BI). Then, introduce the main collections (CEI) of each of the four exhibition halls. In the concluding section, it is pointed out that the museum has organized social activities (SA) and compiled books, as well as made significant academic contributions (AC) to natural science research.

In this way, without adding or deleting the content of the source text (of course, if conditions permit, if the translator is able to obtain relevant information about the museum and to provide HE required for the structure of the English museum introduction in the translation, and align the language expression with the target language specification - detailed later, the translation effect will naturally be better), the modified translation has made structural adjustments to align with the target language compared to the original translation. To be more in line with the reading habits of readers in the target language, the translation naturally appears more"smooth".

In other words, the original translation is completely constrained by the inherent structure of the Chinese genre in terms of structure, without considering the structural aesthetics or norms of the English museum introductions, which naturally appears awkward and indecent in the eyes of readers of the target language. In this way, judging from the perspective of"smoothness" and"elegance", one of the two major parameters for measuring translation quality included in the previously constructed translation quality assessment model, the original translation quality needs to be improved.

8.5.2 Judgment and Improvement Suggestions on the Quality of the Original Translation from the Perspective of Representation Style

The translation should be in line with the norms and habits of the target language to the greatest extent possible, in order to achieve the expected reception effect in the target language society. It needs to be aligned with the corresponding generic texts in the target language at the structural level, and also needs to be similar to them in terms of style and linguistic characteristics.

Here, we also take the English translation of "Shanghai Museum of Natural Sciences" as an example to analyze its linguistic features; Then, based on the linguistic characteristics of foreign English museum introductions summarized in the previous section, criticism and adjustment is to be made to improve the quality of the translation.

As mentioned earlier, the linguistic characteristics of the text can be expanded from transitivity system, mood system and theme system, etc. Next, we will analyze the selected case from these three perspectives.

(1) Transitivity Analysis

The Shanghai Museum of Natural Sciences

(1) The Shanghai Museum of Natural Sciences **is** one of the largest museums of natural sciences in China. (2) Located at downtown Shanghai, the museum **features** some British traditional style and **covers** an area of 12,880 square meters.

(3) Prepared in November 1956, the Shanghai Museum of Natural Sciences **opened** the Division Museum of Animals to the public in 1960, and the Division Museum of Plants in 1984. (4) The building for exhibition of samples **covers** a floor space of 3,053 square meters. (5) The exhibition halls of the museum **are situated** in the Shanghai Botanic Garden and **cover** a total space of 4,726 square meters.

(6) The museum **has** a collection of 240,000 samples, including over 62,000 pieces of animal specimens, 135,000 plant specimens, 700 specimens of the Stone Age, and 1,700 specimens of minerals, which **are** of high value to research on natural evolvement.

(7) The largest exhibit **is** a dinosaur skeleton of over four storeys high. (8) There **are** also some rare species, which cannot **be found** elsewhere outside China, on display, such as a Yellow River mammoth, a giant salamander, a giant panda, and an alligator from the Yangtze River. (9) Besides, the museum **boasts** more than 60,000 volumes of documents

and books on scientific research.

(10) The museum **features** four exhibition halls: the Hall of the History of the Ancient Animals, the Hall of History of Ancient Anthropology, the Hall of Animals and the Hall of Plants.

(11) The Hall of the History Ancient Animals **houses** fossil remains from the Paleozoic, Mesozoic and Cenozoic eras, forming a wordless chronicle of prehistoric life and displaying the evolvement of animals from aquicolous animals to terraneous animals, and from simple formation to complex one. (12) Among the exhibits **is** a restored model of a Mamenxi dinosaur with the length of 22 meters, which **is** 140 million years old.

(13) In the Hall of Ancient Anthropology **is** a huge collection of specimens, restored models and unearthed relics, which **details** the genesis and evolvement of human beings.

(14) The Hall of Animals **displays** invertebrates, fishes, amphibious animals, reptiles, birds and mammals, many of which **are** on the national list of first-class and second-class protected animals. (15) The Hall for Plants **displays** primitive alga, epiphyte, lichen and so on.

(16) The famous Chinese mummies **are exhibited** in the Hall of the Mummies, such as a female mummy unearthed in Loulan of Xinjiang Uygur Autonomous Region.

(17) In addition to permanent exhibitions, the museum often **organizes** other displays, such as Ancient Mummies of China, Rare Animals, Biologic Engineering, Chinese Special Animal - Elk and so on.

(19) The museum **has compiled** a good many of books on animals, plants, human and astronomy such as Research and Study and Nature and Human.

Sentence No.	Process No.	Process Type	Verb Involved
(1)	1	Relational Process	is
(2)	2	Relational Process	features
	3	Relational Process	covers
(3)	4	Material Process	opened
(4)	5	Relational Process	covers
(5)	6	Relational Process	are situated
	7	Relational Process	cover
(6)	8	Relational Process	has
	9	Relational Process	are
(7)	10	Relational Process	is
(8)	11	Existential Process	are

	12	Material Process	be found
(9)	13	Relational Process	boasts
(10)	14	Relational Process	features
(11)	15	Relational Process	houses
(12)	16	Existential Process	is
	17	Relational Process	is
(13)	18	Existential Process	is
	19	Material Process	details
(14)	20	Material Process	displays
	21	Relational Process	are
(15)	22	Material Process	displays
(16)	23	Material Process	are exhibited
(17)	24	Material Process	organizes
(18)	25	Material Process	has compiled

The results are shown in the table below:

From the above table, it can be seen that there are 14 relational processes, 8 material processes and 3 existential processes in the text, no mental, behavioral and verbal processes at all. By analyzing the verbs involved in the process types and their frequency of use in the text, the results are as follows:

Verbs Involved in Process Types and Their Frequency of Use

Verbs Involved in Relational Process	Frequency of Use	Verbs Involved in Material Process	Frequency of Use	Verbs Involved in Existential Process	Frequency of Use
is	3	opened	1	are	1
features	2	be found	1	is	2
cover(s)	3	details	1		
are situated	1	displays	2		
has	1	are exhibited	1		
are	2	organizes	1		
boasts	1	has compiled	1		
houses	1				

Therefore, there are the following problems with the English translation of domestic museum introductions:

Firstly, the repetition rate of some verbs in related types of processes is relatively high, resulting in a singular use of verbs. For example, in existential processes, not only can "be" used, but also "arise", "retain", "happen", "stand", etc. However, only "be" appears in most English translations of Chinese museum introductions but no other similar words. From the perspective of translators, most of the translations are completed by English majors at home. Due to their lack of understanding of the characteristics of similar English genres and the lack of correction and refinement by professionals from English-speaking countries in this field, the translated version lacks the authentic flavor of similar English genres, making it not natural and smooth to read.

Secondly, if the analytical results of Text 4 are compared with the process types of foreign museum introductions summarized from corpus analysis, it is found that foreign museum introductions place more emphasis on describing mental processes, expressing emotions, cognition and vision of the museum, which can better communicate with visitors or readers spiritually and resonate with them. In contrast, the translated version is lacking in this respect.

(2) Mood analysis

Shanghai Museum of Natural Sciences

(1) [1] The Shanghai Museum of Natural Sciences is one of the largest museums of natural sciences in China. (2) Located at downtown Shanghai, [2] the museum features some British traditional style and [3] covers an area of 12,880 square meters.

(3) [4] Prepared in November 1956, [5] the Shanghai Museum of Natural Sciences opened the Division Museum of Animals to the public in 1960, [6]and the Division Museum of Plants in 1984. (4) [7] The building for exhibition of samples covers a floor space of 3,053 square meters. (5) [8] The exhibition halls of the museum are situated in the Shanghai Botanic Garden [9] and cover a total space of 4,726 square meters.

(6) [10] The museum has a collection of 240,000 samples, including over 62,000 pieces of animal specimens, 135,000 plant specimens, 700 specimens of the Stone Age, and 1,700 specimens of minerals, [11] which are of high value to research on natural evolvement.

(7) [12] The largest exhibit is a dinosaur skeleton of over four storeys high. (8) [13] There are also some rare species, [14] which cannot be found elsewhere outside China, on display, such as a Yellow River mammoth, a giant salamander, a giant panda, and an

alligator from the Yangtze River. (9) [15] Besides, the museum boasts more than 60,000 volumes of documents and books on scientific research.

(10) [16] The museum features four exhibition halls: the Hall of the History of the Ancient Animals, the Hall of History of Ancient Anthropology, the Hall of Animals and the Hall of Plants.

(11) [17] The Hall of the History Ancient Animals houses fossil remains from the Paleozoic, Mesozoic and Cenozoic eras, forming a wordless chronicle of prehistoric life and displaying the evolvement of animals from aquicolous animals to terraneous animals, and from simple formation to complex one. (12) [18] Among the exhibits is a restored model of a Mamenxi dinosaur with the length of 22 meters, [19] which is 140 million years old.

(13) [20] In the Hall of Ancient Anthropology is a huge collection of specimens, restored models and unearthed relics,[21] which details the genesis and evolution of human beings.

(14) [22] The Hall of Animals displays invertebrates, fishes, amphibious animals, reptiles, birds and mammals, [23] many of which are on the national list of first-class and second-class protected animals.(15) [24] The Hall for Plants displays primitive alga, epiphyte, lichen and so on.

(16) [25] The famous Chinese mummies are exhibited in the Hall of the Mummies, [26] such as a female mummy unearthed in Loulan of Xinjiang Uygur Autonomous Region.

(17) [27] In addition to permanent exhibitions, the museum often organizes other displays, such as Ancient Mummies of China, Rare Animals, Biologic Engineering, Chinese Special Animal - Elk and so on.

(18) [28] The museum has compiled a good many of books on animals, plants, human and astronomy such as *Research and Study* and *Nature and Human*.

The results are as follows:

Sentence No.	Clause No.	Subject	Infinite	Type of Mood
(1)	[1]	The Shanghai Museum of	is	Indicative
(2)	[2]	the museum	features	Indicative
	[3]	the museum	covers	Indicative
(3)	[4]	(the Shanghai Museum of Natural Sciences)	prepared	Indicative

		[5]	the Shanghai Museum of Natural Sciences	opened	Indicative
		[6]	(the Shanghai Museum of Natural Sciences)	(opened)	Indicative
(4)		[7]	The building for exhibition of samples	covers	Indicative
(5)		[8]	The exhibition halls of the museum	are	Indicative
		[9]	(The exhibition halls of the museum)	cover	Indicative
(6)		[10]	The museum	has	Indicative
		[11]	which	are	Indicative
(7)		[12]	The largest exhibit	is	Indicative
(8)		[13]	There	are	Indicative
		[14]	which	be found	Indicative
(9)		[15]	the museum	boasts	Indicative
(10)		[16]	the museum	features	Indicative
(11)		[17]	The Hall of the History Ancient Animals	houses	Indicative
(12)		[18]	Among the exhibits	is	Indicative
		[19]	which	is	Indicative
(13)		[20]	In the Hall of Ancient Anthropology	is	Indicative
		[21]	which	details	Indicative
(14)		[22]	The Hall of Animals	displays	Indicative
		[23]	many of which	are	Indicative
(15)		[24]	The Hall for Plants	displays	Indicative
(16)		[25]	The famous Chinese mummies	are	Indicative
		[26]	a female mummy	unearthed	Indicative
(17)		[27]	the museum	organizes	Indicative
(18)		[28]	The museum	has	Indicative

The text consists of 28 clauses, all of which are in indicative mood. By analyzing the use of subjects in the text, the following table is obtained:

Subject	Corresponding frequency
The Shanghai Museum of Natural Sciences (the museum)	11
The building for exhibition of samples	1
The exhibition halls of the museum	2
which	4
The largest exhibit	1
There	1
The Hall of the History Ancient Animals	1
Among the exhibits	1
In the Hall of Ancient Anthropology	1
The Hall of Animals	1
many of which	1
The Hall for Plants	1
The famous Chinese mummies	1
a female mummy	1

By comparing the analytical results with the analysis from the corpus of foreign museum introductions, it is found that the problems with the translated versions of domestic museum introductions are:

Among the 28 clauses that make up the text, the subject of 11 clauses is the museum; The subject of 6 clauses is the exhibition hall xx; The subjects of remaining 11 clauses are other matters. On the one hand, the introduction of museums is aimed at providing necessary information to readers or visitors; On the other hand, it is to attract the interest of readers or visitors, which is the goal pursued by genres like museum introduction. Tourists are often used as the subject in introductions o foreign museums in English to narrow the distance with tourists and to attract them to visit. The English translation of domestic museum introductions needs to be strengthened in this regard. In addition, the subject in the English translations of domestic museums is mostly a noun, and the connection between sentences is not close enough, making the writing dull and less authentic.

In addition, according to the previous analysis, although modal verbs are not very much often used in the two corpora, there are indeed more modal verbs in the corpus of foreign museum introductions, that is why introductions of foreign museums read more gently. The English translation of domestic museums needs to be improved in this regard.

(3) Thematic analysis

Shanghai Museum of Natural Sciences

(1) **[1] The Shanghai Museum of Natural Sciences** is one of the largest museums of natural sciences in China. (2) **[2] Located at downtown Shanghai**, the museum features some British traditional style **[3] and** covers an area of 12,880 square meters.

(3) **[4] Prepared in November 1956**, the Shanghai Museum of Natural Sciences opened the Division Museum of Animals to the public in 1960, and the Division Museum of Plants in 1984. (4) **[5] The building for exhibition of samples** covers a floor space of 3,053 square meters. (5) **[6] The exhibition halls of the museum** are situated in the Shanghai Botanic Garden **[7] and** cover a total space of 4,726 square meters.

(6) **[8] The museum** has a collection of 240,000 samples, including over 62,000 pieces of animal specimens, 135,000 plant specimens, 700 specimens of the Stone Age, and 1,700 specimens of minerals, **[9] which** are of high value to research on natural evolvement.

(7) **[10] The largest exhibit** is a dinosaur skeleton of over four storeys high. (8) **[11] There** are also some rare species, **[12] which** cannot be found elsewhere outside China, on display, such as a Yellow River mammoth, a giant salamander, a giant panda, and an alligator from the Yangtze River. (9) **[13] Besides, the museum** boasts more than 60,000 volumes of documents and books on scientific research.

(10) **[14] The museum** features four exhibition halls: the Hall of the History of the Ancient Animals, the Hall of History of Ancient Anthropology, the Hall of Animals and the Hall of Plants.

(11) **[15] The Hall of the History Ancient Animals** houses fossil remains from the Paleozoic, Mesozoic and Cenozoic eras, forming a wordless chronicle of prehistoric life and displaying the evolvement of animals from aquicolous animals to terraneous animals, and from simple formation to complex one. (12) **[16] Among the exhibits** is a restored model of a Mamenxi dinosaur with the length of 22 meters, **[17] which** is 140 million years old.

(13) **[18] In the Hall of Ancient Anthropology** is a huge collection of specimens, restored models and unearthed relics, **[19] which** details the genesis and evolvement of human beings.

(14) **[20] The Hall of Animals** displays invertebrates, fishes, amphibious animals, reptiles, birds and mammals, **[21] many of which** are on the national list of first-class and second-class protected animals. (15) **[22] The Hall for Plants** displays primitive alga, epiphyte, lichen and so on.

(16) **[23] The famous Chinese mummies** are exhibited in the Hall of the Mummies, such as a female mummy unearthed in Loulan of Xinjiang Uygur Autonomous Region.

(17) **[24] In addition to permanent exhibitions**, the museum often organizes other displays, such as Ancient Mummies of China, Rare Animals, Biologic Engineering, Chinese Special Animal - Elk and so on.

(18) **[25] The museum** has compiled a good many of books on animals, plants, human and astronomy such as *Research and Study* and *Nature and Human*.

The thematic analysis in the above text is expressed as follows:

Sentence No.	Clause No.	Type of Theme			Marked Theme	Unmarked Theme
		Textual Theme	Interpersonal Theme	Experiential Theme		
(1)	[1]			The Shanghai Museum of Natural Sciences		√
(2)	[2]			Located at downtown Shanghai	√	
	[3]	and				√
(3)	[4]			Prepared in November 1956	√	
(4)	[5]			The building for exhibition of samples		√
(5)	[6]			The exhibition halls of the museum		√
	[7]	and				√
(6)	[8]			The museum		√
	[9]			which		√
(7)	[10]			The largest exhibit		√

(8)	[11]			There		√
	[12]			which		√
(9)	[13]	Besides		the museum		√
(10)	[14]			The museum		√
(11)	[15]			The Hall of the History Ancient Animals		√
(12)	[16]			Among the exhibits	√	
	[17]			which		√
(13)	[18]			In the Hall of Ancient Anthropology	√	
	[19]			which		√
(14)	[20]			The Hall of Animals		√
	[21]			many of which		√
(15)	[22]			The Hall for Plants		√
(16)	[23]			The famous Chinese mummies		√
(17)	[24]			In addition to permanent exhibitions	√	
(18)	[25]			The museum		√

From the above table, it can be seen that there are in total of 25 thematic combinations in Text 4, of which only 1 is multiple theme and 5 are marked themes. By comparing the analytical results of Text 4 with the previous analysis of the corpus of foreign museum English introductions, it is found that the proportion of multiple theme and marked theme used in foreign museum introductions is higher than that in the translated version, indicating that the translated version is influenced by the Chinese museum introductions, which contains more small and simple clauses and more experiential themes. The use of textual theme and interpersonal theme is not only limited in number, but also limited to a few fixed places, resulting in strong Chinese flavor.

Based on the above comparative analysis, we believe that the following improvements can be made to the translation:

Firstly, the use of verbs related to the same process type should be minimized and the proportion of psychological process can be moderately increased.

Secondly, interpersonal meaning should be highlighted, interaction with readers or visitors should be emphasized, modal verbs and modal adjuncts should be increased; Types of mood other than indicative can be moderately added, such as interrogative and imperative mood.

Thirdly, the types of subject should be diversified, the number of textual themes and interpersonal themes should be increased, more clause complexes can be increased and the number of simple sentences can be reduced.

The following are our modifications to the translation based on this. Italics are used for modifications.

Shanghai Museum of Natural Sciences

(1) [1] The Shanghai Museum of Natural Sciences is one of the largest museums of natural sciences in China. (2) [2] Located at downtown Shanghai, the museum features some British traditional style [3] and covers an area of 12,880 square meters.

(3) [4] Prepared in November 1956, the Shanghai Museum of Natural Sciences opened the Division Museum of Animals to the public in 1960, and the Division Museum of Plants in 1984. (4) *While the building for exhibition of samples takes up* a floor space of 3,053 square meters, [5] *the exhibition halls of the museum, situated in the Shanghai Botanic Garden, cover a total space of 4,726 square meters.*

(5) *Incredibly, there are collected in the museum as many as* 240,000 samples, including over 62,000 pieces of animal specimens, 135,000 plant specimens, 700 specimens of the Stone Age, and 1,700 specimens of minerals, [6] which are of high value to research on natural evolvement.

(7) *What is the the largest exhibit in the museum? (8) It is a dinosaur skeleton of over four storeys high.* (9) There are also some rare species, [10] which cannot be found elsewhere outside China, on display, such as a Yellow River mammoth, a giant salamander, a giant panda, and an alligator from the Yangtze River. (10) *Besides, more than 60,000 volumes of documents and books on scientific research kept herein will definitely challenge the visitors' imagination.*

(11) The museum features four exhibition halls: the Hall of the History of the Ancient Animals, the Hall of History of Ancient Anthropology, the Hall of Animals and the Hall of Plants.

(12) The Hall of the History Ancient Animals houses fossil remains from the Paleozoic, Mesozoic and Cenozoic eras, forming a wordless chronicle of prehistoric life and displaying the evolvement of animals from aquicolous animals to terraneous animals, and from simple formation to complex one. (13) Among the exhibits **stands** a restored model of a Mamenxi dinosaur with the length of 22 meters and **over** 140 million years old.

(14) In the Hall of Ancient Anthropology is a huge collection of specimens, restored models and unearthed relics, **detailing** the genesis and evolvement of human beings.

(15) **Displayed in the Hall of Animals is** invertebrates, fishes, amphibious animals, reptiles, birds and mammals, [16] many of which are on the national list of first-class and second-class protected animals. (16) **In contrast,** primitive alga, epiphyte, lichen and so on **are shown** in the Hall for Plants

(17) The famous Chinese mummies, **such as a female mummy unearthed in Loulan of Xinjiang Uygur Autonomous Region**, are exhibited in the Hall of the Mummies

(18) In addition to permanent exhibitions, **other displays are often organized,** such as Ancient Mummies of China, Rare Animals, Biologic Engineering, Chinese Special Animal - Elk and so on.

(19) The museum has compiled a good many of books on animals, plants, human and astronomy such as *Research and Study* and *Nature and Human*.

The original translation "(4) [5] The building for exhibition of samples covers a floor space of 3,053 square meters." and "(5) [6] The exhibition halls of the museum are situated in the Shanghai Botanic Garden [7] and cover a total space of 4,726 square meters." describe the exhibition of samples and the area of exhibition halls in the museum, both of which belong to the basic introduction of the museum. It is obvious though that the connotations of these two are different, forming a comparative relationship. However, the original translation is simply juxtaposed and cannot reflect this deep logic and the connection is loose. The modified version integrate them two. At the same time, to avoid the repetition of process verbs, "cover" of the second clause in the compound sentence is changed to "take" , namely: "While the building for exhibition of samples takes up a floor space of 3,053 square meters, the exhibition halls of the museum, situated in the Shanghai Botanic Garden, cover a total space of 4,726 square meters."

The original translation"(6) [8] The museum has a collection of 240,000 samples, including over 62,000 pieces of animal specimens, 135,000 plant specimens, 700 specimens of the Stone Age, and 1,700 specimens of minerals, [9] which are of high value to research on natural evolution. "is modified to(6) Incredibly, there are collected in the museum as many as 240,000 samples, including over 62,000 pieces of animal specimens, 135,000 plant specimens, 700 specimens of the Stone Age, and 1,700 specimens of minerals, which are of high value to research on natural environment.

On the one hand, "The museum has a collection of 240000 samples" belongs to typical Chinese English, which is not authentic and needs to be modified; On the other hand, it is necessary to minimize the number of theme type "museum" in the translated version - the original theme type is monotonous and the sentence structure is rigid. In addition, the use of the modal adjunct "incredibly" can not only facilitate interaction with readers, but also enrich the theme types and structure of the translated text.

The original translation "(7) [10] The largest exhibit is a dinosaur skeleton of over four floors high. (8) [11] There are also some rare species, [12] which cannot be found elsewhere outside China, on display,such as a Yellow River mammoth, a giant salamander, a giant panda, and an alligator from the Yangtze River. (9)[13]Besides, the museum boasts more than 60,000 volumes of documents and books on scientific research." is modified to "(7)[10]What is the the largest exhibit in the museum？ It is a dinosaur skeleton of over four storeys high. (8) [11] There are also some rare species, [12] which cannot be found elsewhere outside China, on display, such as a Yellow River mammoth, a giant salamander, a giant panda, and an alligator from the Yangtze River. (9) [13] Besides, more than 60,000 volumes of documents and books on scientific research kept herein will definitely challenge the visitors'imagination (10)".

The original translation is all in indicative mood. By appropriately using interrogative mood, the text structure is enriched and interaction with readers is strengthened, which to some extent compensates for the lack of attention to interpersonal meaning in the original translation. "The museum boasts more than 60,000 volumes" is revised to be "more than 60,000 volumes of documents and books on scientific research kept herein will definitely challenge the visitors' imagination", this not only corrects the monotonous use of the "museum+V" sentence structure in the original translation, but also highlights interpersonal meaning and strengthens the interaction between museums and readers through the use of modal words "will", "defense", and the mental process verb "challenge".

The original translation "Among the exhibits is a restored model of a Mamenxi dinosaur with the length of 22 meters，[17] which is 140 million years old." is revised to be "Among the exhibits stands a restored model of a Mamenxi dinosaur with the length of 22 meters and over 140 million years old." The reason for such a revision is the unitary use of relational process verb 'be' in the original translation and the excessive use of a non restrictive attributive clause'which is'sentence structure.

Similarly, compressing the clause'which details the genesis and evolvement of human beings'into'detailing'phrase is just out of such a consideration.

In the original translation" [20] The Hall of Animals displays invertebrates, fishes, amphibious animals, reptiles, birds and mammals, [21] many of which are on the national list of first-class and second-class protected animals. (15) [22] The Hall for Plants displays primitive alga, epiphyte, lichen and so on.", the monotonous use of SV structure and the juxtaposition of "The Hall of Animals display" and "The Hall for Plants displays" result in monotonous sentence structure, repetitive verbs, unclear internal logical relationships and cohesive expressions between sentences. It reads very much Chinglish. It is revised to be "Displayed in The Hall of Animals is invertebrates, fishes, amphibious animals, reptiles, birds and mammals, many of which are on the national list of first-class and second-class protected animals. In contrast, primitive alga, epiphyte, lichen and so on are shown in the Hall for Plants." In this way, through sentence structure adjustment, the use of the conjunction'In contrast', and the replacement of'show'for'display', not only can overcome the above shortcomings, but also the writing tends to be more consistent with similar English genres.

"(16) [23] The famous Chinese mummies are exhibited in the Hall of the Mummies, such as a female mummy unearthed in Loulan of Xinjiang Uygur Autonomous Region." is revised to be "The famous Chinese mummies, such as a female mummy unearthed in Loulan of Xinjiang Uygur Autonomous Region, are exhibited in the Hall of the Mummies." That is because "The famous Chinese mummies" and "such as a female mummy unearthed in Loulan of Xinjiang Uygur Autonomous Regionare exhibited in the Hall of the Mummies" are in the same position, and the original translation has separated this and weakened the relationship between the two; On the contrary, the revised translation highlights "The famous Chinese mummies—a female mummy unearthed in Loulan of Xinjiang Uygur Autonomous Region".

"(17) [24] In addition to permanent exhibitions, the museum often organizes other displays, such as Ancient Mummies of China, Rare Animals, Biologic Engineering, Chinese Special Animal - Elk and so on." is revised to be "In addition to permanent exhibitions, other displays are also often organized, such as Ancient Mummies of China, Rare Animals, Biologic Engineering, Chinese Special Animal - Elk and so on." On the one hand, it is necessary to avoid the monotonous "the museum+V" structure in the original translation, and at the same time, the subject "other displays" and the "permanent exhibitions" in the initial phrase "In addition to permanent exhibitions" refer to different languages, with a close and natural connection.

After evaluating and revising the quality of the original translation from the perspectives of schematic structure and presentation style, we will integrate this together. However, during the integration process, it is found that there are two moves in the original translation regarding the building information (BI), located at different positions in the text, namely: (**BI**) the museum features some British traditional style and covers an area of 12,880 square meters. (**BI**) The museum features four exhibition halls: the Hall of the History of the Ancient Animals, the Hall of History of Ancient Anthropology, the Hall of Animals and the Hall of Plants. So, from the perspective of the schematic structure, we have made a decision to "integrate similar items" and combine them into one. But from the perspective of style, the sentence structure in this move is the same SV structure: the museum features, which is very monotonous and dull. Therefore, after integrating them, the two sentences are revised to be:

The museum, with an area of 12,880 square meters and characteristic of some British traditional style, features four exhibition halls: the Hall of the History of the Ancient Animals, the Hall of History of Ancient Anthropology, the Hall of Animals and the Hall of Plants.

In this way, we ultimately come up with the following revised translation.

(**D**) Shanghai Museum of Natural Sciences

(**L**) Located at downtown Shanghai, (**EP**) the Shanghai Museum of Natural Sciences is one of the largest museums of natural sciences in China. (**CT**) Prepared in November 1956, the Shanghai Museum of Natural Sciences opened the Division Museum of Animals to the public in 1960, and the Division Museum of Plants in 1984. While the building for exhibition of samples takes up a floor space of 3,053 square meters. the exhibition halls of the museum, situated in the Shanghai Botanic Garden, cover a total space of 4,726 square meters.The building for exhibition of samples covers a floor space of 3,053 square meters. The exhibition halls of the museum are situated in the Shanghai Botanic Garden and cover a total space of 4,726 square meters.

(**CEI**) Incredibly, there are collected in the museum as many as 240,000 samples, including over 62,000 pieces of animal specimens, 135,000 plant specimens, 700 specimens of the Stone Age, and 1,700 specimens of minerals, which are of high value to research on natural evolvement.

The museum has a collection of 240,000 samples, including over 62,000 pieces of animal specimens, 135,000 plant specimens, 700 specimens of the Stone Age, and 1,700 specimens of minerals, which are of high value to research on natural evolvement.

What is the the largest exhibit in the museum? It is a dinosaur skeleton of over four storeys high. There are also some rare species, which cannot be found elsewhere outside China, on display, such as a Yellow River mammoth, a giant salamander, a giant panda, and an alligator from the Yangtze River. Besides, more than 60,000 volumes of documents and books on scientific research kept herein will definitely challenge the visitors' imagination

The largest exhibit is a dinosaur skeleton of over four storeys high. There are also some rare species, which cannot be found elsewhere outside China, on display, such as a Yellow River mammoth, a giant salamander, a giant panda, and an alligator from the Yangtze River. Besides, the museum boasts more than 60,000 volumes of documents and books on scientific research.

（BI）The museum, with an area of 12,880 square meters and characteristic of some British traditional style, features four exhibition halls: the Hall of the History of the Ancient Animals, the Hall of History of Ancient Anthropology, the Hall of Animals and the Hall of Plants.

（CEI）The Hall of the History Ancient Animals houses fossil remains from the Paleozoic, Mesozoic and Cenozoic eras, forming a wordless chronicle of prehistoric life and displaying the evolvement of animals from aquicolous animals to terraneous animals, and from simple formation to complex one. Among the exhibits stands a restored model of a Mamenxi dinosaur with the length of 22 meters and over 140 million years old.

In the Hall of Ancient Anthropology is a huge collection of specimens, restored models and unearthed relics, detailing the genesis and evolvement of human beings.

Displayed in the Hall of Animals is invertebrates, fishes, amphibious animals, reptiles, birds and mammals, many of which are on the national list of first-class and second-class protected animals. In contrast, primitive alga, epiphyte, lichen and so on are shown in the Hall for Plants. The Hall of Animals displays invertebrates, fishes, amphibious animals, reptiles, birds and mammals, many of which are on the national list of first-class and second-class protected animals. The Hall for Plants displays primitive alga, epiphyte, lichen and so on.

The famous Chinese mummies, such as a female mummy unearthed in Loulan of Xinjiang Uygur Autonomous Region, are exhibited in the Hall of the Mummies.

(SA) In addition to permanent exhibitions, other displays are also often organized, such as Ancient Mummies of China, Rare Animals, Biologic Engineering, Chinese Special Animal - Elk and so on.

(AC) The museum has compiled a good many of books on animals, plants, human and astronomy such as *Research and Study* and *Nature and Human*.

8.5.3 Some Thoughts

So far, we have evaluated the quality of the original translation from the perspectives of schematic structure and presentation style, and proposed modification suggestions to address the shortcomings. In this process, we further realize that the schematic structure and presentation style of a discourse are interrelated and mutually constrained; The transitivity, mood, and theme in the presentation style are also interrelated and mutually constrained. This determines that if we want to propose practical and feasible improvement suggestions for the quality of a given text, we often need to comprehensively balance and grasp both the schematic structure and the presentation style, as well as the internal composition of the presentation style.

There is a hierarchical relationship between the schematic structure and the presentation style. The relationship between this level is "embodiment". The schematic structure reflects the entire discourse, while the style reflects clauses. So, when planning the layout of a discourse, we often consider the schematic structure of the discourse first, and then fill the discourse perfectly with appropriate presentation styles. Therefore, when determining the quality of the English translation of domestic museum introductions, we need to determine at the macro level of textual structure whether it converges with the GSP model of similar foreign genres. If there are significant differences, the vocative function played by such genres will be difficult to fully exert in the target language, and the translation effect is not satisfactory. Therefore, from the perspective of the relationship between validity and reliability of the translation (Si, 2009)[1], the quality of the translation is difficult to be recognized.

Due to the fact that the structure of a discourse is reflected by the style of presentation, which itself consists of transitivity system, mood (including modality) system, and theme system, it is naturally necessary to explore into the various sentences and clauses that make up the text from this dimension when determining the quality of a

---

[1] Si Xianzhu. "On the Validity and Reliability of Translation" [J]. *Chinese Translators Journal*, 2009 (3): 60-63.

translation. From the perspectives of transitivity, mood, and theme, it is necessary to determine whether they are similar to the linguistic features of similar genres in the target language, If there is a significant deviation, then the appearance of the translated text will inevitably appear strange, stiff, that is, not authentic and natural. From the perspective of "smoothness" and "elegance" in translation standards, the quality is also not satisfactory. Similarly, from the perspective of reliability and validity, the vocative function of this genre is difficult to fully exert in the target language. Therefore, in order to improve the quality of the translation, it is necessary to follow the linguistic features of similar genres of the target language and make a convergence improvement towards the linguistic features of the target language in the translation. Meanwhile, considering that the participants in the transitivity system are often the subject of the mood system and the theme in the thematic system, the process in the transitivity system is a part of the finite element in the mood system and rheme in the mood system; The circumstance in the transitivity system is a complement or modifier in the mood system, and may also be an experiential, interpersonal, or textual theme in the theme system. Therefore, when making revisions to a translation, it is necessary to coordinate the characteristics and connections of the transitivity system, mood system, and theme system, so that the translation can achieve authentic expression similar to English genres in terms of style, to be "faithful and smooth".

Reference:

[1] Si Xianzhu. "On the Validity and Reliability of Translation" [J]. *Chinese Translators Journal*, 2009 (3): 60-63.

Chapter 9 Conclusion

This chapter, as a conclusion, summarizes the achievements and shortcomings of this study based on a brief analysis of the existing models of translation quality assessment from the perspective of Systemic Functional Linguistics.

The title of this project is "Research on Translation Quality Assessment Model of Applied Generic Discourse", which is the development and improvement of the original research "Construction of Translation Quality Assessment Model - Functional Linguistic Perspective". The aim is to enrich the system of translation quality assessment models, not only to further research on translation quality assessment models, but also to continue translation research from the perspective of Systemic Functional Linguistics.

Since the introduction of linguistics, the study of translation quality assessment model has begun to break free from the characteristics and limitations of casual and impressionistic comments that were previously based on translation principles and translation standards, and has gained systematic, operational, and objective qualities. However, deficiencies still exist. For example, in the face of a vast amount of translation practices for various types and genres of texts, there is no general assessment model that can be universally applied, which can provide scientific and comprehensive quality assessment for a wide range of translated texts. This requires us to explore and establish a more targeted and practical assessment model.

The main achievement of using Systemic Functional Linguistics as the theoretical guidance for the study of translation quality evaluation models is that they have established a relatively complete framework, which is systematic. The existing problems are that, in addition to the obvious lack of detailed research on different genres and insufficient empirical research, the biggest problem is the insufficient attention to the aesthetics or artistry of translated texts. From the two-dimensional perspective of "faithfulness" and "smoothness" in measuring translation quality standards, the existing model fully focuses on whether the translated text is "equivalent" and "faithful" to the source text in terms of ideational and interpersonal meanings. However, it is vague about whether the translated text itself is "smooth" and "beautiful", making it difficult to use the existing model to assess the "smoothnes", "expressiveness, and elegance" that belong to the aesthetic and artistic categories of the translated text.

In view of this, this study discusses the two-stage theory of translation quality assessment based on analyzing the shortcomings of the original model and elaborating on the two-dimensional standards of translation quality. In the first stage, the assessment focuses on the function and significance of the translated work relative to the original work is related to "faithfulness" and "equivalence"; In the second stage, the assessment of whether the language of the translated work itself is smooth and elegant, focusing on "expressiveness and elegance".

The original model, as mentioned earlier, focuses on whether and to what extent the translated text is "equivalent" and "faithful" in terms of ideational and interpersonal meaning to the source text, which can be inherited However, it lacks judgment on whether the translation is smooth and beautiful. Therefore, the new model aims to address this deficiency by adding parameters to assess whether the translated text is smooth and beautiful. Thus, in Chapter 6 of this book, from the perspective of generic analysis, the schematic structure and representation style of the genre are identified as the parameters that determine whether a translation is smooth and elegant.

As mentioned above, what the newly established model has inherited the aspect of the original one that determines whether the quality of the translation is "faithful" to the source text, which has been empirically tested during the construction of the original model (Si, 2007)[1]. Although the empirical evidence is still insufficient, the parameter for assessing the smoothness of the translation—whether the generic analysis path is actually feasible—has not been tested yet. It remains a product of theoretical discussions and can only be considered a hypothetical model at best. To transform this hypothesis into a viable model, practical testing is necessary. Therefore, the second part of this book conducts empirical research on the second stage of the aforementioned model, focusing on how to use generic analytical tools to improve the translation quality of generic discourse. Specifically, it examines the acceptability and appropriateness of the translated text in the target language, which aligns with the traditional translation theory on "smoothness and elegance". To effectively use generic analysis to assess whether a translated text of a given genre is 'elegant', the prerequisite is to have a clear understanding of the schematic structure and stylistic features of the similar genre in the target language. Thus, the main content of Chapters 6, 7, and 8, discusses how to construct a corpus to understand the aforementioned characteristics of several applied genres, it also aims, to grasp the structure and linguistic features of the translated and target language texts involved in

---

[1] Si Xianzhu. *Functional Linguistics and Translation Studies - Construction of Translation Quality Assessment Model*[M]. Peking University Press, 2007:141-185.

translation through textual analysis of the corpus, providing a basis for determining whether the translation is "smooth and beautiful" and how to modify and improve it.

Based on this foundation, we have completed the assessment of the quality of English translation texts for three types of applied genres — corporate profiles, sports news, museum introductions — and discussed how to revise and improve them. We have tested and proven that choosing the schematic structure and presentation style to determine whether the translation is smooth and elegant is effective as a parameter.

9.1 Research Innovation

Firstly, the biggest innovation of this study is the construction of a translation quality assessment model that can evaluate translation quality from the dimensions of "faithfulness" and "smoothness" in measuring translation quality, improving the serious deficiency of the original model in assessing whether the translation is "smooth". This not only makes up for the shortcomings of the original model, but is also the latest progress made in the research of translation quality assessment model at home and abroad so far. According to the investigation of existing translation quality assessment studies in Chapter 2, the existing translation quality assessment models at home and abroad have seriously insufficient or missing attention to the "smoothness" aspect of the translation.

Secondly, in the face of various types and genres of text translation practices, since there is no universally applicable assessment model, it requires us to explore and establish a more targeted and operational assessment model. This study is based on Systemic Functional Linguistics and constructs a translation quality assessment model for applied generic discourses-based generic analysis, enriching the theoretical system of translation assessment and better serving translation practice.

Thirdly, another innovation of this study is that compared to the original model, the newly established assessment model not only compensates for the shortcomings of the original model in evaluating the smoothness and elegance of the translation, but also improves the feasibility of the model.By removing the so-called "positive deviation" from the original model, "the second step at the macro level, from the perspective of form, function, and situational interaction and from aspects of reflecting characteristics, social and cultural environment of the translation of the target language, is to stand at the height of the entire discourse, to re-examine the various" deviation "cases discovered and described at the micro level mentioned above, and exclude those " deviation "cases that have not caused harm to the quality of the translation from the macro perspective (Si,

2007)[1]. " In terms of procedure, what needs to be corrected is the phenomenon that the equivalence between the translation and the source text is at the micro level such as the function/meaning of clauses, but the main function of the discourse is considered to be opposite to the source text; In terms of parameters, it is necessary to add 'negative equivalence', that is, the judgment of 'small equivalence, large inequivalence'(Si, 2008)[2] or 'false equivalence' as mentioned earlier[3], which lacks feasibility. As for how to determine the translation phenomenon of "deviation" referred to in the above evaluation steps and parameters in actual assessment practice, the tools provided by the original model are either abstract— "from the perspective of reflecting characteristics, social and cultural environment of the target language , and other aspects of the translation procedure" , or are at a total loss— "It' s not easy to judge, the factors involved are very complex" (Si, 2007)[4]. The new model provides practical and feasible means—by constructing similar parallel corpora, identifying textual structures and linguistic features of target language, and making judgments on the aforementioned situations in translation, the quality of translation is thereby assessed.

Fourthly, the assessment procedure of the original model has been optimized, and inaccuracies in expression have been corrected. In terms of the assessment procedure, not only has the two-stage theory been proposed and assessment parameters added to determine whether the translation is "smooth ", but it is also reflected in the optimization of the assessment procedure for the original model, which aims to evaluate whether the translation is "faithful" to the source text in terms of meaning - because the explanation of the language framework and its situational, functional, and formal relations of the original model is basically limited to the situational context, that is, the discussion of the equivalence between the translation and the expression of the original meaning at the register level. It is by every means necessary, but it ignores the cultural context, that is, the equivalence and appropriateness of the translated text relative to the source text at the generic level. According to our research, genre is an independent symbolic layer that transcends register and language. The three metafunctions in systemic functional grammar are the organizational levels of language, while the three variables of register are the organizational levels of situational context. The three variables of register closely

---

[1] Si Xianzhu. *Functional Linguistics and Translation Studies - Construction of Translation Quality Assessment Model* [M]. Peking University Press, 2007:137.
[2] Si Xianzhu. "Further Study on the Translation Quality Assessment Model: A Functional Linguistic Perspective" [J]. *Chinese Translators Journal*, 2008 (2): 59.
[3] Si Xianzhu. *Functional Linguistics and Translation Studies - Construction of Translation Quality Assessment Model* [M]. Peking University Press, 2007:188.
[4] Ibid, 174.

correspond to the three metafunctions, namely the ideational function corresponds to the field, the interpersonal function corresponds to the tenor, and the textual function corresponds to the mode. However, none of the metafunctions can fully capture the intention of a particular discourse. Genres have intentions, but cannot generate a one-to-one correspondence with metafunctions. They focus on the overall effects of the three variables of register. Meaning that the implementation of genres is spread among the three major meta functions. So, from the perspective of translation, if the translated work is not equivalent or similar to the original work in terms of genre, its quality cannot be satisfying. Therefore, from the perspective of improving the original model and enhancing its feasibility, it is necessary to change the expression of "situational, functional, and formal analysis at the micro clause level" to "register analysis", and "situational, functional, and formal analysis at macro level" to "genre analysis". This is not only simple and easy to understand, but more importantly, the "generic analysis" section effectively implements the third step in the first stage of assessment, which is to make corrections to the meaning deviation found at the micro level in the second step from the perspective of the influence of genre on meaning construction through register. As for the correction of the inaccuracy in the expression of the original model, it refers to the modification of the "negative equivalence" or "false equivalence" in the parameters of the original model that reflects the phenomenon of "micro equivalence, macro inequivalence" to "mechanical equivalence, stiff and rough", because "equivalence" mainly refers to the faithfulness of the translation relative to the source text at the semantic and functional levels, which is the traditional translation standards of "faithfulness, expressiveness, and eleganc". However, the phenomenon of "false equivalence" referred to in the original evaluation model involves the issue of whether the meaning carried by the source text is sufficiently and appropriately expressed in the translation, while it actually refers to being confined to the structure of the source text with a strong translation tone, which results in little focus on "faithfulness" but more on "expressiveness" and "elegance". (See Chapter 6)

Fifthly, achievements and shortcomings of translation research from the perspective of Systemic Functional Linguistics have been reviewed in Chapter 2, and it is pointed out that "more and more translation theorists are drawing nourishment from functional linguistics, conducting translation research, and have to some extent formed the Halliday School of Systemic Functional Linguistics in translation research, which has promoted the development of translation studies. However, there are also many problems and shortcomings, mainly manifested in: translation studies from the perspective of Systemic

Functional Linguistics focus on situational meaning and its equivalence in translation, while relatively neglecting the aesthetic and artistic aspects of translation." This study, as part of the translation research from the perspective of Systemic Functional Linguistics, has also made positive and beneficial attempts to explore the aesthetic and artistic aspects of translation.

9.2 Defects and Deficiencies

The main shortcomings of this study are as follows:

Firstly, in response to the shortcomings of the original model, this study aims to construct a complete model that not only assesses whether the translation is "faithful" in terms of meaning to the source text, but also evaluates whether the translation is "smooth". With respect to the approach, from the perspective of generic analysis, a targeted assessment model for the translation quality of applied texts is established. This naturally requires analyzing different applied texts to grasp their generic characteristics to provide practical and feasible tools for constructing a translation quality assessment model for this genre. However, how to grasp the norms and characteristics of applied texts in the two languages involved in translation? From the perspective of research methodology, a more practical and feasible approach is to establish corpora of English, Chinese and English translation of the three applied genres of discourses (enterprise profile, sports news report, and museum introduction) that this study focuses on. By analyzing and describing the macro structure (schematic structure, GSP model) and linguistic features (presentation style) of the three types of generic texts included in the corpora, their respective characteristics are summarized, similarities and differences are identified. However, due to time and effort limit, the sampling of established corpora is not large. Therefore, the structural and linguistic features of a certain genre summarized based on limited samples may not accurately reflect the overall picture of that genre. Therefore, judgments on the quality of translations based on this may not be accurate and comprehensive. In addition, the three corpora of applied genres constructed above (corporate profiles, sports news reports, and museum profiles) only include English, Chinese, and English translation of Chinese, and there is a lack of translated corpus from English to Chinese, which needs to be further reinforced in the future.

Secondly, whether it is the structural discrimination and judgment of texts in self-built corpora, or the statistical and descriptive aspects of process types, mood choices, theme types, etc. that belong to presentation style, due to the lack of effective analysis software to be used and the sole relying on manual work, errors are inevitable because of the huge differences and inevitable subjectivity between English and Chinese languages in spite of repeated speculation and verification.

Thirdly, this study addresses the lack of judgment for the parameter of "smoothness" in the translation, which is the biggest deficiency in the original model. From the perspective of genre analysis, the schematic structure and presentation style parameters are established, and on this basis, a two-stage translation evaluation theory is proposed, which constructs a framework that can examine whether the translation is "faithful" in meaning or function relative to the source text. It is also possible to evaluate whether the translation itself presents a complete pattern of "smoothness" and "elegance" compared to similar genres of texts in the target language. However, due to time and energy constraints, this study is unable to address other shortcomings of the original model and to conduct supplementary validation studies to prove its inadequacy. The above-mentioned defects and deficiencies can only be remedied in the future.

References:

[1] Si Xianzhu *Functional Linguistics and Translation Studies - Construction of Translation Quality Assessment Model*[M] Peking University Press, 2007

[2] Si Xianzhu. " Further Study on Translation Quality Assessment Model: A Functional Linguistic Perspective" [J]. *Chinese Translators Journal*, 2008 (2): 57-60.